"Up to date, forward thinking, and highly accessible for students seeking careers in the fast-changing world of communications. A book students will keep well past their graduation."
    Alexandra Wake, *Program Manager Journalism at RMIT University and President, Journalism Education and Research Association of Australia*

"For those navigating the increasingly complex landscape of media law and ethics, there is no better guide than Mark Pearson. Essential reading for all Australian communicators, whether you're an educator, student, or established professional."
    Dr Steinar Ellingsen, *Senior Lecturer in Journalism, Communication and Media, School of the Arts, English, University of Wollongong, Australia*

The Communicator's Guide to Media Law and Ethics

This book offers an introduction to the key legal and ethical topics confronting Australian journalists and strategic communicators both at home and internationally and offers a suite of reflective techniques for navigating them. It starts by positioning morals, ethics, and the law in their historical and philosophical frameworks by tracing the evolution of free expression and professional media ethics. Media law and ethics are then contextualized in their modern international human rights framework.

Readers are equipped with a skill set for reflecting on the law and ethics of professional media dilemmas – including mindful reflection, the Potter Box, journaling, concept mapping, and discussion. Such approaches are then applied to key topic areas, including free expression; reputation; confidentiality; privacy; justice; intellectual property; national security; discrimination and harassment; and conflicted interests. Each is examined in terms of its philosophical underpinnings, relationship to human rights, professional ethical context, international examples, legal principles, key Australian laws, legal cases, and strategies for applying reflective practice techniques. It concludes on a confident note – imploring communicators to engage in constructive and mindful strategic communication with the authority and confidence that results from a working knowledge of media law and ethics.

This handbook is for professional communicators and students in all fields, but particularly in journalism, public relations, corporate communication, media relations, and marketing.

Mark Pearson is Professor of Journalism and Social Media at Griffith University in Queensland, Australia, where he is a member of the Griffith Centre for Social and Cultural Research. He is co-author of *Social Media Risk and the Law: A Guide for Global Communicators* (Routledge, 2022), lead author of *The Journalist's Guide to Media Law: A Handbook for Communicators in a Digital World* (6th ed, Routledge, 2020), author of *Blogging and Tweeting Without Getting Sued* (Allen & Unwin, 2012), and co-editor of *Mindful Journalism and News Ethics in the Digital Era: A Buddhist Approach* (Routledge, 2015). He has worked as a journalist and trainer with several media organisations and as a press secretary to a federal member of parliament. He was Australian correspondent for Reporters Without Borders for a decade and is a life member of the Journalism Education and Research Association of Australia.

The Communicator's Guide to Media Law and Ethics
A Handbook for Australian Professionals

Mark Pearson

LONDON AND NEW YORK

Designed cover image: Getty Image

First published 2024
by Routledge
4 Park Square, Milton Park, Abingdon, Oxon OX14 4RN

and by Routledge
605 Third Avenue, New York, NY 10158

Routledge is an imprint of the Taylor & Francis Group, an informa business

© 2024 Mark Pearson

The right of Mark Pearson to be identified as author of this work has been asserted in accordance with sections 77 and 78 of the Copyright, Designs and Patents Act 1988.

All rights reserved. No part of this book may be reprinted or reproduced or utilised in any form or by any electronic, mechanical, or other means, now known or hereafter invented, including photocopying and recording, or in any information storage or retrieval system, without permission in writing from the publishers.

Trademark notice: Product or corporate names may be trademarks or registered trademarks and are used only for identification and explanation without intent to infringe.

British Library Cataloguing-in-Publication Data
A catalogue record for this book is available from the British Library

ISBN: 978-1-032-44558-8 (hbk)
ISBN: 978-1-032-44557-1 (pbk)
ISBN: 978-1-003-37275-2 (ebk)

DOI: 10.4324/9781003372752

Typeset in Times New Roman
by Newgen Publishing UK

To my wife, Julie.

To my children – Daniel, Ryan, Emily and Sophie – and their partners.

And to my grandchildren – Oliver, Josie, Beatrice, Charlie, Annabelle, Maddox, Harriet, Poppy and Henry.

May you be safe.

May you be well.

May you flourish.

Mark Pearson

Contents

List of figures   *xi*
List of tables   *xii*
Preface: Reflecting upon media law and ethics in a global context   *xiii*
Acknowledgements   *xix*

PART 1
Foundational approaches   **1**

1 Applied ethics 101   3

2 Human rights, ethics and laws   23

3 Tools for reflection in a communication context   49

4 Law and ethics across communication careers: Truth and deception in action   77

PART 2
Key topics in media law and ethics   **99**

5 Reputation and defamation   101

6 Confidentiality, secrets, sources and disclosure   142

7 Privacy and data protection   175

8 Communicating justice   206

PART 3
Challenges in the digital era   241

9   The ethics and law of intellectual property   243

10 Defence, national security, cyber security and anti-terrorism   277

11 Discrimination, cyberbullying and harassment   307

12 Integrity, conflicted interests and the business of
    communication   344

    Index   *372*

Figures

1.1 The adapted Parfit's mountain 12
1.2 The author's moral compass 16
3.1 The author's mindmap of potential risks and options 63

Tables

1.1	The Applied Ethics Matrix	17
2.1	MEAA Journalist Code of Ethics	41
2.2	Public Relations Institute of Australia (PRIA) Code of Ethics	43
3.1	Key professional communication situations and emotions with accompanying ethical and legal risks	54
3.2	Potential problem scenario	65
3.3	Sample specific legal risk analysis for a media release about a client's competitor	72
5.1	Sample specific legal risk analysis for a speech making allegations against a political opponent	134
8.1	Crime reportage time zones	234
9.1	Key questions to ask when using the work of another	264

Preface: Reflecting upon media law and ethics in a global context

Professional communicators can no longer feel comfortable with a rudimentary knowledge of their own country's media law and ethics. Their digital outputs cross borders in an instant, so a globalised and wireless world demands some understanding of laws and ethical practices beyond national boundaries. This book offers an introduction to the key legal and ethical topics confronting Australian journalists and strategic communicators both at home and internationally and delivers a suite of reflective techniques for navigating them.

Communication education and practice have evolved in the 21st century to necessitate a foundational work that covers both media law and ethics – for all communication professionals including journalists, public relations practitioners, strategic and crisis communicators as well as social media and marketing experts. It is now common for graduates' careers to span several or all of these occupations, and even for some hybrid position descriptions to combine elements of all of them. An introductory text on media law and ethics must pay heed to the various guiding principles and social purposes of these differing roles. Journalists, for example, draw on a long tradition of serving the so-called 'public right to know' in their work, with those working in traditional media (particularly in newspapers and public broadcasting) striving to maintain a firewall between their public interest reporting and the commercial interests of their owners. Such boundaries have become blurred in an era when the revenue streams of media outlets are far more complex than the traditional sales of a newspaper or the ratings of the evening news. Sponsorship and advertising are driven by clicks, page views and shares across numerous platforms which complicates the public interest mission of journalism, with both ethical and legal consequences.

Tertiary communication programmes have also evolved in two key ways impacting the approach and content of this book. Firstly, the hybridisation of the various communication careers detailed above has resulted in many courses being adapted to cater to the needs of both communication and journalism students, when these were formerly taught in different cohorts. Secondly, programme streamlining at many institutions has led to the combined offering of media law and media ethics in a single subject – requiring a textbook such as this one that covers both law and ethics across communication careers. Of course, a single book of this length cannot cover all aspects of media law and ethics comprehensively. For that reason, a list of recommended further reading appears at the end of each chapter.

While this is a totally new work, it is designed to replace the author's previous introductory media law text in courses that had prescribed it over its six editions (Pearson and Polden, 2019). It has similarities in its writing style, case selections, reflective approaches and nutshell summaries, although the content has been expanded to cover media law and ethics across communication careers.

We start by positioning morals, ethics and the law in their historical and philosophical frameworks by tracing the evolution of notions of free expression and professional media ethics. Media law and ethics are then contextualised in their modern international human rights framework. Readers are equipped with a skill set for reflecting on the law and ethics of a professional communication dilemma using a range of established and novel techniques. Such approaches are then applied to key media law and ethics topic areas of free expression, reputation, confidentiality, privacy, justice, intellectual property, national security, discrimination and harassment, and conflicted interests.

Each of the key topics is examined in terms of its philosophical underpinnings, relationship to human rights, professional ethical context, international examples, legal principles, key Australian jurisdictional laws, legal cases and strategies for applying reflective practice techniques. Each chapter contains a list of 'Key concepts', an 'In a nutshell' point form summary, and a series of 'Reflect-Research-Review' breakouts which can be used for personal revision or as tutorial exercises.

Part 1 – Foundational approaches – contains the first four chapters, establishing the foundational skills and understandings in media ethics and the law for professional communicators. Chapter 1 – Applied ethics 101 – sets the scene by offering a crucial distinction between morals, ethics and the law in a media context and then tracing the evolution of the moral philosophy which underpins communication ethics. The thinking of some key philosophers whose work has impacted communication law and ethics is introduced, including Aristotle, Kant, Rawls, Bentham and Mill, along with four key approaches to normative ethics including deontology, contractualism, consequentialism and virtue ethics. Key theoretical lenses for viewing applied ethics are examined, such as the human rights-oriented, feminist, environmentalist, post-structuralist, religious, mindful, stakeholder and solutions approaches. Readers are encouraged to reflect upon their moral genealogy to identify their unique 'moral compass' to help equip them with the resilience to tackle the prickly ethical and legal issues that arise in media practice. The approaches are combined into an Applied Ethics Matrix – drawing upon philosophical approaches, laws and professional codes, theoretical lenses, analysis of self-interest versus other interests, and moral compasses to assist in making an ethical decision. Chapter 2 – Human rights, ethics and laws – links human rights with moral philosophy, ethics and the law, with a focus on how the international human right of free expression is balanced against other rights and interests. We look at the philosophical origins of human rights and how rights-oriented rules and laws appear in legal, co-regulatory and self-regulatory communication contexts including legislation and cases, governmental and international regulations and industry codes of practice. Special attention is paid to how the globalised nature of the media in the digital era has eroded the jurisdictional boundaries between nations with regards to human rights. The positioning of media law and ethics in different press systems is considered, with the implications for professional communicators explored. Once the foundations of ethics and law have been established, Chapter 3 – Tools for reflection in a communication context – introduces some key reflective tools and techniques professional communicators can use to help them take a mindful and constructive approach to ethical and legal decision-making – by using their own moral compasses, their profession's ethical standards and the laws and regulations of society as a starting point. The problems of so-called 'moral myopia', 'moral muteness' and 'moral injury' are examined. Moral myopia is where a media professional is blinded to the ethical consequences of their decision, sometimes by rationalising an unethical position, perhaps because there is no explicit law or regulation prohibiting the behaviour. Moral muteness is where there is minimal discussion of ethical issues in the workplace. Moral injury – psychological harm – can occur when professionals breach their moral compasses and ethics without having properly reflected upon their options. Strategies for reflecting initially on a media ethics dilemma are introduced, including Bok's model (Bok, 1978), mindful reflection and journaling – leading into deeper techniques including an 'Applied Ethics Matrix', stakeholder mapping, the Potter Box (Potter, 1972), the TARES test (Baker, 2020) and the Strategic Legal Risk Analysis (Grantham and Pearson, 2022). In Chapter 4 – Law and ethics across communication careers: Truth and deception in action – we examine how the different needs and values of various communication careers impact upon their legal and ethical constraints and decision making. The ethics of truth and deception are foundational to the chapter. Digital and social media communication are considered, including the regulation of new media forms, the meaning and implications of fake news, alternative facts, misinformation, disinformation and malinformation and the use of technological tools like bots and cookies and their impact on job roles such as that of the social media content producer. Strict regulatory regimes for professional communicators in specialist areas like finance are also explained.

In Part 2 – Key topics in media law and ethics – we dive into four of the most important topics facing professional communicators in their work. Chapter 5 – Reputation and defamation – deals with the important topic of reputational damage in both its ethical and legal contexts, where the basic laws and defences of defamation are illustrated via key cases. Attitudes to reputation are traced to their philosophical, cultural and religious origins – and their influences upon the legal action of defamation are assessed. Defamation is considered at an international level, comparing the law in major jurisdictions. Australian law is examined in more detail, including recent reforms covering a new serious harm test and a public interest defence. The defences of most use to professional communicators are outlined with examples. Communicators are offered a pathway to analysing their publications in terms of the potential for reputational damage, from both ethical and legal perspectives. Chapter 6 – Confidentiality, sources, secrets and disclosure – looks at the domain of confidentiality where law and ethics are sometimes at odds because journalists are bound by a professional ethical requirement to protect their confidential sources yet courts sometimes insist that such off-the-record sources be revealed. The moral and ethical origins of confidentiality are considered from a range of philosophical perspectives. The journalist–source confidentiality agreement and the nature of off-the-record interviews and information-sharing is considered from the angles of both reporter and source. Shield laws – legislation designed to protect journalists (but not other communicators) in such situations – are explained. Given that public relations practitioners might sometimes be the confidential sources, their plight as whistleblowers is examined, along with their ethical and legal obligations in this domain. The law of breach of confidence is also examined, as this is relevant to both journalists and corporate communicators who might be tempted to reveal confidential information or material that is commercial-in-confidence. The rationale for freedom of information laws – and the details of their operation – are positioned in terms of the broader philosophical and policy debate over confidentiality versus transparency in government. Chapter 7 – Privacy and data protection – considers the cultural, philosophical and legal evolution of the ethics and law of privacy. It examines key international communication ethical documents for their privacy guidelines. It traces the law of privacy from its early development in France and the United States to its current legal situation across the UK, US, Australia and New Zealand. The human rights, ethics and law of privacy and data protection are all considered, including the digital impact of privacy expectations and laws, with key cases looking at the Cambridge Analytica-Facebook personal data breach scandal, privacy actions involving the Duke and Duchess of Sussex, and the classic Australian Lenah Game Meats case (2001) on privacy, surveillance and trespass. A discussion scenario covering the misuse of a celebrity's private data brings all elements of the topic together. Chapter 8 – Communicating justice – considers the law and ethics of the coverage of crime and violence and how free expression competes with an individual's right to a fair trial. After dealing with how philosophers, criminologists and ethicists have dealt with concepts of justice and media portrayal of violence, it considers how professional communicators and social media managers might navigate various laws in the reporting and public relations management of crime and courts. Solutions journalism is offered as an alternative model, allowing the floating of policies to ease some of the pressures on policing and criminal justice. The chapter also offers guidance to those working in the justice system on ethical ways they might work with the media when an important trial is under way. Featured in the chapter is a handy Crime Reportage Time Zone chart, mapping the stages of the criminal process and how defamation, contempt and reporting restrictions arise.

Part 3 – Challenges in the digital era – applies the knowledge and techniques of the first two parts to important topics facing communicators in the 21st century that have particular relevance to online communications. In Chapter 9 – The ethics and law of intellectual property – the ethical dimensions of plagiarism and the law of intellectual property, particularly copyright, are examined. The philosophical origins of intellectual property are introduced, along with its appearance in various human rights instruments and treaties. In copyright the fundamental principles are covered, along with international differences on how to navigate regimes of the public domain, fair dealing and fair use of the work of others. The gap between the law, ethics and the actual enforcement of intellectual property rights like trade marks and moral rights is discussed. The blurred lines presented by the digital age with implications for artificial intelligence and creations like fan fiction are examined. Australian intellectual property law – particularly copyright – is illustrated in more detail using recent cases and examples. Chapter 10 – Defence, national security, cyber security and anti-terrorism – takes up the concerning ethical and legal issues that arise when communicating about war, defence and national security. It begins with a virtue ethics perspective on the coverage of these highly charged topics where courage is a debated value and truth-telling and free expression come into conflict with national and strategic priorities. Peace journalism is considered as an alternative to conflict-oriented reporting. Human rights of safety and security are weighed against freedom of speech (along with privacy, discrimination and other rights) – fault lines reflected in the development and enforcement of a spate of national security laws internationally since the terrorist attacks on the United States in September 2001. Australian anti-terrorism laws become a point of focus, with the key laws impacting journalists explained and examples given of cases where free expression, open justice and confidential sources have been compromised in the interests of public safety. Chapter 11 – Discrimination, cyberbullying and harassment – looks at these alarming problems in the digital era, with particular emphasis on the online safety of communication practitioners and suggested avenues for them dealing with those who see fit to harass them. The moral, ethical and human rights foundations of discrimination and harassment are covered, along with some of the disturbing implications of such behaviour for marginalised groups, including communicators of diverse backgrounds. Materials on the coverage of mental health and suicide are reviewed. Laws and cases in discrimination, cyberbullying and harassment are detailed at international and national levels. Chapter 12 – Integrity, conflicted interests and the business of communication – considers the law and ethics of integrity, corruption and conflicted interests in professional communication, particularly in a business context. This involves some consideration of ethical codes placing obligations on communicators to disclose vested interests and the related liability under consumer law. The philosophical foundations of integrity and conflict of interests are examined, along with the modern practice of corporate social responsibility (CSR). Anti-corruption structures are surveyed, and Australia's media bargaining laws covered. Special domains of conflicts of interest such as those engaging consumer law and securities law have a special focus with cases and examples.

Overall, the book aims to introduce media law and ethics to professional communicators and students so they have a basic understanding that informs their research and communication across digital platforms. There is no guarantee that such an introductory approach will safeguard them against potential legal action or ethical breaches, but the hope is that the suggested strategies for review and reflection will prompt them to pause at key junctures to consider legal and ethical dilemmas as they arise and learn when to seek counsel from supervisors and lawyers. Actual legal advice is not offered because that is the role of lawyers. The sad reality is that many of the cases and examples in the book could have been avoided if the professional communicators involved had paused to reflect upon the issue and had sought input from colleagues and lawyers on the safest legal or ethical course of action before proceeding to engage in the communication or behaviour that caused the problem.

References

Baker, S. and Martinson, D.L. 2001, 'The TARES Test: Five Principles for Ethical Persuasion', *Journal of Mass Media Ethics*, 16 (2-3), 148–175.

Bok, S. 1978, *Lying: Moral Choice in Public and Private Life*, Pantheon Books, New York.

Grantham, S. and Pearson, M. 2022, *Social Media Risk and the Law: A Guide for Global Communicators*, Routledge, London and New York.

Potter, R.B. 1972, 'The Logic of Moral Argument', *Toward a Discipline of Social Ethics*, Deats, P. ed., Boston University Press, Boston, 93–114.

Swain, K. 1994, *Beyond the Potter Box: A Decision Model Based on Moral Development Theory*. AEJMC conference paper.

Cases cited

Lenah Game Meats case: *ABC v Lenah Game Meats Pty Ltd* [2001] HCA 63; 208 CLR 199; 185 ALR 1; 76 ALJR 1 (15 November 2001), <www.austlii.edu.au/au/cases/cth/high_ct/2001/63.html>.

Acknowledgements

My greatest thanks go to my wife, Julie, who has been incredibly supportive throughout this process. Numerous colleagues have assisted as collaborators over the decades and have thus contributed to my knowledge of the topic areas. They include my co-authors for my two most recent books, Susan Grantham and Mark Polden, and other collaborators including Jane Johnston, Joseph Fernandez, Patrick Keyzer and Virginia Leighton-Jackson, who has also kindly performed referencing assistance. Friend and colleague Roger Patching has been of continuous help by sending me snippets of the latest cases and readings. International colleagues David Goldberg, Kyu Ho Youm, Judith Townend and Dirk Voorhoof have offered useful global comparisons. A special thanks to the friends who have indulged me with deep and meaningful conversations about philosophy, morals and ethics, including Michael Smith, Lydia Lessing, Steve Hodgson, Mark Chellew and Kerrie Foxwell-Norton. Buddhist teachers Steve and Rosemary Weissman and friends in that meditation group have offered guidance on that perspective, while Graeme Cole and members of the Australasian Religious Press Association gave me feedback on mindfulness-based meditation for Christians. I am indebted to Muslim colleagues who worked with me on the Reporting Islam Project (2014–2016) for insights into Islamic philosophy, particularly Dr Abdi Hersi. Administrative and teaching colleagues at Griffith University have been supportive and helpful – especially those in the School of Humanities, Languages and Social Science headed by Professor Michael Ondaatje and in the Griffith Centre for Social and Cultural Research headed by Professor Susan Forde, which generously funded the book's referencing. Thanks also to the reviewers of the book proposal for their useful suggestions of topics and examples. The production of the book by the Routledge team also deserves acknowledgment. Thanks to senior editors Lucy Batrouney and Lucie Bartonek, senior publisher Katie Peace, senior editorial assistant Payal Bharti, editorial assistant Georgia Oman, senior production editor Ed Gibbons and copyeditor Jonathan Merrett.

Finally, special thanks go to the hundreds of media professionals and students I have trained and taught over the years whose questions, insights and case examples have earned their place in this book.

Part 1
Foundational approaches

1 Applied ethics 101

Key concepts

Normative ethics: The branch of philosophy examining how people should act in a moral sense with regard to the rightness or wrongness of actions.
Deontology: A rules-based approach to ethics applying a system of duties and moral obligations.
Contractualism: An ethical approach centred upon the notion of a moral social contract between all citizens that we should do the right thing by each other.
Consequentialism: The approach to ethics requiring us to foresee and reflect upon the potential moral consequences of any action and to choose that which brings the greater benefit to the most people.
Virtue ethics: The area of moral philosophy focusing on enhancing and developing the most virtuous aspects of character via ethical decisions and upon minimising vices.
Theoretical lens: An underlying belief, approach or motivation a protagonist must acknowledge in their ethical decision-making.
Egoism: The view that self-interest drives, or is a key factor in, all moral decision-making.
Altruism: The position that an interest in the welfare of others, as opposed to self-interest, is crucial to an ethical decision
Moral compass: The individual's unique approach to ethical decision making as informed by their own background and values within the boundaries of their professional ethical codes.

Setting the scene

> I have gained this from philosophy: that I do without being commanded what others do only from fear of the law. – Aristotle

Whether you are a journalist, a public relations practitioner, a social media moderator or a marketing executive, your professional conduct is underpinned

DOI: 10.4324/9781003372752-2

by a web of moral, ethical and legal requirements. While these vary with time and place, they are universal in their existence. A broad definition of 'media law and ethics' even accommodates ancient cultures. Indigenous societies all had laws and protocols controlling the flow of information between members of their communities and beyond. For example, Aboriginal Australians had (and continue to have) customary laws that vary between communities related to intellectual and cultural property, including who might own and share 'songs, stories, dances and ceremonies, medicinal knowledge, and knowledge relating to land care and management' (Janke and Quiggan, 2005: 452). Traditional Samoan protocols banned even the direct questioning of an elder (Masterton, 1985). The law and ethics of professional communication in the modern world are as deeply steeped in their cultural and religious origins, predominantly via Western traditions. In this chapter we start by visiting those origins in history, philosophy, religion and jurisprudence (legal theory) to position media law and ethics to help the 21st century practitioner and student understand it in relation to their own cultural traditions and moral compasses. This understanding is crucial to the process of reflecting upon a communication dilemma to be able to navigate a safe legal pathway within the bounds of professional ethical guidelines.

Why is there a need to reflect on the ethics of media decisions?

Reflection upon the fundamental morality, ethical integrity and legality of their decisions is what sets media professionals apart from mere media workers, 'content creators' and 'hacks'. As we explore in coming chapters, each media role plays an important function in society but the work can impact other people's lives in a litany of ways. Public relations practitioners might help publicise a product or service that could damage someone's health. Journalists might cover a story that could create alarm in the financial markets. Social media moderators might encourage discussion on a topic that could prejudice someone's criminal trial. Each of these actions can have moral, ethical and legal consequences and it is vital that media professionals learn to anticipate potential issues and come to a reasoned decision on their course of action. In summary, these are the three key reasons media professionals need to reflect on potential moral, ethical or legal dilemmas:

- Ethical reflection and accountability are fundamental ingredients of professional behaviour;
- Justification for difficult ethical and legal decisions can be required by professional self-regulatory bodies and the courts; and
- The process of carefully weighing ethical options has been proven to bolster the mental health resilience of media professionals in situations when others suffer as a result of those decisions (Pearson et al., 2021).

> **Reflect – Research – Review:**
>
> Identify a social media 'influencer' and identify three aspects of their behaviour and publishing that might indicate whether they reflect upon the moral integrity, ethics and legality of their posts. Give an example to support your view.

Philosophical approaches

Philosophers have long pondered the notion of morals and ethics. The word 'ethics' comes from the Greek *ēthikos* meaning 'ethical, pertaining to character', while 'morals' originates from the Latin *mores*, meaning 'customs, manners or morals' (Harper, 2022). The terms have often been used interchangeably but for our purposes in this book we draw a distinction between an individual's sense of right and wrong ('morals') and the code of behaviour expected of certain professionals ('ethics'). Each can differ from the other and both can be at odds with a society's rules and regulations ('laws'). This book is structured so that we first explore philosophical approaches to morality so we can help you locate your own 'moral compass' – the influences upon your decision-making about what is the right or wrong thing to do. It is vital to acknowledge this because it will be a key reference point for you when you are reflecting on an ethical dilemma confronting you in your communication practice. The second ingredient in ethical decision making is the actual code of practice or behaviour (written or implied) that guides communicators in their specialist fields – be that journalism, public relations, marketing or social media moderation. The third is the law itself – the legislation, regulations and court decisions that determine whether your communication activities conform with the formal rules of society.

Moral philosophy

'Moral philosophy' is the umbrella term covering a litany of approaches to morals and ethics by philosophers throughout the millennia. It is just one branch of the broader study of philosophy which takes up the systematic study of all things of concern to human existence, including existence itself, thinking and reasoning, language, consciousness, power relationships and values. Moral philosophy – commonly just called 'Ethics' – is broadly divided into three areas: 'meta-ethics' (theories of moral propositions and truths), 'normative ethics' (practical guidelines on moral decision-making) and 'applied ethics' (how people should act in particular situations or occupations). Of course, the thrust of this book is upon the latter (decision-making and applied ethics) because the field of applied ethics provides guidance on how professional communicators might navigate ethical dilemmas in their practice. Before we

6 Foundational approaches

can venture far down the applied ethics path, we must first consider how some of the world's greatest philosophers have approached normative ethics – the fundamental moral decision-making process.

Normative ethics

Normative ethics is the overarching branch of philosophy examining how people should act in a moral sense with regard to the rightness or wrongness of actions. Driver (2009: 31) described normative ethics as an 'enormous field' and defined it as '…the articulation and the justification of the fundamental principles that govern the issues of how we should live and what we morally ought to do. Its most general concerns are providing an account of moral evaluation and, possibly, articulating a decision procedure to guide moral action'. There have been numerous approaches and sub-approaches to moral decision-making in philosophical history, but in this book we focus on four key categories that offer the most value to professional communicators: Deontology, Contractualism, Consequentialism and Virtue Ethics. While they are often portrayed as being distinctive and autonomous, with each having flaws exposed by theoretical moral philosophers, some have agreed they actually share substantial common ground (Guinebert, 2020). The great modern philosopher Derek Parfit (1942–2017) put it this way: '(It) has been widely believed that there are … deep disagreements between Kantians, Contractualists, and Consequentialists. That, I have argued, is not true. These people are climbing the same mountain on different sides' (Parfit, 2011: 419). All approaches can inform ethical decision-making by media professionals, as we see below when we consider frameworks that can be used to apply them, including an attempt at putting Parfit's 'mountain' into practice in Figure 1.1.

Deontology

Deontology has strong similarities with the law in that it centres upon a system of rules about duties and moral obligations. The word stems from the Greek *deon*, meaning 'duty', and it is a rules-based approach to morality (Alexander and Moore, 2020). Perhaps the most famous advocate of deontology was the German philosopher Immanuel Kant (1724–1804) who developed his 'Categorical Imperative' which was a system of binding moral laws that everyone must follow regardless of their consequences. Kant's test of whether an action met the standard for a categorical imperative of morality was whether that course of action should be made a universal law. If you did not believe it should be applied universally endorsing everyone to do it, then it would not meet the required standard. The second formulation of the categorical imperative declares people should never be treated as simply a means to an end – and that they should be treated as ends 'in and of themselves' (Lipari, 2017). A simplified Christian version of the approach is known as the 'Golden Rule'. It can be found in the biblical verses Matthew 7:12 and Luke 6:31 where

Jesus exhorts followers to treat others as they themselves would like to be treated: 'Do unto others as you would have them do unto you'. Kant extended this from a transactional interpersonal obligation to a universal one where the individual should envisage what would happen if everyone agreed they could treat everyone else that particular way. Kant's philosophies have been extended over generations to the moral qualities driving the actions (a virtue ethics perspective) and to the rights and duties of those doing and subject to an action (a contractualist/human rights/justice perspective).

Media ethics application

Journalists, public relations practitioners and marketing executives typically operate under an overarching code or charter of ethics applying to their professions. In fact, the French translation of 'code of ethics' includes the word 'deontology' because of its rule-based approach: *code de déontologie*. A media example of such a moral 'law' might be found in the non-negotiable obligation of journalists to protect the identity of their confidential sources which has found its way into journalism ethical codes internationally. As we learn in Chapter 6, journalists are expected to meet this obligation even if it risks the journalist being jailed for refusing a court order to reveal their source and perhaps even if the lives or liberty of others are endangered by not revealing the source.

Contractualism (Social Contract Theory)

Social contract theory – which developed into 'contractualism' – is an ethical approach centred upon the notion of a moral social contract between all citizens that we should do the right thing by each other. It was a development from deontology which can be traced back to Socrates (470–399BC) in Ancient Greece, but developed by the likes of Thomas Hobbes, John Locke and Jean-Jacques Rousseau, and finally modernised by John Rawls and T.M. Scanlon. The gist of Socrates' social contract argument was that he had lived by – and benefited from – the laws of the city of Athens. He had been free to leave but had chosen to stay. Thus, he was contracted to obey those laws even when they ruled against him – in his case when he was imprisoned facing the death penalty. In other words, one should be willing to take the bad with the good once one has agreed to a rule-based moral regime (Friend, 2022).

This social contract theory was extended in the seventeenth century by British philosopher Thomas Hobbes (1588–1679) who argued that all people would agree to a set of moral and political rules that prevented them returning to the 'State of Nature' – a situation of chaos and war, every person for themselves. That implied all citizens would be willing to apply their rationality to abide by society's rules – both in the form of morality and of justice (Friend, 2022). English philosopher John Locke (1632–1704) extended the notions of both human reason and the social contract in his *Essay Concerning Human*

Understanding and his *Two Treatises of Government*. There he argued that men had no innate knowledge of moral truths, but that they acquired them via introspection (Flew, 1984: 206). (Introspection – or 'reflection' – is a central theme of this book, explored in Chapter 3.) In Locke's second *Treatise*, he argued that in the state of nature man is free and equal, but a Law of Nature ordained by God demanded that people regulate their behaviour. Everyone has certain natural rights – such as to life and liberty – so long as their exercise of those rights does not infringe the rights of others. The prevention of such infringement requires them to enter into a 'social contract' – where a government ensures people can enjoy their natural rights and decide upon disputes. With regard to rights other than natural rights, majority opinion should prevail, a concept that fed significantly into the democratic ideals of both the American and French revolutions (Flew, 1984: 207).

Genevan philosopher Jean-Jacques Rousseau (1712–1778) made important contributions to both social contract theory and moral psychology. Under *The Social Contract*, Rousseau posited that the citizen reconciles their own free will and the authority of the state under law in recognition of the need for co-operation and interdependence in society. He developed the notion of the 'general will' – the overall will of the total citizenry. By obeying it of their own free will, all citizens maintained their freedom. Rousseau's contribution to moral psychology was also helpful. He argued morality is made possible by people's consciousness of their role as social beings. While sympathy for others might be instinctual, its development into a moral consciousness depends on applying reasoning to social relations and actions. However, he warned that people could deceive themselves about their own level of morality – a caution media practitioners should bear in mind when making ethical decisions, and a key reason for our systematic approach to ethical and legal decision making in this book (Bertram, 2017).

One of the 20th century's greatest philosophers, American John Rawls (1921–2002), extended social contract theory by arguing moral acts were the acts we would all agree to abide by if we did not hold any biases. His theory of a just liberal society, called 'justice as fairness', was detailed in his 1971 book *A Theory of Justice* (Rawls, 1971). In establishing a model for social justice, Rawls stated what he called the 'original position' as a question: 'What terms of co-operation would free and equal citizens agree to under fair conditions?' Importantly, such a question should be posed from behind a 'veil of ignorance' – where those deciding on the moral course of action should be ignorant of the circumstances of those performing the action and those impacted by it – minimising bias over race, natural talents, social status, religion, wealth, gender, sexual preference and so on (Wenar, 2021). Two important principles – liberty and difference – underpinned the theory. Under the liberty principle, a social contract should aim to offer everyone the maximum liberty possible without reducing the freedom of other citizens. Under the difference principle, everyone should have an equal right to flourish regardless of their standing. Those who are worse off should stand to benefit from the contract. Harvard philosophy professor T.M. Scanlon worked from these foundations to develop the moral theory of 'Contractualism' which delved further into reasons and approaches to reasoning, assumed all citizens could agree autonomously, required justification for the pursuit of individual interests, and focused on aggregating individual interests into a mutual 'common interest' (Ashford and Mulgan, 2018).

Media ethics application

While they were not designed to be used in ethical decision-making, social contract theories offer a useful prism for media professionals trying to navigate an ethical dilemma by encouraging them to assess the justice and fairness of a situation by disregarding the vested interests of the various stakeholders – including the media practitioner. Further, Rawls' theorising around decisions favouring the maximum liberty for all citizens feeds into both human rights and the public communication of media professionals – particularly journalists who are exposing inequities and corrupt decision making by public officials.

Consequentialism

The area of ethics and moral philosophy called 'consequentialism' requires us to reflect upon the moral consequences of any action and foresee the path that brings the greater benefit to the most people before deciding whether to act. Consequentialism is often compared with 'teleology' which comes from the Greek *telos*, meaning 'end, purpose or goal', and *logos*, meaning 'explanation or reason' (Ethics Centre, 2022). In media terms, however, teleology serves a different purpose from consequentialism. It can help by assisting us to identify wholesome purposes in our pursuit of a particular activity – such as social justice, improved health, environmental benefits and so on (Ethics Centre, 2022). While it might be uplifting to know you have done something for a noble purpose, your performance and reputation will more likely be judged by the consequences of your actions, particularly if you are publishing something that might hurt others. We return to purpose or 'intent' when we consider the virtue ethics approach and the notions of 'egoism' and 'altruism'. The driving force of consequentialist decision-making is that an act – and the intentions behind an act – should be assessed on the extent to which they increase what is called 'The Good' (Sinnott-Armstrong, 2019). Morally correct choices are those that have the consequence of bringing about more good.

The most famous branch of consequentialism – Utilitarianism – was developed by the British philosophers Jeremy Bentham (1748–1832) and John Stuart Mill (1806–1873). [We revisit both of them for their views on free expression in Chapter 2.] Each represented the hallmark attributes of the Enlightenment era – an age of reason where rationality would be applied to arrive at calculated solutions to philosophical and social problems, echoing the advances of the time in maths, science and engineering. Their primary focus in moral decision making was upon the extent to which pleasure or happiness could be increased (or diminished) by an action (Alexander and Moore, 2020). There were open questions as to whether certain acts might increase the average happiness of everyone, yet make certain individuals miserable. Bentham applied his utilitarian theories to the practice of law-making as a prominent jurist. He argued that judges and legislators needed to employ the basic calculation that the benefits for the majority should be achieved with the minimal necessary pain for the few. The best policies were justified by such a calculation of pain versus happiness. He refined it by implementing the egalitarian commitment that every citizen's interests must count equally in arriving at such policies (Crimmins, 2021). In his book *Utilitarianism* (1861), Mill made it clear that utilitarianism simply offered a standard for acting morally, but not an actual procedure for calculating how to do so. He argued the actual reasoning in a particular case should be guided by foundational moral principles like fidelity, fair play and honesty, and that calculations of the greater happiness for the most people should only be undertaken when principles conflict or when some would suffer (Brink, 2022). Mill also applied his thinking on utilitarianism in his other major work, *On Liberty* (1959), where he linked the greater good to the implementation of three basic liberties: liberties of conscience and expression; liberties of tastes, pursuits, and life-plans; and liberties of association (Brink, 2022). It is the first of these that occupies much of our attention when we examine human rights and the media in Chapter 2. At its extreme, consequentialism can be confused with the moral philosophy of Machiavelli (1469–1527), 'the end justifies the means', which might excuse any method of getting to a desired goal, no matter how immoral the action.

Media ethics application

How do we apply a consequentialist approach in a media sense? The reporting of chronic homelessness on national television evening news could well diminish most viewers' pleasure or happiness as they dine. But in the longer term the reporting on the misery of homelessness might prompt policy changes that result in a reduction in homelessness, thus increasing the overall happiness of society. Public relations practitioners and crisis communicators use a version of the consequentialist approach when they apply models of stakeholder theory to their decision-making. Stakeholder theory requires communicators to assess the consequences of an action upon the many and various stakeholders in an organisation, often in tandem with the entity's corporate social responsibility (CSR) obligations (Grantham and Pearson, 2022, p16).

Virtue ethics

While types of normative ethics help guide our choices about how to make an ethical choice in a situation, virtue ethics are more to do with helping us determine the kind of person we are and aspire to be (Alexander and

Moore, 2020). This is the area of moral philosophy focusing on enhancing and developing the most virtuous aspects of character via ethical decisions, and upon minimising vices. It is well summed up in a quote often attributed to Aristotle (though probably not actually spoken by him): 'We are what we repeatedly do. Excellence, then, is not an act, but a habit'. He and other classical philosophers explored virtue ethics, often with a teleological lens. One's purpose or intent in committing an action is often closely associated with one's virtues (Ethics Centre, 2022). Virtue ethics started with Socrates and further developed with variations by Plato (428–348BC), Aristotle (384–322 BC) and the Stoics (340BC–180AD). Aristotle proposed that 'a life well lived' abided by the development of certain virtues (called *arête*) via *phronesis* (practical or moral wisdom) – leading to a state of *eudaimonia* (flourishing or happiness) (Hursthouse and Pettigrove, 2022). The virtues Aristotle listed included the intellectual qualities of wisdom, understanding and prudence, applied to the moral virtues of courage, justice and truthfulness. Each involved striking a moderating equilibrium between two extremes, known as Aristotle's 'Golden Mean'. For example, the virtue of courage sat between the extremes of rashness and cowardice. Such an approach of moderation has equivalents across other philosophies including the 'Middle Way' in Buddhism and the 'doctrine of the mean' in Confucianism (Flew, 1984: 134). While virtue ethics evolved from Ancient Greece, even Kant as a deontologist and modern consequentialists have paid close attention to the virtues (Crisp, 2020; Hursthouse and Pettigrove, 2022). In the 20th century virtue ethics underwent a resurgence and it has earned its place in prominent guides to ethics for communicators (Patching and Hurst, 2022: 158–159). We consider it as a separate approach here because it prompts a foundational reflection by the professional communicator upon the character virtues they wish to develop in their lives and careers.

Media ethics application

The pursuit of a virtuous career requires an ongoing process of reflection where pausing to challenge moral decisions will position you as an ethical practitioner. Nobody is perfect, and many great journalists and communicators have succumbed to temptations or committed ethical breaches at some stage of their careers, but they are admired for their overall professionalism and ethical stances across the breadth of their careers and at crucial moments when they have been in the public eye.

> **Reflect – Research – Review:**
>
> What character virtues should you strive for in your field of professional communication and why? Rank the top five virtues in order. What opposing vices should you strive to avoid or minimise?

12 Foundational approaches

Climbing the mountain

While virtue ethics is often listed with deontology, contractualism and consequentialism as the main ethical schools, they all merge to some degree. It is possible for communication professionals to reach ethical decisions using one – or some combination – of the four approaches explained above (Crisp, 2020). When discussing the deontological, consequentialist and contractualist schools, the philosopher Derek Parfit suggested all were 'climbing the same mountain' from different sides (Parfit 2011: 419). Parfit argued in his 'triple theory' there was potential in each of the key approaches to accommodate the others. When we add virtue ethics to the equation, analysing an ethical action in terms of societal rules, consequences or the social contract can be performed while considering how a decision sits within the framework of character virtues a professional strives to accomplish. (See Figure 1.1).

Egoism versus altruism

A simple consideration in most ethical decisions is the extent to which self-interest – or respect for the interests of others – is the driving force. Of course, most difficult decisions include a combination of these factors. All the above approaches include some process for weighing them. Egoism is the view that self-interest drives, or is a key factor in, all moral decision-making while altruism is the position that an interest in the welfare of others, as opposed

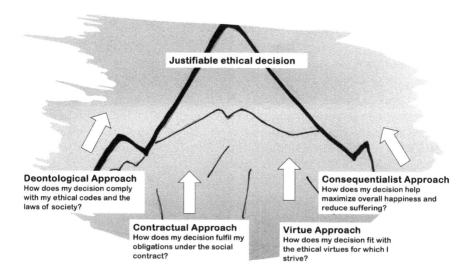

Figure 1.1 The adapted Parfit's mountain (2011: 419) – how four key ethical approaches can be followed to reach the same justifiable ethical decision.

(Graphic © Mark Pearson 2022).

to self-interest, is crucial to an ethical decision. Many view self-interest as a negative factor in moral decision-making. However, there have been many ways philosophers have viewed the ego and self-interest. The great pessimist German philosopher Arthur Schopenhauer (1788–1860) identified the greatest driving force of humanity as that of the 'will' – or incessant desire – which fed into every aspect of life including decision-making on matters of good and bad, right and wrong (Schirmacher, 1996: 146–147). Logically, then, the will (or self-interest) could not be discounted as a consideration in weighing moral and ethical choices. The philosophy poster child of the libertarian movement (and more recently US ultra-conservatives) was Ayn Rand (1905–1982). Her guiding ethical principle was 'rational egoism'. She described self-interest as a positive in her book *The Virtue of Selfishness – A new concept of egoism* (1964). Egoists assert that there are dimensions to self-interest, including the direct and indirect and the long term and short term. For example, it is in our self-interest that moral order be maintained in society, so we might make some individual sacrifices to attain an overall goal of benefit to ourselves. Altruism is essentially the opposite of egoism. Altruists argue that moral decisions cannot be reduced to self-interest and that a key ingredient of morality is an interest in the welfare of others (Flew, 1984: 10).

Media ethics application

The relative importance of self-interest (egoism) and the interest of others (altruism) is implicit in many communication ethics decisions. Journalists encounter it in the relationship with their sources and it impacts all communication professionals at moments when their individual career advancement is being weighed against the interests of other stakeholders, including sources, clients and customers.

> **Reflect – Research – Review:**
>
> List and justify three acceptable self-interest (egoism) factors that might influence a communication ethics decision. Then list and justify three altruistic factors – those that might put the welfare of others at the forefront of your thinking. How can you resolve any differences between them?

Theoretical lenses and perspectives

While these are the key traditional moral philosophy positions on ethics, many professional communicators will have their own perspectives that can be acquired from their educational, social or political standpoints. These can inform your judgment about the communication career you choose and the decisions you make within it. As long as your behaviours and beliefs do not conflict with your occupational ethical codes or the laws of society, they can be a useful device in your ethical toolkit. However, there is an obligation for you to be transparent about any such beliefs and perspectives you might hold – with your employer, your audiences and, just as importantly, with yourself. In summary, what we call a 'theoretical lens or perspective' is an underlying belief, approach, mission or motivation a communication professional must acknowledge in their ethical decision-making.

Human rights-centred lens

Each of the main approaches to ethics detailed above can be viewed through a human rights lens, explored further in Chapter 2. Many professional ethical codes take up fundamental human rights frameworks as a starting point for their guidance. For example, most journalism ethical codes in Western democracies counsel against all forms of discrimination, privacy invasion and plagiarism – although they typically ask journalists to balance these against the other human right of free expression. Professional communicators working for non-government organisations (NGOs) on the international stage will often use a human rights lens to assist with ethical decisions, likely driven by charters like the *Universal Declaration of Human Rights* (United Nations, 1948).

Feminist lens

A feminist lens on ethics focuses on the human right of not being discriminated against because of one's gender. It sets out to identify and correct the binary view of gender, historic male privileges and social orders that oppress women and girls (Norlock, 2019). The approach can be traced back at least until the 18th century when Mary Wollstonecraft (1759-1797) penned the trailblazing work of feminism *A Vindication of the Rights of Woman* in 1792, arguing that all women required better education to elevate their status and role in society. The approach has swept through society and academia since the 1960s and now extends beyond male-female gender issues and embraces ethical decision-making on issues across the full LGBTQI+ spectrum.

Environmental lens

As UN Secretary-General Antonio Guterres told world leaders at COP27 in 2022: 'The global climate fight will be won or lost in this crucial decade – on our watch' (UN, 2022). Many professional communicators adopt an environmental perspective in their careers, assignments and individual ethical judgments. Some choose to adjust the basic theories of deontology, contractualism, consequentialism and virtue ethics to meet ecological ends.

Marxist, structuralist, post-structuralist and postmodernist perspectives

Some people's views of the world are informed by the tools of analysis offered by key intellectual thinkers in the areas of economics, politics, power relations and communication. These include the economics and class-oriented writings of Karl Marx (1818–1883) and Friedrich Engels (1820–1895), the analysis of power in social structures and language of Michel Foucault (1926–1984) and the critical public sphere and media analysis of Jürgen Habermas (1929–). Each offers a different lens on the types of communication careers and topics that might be important to a more equitable world.

Christian perspective

The ethical decision-making of communicators operating in Western societies has inevitably been influenced by Christianity – either explicitly through a practitioner's adherence to a Christian faith and its associated moral code or implicitly via familial influences and the centuries-long impact of the church-state relationship, particularly in the UK and its former colonies. It is vital that this be identified and acknowledged for the benefit of the practitioner and stakeholders.

Other theistic lenses

While Christianity has undoubtedly had the strongest influence on the laws and ethics of Western democracies, we need to acknowledge in a globalised and multicultural world that many other religions can shape our moral compasses. Generational influences of Judaism, Hinduism, Buddhism, Islam, Confucianism and a host of other religions and philosophies can affect our approach to moral and ethical decision-making and the relative importance of various values. Worth a special mention is Buddhism because of its influence on the philosophy and psychology of millions of followers in various cultures over 2,500 years – and its impact upon Western societies via mindfulness-based approaches to mental health and well-being in recent decades. This might take the form of a highly ritualised and culturally based view of Buddhism as a religion, or a more secular application of its key tenets as an ethical framework. We adapt some of the techniques of mindfulness-based reflection (Pearson, 2014) to ethical decision-making in Chapter 3 as one of several approaches examined.

Solutions approach

A recent trend in communication practice – particularly in journalism – has been towards communicating to help forge a solution to important social problems rather than just reporting their negative and critical aspects. It stemmed in North America from the 1970s and 1980s approaches of 'public journalism' and 'civic journalism'. Solutions journalism – and 'constructive journalism' – involves identifying community concerns and helping improve social justice, sometimes as a campaign involving a news outlet or a non-government organisation (Parisi, 1997; Solutions Journalism Network, 2023).

Reflect – Research – Review:

Applied ethics in action: mapping your unique moral compass

We call an individual's unique moral pedigree their 'moral compass' – which can come from a range of sources, including their cultural backgrounds, family upbringing, religion, political preferences, passions, interests and stances. It is informed by their own background and values within the boundaries of their professional ethical codes. Sit for a few moments to reflect on influences upon your own moral decision-making and then draw your unique moral compass, attributing the four main points on the compass to the four prime influences on your moral decisions, with the lesser points representing other factors. As an example, the author's moral compass is illustrated at Figure 1.2.

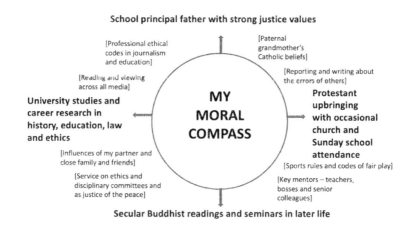

Figure 1.2 The author's moral compass.

Applying your moral compass to ethical decisions

Potential biases need disclosure and differences between your moral compass and your professional ethical codes or the law need to be resolved. Strong influences upon moral compasses can come from the theoretical lenses

Table 1.1 The Applied Ethics Matrix – combining philosophy, laws and professional codes, theoretical lenses, relative interests and moral compass to assist in making a communication decision

Applied Ethics Matrix steps	Questions to ask
a. Philosophical approaches	Deontological: What if everyone acted this way? Should this approach become the rule? What duties do I owe to others?	Consequentialist: Does my proposed action lead to the greatest benefit for most stakeholders?	Contractualist: How are the rights and interests of various stakeholders affected by this action?	Virtue Ethicist: What virtues or vices are evident in this action? How does it shape my character?
b. Ethical code and legal constraints	What clauses from a professional communication ethical code apply to this situation and what guidance is given? How does the action sit with the laws of society?
c. Theoretical lens	How does the dilemma sit with a theoretical perspective I have adopted, such as feminism, environmentalism or Marxism (or some combination)?
d. Egoism v altruism	Which of my self-interests is this decision serving as opposed to, or in combination with, the interests of others?
e. Unique moral compass	What does my unique moral compass contribute to my deliberations? That is, how does my culture, family values, religion or political persuasion factor into it? Does a potential bias need consideration or disclosure?

18 *Foundational approaches*

identified above, but also from an individual's family upbringing, schooling, religion and politics. The professional communicator – when faced with an ethical dilemma – might:

a. apply the key questions suggested by the world's greatest philosophers;
b. reference the situation against the law of the land and their own occupation's ethical code;
c. cross-correlate the likely approach against their own theoretical lens;
d. analyse their self-interests versus the interests of others; and
e. consider their own 'moral compass' as a touchstone.

To some extent, the five are not mutually exclusive and components of decisions might overlap. Further, it is not necessarily a step-by-step or linear approach. However, it is worth treating it as such until you get familiar with each of the factors and its application to a communication context. Table 1.1 suggests an 'Applied Ethics Matrix' for reaching an ethical decision via a situational analysis considering each of the five key tools. We then put these into practice in Case Study 1.1.

Case Study 1.1: The marketing executive and the high roller

Consider the relationship between the casino marketing executive Richard Wilk and a high rolling gambler from Canada who play key roles in Louis Theroux's 2007 documentary 'Gambling in Las Vegas' (Theroux, 2007). Wilk's role as executive director of player development at the Las Vegas Hilton was to look after every need of the biggest gambling customers. The self-interest versus altruism tension in the ethics of that role became clear when Wilk answered Theroux's question about their relationship: 'He's a friend of mine, he's a high roller. He's also godfather to my little girl too'. Communication professionals often develop friendships with their clients, sources or customers, and this represents a key ethical juncture. Before embarking on such relationships, they might ask the crucial questions: Is this a genuine friendship of mutual benefit? Would the friendship survive if the professional relationship ended? To what extent is the friendship serving my own career and personal interests rather than the needs and welfare of the other party?

Reflect – Research – Review:

1. Apply each of the four moral approaches outlined above to this situation and answer the following:
   a. Deontology: How might Kant's categorical imperative of universal application apply to this situation?

b. Contractualism: What elements of a hypothetical 'social contract' are being honoured or broken in such a relationship?
c. Consequentialism: How might we project the potential consequences for the parties to this relationship, primarily the marketing executive and the high roller. [Those pursuing journalism as a career might also wish to project the potential consequences for the journalist and the subjects of the story.]
d. Virtue ethics: What does the scenario say about the virtues (and perhaps vices) of the marketing executive as a communication professional?
2. Explore further how the egoism/altruism analysis of the relationship might inform the communication ethics of the situation.
3. Finally, extend the above analysis by applying the rest of the Applied Ethics Matrix in Table 1.1 to the situation – combining philosophy, laws and professional codes, theoretical lenses and moral compass to assist in making a justifiable communication decision on the issue of friendship with clients or sources.

Reflect – Research – Review:

Now take the Applied Ethics Matrix and apply it to one of the following four professional communication dilemmas:

- A social media campaign in favour of a new commuter motorway that will reduce driving time and minimise accidents but will likely destroy an endangered fauna habitat.
- A tourism agency's sponsorship of a travel journalist's five-star vacation to an island resort.
- A marketing campaign to teenagers encouraging the drinking of zero alcohol beer.
- A phone call to the parents of a child who has just been killed in a train accident seeking a television interview about the incident and its effect on them.

In a nutshell
- There are important differences between morals (personal values about right actions), ethics (decisions related to professional ethical codes) and laws (society's rules of behaviour).
- Deontology is a rules-based approach to ethical decision making applying a system of duties and obligations. Under Kant's Categorical Imperative,

something should not be done unless you would be happy for there to be a universal rule requiring everyone to act that way.
- Contractualism suggests there is a moral social contract between all citizens demanding we treat each other well. It feeds into human rights-based approaches to ethical decisions.
- Consequentialism – stemming from Bentham's and Mill's utilitarianism – demands we look ahead to the potential consequences of an action and choose the approach that brings the greatest benefit to the most people.
- The virtue ethics approach can be combined with others because it focuses on the identification and development of the most virtuous elements of character, and upon taking actions that build good character.
- Ethical decisions can be shaped by a range of theoretical beliefs, approaches or motivations and these need to be identified and made known. These can include environmentalist, feminist, political, critical, mindful and solutions-oriented lenses, among others.
- The notions of egoism and altruism feed into ethical decision making. Not all egoistic decisions are wrong. In fact, self-interest is a part of all decision making but must be acknowledged and weighed against the impact upon others. Altruistic decisions place more emphasis on doing good for others.
- Professional communicators need to self-assess the elements of their own 'moral compass' – influences on their morality from their family or cultural background, religion or social networks. Potential biases need disclosure and differences between their moral compass and professional ethical codes or the law need to be resolved.
- The Applied Ethics Matrix combines philosophical approaches, laws and professional codes, theoretical lenses, respective interest analysis and moral compasses to assist in making a communication decision.

References and further reading

Alexander, L. and Moore, M. 2020, 'Deontological ethics', *The Stanford Encyclopedia of Philosophy*. Zalta, E.N. ed., <https://plato.stanford.edu/entries/ethics-deontological/>.

Ashford, E. and Mulgan, T. 2018, 'Contractualism', *The Stanford Encyclopedia of Philosophy*, Summer 2018 edn, Zalta, E.N. ed., <https://plato.stanford.edu/archives/sum2018/entries/contractualism/>.

Bertram, C. 2017, 'Jean Jacques Rousseau', *The Stanford Encyclopedia of Philosophy*. Zalta, E.N. ed., <https://plato.stanford.edu/entries/rousseau/>.

Brink, D. 2022, 'Mill's Moral and Political Philosophy', *The Stanford Encyclopedia of Philosophy*, Fall 2022 edn, Zalta, E.N. and Nodelman, U. eds, <https://plato.stanford.edu/archives/fall2022/entries/mill-moral-political/>.

Crimmins, J.E. 2021, 'Jeremy Bentham', *The Stanford Encyclopedia of Philosophy*, Winter 2021 edn, Zalta, E.N. ed., <https://plato.stanford.edu/archives/win2021/entries/bentham/>.

Crisp, R. 2020, 'Are we climbing the same mountain?', *ZEMO*, 3, 269–278, <https://doi.org/10.1007/s42048-020-00076-2>.

Driver, J. 2009, 'Chapter 2 – Normative Ethics', *The Oxford Handbook of Contemporary Philosophy*, Jackson, F. and Smith, M. eds, Oxford University Press, Oxford, 31–62.

Ethics Centre. 2022, *Ethics explainer – teleology*, Ethics Centre, Sydney, <https://ethics.org.au/teleology/>.

Flew, A. 1984, *A Dictionary of Philosophy*, revised 2nd edn, St Martin's Press, New York.

Friend, C. 2022, 'Social Contract Theory', In *Internet Encyclopedia of Philosophy – A Peer-Reviewed Academic Resource*, <https://iep.utm.edu/soc-cont/#H1>.

Grantham, S. and Pearson, M. 2022, *Social Media Risk and the Law: A Guide for Global Communicators*, Routledge, London and New York.

Guinebert, S. 2020, 'How do moral theories stand to each other?', *ZEMO*, 3, 279–299, <https://doi.org/10.1007/s42048-020-00077-1>.

Harper, D.R. 2022, *The Online Etymology Dictionary*. <www.etymonline.com/>.

Hursthouse, R. and Pettigrove, G. 2022, 'Virtue Ethics', *The Stanford Encyclopedia of Philosophy*, Winter 2022 edn, Zalta, E.N. and Nodelman, U. eds, <https://plato.stanford.edu/archives/win2022/entries/ethics-virtue/>.

Janke, T. and Quiggin, R. 2005, *Background paper 12: Indigenous cultural and intellectual property and customary law*, Law Reform Commission of Western Australia, 451–506, <www.wa.gov.au/system/files/2021-04/LRC-Project-094-Background-Papers.pdf>.

Lipari, L. 2017, 'Communication Ethics', *Oxford Research Encyclopedia of Communication*, <https://oxfordre.com/communication/view/10.1093/acrefore/9780190228613.001.0001/acrefore-9780190228613-e-58>.

Masterton, M. 1985, 'Samoa, where questioning is taboo', *Australian Journalism Review*, 7 (1&2), 114–115.

Norlock, K. 2019 'Feminist Ethics', *The Stanford Encyclopedia of Philosophy*, Summer 2019 edn, Zalta, E.N. ed., <https://plato.stanford.edu/archives/sum2019/entries/feminism-ethics/>.

Parfit, D. 2011, *On What Matters*. Oxford University Press, Oxford.

Parisi, P. 1997, 'Toward a 'Philosophy of Framing': News Narratives for Public Journalism', *Journalism & Mass Communication Quarterly*, 74 (4), 673–686.

Patching, R. and Hirst, M. 2021, *Journalism Ethics at the Crossroads: Democracy, Fake News, and the News Crisis*, Routledge, London and New York.

Pearson, M., McMahon, C., O'Donovan, A., and O'Shannessy, D. 2021, 'Building journalists' resilience through mindfulness strategies', *Journalism*, 22 (7), 1647–1664, <https://doi.org/10.1177/1464884919833253>.

Pearson, M. 2014, 'Towards 'mindful journalism': Applying Buddhism's Eightfold Path as an ethical framework for modern journalism', *Ethical Space* 11 (4), 38–46.

Rand, A. and Branden, N. 1964, *The Virtue of Selfishness: A new concept of egoism*, New American Library, New York.

Rawls, J. 1971, *A Theory of Justice* [TJ], Harvard University Press, Cambridge, MA.

Schirmacher, W. ed. 1996, *Arthur Schopenhauer – Philosophical Writings*. Continuum, New York.

Sinnott-Armstrong, W. 2019, 'Consequentialism', *Stanford Encyclopedia of Philosophy*, <https://plato.stanford.edu/entries/consequentialism/>.

Solutions Journalism Network. 2023, [Online]. <http://solutionsjournalism.org/>.

Stanford Encyclopedia of Philosophy <https://plato.stanford.edu/contents.html>.

Theroux, L. 2007, *Louis Theroux: Gambling in Las Vegas*, [film] Directed by Theroux, L., Las Vegas/London, BBC2.

United Nations (UN). 1948, *Universal Declaration of Human Rights*, <www.un.org/en/about-us/universal-declaration-of-human-rights>.

United Nations (UN). 2022, *Secretary-General's remarks to High-Level opening of COP27 – as delivered*, Media release 7 November, <www.un.org/sg/en/content/sg/statement/2022-11-07/secretary-generals-remarks-high-level-opening-of-cop27-delivered-scroll-down-for-all-english-version>.

Wenar, L. 2021, 'John Rawls', *Stanford Encyclopedia of Philosophy*, Zalta, E.N. ed., <https://plato.stanford.edu/entries/rawls/>.

2 Human rights, ethics and laws

To deny people their human rights is to challenge their very humanity. – Nelson Mandela, 1990

Key concepts

Human rights: Human rights are rights inherent to all human beings, regardless of their race, sex, nationality, ethnicity, language, religion or other status. They include the right to life and liberty, freedom from slavery and torture, freedom of opinion and expression, the right to work and education, and others.

Freedom of expression: The ideal that all human communication in a democratic society should be unshackled by laws or censorship – subject to the impact upon other human rights.

Freedom of the press: The term that applied to freedom of the media for more than five centuries since the invention of Gutenberg's printing press in 1440. Today, the expression is used interchangeably with 'media freedom'.

Co-regulation: A combination of the law (regulation) and self-regulation, usually administered by an overarching government agency.

Self-regulation: A particular profession's system of rules and procedures, usually centred on an ethical charter, where it can manage complaints internally without involving the legal system.

Codes of ethics and practice: Documents listing the ethical rules and expectations of members or employees, most notably for our purposes in the professional communication fields of journalism and public relations.

Press systems: Classifications of the functions of the press within different government systems. Siebert, Peterson and Schramm's (1963) *Four Theories of the Press* categorised press systems into 'Authoritarian', 'Libertarian', 'Soviet-Communist' or 'Social Responsibility' categories. (These were extended to include development and democratic-participant models.)

First Amendment: The words added to the US Constitution via the Bill of Rights prohibiting Congress enacting laws abridging freedom of religion, freedom of speech or freedom of the press. The term is sometimes used as a synonym for 'free expression'.

DOI: 10.4324/9781003372752-3

Philosophical and historical background to the human rights context of free expression

Professional communicators need to understand how a respect for human rights feeds into their ethical decisions and into the laws that impact their practices. The historical foundations of human rights as an ethical and legal framework have been traced back to ancient Greece and Rome (Piotrowicz and Kaye, 2000: 11). Greek philosopher Herodotus (484–425BCE) even developed a list of fundamental privileges citizens should be afforded, including equality before the law, equal respect for all and equal freedom of speech. The Roman philosophers Cicero (106–43BCE) and Ulpian (170–circa 223BCE) thought the state took its authority for lawmaking from an innate law of equality of all. The notion of fundamental human rights was fine-tuned over centuries until their first formulation in King John's *Magna Carta* ('Great Charter') in England in 1215 which included key justice principles such as the writ of habeas corpus requiring a citizen's release unless they were being detained with due process (Courtland et al., 2022). The next great human rights document was the *Declaration of Rights* – now known as the 'Bill of Rights' – read to the English Parliament in 1689 after a crisis in the succession of kings led to the replacement of those believing they ruled by divine right. It established basic rights and freedoms of citizens including the freedom of election, freedom of speech (in Parliament) and the establishment of jury trials (Piotrowicz and Kaye, 2000: 11). The Bill of Rights implemented some of the philosophy of universal 'natural rights' espoused by Thomas Hobbes (1588–1679) and John Locke (1632–1704), philosophers who had turned their minds to the notion of human rights and then to the right of free expression. The US *Declaration of Independence* in 1776 summed up the idea of natural rights in this famous passage:

> We hold these truths to be self-evident, that all men are created equal, that they are endowed by their Creator with certain unalienable Rights, that among these are Life, Liberty and the pursuit of Happiness.
> (*US Declaration of Independence*, 1776)

Those words have been attributed mainly to future US President Thomas Jefferson (1743–1826) but they built on the thinking of Hobbes, Locke and the French philosopher Jean Jacques Rousseau (1712–1778). Their key principles fed through into the key constitutional documents and international human rights instruments we examine in this chapter. The great thinkers saw freedom of speech as a vital component of every citizen's right to liberty.

If we return to the four classical philosophical approaches to ethical decision making outlined in Chapter 1, we can see that three sit comfortably with the notion of individual and universal human rights:

Deontology: Human rights are a good fit with Kant's 'Categorical Imperative' – a system of binding moral laws that everyone must follow regardless of their consequences. Modern international human rights frameworks operate as a universal rule-based approach to honoring the rights of others.
Contractualism: The concept of a moral social contract between all citizens also sits well with the modern approach to human rights.
Virtue ethics: Key virtues include justice, charity and generosity – each evident to some extent in human rights. Recognition of the rights of others has a fundamental moral character component. Empathy, compassion and acting to address the impact on others are all part of virtuous conduct linked with human rights.

However, at face value the Consequentialist approach – aiming for the greatest happiness overall and the end justifying the means – can lead to sacrificing the rights of a few for the good of the many. This might, for example, excuse the infringement of important fundamental human rights for some – perhaps their liberty, their safety or their privacy – in order to attain the maximum benefit for the majority. In communication ethics, the best examples can be drawn from the strict libertarian approach to freedom of expression – an attitude of 'publish and be damned' – that many editors and publishers read into the philosophies of the leading Utilitarians (Consequentialists) like John Milton and John Stuart Mill, as we see later in this chapter. That said, most acknowledge some rights are in contest with others and that sometimes it is necessary to infringe upon the rights of some for the greater good. A recent example was in the midst of the COVID-19 pandemic when individuals' rights to freedom of movement were sacrificed in the interests of general public health, an action endorsed by international bodies but opposed by a vocal minority.

Not all leading philosophers have been in favour of a rights-driven system. French philosopher Simone Weil (1909–1943) argued the focus should be on a citizen's obligation to do good to others rather than upon their individual rights:

> The possession of a right implies the possibility of using that right for either good or bad. Rights are therefore alien to the good. On the contrary, the accomplishment of an obligation is always good, everywhere. Truth, beauty, justice, compassion are always good, everywhere.
> (Weil, 2015: 108)

Freedom of speech as a human right is central to the work of professional communicators. However countless people have been killed throughout history for expressing religious or political views. Many more have been imprisoned, tortured or punished for exercising their free speech. In 399BCE, Socrates elected to drink a poison – hemlock – rather than recant his philosophical questioning of the edicts of his city-state, Athens (Brasch and Ulloth, 1986: 9). The history of freedom of expression can equally be viewed as a history of censorship, because intellectuals have been called upon to defend it when free expression has been threatened by government gagging. It was Johann Gutenberg's invention of movable type in about 1440, and the massive growth in the publishing industry over the next two centuries in the form of newsbooks and political pamphlets, that first triggered repressive licensing laws and the accompanying movement for press freedom (Feather, 1988: 46). It is interesting that these small radical 'pamphleteers' were similar to the social media posters we know today – often highly opinionated and quick to publish speculation and rumour.

Political philosopher and poet John Milton (1608–1674) – himself a pamphleteer – targeted print licensing laws in 1644 with *Areopagitica*, a speech to the parliament appealing for freedom of the presses. He went on to utter the famous free speech principle, 'Give me the liberty to know, to utter, and to argue freely according to conscience, above all liberties' (Patrides, 1985: 241). Milton inscribed his name on the title page of his unlicensed work in bold defiance of the law he was criticising. With this act, the principle of free expression had given birth to its offspring: press freedom. Milton's argument featured what he called the 'marketplace of ideas' – the principle that truth would win out eventually in a battle with falsehood. This proposition of a contest between truth and falsehood was often used during the 17th and 18th centuries to justify freedom of expression (Smith, 1988: 31). It continues in public discourse today and is cited frequently by libertarians opposing any limitations on free speech.

Freedom of expression was also central to John Locke's social contract theory, under which the primary role of governments was to serve the people (Overbeck, 2001: 36). Of the temptation to suppress truth and new ideas, Locke (1690) wrote in his preamble to an *Essay Concerning Human Understanding*:

> Truth scarce ever yet carried it by vote anywhere at its first appearance: new opinions are always suspected, and usually opposed, without any other reason but because they are not already common. But truth, like gold, is not the less so for being newly brought out of the mine. It is trial and examination must give it price.

Like Milton, Locke campaigned to abolish the printing licence system, which ended in 1694 (Overbeck, 2001: 36).

One of the great legal minds of the 18th century, Sir William Blackstone (1765–1769: 151–152), had a great impact on the evolution of press freedom in his *Commentaries on the Laws of England* by defining it as the absence of 'previous restraints upon publications'. Blackstone's principle of 'prior restraint' underscored the development of media law in the US. The idea was that freedom of the press could tolerate no restrictions prior to actual publication, such as licensing and taxes that had been imposed in Britain, but that the law should be allowed to take its course and be imposed after publication to punish those who abused this freedom. In other words, publications should be tax and licence free, but could be subject to laws like defamation and contempt once published.

England's foremost philosopher of the late 19th century, John Stuart Mill (1806–1873) articulated the need for free speech in a liberal democratic society in *On Liberty*, first published in 1859. He wrote:

> The time, it is to be hoped, is gone by, when any defence would be necessary of the 'liberty of the press' as one of the securities against corrupt or tyrannical government. No argument ... can now be needed, against permitting a legislature or an executive, not identified in interest with the people, to prescribe opinions to them, and determine what doctrines or what arguments they shall be allowed to hear.
>
> (1991: 20)

Mill's *On Liberty* defined the boundaries of freedom of expression in the modern democratic nation-state.

During the 17th to 19th centuries the movement for civil rights and individual liberties spread throughout Western Europe, epitomised by the French Revolution in 1789, implanting a legacy of press freedom throughout that region and in its colonial outposts. The key document of the French Revolution was the *Declaration of Rights of Man*, approved by the National Assembly of France on 26 August 1789. Its Article 11 stated (Avalon Project, 2002):

> The free communication of ideas and opinions is one of the most precious of the rights of man. Every citizen may, accordingly, speak, write, and print with freedom, but shall be responsible for such abuses of this freedom as shall be defined by law.

Note the important qualification: people should be responsible for abuses of this freedom 'as defined by law', a common theme to such provisions and a central thread in our study of media law. Nowhere has there ever been unshackled free speech or a completely free media: we operate on an international and historical continuum of free expression through to censorship.

It is only over the past century that the notion of free expression and a free media has gained traction on a broader international scale. Professional communicators can only work effectively if they have a deep understanding of the level of free expression tolerated in the societies in which they work. Public relations practitioners will often have to explain to managers and clients why journalists are able to pursue stories so vigorously and why it is important to be transparent and truthful in the midst of a crisis. Lawyers will need to understand this principle to defend a media client and when opposing a suppression order in court.

The human right of free expression will trump other rights such as privacy, reputation and a fair trial when so-called 'public interest' and 'the public's right

28 *Foundational approaches*

to know' demand it takes precedence. For editors, the notion of 'public interest' sometimes amounts to no more than public curiosity and ratings, but the term also finds its way into ethical codes and the law in the form of defences to some legal actions, as we learn in Part 2.

Freedom of the press through the lens of press systems theory

'Press systems' are classifications of the functions of the role of the press and their relative levels of freedom within different government systems. The seminal Siebert, Peterson and Schramm's *Four Theories of the Press* (1963) categorised press systems into 'Authoritarian', 'Libertarian', 'Soviet-Communist' or 'Social Responsibility'. Others have added further categories, including McQuail's (1987) 'Development' and 'Democratic-participant' models. When used to describe media regulation by governments, the libertarian model has most commonly been associated with private ownership of newspapers and other news media and their active watchdog role as the 'Fourth Estate'. But liberal democratic societies have also adopted a 'Social Responsibility' approach to the regulation of broadcast media, originally based on public or collective interest in control of what was in the pre-digital era the scarce resource of analogue broadcasting licences (Feintuck and Varney, 2006: 57). Proposals by inquiries into media regulation in the UK (Leveson, 2012) and Australia (Finkelstein, 2012) would have extended the social responsibility model to print and new media regulation. Communication theories of press systems provide mechanisms to help contextualise media regulation and to explain why media laws condone or prohibit certain media practices. Media regulations originated from an Anglo-American approach to journalism, shaped largely by the libertarian positioning of the press in those countries (the public's right to know and source confidentiality) and refined somewhat by the social responsibility pressures of the late 20th and early 21st centuries (concerns over broadcast licences as a public resource, and rights such as those of privacy and against discrimination).

New approaches to journalism such as 'peace journalism' (Lynch, 2010), 'solutions journalism' (Parisi, 1997; Solutions Journalism Network, 2023), and 'mindful journalism' (Gunaratne et al, 2015) are also attempts to move Western media towards a greater emphasis on the social responsibility approach – paying heed to the impacts of public communication on the rights and interests of others rather than placing more emphasis on the liberty of the press.

The level of free expression will depend on where policymakers believe the balance should rest after considering a host of other factors including competing rights, political and economic interests and sometimes even vested interests and corruption. Some countries justify their stricter regulation of the press, and limitations of media freedom, on religious, cultural or economic grounds, in line with the 'Development' model of press systems (McQuail, 1987). There has been debate about the lack of press freedom in the Asia-Pacific region: Malaysia, Singapore, Brunei and Fiji have state licensing systems in place for their newspapers, justified by a 'Development' model for the media 'to support the government in its quest to promote harmony, solidarity, tolerance and prosperity' (Dutt, 2010: 90).

Law of free expression and human rights internationally

The United Nations and its foundational documents give clear statements on human rights that offer professional communicators a yardstick for considering where free expression might be in competition with other rights. The *Universal Declaration of Human Rights* (United Nations, 1948) speaks of the 'inherent dignity' of all people in its Preamble. Articles especially relevant to media ethical decisions include:

Article 1: 'All human beings are born free and equal in dignity and rights';
2: '…without distinction of any kind, such as race, colour, sex, language, religion, political or other opinion, national or social origin, property, birth or other status';
7: against any discrimination or incitement to discrimination;
10: 'Everyone is entitled in full equality to a fair and public hearing';
11: 'Everyone charged with a penal offence has the right to be presumed innocent until proved guilty';
12: Prohibiting 'arbitrary interference with his privacy, family, home or correspondence, nor to attacks upon his honour and reputation. Everyone has the right to the protection of the law against such interference or attacks';
18: Guaranteeing 'freedom of thought, conscience and religion'; and,
27: Establishing 'the right freely to participate in the cultural life of the community' (United Nations, 1948).

These are all potentially at odds with Article 19, enshrining:

> the right to freedom of opinion and expression; this right includes freedom to hold opinions without interference and to seek, receive and impart information and ideas through any media and regardless of frontiers.
> (United Nations, 1948)

The Declaration was followed in 1966 by the *International Covenant on Civil and Political Rights* (UN Human Rights Office, 1966). This is a multilateral treaty that commits states to respect the civil and political rights of individuals and has a similar list of articles to the *Universal Declaration*, although sometimes with slightly different wording. Again, Article 19 guarantees the right to hold opinions without interference along with the right to freedom of expression across borders and in any medium (UN Human Rights Office, 1966). At face value, Article 19 appears to give all the world's citizens a right

30 *Foundational approaches*

to free expression. While this is a lofty goal, it has many limitations such as the fact that many countries either have not ratified the covenant or have not incorporated its provisions to make them part of their domestic law. Meanwhile, special efforts have been made to protect journalists at a UN level. The UN Secretary-General reported that in July 2019, at the Global Conference for Media Freedom, the Media Freedom Coalition was formed (UN, 2021: 8). This is a partnership of states working together to advocate for media freedom online and offline, and for the safety of journalists. At that point, 49 member states had signed the global pledge on media freedom – a written commitment to improve media freedom at the national level and to collaborate at the international level.

Reflect – Research – Review:

Review the key human rights protected under the *Universal Declaration of Human Rights*. Select three of them and explain how the work of a professional communicator could infringe them.

Guarantees of free expression also appear in many foundational legal documents internationally, but again they vary markedly in their application. At least four major democratic English-speaking nations have Bills of Rights enshrining free speech. The First Amendment to the US Constitution in 1791 guaranteed free speech and a free press. The *Canadian Charter of Rights and Freedoms* (1982), at s2(b), confers upon every citizen 'freedom of thought, belief, opinion and expression, including freedom of the press and other media of communication'. Rights instruments in the United Kingdom and New Zealand do not mention media freedom, opting instead for the broader term 'freedom of expression'. New Zealand enshrined free expression at s14 of its *Bill of Rights Act 1990* (BoRA).

Case example:

Flag Burning case, 2011: The New Zealand Supreme Court decided the right to free expression in the *NZ Bill of Rights Act* protected Valerie Morse, an anti-war protester who burned her country's flag during a dawn memorial service in Wellington. Her conviction for offensive behaviour was set aside.

The European Convention on Human Rights has had a strong impact on the laws of countries on that continent, as well as in the United Kingdom via the *Human Rights Act 1988*. Free expression is protected in Article 10, and it carries with it similar responsibilities to those in the *Universal Declaration of Human Rights* (United Nations, 1948). European countries vary greatly in their levels of free expression. In 2022, they occupied nine of the top ten places in the Reporters Without Borders World Press Freedom Index (Reporters Without Borders, 2022).

British and European liberal ideals found their way into the wording of the *American Declaration of Independence* in 1776, the *US Constitution* in 1789 and the *US Bill of Rights* in 1791. Central to the *Bill of Rights* was the First Amendment to the *US Constitution*:

> Congress shall make no law respecting an establishment of religion, or prohibiting the free exercise thereof; or abridging the freedom of speech, or of the press; or the right of the people peaceably to assemble, and to petition the Government for a redress of grievances.

The First Amendment has allowed the US media to act with fewer restraints than their colleagues in almost any other country. Nevertheless, their behaviour is not unrestricted and in the two centuries since it was enacted there have been court and parliamentary battles against attempts to read it narrowly. Many such contests have been lost, with courts and legislatures maintaining that other rights – like national security – take precedence.

The most significant First Amendment case was Sullivan's case (1964) (see Key Case 2.1). The US Supreme Court invoked the First Amendment to rule that public officials had to pass tough new tests before they could succeed in a defamation action, even if the allegations were false.

Key Case 2.1: Sullivan's case

New York Times v Sullivan (1964) 376 US 254

Facts

Civil rights activists took out a full-page advertisement in *The New York Times* in 1960 which made accusations against the police department in Montgomery, Alabama over its treatment of protesters. Some of the facts they stated were untrue. The elected police commissioner, L.B. Sullivan, took umbrage at the false allegations and sued the newspaper for defamation in an Alabama court. He argued the advertisement implied police under his supervision were violent and intimidating towards African-American civil rights protesters. The Alabama court and the state Supreme Court each found in favour of Sullivan but *The New York Times* appealed to the US Supreme Court claiming any reputational damage was unintentional and that the speech in the advertisement should be protected by the First Amendment.

32 Foundational approaches

> *Law*
>
> In a unanimous decision, the US Supreme Court found in favour of *The New York Times*. It agreed all communications were protected by the First Amendment and that public officials had to demonstrate that defamatory comments about them were made with 'actual malice' – either 'with knowledge that it was false or with reckless disregard for the truth'.
>
> *Lesson for communicators*
>
> The *NY Times v Sullivan* decision is a landmark communication law case because it showed the extent to which US law can protect public communication – even when material is both damaging and untrue. It also showed how different jurisdictions can choose to strike a balance between free expression and other human rights – in this case a public official's right to their untarnished reputation.

For many truth-seekers and truth-tellers, the commitment to free expression has taken the form of danger, physical injury and even death. The Committee to Protect Journalists (CPJ) lists more than 2,193 journalists and media workers confirmed as killed in the course of their work since 1992 (CPJ, 2023). Many others experience violence or are imprisoned for what they report. Some have suffered as the victims of lawsuits by those who set out to gag them. International free expression groups such as the Electronic Frontier Foundation, Amnesty International, Transparency International, Reporters Without Borders, Freedom House, the Committee to Protect Journalists, Article 19 and IFEX all operate as important non-government organisations dedicated to the freedom of communication and transparency of government processes globally.

> **Reflect – Research – Review:**
>
> Go to the website of one of the leading non-government organisations defending free expression, such as Reporters Without Borders. Find a recent example of where a professional communicator's media freedom has been threatened and write a 150-word case summary.

Professional ethical dilemmas, co-regulation and self-regulation

Rules governing the behaviour of professional communicators typically fall into one of three categories: laws, co-regulation or self-regulation. The term 'self-regulation' usually refers to a profession's system of rules and procedures, including for ethical complaints that it can handle internally without involving the court system. Such self-regulatory processes might be contained within a particular corporation or apply across a whole industry. For example, press councils internationally feature codes of practice that should be followed by their member publishers. Journalists' unions and professional associations have codes of ethics. Particular media corporations or platforms often have their own internal ethical guidelines. Complaints might be variously adjudicated by a disciplinary or complaints committee or perhaps an ombudsman. The biggest criticism of self-regulatory approaches is that they are renowned for not having strong enforcement regimes in place and they are often adjudicated by industry or corporate 'insiders' with no great incentives for transparency or penalties.

Co-regulation involves a combination of the law (regulation) by governments or their agencies and self-regulation by media industry groups. For example, a communication regulator like the Australian Communications and Media Authority (ACMA) has power to intervene when self-regulation in the broadcast media via their industry codes of practice has failed or a decision has been appealed.

Society's laws take the form of a combination of formal legislation and court decisions, typically enforced by either criminal penalties such as jail terms or fines or civil remedies like an award of damages or the issuing of a court order (injunction) demanding or prohibiting some action. In democracies self-regulatory mechanisms are often proposed by professional communication bodies as alternatives to proposed laws or regulations. The extent to which governments encroach upon the work of communicators – particularly in the realm of their freedom of expression – will often reflect the type of press system in place in that nation.

The contest between the human right of free expression and the rights and interests of other citizens is at the crux of many professional communication ethical codes and their regulation. Communication professional groups and industry organisations usually have a document listing the ethical rules and expectations of their members. Examples internationally include the Society of Professional Journalists' (SPJ) Code of Ethics in the US and the Chartered Institute of Public Relations Code of Conduct in the UK. Australian equivalents are the MEAA Australian Journalists Association Code of Ethics and the Public Relations Institute of Australia's Code of Ethics (see Tables 2.1 and 2.2). Free but responsible communication is at the heart of journalists' ethical codes that typically weigh free expression and a free press against other rights featured over the balance of this book – reputational damage, confidentiality of sources, invasion of privacy, the right to a fair trial, plagiarism, national security, discrimination and harassment. Public relations practitioners also have ethical codes focussed less on freedom of speech and more upon setting behavioural boundaries in the areas of truth-telling, bias, disclosure of vested interests, secret payments, misleading and deceptive conduct and misrepresentation. The professional ethics of other communicators often reflects their organisations' corporate social responsibility (CSR) policies.

Global platform self-regulation

One type of self-regulation exists within social media platforms. Human rights become complicated in the digital era when important decisions to do with privacy, freedom of expression, discrimination and personal safety are adjudicated by large globalised corporate entities. Their self-regulatory processes typically pay heed to such important human rights (and simultaneously to their own commercial interests) via their 'terms of use' (or 'terms of service'), their content moderation practices and their complaints and disciplinary procedures. Social media is now so integral to professional communication practice that journalists and public relations practitioners need to be familiar with their rules and processes. A social media company has the right to suspend an account for what it deems to be misuse or misbehaviour. This can involve something as serious as cyberbullying or posting offensive or untrue material, through to setting up an account in a false name. However, terms of service also represent a non-legal avenue of recourse for professional communicators wanting redress against trolls and troublesome users who might be damaging their brands and reputations on social media. For example, a common clause in terms of service states:

> We may also remove or refuse to distribute any Content on the Services, suspend or terminate users, and reclaim usernames without liability to you.
> (Twitter/X, 2023)

Platforms vary in their appeal processes for disabled or terminated accounts. A good example of self-regulation within a social media platform can be found at Meta, which claims more than 15,000 reviewers worldwide review potential violations on Facebook and Instagram, reviewing content in more than 50 languages (Meta, n.d.). The extent of resources and personnel allocated by such platforms to content control, moderation and complaints handling became evident after entrepreneur Elon Musk bought Twitter (now 'X') for $US44 billion in 2022. The platform became 'less safe' after he sacked hundreds of staff in the content moderation team, including its head (Fung, 2022).

Basic Australian legal principles in human rights and free expression

Prior to European settlement, communication and storytelling within and between Aboriginal and Torres Strait Islander peoples were navigated through a range of socio-linguistic, cultural and religious conventions related to seniority, gender, place, traditions and purpose (Klapproth, 2004: 6). In that sense, codes of communication behaviour ('ethics') varied in accordance with social roles and generational status. Human rights were indeed 'natural rights' and were determined in accordance with cultural norms of the peoples. 'Communication law' was markedly different from the laws we consider in this book, yet similar in that it was socially determined over thousands of years according to the various rights of the individuals communicating in the many cultures and places where that communication took place.

When Australia became a British colony, freedom of the press shadowed its development in England. Mayer (1964: 10) recorded that Australia's first newspaper, the *Sydney Gazette* (1803–42), was published 'By Authority', indicating the censorship powers of the governors of the day. Pullan (1994) wrote a colourful account of the early instances of censorship in colonial Australia. It was a litany of prosecutions for sedition, criminal libel and contempt as governors attempted to force their will on the fledgling press. An excerpt from the *Newspaper Acts Opinion* in 1827 captured a crucial moment in the development of press freedom in Australia: the dispute between NSW Governor Ralph Darling and Chief Justice Sir Francis Forbes over newspaper licensing. Former NSW Chief Justice James Spigelman (2002) described the episode as 'the most serious conflict between the judiciary and the executive that has ever occurred in Australian history' because there were 'fundamental principles at stake involving the rule of law, the independence of the judiciary and the freedom of the press'. Communication law over the ensuing 200 years in Australia has continued to be a tussle between those values, as we see in the Australian-related content in this book.

Unlike other Western democracies, Australia has no equivalent to the US First Amendment and no written law enshrining freedom of the press at a national level. (However, some state and territory charters are detailed below.) The Australian Constitution did not explicitly mention freedom of speech or of the press at Federation in 1901. Nevertheless, Australian laws affecting press freedom deviated little from the British system. It was not until the 1990s that major High Court decisions held that the Australian Constitution contained an implied, albeit limited, right to freedom of communication on matters of politics and government.

Under the leadership of Dr H.V. Evatt, Australia was one of just eight nations involved in the drafting of the landmark *Universal Declaration of Human Rights*. Australia voted in favour of the Declaration in 1948. Although it is not formally binding, the *Universal Declaration of Human Rights* is certainly influential in Australian law, with it being referenced in at least 50 judgments by the High Court of Australia by 2022. Despite signing the *International Covenant on Civil and Political Rights* (ICCPR) in 1972 and ratifying it in 1980, Australia has never adopted it in full into domestic law (Parliament of Australia, 2019: para 2.4). Nevertheless, it is more influential than the Declaration and it has been referenced in 141 High Court cases between 1978 and 2022.

Specific guidelines for public servants advise them that they must consider the right to freedom of opinion and expression when developing legislation, policies and programmes that do any of the following:

36 Foundational approaches

- regulate the content of any speech, publication, broadcast, display or promotion;
- regulate the format or manner of any form of expression;
- restrict or censor media coverage, including in relation to political matters;
- require material to be approved before it may be published;
- attach criminal or civil liability to the publication of opinions or information;
- regulate or restrict access to information, including on the internet;
- impose censorship or provide for classification of entertainment content; or
- regulate commercial expression (such as advertising)
  (Australian Government Attorney-General's Department, n.d., para 3).

Key laws on human rights in Australia

Although Australia has no Bill of Rights enshrining human rights at the Commonwealth level, three Australian jurisdictions do feature bills or charters of rights. Queensland, Victoria and the Australian Capital Territory (ACT) have their own human rights legislation, which grants rights of freedom of expression to individuals among a host of other rights. Queensland's *Human Rights Act 2019* protects 23 rights, including freedom of expression and the often-competing rights of privacy, reputation, a fair hearing, religion and belief. Breaches of rights not dealt with adequately by a government agency after 45 days can be filed with the Queensland Human Rights Commission.

Section 16 of the Australian Capital Territory's *Human Rights Act* 2004 states that everyone has the right to right to freedom of expression, including the right to impart information and ideas orally, in writing or in print, or in another way, subject only to reasonable limits set by Territory laws that can demonstrably be justified in a free and democratic society.

In Victoria, s15 of the *Charter of Human Rights and Responsibilities Act* 2006 (Vic) expresses the right in very similar terms, subject to lawful restrictions reasonably necessary to respect the rights and reputation of other persons; or for the protection of national security, public order, public health or public morality (Pearson and Polden, 2019: 49). The Victorian Equal Opportunity and Human Rights Commission offers complaints channels for employee and workplace rights, aboriginal rights, disability rights, LGBTQI+ rights, older people's rights, racial and religious rights, youth rights and women's rights, all linked to human rights listed in that state's Charter and other state-based human rights legislation.

A host of Australian laws protect various human rights via legislation or case law decided by superior court judges (known as the 'common law' or 'general law'). Most go some way towards striking a balance between free expression and the particular human right in question, by featuring either a public interest defence or a media exception to the legislation. In Chapter 11 we look more closely at anti-discrimination and cyberbullying laws. The *Racial Discrimination Act* prohibits behaviour (including publications) that offend on the grounds of race, colour, nationality or ethnicity, but a fair comment defence is available if the opinion is fair and based on provable facts. The *Privacy Act 1988* (Chapter 7) seeks to protect the human right of privacy via strict data protection laws but the media have an exemption if they are signatories to privacy provisions via their own industry groups. The universal human right to not have one's reputation unfairly damaged is protected by a combination of the *Defamation Act 2005* and common law developed over centuries, with media defences outlined in Chapter 5. Media law topics of national security and justice have similar balancing features. In short, that balancing process between free expression and competing human rights is at the heart of all areas of communication law featured in this book.

Key Australian cases in freedom of expression

Although Australia has no written constitutional protection of freedom of expression, in a series of cases from 1992 the High Court has found there is an implied freedom to communicate on matters of politics and government in the Constitution. An 'implied freedom' is one that is not explicitly stated in the Constitution, but has been implied by High Court judges to exist because of the context and conventions of a democratic system of responsible and representative government. The High Court has, however, allowed for that implied freedom to be impinged upon by reasonably appropriate laws.

Case examples: Cases on the implied freedom to communicate on matters of government have included:

ACTV case (1992): The Commonwealth government's power to prohibit political advertising on radio and television on the eve of an election was challenged successfully under the implied freedom.

Stephens' case (1994): Three articles published in 1992 by *The West Australian* newspaper about travel by six Western Australian politicians quoted an MP describing the trip as a 'mammoth junket' and a 'rort' – a waste of public funds done without parliament's knowledge. When the politicians sued for defamation, the High Court broadened a defence called 'qualified privilege' to apply to the media if the defamation happened while discussing government or politics.

Theophanous's case (1994): When a Victorian RSL president had published a letter in the *Sunday Herald Sun* imputing that a Labor MP was biased towards Greeks as migrants and that he was an 'idiot', the politician sued for defamation. The court developed a new defamation defence based on the implied freedom.

Lange's case (1997): Former New Zealand Prime Minister David Lange sued the ABC over a broadcast on *Four Corners* about political donations. On appeal, the High Court described the new freedom to communicate as a brake on the efforts of government or legislators to limit what people might say – as distinct from a positive 'right'. The question in each case was, if a particular law like defamation was a burden on communication about government and political matters, whether the law served a legitimate end. In defamation, this meant a 'reasonableness' test would be applied to a defamatory publication on a political matter.

Palm Island Parole case (2012): Indigenous parolee – activist Lex Wotton – wished to make comments in the media. However, Queensland law banned prisoners on parole attending public meetings and being paid for media appearances. The High Court majority decided the legislation was a reasonable burden on the freedom to communicate on matters of government or politics and served a legitimate end.

Mall Preachers case (2013): Adelaide City Council tried using a local government by-law to stop evangelical members of a fundamentalist 'Street Church' preaching in Adelaide's busy Rundle Mall in a confronting style that bothered passers-by. The High Court held that even though the preachers' political communication was burdened, the constraints were legitimate for the good rule and government of the area.

Afghan Letters case (2013): The High Court split 3–3 over whether a law restricting the use of the postal service to distribute offensive materials was invalid because it was inconsistent with the implied constitutional freedom of political communication. An anti-war protester, Man Haron Monis (who later died conducting a siege in the Lindt Café in Sydney), sent at least 12 insulting letters and a recorded message to the families of Australian soldiers killed in action in Afghanistan, and to the mother of an Austrade official killed in Indonesia. All High Court justices agreed a NSW postal law under which Monis was charged did restrict political speech, but were split on whether the legislation was legitimate or was compatible with Australia's system of representative and responsible government.

Protesters' case (2017): The High Court held a Tasmanian law empowering police to direct protesters to leave business premises under pain of arrest and criminal penalties, was invalid to the extent that it impermissibly burdened the implied freedom of political communication.

Anonymous Tweets case (2019): An employee of the Commonwealth Department of Immigration and Citizenship was dismissed after it was discovered she had used the anonymous Twitter handle '@LaLegale' to broadcast more than 9,000 tweets critical of her department. The High Court held the public service provisions were reasonably appropriate to their purpose of keeping public servants apolitical and did not impose an unjustified burden on the implied freedom.

LibertyWorks Case (2021): A 5–2 majority of the High Court held that the *Foreign Influence Transparency Scheme Act 2018* (Cth) did not impermissibly burden the implied freedom by requiring individuals or entities to register if they were conducting lobbying, communications activity, or making payments on behalf of a foreign principal aimed at influencing politics or government. The court applied a three-step proportionality test: whether a law was suitable, necessary and adequate in its balance. One justice questioned whether the implied freedom should exist at all.

Animal Cruelty case (2022): An animal rights corporation and its director failed to have NSW surveillance legislation overturned on the basis of the implied freedom. A 4–3 majority of the High Court applied the three-step proportionality test to decide that it was not an unreasonable imposition on the implied freedom that legislation could prohibit the publication of animal cruelty footage obtained by trespass to a farm.

In short, the High Court is still fine-tuning the implied constitutional freedom to communicate on matters of politics and government but has set a high bar when considering whether that freedom should trump legitimate public policies.

Self-regulation and co-regulation of Australian media: where ethics and law converge

Other mechanisms impact on the research and publishing activities of professional communicators – either in tandem with laws as 'co-regulation' or independently of the legal system via corporations or industry groups as 'self-regulation'. In the newspaper industry (and its online iterations) and in public relations, the trend has been towards self-regulatory mechanisms, including media organisations' in-house codes of practice, the Media, Entertainment and Arts Alliance (MEAA) ethics processes, the industry-funded Australian Press Council and the disciplinary powers of the Public Relations Institute of Australia (PRIA). Here we summarise some of the key co-regulatory and self-regulatory players.

Australian Communications and Media Authority (ACMA)

Broadcast media are regulated by the *Broadcasting Services Act 1992* in a system of 'co-regulation'. Section 51(v) of the Constitution granted the Commonwealth parliament control over 'postal, telegraphic, telephonic, and other like services', which for more than four decades was interpreted to include broadcasting, giving rise to this Commonwealth agency. The ACMA regulates broadcasting, radio communications, telecommunications and online content. It regulates the operations of all broadcast media except the national public broadcasters, although it can review their handling of complaints. Under s123, the responsibility for the development of codes of practice was devolved to the main radio and television industry groups, which include Free TV Australia and Commercial Radio Australia. Other codes of practice cover community broadcasting, narrowcasting, subscription television and internet services. Such codes are meant to cover a range of topics (many of which deal with human rights related to children, women, discrimination and privacy), and include 'promoting accuracy and fairness in news and current affairs programmes' and the development of complaints-handling protocols. Examples include the Commercial Television Industry

40 *Foundational approaches*

Code of Practice (Free TV Australia, 2015) and Commercial Radio Code of Practice (Commercial Radio Australia, 2017), covering accuracy and fairness in news and current affairs programmes. ACMA's rules for radio and television broadcasters can be found at <www.acma.gov.au/tv-and-radio-broadcasters>. (The ABC and SBS have their own codes of practice, which are notified to ACMA.)

Australian Press Council

The Australian Press Council (APC) is a non-profit organisation funded by print and digital media publishers. It was established in 1976, in the midst of political pressure for greater regulation of the press. It aims to promote freedom of speech 'through responsible and independent print and digital media and adherence to high journalistic and editorial standards'. It manages a complaints regime where citizens can seek an adjudication against a member publisher which it would then be obliged to publish. It has no actual punitive powers. Its key documents for ethical self-regulation are its Statements of Principles, covering fundamental values like accuracy, fairness, privacy and integrity; specific standards for covering sensitive issues like suicide and interviews with hospital patients; and Advisory Guidelines on specific areas of reporting and publishing practice. Its latest processes and membership, along with recent adjudication decisions, can be found at <www.presscouncil.org.au>. Seven West Media withdrew from the APC in 2012 and has since operated a separate Independent Media Council for West Australian newspapers. (See <www.independentmediacouncil.com.au/>). In 2021 the MEAA gave notice it would be leaving the Council in 2025 (MEAA, 2021).

MEAA Ethics Complaints Panel

The ethics panel of the MEAA has actual disciplinary powers at its disposal for use against individual members of the journalism union who breach its Code of Ethics – but it rarely uses them. Members of the MEAA are required to abide by the Code of Ethics (see Table 2.1). This is the primary document cited whenever an ethical issue to do with journalism arises and is relevant in this book to the areas of secrets, confidentiality, intellectual property, privacy and discrimination. Its twelve items demand honesty, fairness, independence and respect for the rights of others. The MEAA's ethical complaints procedures are outlined online (MEAA, 2018). If a complaint is upheld, the infringing journalist may be liable to a range of penalties including: warning, reprimand, fine (maximum $1,000), membership suspension (for up to one year) and expulsion from membership. The processes do not apply to non-members of the union, but the Code of Ethics is considered the primary ethical document for all Australian journalists.

Table 2.1 MEAA Journalist Code of Ethics

Respect for truth and the public's right to information are fundamental principles of journalism. Journalists search, disclose, record, question, entertain, comment, and remember. They inform citizens and animate democracy. They scrutinise power, but also exercise it, and should be responsible and accountable. MEAA members engaged in journalism commit themselves to:

honesty
fairness
independence
respect for the rights of others

Journalists will educate themselves about ethics and apply the following standards:

1. Report and interpret honestly, striving for accuracy, fairness and disclosure of all essential facts. Do not suppress relevant available facts, or give distorting emphasis. Do your utmost to give a fair opportunity for reply.
2. Do not place unnecessary emphasis on personal characteristics, including race, ethnicity, nationality, gender, age, sexual orientation, family relationships, religious belief, or physical or intellectual disability.
3. Aim to attribute information to its source. Where a source seeks anonymity, do not agree without first considering the source's motives and any alternative attributable source. Where confidences are accepted, respect them in all circumstances.
4. Do not allow personal interest, or any belief, commitment, payment, gift or benefit, to undermine your accuracy, fairness or independence.
5. Disclose conflicts of interest that affect, or could be seen to affect, the accuracy, fairness or independence of your journalism. Do not improperly use a journalistic position for personal gain.
6. Do not allow advertising or other commercial considerations to undermine accuracy, fairness or independence.
7. Do your utmost to ensure disclosure of any direct or indirect payment made for interviews, pictures, information or stories.
8. Use fair, responsible and honest means to obtain material. Identify yourself and your employer before obtaining any interview for publication or broadcast. Never exploit a person's vulnerability or ignorance of media practice.
9. Present pictures and sound which are true and accurate. Any manipulation likely to mislead should be disclosed.
10. Do not plagiarise.
11. Respect private grief and personal privacy. Journalists have the right to resist compulsion to intrude.
12. Do your utmost to achieve fair correction of errors.

Guidance Clause
Basic values often need interpretation and sometimes come into conflict. Ethical journalism requires conscientious decision-making in context. Only substantial advancement of the public interest or risk of substantial harm to people allows any standard to be overridden.

Source: Media Entertainment and Arts Alliance, Sydney, 2022 <www.meaa.org/meaa-media/code-of-ethics/>

42 *Foundational approaches*

Corporate codes of practice

Internal complaints-handling protocols vary across media outlets, partly because of their own corporate policies and partly because some media sectors are obliged to have such processes, while for others it is purely voluntary. Newspapers and their new digital products operate in a voluntary self-regulatory environment, so their complaints-handling processes might range from an editor's review through to a formal corporate policy. Some former newspaper and online news groups have established codes of practice for journalists within their own newsrooms. An example is the News Corp Australia Editorial Professional Conduct Policy (*The Australian*, 2022) which covers a host of unethical practices read in conjunction with other policies. ABC journalists operate under a suite of standards including their Editorial Policies, Editorial Guidelines, Classification Standards and Code of Practice, with accompanying complaints, internal review and disciplinary processes (ABC, 2022).

ABC's Media Watch – public shaming via national television

Regulatory bodies vary markedly in their powers and influence over journalists and their behaviour. However, the institution that many journalists fear most – and that many quite simply despise – is the ABC's weekly programme *Media Watch*, which was first screened in 1989. Its website promotes it with the tag line 'Everyone loves it until they're on it'. *Media Watch* has exposed some spectacular ethical breaches. These include blatant instances of untruths, plagiarism, deception, bias, privacy invasion, undisclosed payments for coverage and shameless self-promotion by news outlets. While *Media Watch* itself has no sanctions available, the power of the programme lies in the fact that ethical breaches and glaring errors are exposed on national television and the journalists and their outlets are shamed publicly, sometimes prompting other disciplinary action against them.

PRIA codes and disciplinary processes

The Public Relations Institute of Australia (PRIA) is a self-regulatory professional body with disciplinary powers over its members for breaches of its Code of Ethics (see Table 2.2) and the organisation's Consultancy Code of Practice (applying to full professional members who are registered consultancies). These documents are detailed at <www.pria.com.au>. They require ethical practice in relation to honesty, confidentiality, conflict of interest, fee charging practices, transparency of funding, exaggerated claims, misrepresentation and injury to other practitioners. Given the lack of laws requiring the registration, licensing or accreditation of public relations personnel in Australia, there are no statutory sanctions for misconduct. Instead, PRIA has power to censure, fine, suspend and expel members who have breached the code – and to 'suitably

Table 2.2 Public Relations Institute of Australia (PRIA) Code of Ethics

Public Relations Institute of Australia (PRIA) Code of Ethics

PRIA is a professional body serving the interests of its members. PRIA is mindful of the responsibility which public relations professionals owe to the community as well as to their clients and employers.

PRIA requires members to adhere to the highest standards of ethical practice and professional competence. All members are duty-bound to act responsibly and to be accountable for their actions.

The following code of ethics binds all members of PRIA:

1. Members shall deal fairly and honestly with their employers, clients and prospective clients, with their fellow workers including superiors and subordinates, with public officials, the communication media, the general public and with fellow members of PRIA.
2. Members shall avoid conduct or practices likely to bring discredit upon themselves, the Institute, their employers or clients.
3. Members shall not knowingly disseminate false or misleading information and shall take care to avoid doing so inadvertently.
4. With the exception of the requirements of Clause 9 members shall safeguard the confidences of both present and former employers and clients, including confidential information about employers' or clients' business affairs, technical methods or processes, except upon the order of a court of competent jurisdiction.
5. No member shall represent conflicting interests nor, without the consent of the parties concerned, represent competing interests.
6. Members shall refrain from proposing or agreeing that their consultancy fees or other remuneration be contingent entirely on the achievement of specified results.
7. Members shall inform their employers or clients if circumstances arise in which their judgment or the disinterested character of their services may be questioned by reason of personal relationships or business or financial interests.
8. Members practising as consultants shall seek payment only for services specifically commissioned.
9. Members shall be prepared to identify the source of funding of any public communication they initiate or for which they act as a conduit.
10. Members shall, in advertising and marketing their skills and services and in soliciting professional assignments, avoid false, misleading or exaggerated claims and shall refrain from comment or action that may injure the professional reputation, practice or services of a fellow member.
11. Members shall inform the Board of the Institute and/or the relevant State/Territory Council(s) of the Institute of evidence purporting to show that a member has been guilty of, or could be charged with, conduct constituting a breach of this Code.
12. No member shall intentionally injure the professional reputation or practice of another member.
13. Members shall help to improve the general body of knowledge of the profession by exchanging information and experience with fellow members.
14. Members shall act in accord with the aims of the Institute, its regulations and policies.
15. Members shall not misrepresent their status through misuse of title, grading, or the designation FPRIA, MPRIA or APRIA.

Source: PRIA, Sydney, 2009 <www.pria.com.au/about-pria/code-of-ethics-privacy/code-of-ethics/>

44 *Foundational approaches*

publicise' its decisions. All members are required to agree in writing that they will adhere to the Code of Ethics upon joining PRIA. Ethics complaints are adjudicated by the national council of PRIA's College of Fellows – a committee of the industry's senior practitioners. The complaints procedure is detailed in the *Code of Ethics Administration Procedure Manual* (PRIA, 2003).

Social media policies

One of the most important self-regulatory systems in place in the modern workplace is the social media policy of the organisation that employs professional communicators. These can vary from just a few dot points through to highly legalistic industrial regulations. Decisions by the Fair Work Commission have instructed employers on what constitutes an effective social media policy. Such policies need to offer guidance on public versus private social media use, be kept up to date, be reasonable and staff must be offered training on their requirements (Grantham and Pearson, 2022). Use of social media accounts to harass or infringe upon the rights of others will normally invoke serious disciplinary repercussions.

Reflect – Research – Review:

Freedom of communication could be limited in different ways for journalists and public relations practitioners. Explain how and why.

Reflect – Research – Review:

Compare the code of ethics of a journalism professional association with that of a public relations professional association. Identify three important differences in their guidelines.

In a nutshell
- The origins of free speech (and censorship) can be traced back at least to the time of Socrates, though the battle for a free press was taken up by libertarians like Milton, Locke, Mill and Jefferson through the 17th, 18th and 19th centuries.
- US government attempts to restrain publications in the national interest have often failed on First Amendment grounds.
- Other countries have taken a range of approaches to press freedom, varying markedly according to their political, cultural and historical backgrounds.

- Article 19 of the *Universal Declaration of Human Rights* gives all world citizens the right to freedom of opinion and expression and the right to 'receive and impart information and ideas through any media and regardless of frontiers'.
- Australia has no equivalent to the US First Amendment enshrining freedom of the press. However, in recent decades the High Court has recognised an implied freedom to communicate on matters of politics and government and there is some limited protection in charters of rights in the ACT, Victoria and Queensland.
- The enforcement of media codes of behaviour come from a combination of laws and regulations, co-regulation and self-regulation.

References and further reading

ABC. 2022, *Editorial Policies and Guidance*, ABC, Sydney, <https://about.abc.net.au/how-the-abc-is-run/what-guides-us/abc-editorial-standards/editorial-policies/>.

The Australian. 2022, *News Corp Australia Editorial Professional Conduct Policy – Editorial Code of Conduct*, News Corporation, Sydney, <www.theaustralian.com.au/editorial-code-of-conduct>.

Australian Government Attorney-General's Department. (n.d.), *Right to Freedom of Opinion and Expression*, Canberra, <www.ag.gov.au/rights-and-protections/human-rights-and-anti-discrimination/human-rights-scrutiny/public-sector-guidance-sheets/right-freedom-opinion-and-expression#where-does-the-right-to-freedom-of-opinion-and-expression-come-from>.

Avalon Project, Yale Law School. 2002, *Declaration of the Rights of Man 1789*, <http://avalon.law.yale.edu/18th_century/rightsof.asp>.

Blackstone, W. 1765–1769, *Commentaries on the Laws of England*, The Avalon Project, Yale Law School, <http://avalon.law.yale.edu/subject_menus/blackstone.asp>.

Brasch, W.M. and Ulloth, D.R. 1986, *The Press and the State: Sociohistorical and Contemporary Interpretations*, University Press of America, Lanham, MD.

Committee to Protect Journalists (CPJ). 2023, *2195 Journalists and Media Workers Killed*, The John S. and James L. Knight Foundation Press Freedom Center, <https://cpj.org/data/killed/?status=Killed&motiveConfirmed%5B%5D=Confirmed&motiveUnconfirmed%5B%5D=Unconfirmed&type%5B%5D=Journalist&type%5B%5D=Media%20Worker&start_year=1992&end_year=2023&group_by=year>.

Courtland, S. D., Gaus, G. and Schmidtz, D. 2022, 'Liberalism', *The Stanford Encyclopedia of Philosophy*, Spring 2022 edn, Zalta, E.N. ed., <https://plato.stanford.edu/archives/spr2022/entries/liberalism/>.

Dutt, R. 2010, 'The Fiji media decree: A push towards collaborative journalism', *Pacific Journalism Review*, 16 (2), 81–98.

Feather, J. 1988, *A History of British Publishing*, Routledge, London.

Feintuck, M. and Varney, M. 2006, *Media Regulation, Public Interest and the Law*, 2nd edn, Edinburgh University Press, Edinburgh.

Finkelstein, R. 2012, *Report of the Independent Inquiry Into the Media and Media Regulation*, Department of Broadband, Communications and the Digital Economy, Canberra, <www.dbcde.gov.au/__data/assets/pdf_file/0006/146994/Report-of-the-Independent-Inquiry-into-the-Media-and-Media-Regulation-web.pdf>.

Fung, B. 2022, Twitter is less safe due to Elon Musk's management style, says former top official. *CNN Business*, 30 November, <https://edition.cnn.com/2022/11/29/tech/yoel-roth-twitter-elon-musk/index.html>.

Grantham, S. and Pearson, M. 2022, *Social Media Risk and the Law: A Guide for Global Communicators*, Routledge, London and New York.

Gunaratne, S., Pearson, M. and Senarath, S. 2015, *Mindful Journalism and News Ethics in the Digital Era: A Buddhist Approach*, Routledge, London and New York.

Inglebart, L.E. 1987, *Press Freedoms: A Descriptive Calendar of Concepts, Interpretations, Events, and Court Actions, from 4000 BC to the Present*, Greenwood Press, New York.

Klapproth, D.M. 2004, *Narrative as Social Practice: Anglo-Western and Australian Aboriginal Oral Traditions*, Walter de Gruyter & Co., Berlin.

Leveson, B. 2012, *Report of an Inquiry into the Culture, Practice and Ethics of the Press*, The Stationery Office, London.

Locke, J. 1690, 'Preamble' to *Essay Concerning Human Understanding*, <www.rbjones.com/rbjpub/philos/classics/locke/ctb0prea.htm>.

Lynch, J. 2010, 'Peace Journalism', *Routledge Companion to News and Journalism*, Allen, S. ed., Routledge, London and New York, 542–554.

Mayer, H. 1964, *The Press in Australia*, Lansdowne Press, Melbourne.

McQuail, D. 1987, *Mass Communication Theory: An Introduction*, Sage, London.

Media Entertainment and Arts Alliance (MEAA). 2018, *How MEAA's Journalist Code of Ethics complaints process works*, Sydney. <www.meaa.org/download/how-meaas-journalist-code-of-ethics-complaints-process-works/>.

Media Entertainment and Arts Alliance (MEAA). 2021. 'Journalists' union gives notice to quit Australian Press Council'. <www.meaa.org/mediaroom/journalists-union-gives-notice-to-quit-australian-press-council/>.

Meta. (n.d.), 'Detecting violations', *Meta Transparency Center*, <https://transparency.fb.com/en-gb/enforcement/detecting-violations/>.

Mill, J.S. 1991, *On Liberty and Other Essays*, Oxford University Press, Oxford.

Overbeck, W. 2001, *Major Principles of Media Law*, Harcourt, Fort Worth, TX.

Oversight Board. 2022, 'Board decisions', *Case decisions and policy advisory opinions*, 5 August, <https://oversightboard.com/decision/>.

Parisi, P. 1997, 'Toward a 'Philosophy of Framing': News Narratives for Public Journalism', *Journalism & Mass Communication Quarterly*, 74 (4), 673–686.

Parliament of Australia. 2019, *Inquiry into the Status of the Human Right to Freedom of Religion or Belief*, International Human Rights Law, 11 April, <www.aph.gov.au/Parliamentary_Business/Committees/Joint/Foreign_Affairs_Defence_and_Trade/Freedomofreligion/Interim_Report/>.

Patrides, C.A. ed. 1985, *John Milton: Selected Prose*, rev. edn, University of Missouri Press, Columbia, MO.

Piotrowicz, R. and Kaye, S. 2000, *Human Rights in International and Australian Law*, Butterworths, Sydney.

Public Relations Institute of Australia (PRIA). 2003, *Code of Ethics Administration Procedure Manual*, 2nd edn, PRIA, Sydney.

Pullan, R. 1994, *Guilty Secrets: Free Speech and Defamation in Australia*, Pascal Press, Sydney.

Reporters Without Borders (RSF). 2022, World Press Freedom Index, <https://rsf.org/en/index>.

Siebert, F.S., Peterson, T. and Schramm, W. 1963, *Four Theories of the Press*, University of Illinois Press, Urbana, IL.
Smith, J.A. 1988, *Printers and Press Freedom: The Ideology of Early American Journalism*, Oxford University Press, New York.
Solutions Journalism Network. 2023, [Online]. <http://solutionsjournalism.org/>.
Twitter/X. 2023, *Twitter User Agreement*, <https://cdn.cms-twdigitalassets.com/content/dam/legal-twitter/site-assets/privacy-policy-new/Privacy-Policy-Terms-of-Service_EN.pdf>.
United Nations (UN). 1948, *Universal Declaration of Human Rights*, <www.un.org/en/about-us/universal-declaration-of-human-rights>.
United Nations (UN). 2020, *Global Issues – Human Rights*, <www.un.org/en/global-issues/human-rights>.
United Nations (UN). 2021, *Safety of journalists and the issue of impunity: Report of the Secretary-General (A/76/285) [EN/AR/RU/ZH]*, General Assembly, 12 August, <https://reliefweb.int/report/world/safety-journalists-and-issue-impunity-report-secretary-general-a76285-enarruzh>.
United Nations (UN) Human Rights Office. 1966, 'UN General Assembly resolution 2200A (XXI)', *International Covenant on Civil and Political Rights*, <www.ohchr.org/en/instruments-mechanisms/instruments/international-covenant-civil-and-political-rights>.
United States Declaration of Independence. 1776, *Declaration of Independence: A Transcription*, US National Archives, <www.archives.gov/founding-docs/declaration-transcript>.
Weil, S. 2015, 'What Is Sacred in Every Human Being? (La Personne et le sacré)', *Simone Weil: Late Philosophical Writings*, Springsted, E.O. ed., University of Notre Dame, Indiana, 96–117.

Cases cited

ACTV case: *Australian Capital Television Pty Ltd v Commonwealth* [1992] 177 CLR 106 (30 September 1992), <www.austlii.edu.au/cgi-bin/viewdoc/au/cases/cth/HCA/1992/45.html>.
Afghan Letters case*: Monis v The Queen* [2013] HCA 4 (27 February 2013), <www.austlii.edu.au/cgi-bin/sinodisp/au/cases/cth/HCA/2013/4.html>.
Animal Cruelty case: *Farm Transparency International Ltd v New South Wales* [2022] HCA 23 (10 August 2022), <www.austlii.edu.au/cgi-bin/viewdoc/au/cases/cth/HCA/2022/23.html>.
Flag Burning case: *Valerie Morse v The Police* [2011] NZSC 45 (6 May 2011), <www.nzlii.org/cgi-bin/sinodisp/nz/cases/NZSC/2011/45.html>.
Lange's case: *Lange v Australian Broadcasting Corporation* [1997] 189 CLR 520 (8 July 1997), <www.austlii.edu.au/cgi-bin/viewdoc/au/cases/cth/HCA/1997/25.html>.
LibertyWorks case: *LibertyWorks Inc v Commonwealth of Australia* [2021] HCA 18; 95 ALJR 490; 391 ALR 188 (16 June 2021), <www.austlii.edu.au/cgi-bin/viewdoc/au/cases/cth/HCA/2021/18.html>.
Mall Preachers case*: Attorney-General (SA) v Corporation of the City of Adelaide* [2013] HCA 3 (27 February 2013), <www.austlii.edu.au/cgi-bin/sinodisp/au/cases/cth/HCA/2013/3.html>.
Newspaper Acts Opinion [1827] NSWSC 23 (1 April 1827), SCNSW, Forbes CJ, April 1827. Forbes CJ to Governor Darling, 16 April 1827, Historical Records of Australia,

Series 1 (13), 282–285; Mitchell Library, A 748, Reel CY 1226: 24–28, 63–66, <www.austlii.edu.au/au/other/NSWSupC/1827/23.html>.

Palm Island Parole case: *Lex Patrick Wotton v The State of Queensland & Anor* [2012] HCA 2, <www.austlii.edu.au/cgi-bin/sinodisp/au/cases/cth/HCA/2012/2.html>.

Protesters' case: *Brown v Tasmania* [2017] HCA 43 (18 October 2017), <www.austlii.edu.au/cgi-bin/viewdoc/au/cases/cth/HCA/2017/43.html>.

Stephens' case: *Stephens v West Australian Newspapers Ltd* [1994] 182 CLR 211 (12 October 1994), <www.austlii.edu.au/cgi-bin/viewdoc/au/cases/cth/HCA/1994/45.html>.

Theophanous's case: *Theophanous v Herald and Weekly Times Ltd* [1994] 182 CLR 104 (12 October 1994), <www.austlii.edu.au/cgi-bin/viewdoc/au/cases/cth/HCA/1994/46.html>.

3 Tools for reflection in a communication context

Key concepts

Moral injury: In the psychological literature this has been defined as 'injury done to a person's conscience or moral compass by perpetrating, witnessing, or failing to prevent acts that transgress personal moral and ethical values or codes of conduct'.

Moral myopia: Where one is blinded to the ethical consequences of one's decision, sometimes by rationalising an unethical decision, perhaps because there is no explicit law or regulation prohibiting the behaviour.

Moral muteness: The situation where there is minimal discussion of ethical issues in the workplace.

Reflection-in-action: The ability of the professional to reflect on some problem in the midst of their work.

Mindful reflection: The meditation-based technique used to pause to engage in 'reflection-in-action' using an approach helping explore the ethical and legal dimensions of an issue or problem.

Journaling: The formal or informal reflective writing about the ethical or legal decision-making process.

Mindmapping: An effective means to brainstorm ethical and legal dilemmas by using a combination of drawn shapes and notes to conceptualise a situation and to help navigate a pathway from theory into practice.

Stakeholder mapping: A grid used to compare the various stake and power levels of all identifiable stakeholders in a given ethical or legal scenario.

Potter Box: A model of social responsibility ethics used for analyzing situations and reaching responsible conclusions.

TARES test: An approach which prompts advertising and PR professionals to pause to go through key steps of ethical analysis in the midst of action: in terms of its truthfulness, authenticity, respect, equity and social responsibility.

Specific Legal Risk Analysis: A five-step process recommended for diagnosing and acting upon a media law issue arising in the workplace.

DOI: 10.4324/9781003372752-4

50 *Foundational approaches*

Important reasons for ethical reflection-in-action

The unexamined life is not worth living – Socrates.

As Socrates famously noted, self-examination is central to a virtuous life. Now that the foundations of ethics and human rights have been established, this chapter introduces some key reflective tools and techniques professional communicators can use to help you take a mindful and constructive approach to ethical and legal decision-making. It uses your developed moral compass, your profession's ethical standards and the laws and regulations of society as a starting point.

The ability to 'reflect-in-action' is a hallmark quality of professionals across a range of fields – and is vital for communicators. The work of educationalist Donald Schön aimed to equip professionals with the ability to make crucial decisions in the midst of practice. Schön (1987: 26) coined the expression 'reflection-in-action' to describe the ability of the professional to reflect on some problem in the midst of their work. Such reflection is crucial to a considered review of a legal or ethical dilemma in a professional communication context. For a host of reasons, it is essential for a journalist or public relations practitioner to have gone through such a process if they are later called to account.

Unfortunately, there are sometimes psychological or organisational barriers to effective reflection upon ethical problems. Some professional communicators encounter 'moral myopia' – effectively blinding them to the ethical consequences of their decision, sometimes by rationalising an unethical decision, or perhaps because there is no explicit law or regulation prohibiting the behaviour. At an organisational level, 'moral muteness' is where there is little if any discussion of ethical issues in the workplace (Drumwright and Murphy, 2013). Some have even argued that the strong libertarian tradition of the media as the Fourth Estate we examine in Chapters 2 and 4 – epitomised by the US First Amendment protection of freedom of the press – has led to a 'moral minimalism' in journalism. Borden (2008: 26) argues that if journalism focussed less on its political function and its legal mandate, and instead strived for intellectual virtue and civic participation, it would be doing more to fulfil its moral mission of aiding human flourishing in the public sphere.

There is no doubt that inadequate reflection upon the ethical and legal consequences of your professional communication actions can lead to unnecessary harm to others. Unethical behaviour can exacerbate the trauma victims have already encountered in shocking news events. As we will discover in the ensuing chapters, unlawful practice can bring reputational or financial damage to others and awards of damages or even jail terms for the offending communicators.

Building resilience through ethical practice

There is another crucial reason why it is important to engage in some method of careful reflection before making an ethical or legal decision: the mental health of the communication professionals themselves. We learned in Chapter 1 about the importance of identifying your own unique 'moral compass' – your sense of right and wrong behaviour that can stem from a combination of a host of factors including your upbringing, religion, and values within your own professional ethical codes. Psychological studies of trauma have revealed the relatively new concept of 'moral injury' – where media professionals might encounter mental health issues because they feel they have compromised their moral compasses by engaging in unethical or immoral behaviour in the line of duty. One definition of 'moral injury' is:

> The injury done to a person's conscience or moral compass by perpetrating, witnessing, or failing to prevent acts that transgress personal moral and ethical values or codes of conduct.
> (Feinstein and Storm, 2017)

Some have linked moral injury to some versions of the 'moral muteness' we identified earlier. Shay (2014) suggested moral injury occurred when someone in authority forced a staff member to breach their moral compass – essentially where the workplace was out of synch with the moral standards of the employee. An example can include the journalist who is ordered to conduct a so-called 'death knock' – an intrusion into the privacy of the grieving relatives of someone who has died in tragic circumstances – despite the gut feeling derived from their moral compass that these people should be left to grieve undisturbed. Others have defined moral injury more broadly, to take in both situations where someone has been instructed to breach their moral compass and situations where they have chosen to do so themselves (Litz et al., 2009). Backholm and Idås (2015) found the guilt of possibly causing further harm to terrorism victims was a contributing factor in post-traumatic stress among journalists which might have been minimised if employers had offered better training on handling ethical dilemmas when reporting. Muller (2010) has argued that media professionals' resilience to mental health difficulties and trauma can be improved by developing strong moral and ethical compasses and by adhering to professional values.

In summary, the research appears to be suggesting that a routine and systematic method of analysing the ethical dimensions of a communication issue might offer some level of resilience or protection against the mental health consequences of moral injury (Pearson et al., 2021). In other words, if you weigh up all the options in a complex ethical scenario and make a calculated decision based on one of the frameworks outlined here, then you might be less likely to feel the guilt that can contribute to such psychological impacts.

Case example:

Court reporter's case (2019): An important Australian legal decision in 2019 upheld an *Age* journalist's claim of negligence against her employer when she was moved to a court reporting round after she had reported post-traumatic stress disorder after six years of covering crime, including Melbourne gangland murders. According to the Victorian Court of Appeal, this caused a significant deterioration in her health and constituted a breach of duty by the newspaper employer. The news group then offered her an undisclosed out of court damages settlement.

> **Reflect – Research – Review:**
>
> Outline one potential scenario where moral injury, moral muteness or moral myopia might occur in a professional communication context, and explain how a more ethical approach might minimise the consequences.

A toolkit for ethical and legal reflection

> Freedom is the capacity to pause in the face of stimuli from many directions at once and, in this pause, to throw one's weight toward this response rather than that one – Rollo May, *Freedom and Destiny*, 1981: 54.

Psychological harm to the professional communicator and other stakeholders can be minimised or countered if they structure a routine process of reflection into ethical and legal decisions. Such approaches can help sound the alarm bells to warn of an ethical or moral dilemma. Further strategies offer the tools for actually working through such a problem. Here we consider a range of options. You are invited to consider the menu and select the approaches according to the particular problem at hand, your own style of learning, the complexity of the issue, and the amount of time available for reflection. We return to each of them in later chapters as part of exercises in ethical and legal reflection on particular issues.

So how can you learn to identify a potential ethical or legal issue in the midst of researching or writing? Given that a journalist or public relations consultant might be working on numerous stories, investigations, production or communication tasks in any single day, what might indicate to you the 'red flags' that indicate a situation that is worthy of reflection or advice from supervisors or lawyers?

The answer lies in developing a routine system of reflection to identify the situations and emotions that require nuanced ethical and legal decision making. The author has identified over decades of training and advising professional communicators the key junctures requiring ethical reflection. They are the crucial moments that Patching and Hirst (2022: 123) call the 'fault lines' – points at which clashing rights and interests intersect to trigger an ethical or legal dilemma. Examples include: a court's demand a journalist reveal a confidential source versus the reporter's ethical obligation to that source; the public interest in getting objective coverage versus the news organisation's profit imperative; and, the citizen's right to truthful electoral information versus the media adviser's desire to get their political boss re-elected.

Situations like these need to be recognised so you can pause to reflect on their ethical and legal dimensions. Equally, you need to pause to think through situations that have triggered your emotions, because they are also moments where ethical or legal errors can arise. Table 3.1 presents some key professional communication situations and emotions mapped against the areas of media ethics and law that might become relevant when that situation or emotion arises. Later in the book we look at more specific situations that map against particular areas of media law, such as the litany of legal and ethical challenges in covering the justice system, race and national security. The important thing here is that you are aware of some of the situations and emotions that might trigger law and ethics risks or fault lines and use that recognition to embark upon one of the practices of reflection and analysis outlined in this chapter.

Obviously, the key here is being able to identify a problematic emotion or situation, red flag it, then pause to weigh an appropriate ethical and legal course of action. Several strategies for reflecting on media ethical and legal dilemmas are covered in this chapter, including Bok's model (1978), mindful reflection, journaling, mindmapping, stakeholder mapping (Grantham and Pearson, 2022: 18–19), the Potter Box approach (Potter, 1972) and its updated iterations including the TARES test (Baker, 2020; Swain, 1994). For legal dilemmas, the Specific Legal Risk Analysis approach (Grantham and Pearson, 2022) is explained. Each approach is demonstrated using a problem scenario.

A. Moving beyond the Applied Ethics Matrix

When we considered the key philosophical approaches to morality and ethics in Chapter 1 we presented the Applied Ethics Matrix as Figure 1.2 – combining philosophy, laws and professional codes, theoretical lenses, relative interests and moral compasses to assist in making a communication ethics decision. It included key questions a professional communicator might ask themselves when confronting an ethical dilemma. If every communication professional worked through those questions each time they faced an ethical or a legal dilemma there would be far fewer cases before self-regulatory bodies and the courts. However, professional self-examination does not need to stop there. Philosophers and communication scholars have turned their minds to the problem of recognising legal and ethical dilemmas and then to the systematic analysis of the pathways to a suitable course of action.

54 *Foundational approaches*

Table 3.1 Key professional communication situations and emotions with accompanying ethical and legal risks

Situation or emotion	Ethical risks	Legal risks
You are too rushed to check or you feel you are out of your depth.	Feeling rushed or ill-equipped can lead to a range of ethical breaches. Taking short-cuts can result in a disregard for the truth of a matter, temptations to plagiarise, and a disregard for fairness by skipping an interview or disregarding information that might convey an alternative viewpoint.	All areas of media law, including the main ones of defamation, contempt of court and breach of court reporting rules, can result from feeling rushed or pressured. Learn to recognise when you are feeling that way – then pause and reflect. [See Chapters 5 and 8].
You are broadcasting live or have direct publishing authority without checks or editing.	The pressure of live or unsupervised coverage can lead to inaccuracies compromising the truth, unfairness, or inappropriate speech that can impact the rights and interests of others.	A danger zone for defamation, contempt, identification restrictions and other laws. All journalism and professional communications should be checked or edited by others. Live broadcasts should be cautious and only conducted by experienced practitioners abreast of media law. [See Chapters 5 and 8].
You have a vested interest or strong opinion on the matter or the item relates to advertising or promotion.	Personal biases or vested interests such as commercial incentives are key ethical factors featured as problematic in most ethical codes.	Defamation defences can be lost if you are biased or partisan. News reporting protections can be forfeited under consumer law. [See Chapters 5 and 12].
It involves secret recordings, surveillance, tapping, hacking, disguise, deception or entry onto private property.	Lying and deception are foundational ethical principles that most professional codes warn against unless there is an overriding public interest at play. Respect for the privacy of others can also be compromised.	Be specially aware of the laws of trespass, breach of confidence, surveillance devices legislation, and of gathering evidence, which might not be admissible for a defamation defence. [See Chapters 5, 6 and 7].
You are exposing wrongdoing or misconduct.	The public interest in such exposure of corruption or illegality has to be weighed against the implications of other stakeholders and their families, colleagues and employees.	Defamation and contempt are potential issues. Seek legal advice on requirements of defences like truth, fair report and qualified privilege. [See Chapters 5, 8 and 12].

Tools for reflection in a communication context 55

You are feeling angry, exhausted, annoyed, betrayed or emotional, or you have been drinking, using substances or are mentally unwell.	Emotions like these can lead to rash or thoughtless communications that can affect the rights, lives and interests of others and can spark falsities, inappropriate language or reputational damage.	This is no time to publish or use social media. Your state of mind increases legal risk, impacts your media law assessment of the situation, and can leave you exposed to allegations of malice, lack of belief in the truth of what you have published and failure to establish reasonableness, thus losing key defamation defences and exposing you to dismissal for misuse of social media. [See Chapters 5 and 12].
It 'feels wrong', or you get that feeling that you wouldn't want to be the person mentioned.	The internal moral compass – Bok's 'conscience' (1978: 94) is a wonderful starting point for ethical reflection.	Deeper consideration might reveal a risk of defamation, contempt or breach of confidence/privacy. [See Chapters 5–12].
It sounds sensational or unbelievable.	Truthfulness and honesty are foundational ethical virtues and any suspicion that a communication falls short on these fronts should be the subject of reflection, analysis and further investigation.	If the story seems far-fetched, it probably isn't true: unverified claims present major problems in defamation and contempt of court. They raise real problems with defamation defences, where the item may carry defamatory meanings you or the person being quoted did not realise or intend to convey. [See Chapters 5 and 8].
The material concerns sex, nudity or sexuality.	Privacy is a fundamental human right and a key ethical consideration.	This requires special care, as it can raise legal issues around defamation, breach of confidence, court reporting restrictions, privacy and indecency. [See Chapters 5–8].
It generalises, stereotypes, or is offensive to religions or cultures.	All people have the right not to be discriminated against on a range of grounds and all ethical codes respect that right.	This can be defamatory if certain individuals are identifiable, and might also breach discrimination and vilification laws. [See Chapter 11.]
It criticises someone's performance or competence.	Truth and honesty are crucial ethical factors, and a person's right to have their good reputation preserved is respected internationally.	Defamation defences – particularly the requirements of the truth and honest opinion/fair comment defence – should be checked and legal advice must be sought: the factual basis for the criticism must be set out or adequately referred to. [See Chapter 5].
It relates to someone's mental health or other vulnerability, or involves children.	Vulnerability because of age or mental illness deserves universal caution and care.	Special restrictions apply to mental health and some coroners' proceedings, and both defamation and breach of confidence could be in play. [See Chapters 5, 8 and 11].

56 *Foundational approaches*

Reflect – Research – Review:

Potential problem scenario: A simple situation confronting a communication professional is whether to mislead or deceive in their line of work. In Chapter 4 we look more closely at ethical and legal conceptions of 'truth' and consider communication and social media contexts where they become an issue. One classic situation is whether to deceive in a communication – spoken or written – for the benefit of yourself or your client at the expense of another party (the public, the audience, an advertiser or other stakeholder). Let's take a very simple but common situation and view it through the lens of the Applied Ethics Matrix. The survival of your news media venture depends on attracting advertising. A potentially major advertiser will only enter a contract with you if it includes regular 'advertorials' about its business – essentially sponsored content disguised as normal news coverage. Let's view it through the Applied Ethics Matrix:

- What if everyone acted this way? Should this approach become the rule? What duties do I owe to others? (deontological): *If everyone acted this way and such behaviour became the rule then audiences could never trust news products as being independent of vested interests. News outlets owe it to their audiences to be transparent about any advertising.*
- Does my proposed action lead to the greatest benefit for most stakeholders? (consequentialist): *Such deception would benefit your news operation and its shareholders – and perhaps the advertiser – but this would likely be outweighed by potential damage done to its reputation and the broader reputation of news outlets generally via the erosion of public trust. Audience members could be harmed by making ill-informed decisions about the product or service being promoted.*
- How are the rights and interests of various stakeholders affected by this action? (contractualist): *You and your news outlet have a social contract with your audience to provide independent and unbiased news. The interests of a few stakeholders might be advanced but the interests of many might be damaged. There can also be unanticipated brand damage to your business once the deception is discovered, or perhaps even legal action by the authorities for misleading conduct.*
- What virtues or vices are evident in this action? How does it shape my character? (virtue ethicist): *Honesty is widely regarded as a 'cardinal virtue' – and lying and deception are its opposites in the form of vices. Ethical professionals avoid such practices and strive to imbue themselves with the virtues of honesty and transparency.*
- What clauses from a professional communication ethical code apply to this situation and what guidance is given?: *All professional*

Tools for reflection in a communication context 57

> *communication codes of ethics encourage honesty. Such opaque practices like disguised advertising are seen as unethical behaviour.*
> - How does the action sit with the laws of society?: *As mentioned, various laws could come into play here, particularly consumer laws prohibiting misleading and deceptive conduct by businesses and a host of advertising regulations.*
> - How does the dilemma sit with a theoretical perspective I have adopted, such as feminism, environmentalism or Marxism (or some combination)?: *This is one for you to answer, but most – if not all – theoretical perspectives are underpinned by integrity and transparency. Many will, however, contest the notion of 'truth'.*
> - What self-interests is this decision serving as opposed to, or in combination with, the interests of others?: *Clearly, self-interest is dominating this decision, with the livelihood of the particular communicator and the survival of your news outlet being preferred over the interests of the audience and the wider public.*
> - What does my unique moral compass contribute to my deliberations? That is, how do my culture, family values, religion or political persuasion factor into it? Does a potential bias need consideration or disclosure?: *Some people have been raised in families where lying and deception is common. Sadly, some institutionalised religions and politicised cultures have also been corrupted by dishonesty and the admonishment of those who speak truth to those in power. For some the sheer weight of economic necessity prompts the compromise of ethical values. Decisions made on this basis require special reflection and perspective.*

B. Bok's model of ethical decision-making

Swedish-American moral philosopher Sissela Bok (1934–) has proposed a relatively simple three-step approach to ethical decision-making in her account of the process involved in justifying lying and deception (Bok, 1978: 94–103). As Patterson and Wilkins (1997: 4) explain, the Bok model is premised on two foundational qualities – empathy for people and the maintenance of social trust. Bok's three steps are:

a. Consult your conscience – go through the process of 'soul searching' about the rightness of your action. Bok quotes the ancient Stoic philosopher Seneca calling such a process becoming 'a guardian over oneself' (Bok, 1978: 94).
b. Go beyond your own 'thought experiment' to consult others for advice on the course of action that might constitute an ethical breach, such as friends, colleagues and even experts in ethics, and to consider precedents that might shed light on a viable alternative pathway (Bok: 96).

58 *Foundational approaches*

c. Consult widely and publicly among all possible people of a variety of allegiances in open dialogue – 'wider than our own conscience and more critical than the imagined audience' (Bok, 1978: 100). Such a test of publicity might be applied in advance to hypothetical cases to allow a future ethical decision on similar facts to be made with more authority. Of course, it might best be conducted at a corporate level where a media organisation or industry group flags potential ethical breaches for public discussion. But it can also be undertaken via a conversation with oneself taking on the role of the various stakeholders (Patterson and Wilkins: 6).

Reflect – Research – Review:

Potential problem scenario: Let's now apply Bok's model to the earlier scenario – selling advertising on the undertaking we devote some news coverage to the advertising client without disclosing the relationship.

a. Consult your conscience: *Any process of 'soul searching' by an ethical practitioner would sound the alarm bells that such undisclosed sponsorship of news is wrong.*
b. Go beyond your own thinking to consult others on the situation such as friends, colleagues and experts in ethics: *You might find your close work colleagues are familiar with the practice and have accepted this compromise to their ethics because of their own moral myopia or moral muteness in their workplace. If you venture more broadly you will find ethical outlets where alternatives have operated successfully – perhaps a policy of transparency where sponsored content is marked as advertising so audience members can distinguish it from independent news material.*
c. Consulting widely and publicly: *It is likely your professional or industry association has produced research and policies on this practice with an array of alternative courses of action recommended. Regulatory bodies and the courts will have bodies of precedent where the practices of others have been considered in like situations. Public forums on the topic could be arranged to debate the issue, in person or online.*

Even Bok's relatively simple recipe for making an ethical decision requires a starting point of self-reflection, where you become the 'guardian over yourself' and consult your own conscience. What techniques can be used to engage in such 'soul-searching'? Here we consider some approaches that might suit different types of communication professionals – the processes of 'mindful reflection', journaling and mindmapping.

C. Mindful reflection

> Reflection (is) that notice which the mind takes of its own operations – John Locke, *An Essay Concerning Human Understanding*: 124.

In the above quote the English philosopher John Locke (1632–1704) was summing up the practice we now know as 'metacognition' (Tarricone, 2011) or 'reflection-in-action' (Schön, 1987) – being consciously aware of one's own thinking and doing. About 2500 years ago the Buddha had explained the foundations of what we now call 'mindfulness' in a similar way. Speaking of a monk, he was purported to say:

> In this way he remains focused internally on the mind in and of itself, or externally on the mind in and of itself, or both internally and externally on the mind in and of itself.
> (Thanissaro Bhikkhu, 2018)

The term 'mindfulness' is commonly used in modern Western societies – and is a practice recommended by many psychologists and counsellors – but it originated in Buddhism. Its application to professional ethics has synergies with the step of 'right conduct' in Buddhism which involves 'a call to understand one's behaviour more objectively before trying to improve it' and 'to reflect on actions with an eye to the motives that prompted them' (Smith and Novak, 2003: 43). This has parallels with the secular approach developed by educationalist Donald Schön, whose research aimed to equip professionals with the ability to make crucial decisions in the midst of practice, which he called 'reflection-in-action' (Schön, 1987: 26). French philosopher and mystic Simone Weil (1909–1943) proposed that the only way to reach the perfection of truth and beauty was via precise attention – in solitude:

> What is sacred in science is truth. What is sacred in art is beauty. Truth and beauty are impersonal. All that is too obvious... Perfection is impersonal... Passage into the impersonal only comes about by attention of rare quality, and is only possible in solitude. Not only actual solitude, but moral solitude.
> (Weil, 2015a: 100)

Weil took it even further by suggesting a religious quality results from consummate attention that can create great art and science – in a similar way to a concert pianist or professional athlete getting 'in the zone' or 'in the flow':

> Intuitive attention in its purity is the unique source of perfectly beautiful art, of scientific discoveries that are truly luminous and new, of philosophy that truly moves towards wisdom, of love of the neighbor that is truly helpful; and when turned directly towards God, it constitutes true prayer.
> (Weil, 2015b: 125–126)

60 Foundational approaches

In Buddhism this ultimate state of attention is called Right Concentration ('*samadhi*') – and is the final step in that religion's path to enlightenment. The 20th century philosopher Iris Murdoch was influenced by both Weil and by Buddhism in her writings about the search for space to reflect on important decisions, with an accompanying need to identify and diminish the power of the ego. She argued that it is difficult to rid ourselves of emotions, attachments and motives that combat our desire to act morally. Murdoch then describes a process of 'unselfing' (borrowed from Weil and Buddhism) so we might obtain the distance needed to make the right decision (Blum, 2022).

Basic mindfulness meditation practices can equip communication practitioners with a toolkit of techniques for inward reflection they can use to assess their thought processes, emotional states, workplace situations, learning and, most importantly, their ethical and legal decision-making. It is beyond the scope of this book to provide detailed instructions on the many kinds of meditation that could be used to find the mental space to engage in purposive reflection on an ethical or legal issue. Some of you would already have experimented with some techniques in counselling sessions or while on holiday retreats, and many will have already built some type of meditation practice into your lives. Those with a religious background might already undertake it regularly in the form of 'prayer', which can also be directed to work through an ethical dilemma (Trammel, 2015). You should have listed that in your moral compass as it draws upon centuries of refinement by clerics in Christianity, Judaism, Islam and other religions.

Riskin and Wohl (2015) explained the widespread use of mindfulness meditation techniques in US law schools and conflict management courses, with a strong focus on concentration practices. The approach typically involves finding seclusion and stillness by sitting to focus firstly on the breathing and then on the bodily sensations, emotions and thoughts (Riskin and Wohl, 2015: 136–137). A routine habit of such reflection allows easy entry into concentration upon a particular legal or ethical dilemma, a practice Riskin and Wohl (2015: 149) labelled their 'STOPS and Take STOCK' tool. They encouraged lawyers to take time prior to a difficult negotiation or meeting to 'Stop; Take a breath; Observe body sensations, emotions, thoughts; Proceed to …; Set a clear and simple intention' ('STOPS'). Then, in the midst of the activity, they should again 'Stop; Take a breath; Observe their body sensations, emotions, thoughts; Consider [their intention and re-evaluate it]; Keep going'. ('STOCK'). In a similar vein, throughout this book we ask you to 'Reflect – Research – Review' at various junctures where we pose ethical or legal questions requiring you to think about a dilemma.

Communication professionals can adapt this practice to help them pause and reflect on an ethical or legal problem in the midst of a busy newsroom or public relations consultancy practice. It is certainly possible to find time out even in the noisiest and most time-pressured situation. Approaches to mindful reflection have been incorporated into many communication teaching programmes and in actual newsrooms. In-depth journalism platform News

Deeply ran a 'gratitude practice' at the start of its editorial meetings so that its reporters could show their appreciation for good things in their lives. Salon.com writer Mary Elizabeth Williams has spoken about how meditation helped her get through difficult assignments like covering the Manchester Arena bombing in the UK in 2017 (Faizer, 2017).

Case study 3.1: Potential problem scenario – Mindful reflection in the BBC newsroom

Former BBC journalist turned Buddhist nun Sister True Dedication addressed a mindfulness symposium for journalists at Columbia University in New York, sponsored by the Dart Center for Journalism and Trauma. She explained the importance of mindful reflection in the midst of a busy newsroom:

> Our capacity to write the kinds of stories or make the kinds of programme packages that we would like to make depends on our capacity to generate insight, clarity and calm when we need it. ... So that when things hit the fan, when things are under pressure, when moments are difficult, we will have the kind of response that we would like to have.
>
> I worked in the politics newsroom in Westminster in London. And my own experience is you never know when things are going to happen or explode. One minute everything is fine and 60 seconds later everything is not fine.
>
> So mindfulness is a kind of training, an energy that we can generate, that gives us space in difficult moments. And it is the kind of energy that we can generate right there in our workplace.
>
> One of the challenges we have in the field of journalism is we are consuming huge amounts of information [and] we need to learn how to stop the mind spinning for short moments throughout the day so that we can get some space and clarity to actually get what we call insight. And in order to get insight we need space. I found ways in my own working day to create these pauses, these moments for insight to arise.
>
> I would get off the bus a few stops early and walk the last distance to work. I made a commitment to myself to walk those 200 yards in peace and freedom every morning. We also have water coolers (water fountains) in most of our places of work. So I made a promise to myself that every step from my desk to the water fountain, I would take each step in freedom. Sometimes the best thing to do is just take time out. And there's one place you could always take time out when no one will disturb you. That is the bathroom. I made a very good use of those 10 minutes. I stopped, I followed my breathing, I did the exercise ... with a body scan to calm my mind to come into contact with my breathing. So the trick is to stop thinking, stop the fast cogitating to come back to establish ourselves in calm in the present moment. And in that moment, insight will arise [about] what to do next and what not to do. (Used with permission. For the full presentation, see <https://dartcenter.org/event/training-mindfulness-for-journalists>)

62 *Foundational approaches*

> **Reflect – Research – Review:**
>
> Think of three other innovative ways a working communication professional could take time out for mindful reflection in the midst of a busy 24/7 newsroom or communications consultancy.

D. Journaling and mindmapping

Alternative or complementary approaches to mindful reflection can take the form of actually noting down all of the dimensions of an ethical or legal issue ('journaling') or using diagrams and sketches to illustrate the different aspects of a problem ('mindmapping'). Each has been used to effect in different professional contexts, including education (Bates and Wright, 2019) and health (Bzowyckyj et al., 2017 and Kottler, 2012).

Journaling

Communication professionals are usually adept at writing, so the diarising of an ethical or legal problem and its dynamics can be an effective method of working your way through to a solution. Recording the pros and cons, potential consequences and likely harms – along with your own thoughts and emotions on this issue – can be combined with a recording of research and documentation to support your stance. This might include references to ethical codes or academic writing on the topic, or perhaps regulatory or legal cases and examples about a similar situation.

> **Reflect – Research – Review:**
>
> Use a journaling approach to work through the ethical and legal implications of an exclusive news story about a rumoured food safety issue – glass fragments purportedly found in a popular brand of ice cream.

Mindmapping

Some communication professionals are more visual in their orientation. Perhaps you work more in the audio-visual production end of media industries or simply find benefits in the practice of drawing and doodling using shapes and images to represent ethical positions and concepts in a decision. There are many approaches to mindmapping. It can be conducted using pen and paper or digitally, even using specialised applications for the purpose. Burch et al. (2015: 489) offered the example of a mind map for ethical decision making in

Tools for reflection in a communication context 63

management, including key concepts such as values, responsibility, principles, right/wrong, fair and moral.

Potential problem scenario

Mindmapping a conflict of interest between competing public relations clients in the sports supplement industry. A PR consultancy has discovered two of its valued clients are actually competing in the same market. How should this conflict be managed ethically? A mindmap like the one by the author in Figure 3.1 might flesh out some of the possibilities and solutions. Make your own attempt.

> **Reflect – Research – Review:**
>
> Construct a mindmap around the ethical considerations facing a public relations practitioner giving confidential information on a matter of public interest to a journalist.

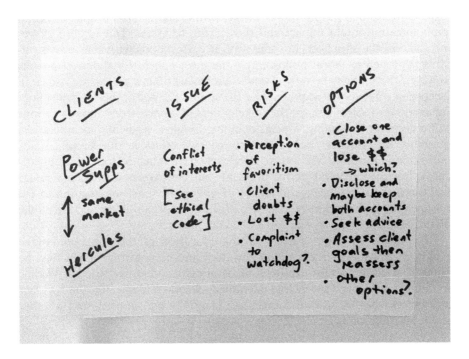

Figure 3.1 The author's mindmap of potential risks and options related to the ethical dilemma of a PR consultancy representing two clients with products competing in the same market. How would you map it?

64 *Foundational approaches*

E. Stakeholder mapping

Professional communicators are encouraged to consider the implications of all actions upon the various stakeholders in an organisation – particularly in the management and public relations literature. As Crane and Ruebottom (2011) explain, the identities and interests of stakeholders can be far more complex than the traditional view which limits them to the simple categories of shareholders, customers and management. Now their various social identities need to be factored into any consideration about the impact of an ethical dilemma – and such social identities can overlap. As Grantham and Pearson (2022: 18) explain, the process of stakeholder mapping involves weighing the relative power and stake in an important organisational decision. When ethical considerations are taken into account, it is important to avoid giving in to power for power's sake and to take measures to reflect the interests of those who might have little power but a high stake in a communication decision.

Professional communicators should pause to reflect not only on the legal risks involved, but also on the implications of their actions upon others – the people who are the subjects of their stories, others who might be impacted, the effects upon their own reputations and the community standing of others, and the public benefits ensuing from this particular truth being told in this way at this time.

Stakeholder mapping involves firstly composing a list of all those that a communication might impact and then trying to assess their level of power and stake in the situation. In some ways it corresponds with the consequentialist approach in moral philosophy – the most benefit for the most people. However, there might be only a small number who have a very high stake in the coverage but very little power over the communicator or their organisation. For example, Table 3.2 maps the stakeholders in a news story about a serious traffic accident, including sources, victims, families, audience members, the journalist, the publisher, police and emergency services, health workers, roads and traffic authorities. Victims would clearly have much to lose by an unethical or intrusive account of the accident, but consequentialist theory might play down their significance in favour of giving the most information to the most people, to the commercial benefit of the news organisation and the public relations benefit of the police and emergency services.

Of course, you might argue with the allocation of the power and stake level in each instance. Elements of the story and its reportage might then be adjusted, with important decisions made about matters like whether victims or families are interviewed and identified, whether blame for the incident is assigned, whether official sources are identified and quoted, and whether health information is included.

Table 3.2 Potential problem scenario: Stakeholder mapping a news story allocating responsibility for a serious traffic accident and giving medical details about victims

Stakeholder	Power	Stake	Consequences
Journalist	High	High	Reputation, promotion
Publisher	High	Medium	Profit, brand
Sources	Varying	Varying	Praise, humiliation
Victims	Low	High	Loss of privacy, dignity, reputation, trauma
Victims' families	Low	Medium	Loss of privacy, added trauma
Health workers	Low	Medium	Reputation
Emergency services	Low	Medium	Reputation, scrutiny
Police	High	High	Public relations, scrutiny
Roads and traffic authority	Low	Low	Scrutiny
Audience	Low	Medium	Being informed and educated

Reflect – Research – Review:

Your client asks you to create a political advertising campaign to support a candidate who wants to reduce the environmental regulations for the mining industry. Conduct a stakeholder mapping exercise to determine the potential ethical and legal impacts on stakeholders and their relative stakes and power in the situation.

F. The Potter Box approach (Potter, 1972)

One of the most common ethical decision-making tools recommended for communication professionals is the Potter Box – a model devised by social ethics Professor Ralph Potter at Harvard Divinity School (Potter, 1972). It has four key components, often displayed as a quadrant as outlined by Patterson and Wilkins (1997: 90) and Christians et al. (2011):

Facts	Loyalties
Values	Principles

While the Potter Box appears simple, each of its four categories can be discussed at length because each potentially has numerous sub-topics ripe for analysis.

1. *Facts*: Understanding the facts is crucial to any ethical situation. As we learn in Chapter 4, some facts are commonly misinterpreted while others are ignored to suit the purposes of the decision maker. Just as with Bok's

model, this identification of facts requires some level of cross-referencing and acknowledging the interpretations and weightings of others.
2. *Values*: As we learned in Chapter 1, our values can come from a range of sources informing our moral compass, including our cultural background and upbringing, religion, political persuasion, passions, interests and stances on social issues. Our respect for the fundamental human rights of others also feeds into our values. Professional values are a crucial consideration here – such as a journalist's obligation of confidentiality to a source and a public relations practitioner's duty to honour the interests of their client.
3. *Loyalties*: To some extent, the notion of loyalties overlaps with both values and the notion of stakeholder we mapped earlier. In the Potter Box, the primary loyalty consideration is the weighing up of obligations the professional communicator might have towards those who might benefit from the decision – yourself, your employer or client, your audience and the public. Under the social responsibility theory we examined in Chapter 2, we might also feel a loyalty to those who are disadvantaged or disempowered in some way – perhaps the migrant or the person with a disability who might be impacted by the communication or who is invested in the story we are telling. All loyalties need to be articulated clearly, perhaps using the journaling or mindmapping methods detailed above.
4. *Principles*: Here Potter is referring mainly to philosophical principles at play. Again, these can overlap significantly, but all are featured in the Applied Ethics Matrix we presented in Chapter 1 and above: rules and duties (deontological); greatest benefit for most (consequentialist); rights and interests of stakeholders (contractualist); and character-shaping actions (virtue ethics).

Christians et al. (2011: 5) suggest the Potter Box process be viewed 'organically' rather than as a four-step linear process. They recommend a feedback loop where each of the four elements is reconsidered in light of advice and then the key issues are conferenced as they apply to the fact situation in question. They demonstrate how different news organisations applying the Potter Box reasoning to exactly the same fact situation can reach different ethical judgments, depending upon their own loyalties and values. Each could be justifiable in context. They also suggest the Potter Box can be used as a tool to develop organisational policy stances to be applied to the coverage of common issues raising ethical dilemmas (Christians et al, 2011: 7).

Reflect – Research – Review:

Potential problem scenario: How we might apply the Potter Box to a decision by a television news executive on whether to show mobile phone footage taken by a shooter during a mass killing at a high school.

1. *Facts*: What are the facts of the story and the circumstances of the network acquiring this footage? Has it been released by police? Was it really recorded by this suspect? Have any advisories been issued by authorities about its use? What is the organisation's policy on the use of such footage? Do any laws prohibit it?
2. *Values*: What is your gut feeling about broadcasting such violent material? Can you reflect mindfully about why you feel a certain way about it? Does that stem from your moral compass: your cultural background or upbringing, religion, political persuasion, passions, interests and stances on social issues? What does your code of ethics counsel on such material? If the public interest and the public's right to information are important, how necessary is this footage to those values?
3. *Loyalties*: Who are the stakeholders here and what loyalty do you owe them? The footage might be exclusive to your network and your loyalty to your employer is to increase ratings and commercial success, but what about your loyalties to audience members who might be traumatised or perhaps motivated to conduct a copycat episode?
4. *Principles*: If you broadcast this, could you envisage a universal rule where all networks were required to broadcast such violent footage? (Deontological). Does the overall benefit of broadcasting it outweigh the possible harms resulting? (Consequentialist); What are the rights and interests of all identifiable stakeholders, including their human rights? (Contractualist). Does this decision make you a better person and a more ethical news professional? (Virtue ethics).

This example explores only some of the ramifications under each Potter Box category. Try to think of some more.

F. The TARES test

Public relations and advertising involve considerable persuasion, which can create an ethical tension if vested or commercial interests are allowed to dominate other moral considerations. Baker and Martinson (2001) took up this challenge by drawing upon virtue ethics (Baker, 2020: 157) to devise what they called the 'TARES Test' – with the acronym standing for their five recommended stages of ethical persuasion:

- Truthfulness (of the message)
- Authenticity (of the persuader)
- Respect (for the persuadee)
- Equity (of the persuasive appeal)
- Social responsibility (for the common good)

They argue that advertising and public relations professionals can serve the public good by offering important information to consumers, but that role is too often corrupted by misinformation, inflated costs and the persuasion of people to buy products and services that are not in their best interest. They propose that applying Bok's level of 'public justification' outlined above would counter the tendency to self-interest or 'moral myopia' in what they call the 'persuasion professions' of advertising and public relations. This prompts the need for special steps of reflection to ensure that any attempt at persuasion is conducted ethically.

Baker and Martinson offer extended advice under each of the five categories of their TARES test (based on crucial questions from the academic literature) and their articles are essential reading for advertising and public relations professionals because we cannot go into every aspect here. Some highlights of the approach are:

- *Truthfulness (of the message)*: They suggest a broader standard than simple literal truth because deception is possible without actual lying. It requires an 'intention not to deceive, the intention to provide others with the truthful information they legitimately need to make good decisions about their lives' (Baker and Martinson, 2001: 160)
- *Authenticity (of the persuader)*: They draw on virtue ethics to propose 'a cluster of related issues including integrity and personal virtue in action and motivation; genuineness and sincerity in promoting particular products and services to particular persuadees; loyalty to appropriate persons, causes, duties, and institutions; and moral independence and commitment to principle' (Baker and Martinson, 2001: 161).
- *Respect (for the persuadee)*: In a subsequent article, Baker (2020: 155) suggests these crucial questions on this issue: 'Have I respected the interests of others? Have I given them substantially complete information so they can make good decisions? Have I made them aware of the source of this message?'
- *Equity (of the persuasive appeal)*: Baker (2020: 5) offers these questions to the public relations practitioner on fairness: 'Is this campaign fair? Does it take unfair advantage of receivers of the message? Is it fair to targeted or vulnerable audiences? Have I made the communication understandable to those to whom it is directed? Have I fairly communicated the benefits, risks, costs, and harms?'
- *Social Responsibility (for the common good)*: Here, the TARES test proponents hark back to the social responsibility model flagged in Chapter 2, with these crucial questions: 'Will the cause I am promoting result in benefits or harm to individuals or to society? Is this cause responsible to the best interests of the public?' (Baker, 2020: 155).

Reflect – Research – Review:

Potential problem scenario: *Here we apply the TARES Test to a PR or advertising campaign promoting a cereal product to children. Add your own points under each category.*

- *Truthfulness:* Be transparent about all the nutritional aspects of the product without just focusing on the positives (fibre, proteins and minerals) with total disregard of the negatives (amount of fats and sugars).
- *Authenticity:* Virtue ethics and commitment to principle might force you to question whether you even take on this account in the first place. If you decide to proceed, then your integrity will demand you handle it better than competitors might have.
- *Respect*: Place children's health and wellbeing at a premium and respect the interests of children and their families. Include enough information for them to decide on the nutritional value of the product.
- *Equity*: It is easy to take advantage of the vulnerable, particularly children. Ensure the focus is not on colourful and entertaining distractions at the expense of useful information on the benefits, risks, costs and potential harms.
- *Social Responsibility:* Promotion of children's health and nutrition is a responsibility for us all and is in the best interests of each child and society more generally in the form of long-term costs to the health system.

Now think of a different advertising or public relations campaign decision that involves an ethical dilemma and work through the TARES test considerations to reach your decision on how to proceed.

G. *The Specific Legal Risk Analysis approach (Grantham and Pearson, 2022)*

A *legal* right to free expression cannot do away with the need for *moral* scruples in choosing what to publish. – Moral philosopher Sissela Bok (1989: 255) [Emphasis in original].

As Bok notes in the above quotation, reflection upon the morals and ethics of a situation is essential prior to a legal evaluation. While they do not always correlate, the moral framework usually sets the backdrop for a legal analysis. When a problem or dilemma has a potential legal dimension a targeted legal risk analysis has to be implemented, addressed at the specific area of media law identified. Grantham and Pearson (2022: 48–51) outlined an approach to the analysis of specific legal risks, with a particular emphasis on social media risk exposure but this is easily adapted to broader media law risk assessment. They identify five key steps to specific legal risk analysis (Grantham and Pearson, 2022: 51–53):

1. *Identifying the potential (or existing) legal problem*: Pausing to reflect on potential problems is vital here, using mindful reflection, journaling or mindmapping. The balance of this book should prepare professionals well enough to sound the alarm bells on potential legal issues arising in the many forms of communication they practice. It is vital they have the foundational knowledge to be able to identify potential reputational damage, privacy invasion, hazards in the justice system, hate speech, social media moderation dangers and intellectual property issues. This approach becomes crucial as you work through each legal dilemma in this book and in the workplace.
2. *Reviewing the areas of the law involved*: After the alarm bells sound, the communication professional then needs to revise the foundational elements and defences applying to that area of the law, with a special focus on the laws applying in the jurisdictions in which they and any relevant stakeholders are based. They need to look at each of the required elements of any legal action to assess whether they might apply in this situation, along with the elements of likely defences that might be available to them. That is why each chapter on a substantial legal topic covers these crucial considerations.
3. *Projecting the possible consequences for stakeholders*: The ethical approaches considered earlier should also factor into legal analysis. Just because something is in breach of a law does not mean it can't be published – just as there are sometimes sound reasons for publishing something that is legally defensible but problematic ethically. This is where a thorough analysis of the potential impacts on a range of stakeholders comes into play and necessitates the kind of stakeholder mapping process described earlier to consider the impact on those mentioned in the communication along with audience members, customers, clients, management, shareholders, policy makers, regulators, industry organisations, advocacy groups and the broader public.
4. *Seeking advice/referring upward*: If there are any doubts about whether (or how) the material should be communicated then the advice of colleagues, supervisors and lawyers might be necessary. In the first instance, seeking comment from some close colleagues is a wise step, particularly if they have more experience or expertise. Every organisation has a policy around the steps necessary when a matter could have legal repercussions – often called a 'legal escalation policy'. This obliges you to check the communication with a supervisor who likely has the power to authorize legal advice if they deem it necessary. You should diarise all

such interactions so you can show the steps you took if the matter comes under subsequent review.
5. *Publishing/amending/deleting/correcting/apologizing/compensating*: You would proceed to publish or communicate the material only after considering the advice (and perhaps the instructions) of colleagues, supervisors and perhaps even lawyers. They might recommend publication within the bounds of one or more of the defences available, or perhaps require you to amend or delete some of the material that might invite legal action. If the scenario involves a complaint or perhaps a threat of legal action then you would take the advice of lawyers on how to word any correction, apology or offer of settlement.

Potential problem scenario

The five-step process is illustrated in the step/status/action approach exemplified in Table 3.2.

Reflect – Research – Review:

Your intern wants to cut and paste the cover illustration of a children's book for a social media advertising campaign. Skim Chapter 9 and then work through the Specific Legal Risk Analysis to come up with a recommended course of action.

Putting it all together in communication practice

No single ethical or legal decision-making framework will suit all communication professionals – but the use of any of the above tools is always going to be better than using none of them. Each has a simple entry point with further layers of complexity depending on the time available to the practitioner and the level of deeper analysis required for the problem at hand. All the tools outlined above rely on the practitioner being able to raise the red flag when an ethical issue arises – perhaps via the situational and emotional signposts of mindful reflection – and then enter into one of the processes of ethical or moral analysis. Only by trialling each of them on realistic ethical scenarios will you become adept at making justifiable decisions in a professional context – and thereby increase your protection against professional and public shaming, enhance resilience against moral injury, and minimise the risk of legal actions against you.

72 *Foundational approaches*

Table 3.3 Sample specific legal risk analysis for a media release about a client's competitor. Based on approach detailed in Grantham and Pearson (2022: 51–53)

Specific legal risk analysis	Status	Action required
1. Identifying the potential (or existing) legal problem	A junior in your public relations consultancy has drafted a media release about your pharmaceutical company client's new blood pressure medication, stating it 'works better than the leading brand on the market'.	Your media law studies have made you wary of any claims about a product or service, particularly if it is claiming superiority to competitors who might be litigious. First step is to check the accuracy of the claim and gather any supportive evidence – research results, government documents, expert opinions etcetera.
2. Reviewing the areas of the law involved	Your recollection of your media law studies prompt you to research three areas of law in particular – the reputational laws of defamation and injurious falsehood (slander of goods) along with consumer law related to false representations or misleading and deceptive conduct. You also recall the drug industry has special regulations prohibiting unjustified claims.	The law of your own jurisdiction and those where you are publishing will outline the elements of these legal actions, their defences and any relevant regulatory requirements. You would research each of them to help decide on your course of action. [See Chapters 5 and 12].
3. Projecting the possible consequences for stakeholders	Clearly a lawsuit or the attention of the pharmaceuticals regulator could have devastating consequences for your own public relations consultancy, your client drug company, consumers and other citizens.	The action required here is to undertake a full stakeholder mapping process to help weigh the impact upon all stakeholders as a means of informing the decision on whether to proceed.

Tools for reflection in a communication context 73

4. Seeking advice/ referring upward	Given the potential legal and regulatory implications, further advice is absolutely essential.	In the first instance you should show some close colleagues the draft media release for their input. Then, if you are deciding to proceed with the claim you would need to alert your supervisor to the potential legal problems who might in turn engage lawyers. You need to keep a diary note of all communications at this stage to help protect you if trouble arises later.
5. Publishing/ amending/ deleting/ correcting/ apologizing/ compensating	Pre-publication there are opportunities to make changes to the wording, or perhaps even deleting that section of the press release altogether. Once publication has occurred then any corrections or apologies must be handled carefully.	Supervisors and lawyers must be consulted if strategic legal risks are being taken that could have financial or reputational consequences for the organisation. Every amendment or deletion should be weighed for its own implications. If the material is communicated and then legal demands are made, then lawyers must be engaged to assist with any corrections, apologies or compensation.

In a nutshell

- A sound framework for ethical and legal decision-making can help prevent moral injury by increasing a practitioner's psychological resilience.
- Professionals can reduce moral myopia and moral muteness by using decision-making frameworks and reflection techniques to consider the consequences of their decisions and by taking leadership to encourage more ethical dialogue in the workplace.
- Mindful reflection, journaling and mindmapping are three techniques professional communicators can use to help recognise and reflect upon an ethical or legal dilemma.
- Bok's model for ethical reflection provides a useful starting point.
- Stakeholder mapping is an excellent technique for considering the interests of everyone potentially impacted by an ethical or legal decision.
- The Potter Box offers a four-point framework for the appraisal of an ethical dilemma, focussing on Facts, Values, Loyalties and Principles.
- The TARES Test has been designed specifically for advertising and public relations professionals to assess their persuasive communication in terms of its truthfulness, authenticity, respect, equity and social responsibility.
- The Specific Legal Risk Analysis maps out a five-step process for analysing and acting upon a media law problem.

References and further reading

Backholm K. and Idås T. 2015, 'Ethical dilemmas, work-related guilt, and post-traumatic stress reactions of news journalists covering the terror attack in Norway in 2011: Ethical dilemmas experienced by journalists', *Journal of Traumatic Stress 28* (2), 142–148.

Baker, S. and Martinson, D.L. 2001, 'The TARES Test: Five Principles for Ethical Persuasion', *Journal of Mass Media Ethics*, 16 (2-3), 148–175.

Baker, S. 2020, 'The ethics of advocacy: Moral reasoning in the practice of public relations', *The Routledge Handbook of Mass Media Ethics*, Wilkins, L. and Christians, C.G. eds, Routledge, London and New York, 148–162.

Bates, S. and Wright, V. 2019, 'Adopting a Janus perspective: moving forwards and backwards through our teacher professional experiences', *International Journal of Lifelong Education*, 38 (3), 241–253.

Bhikkhu, T. 2018, 'The Buddha's original teachings on mindfulness', *Tricycle – The Buddhist Review*, 5 March, <https://tricycle.org/article/satipatthana-sutta-mindfulness/>.

Blum, L. 2022, 'Iris Murdoch', *The Stanford Encyclopedia of Philosophy*, Winter 2022 edn, Zalta, E.N. and Nodelman, U. eds, <https://plato.stanford.edu/archives/win2022/entries/murdoch/>.

Bok, S. 1978, *Lying: Moral Choice in Public and Private Life*, Pantheon Books, New York.

Bok, S. 1989, *Secrets: On the Ethics of Concealment and Revelation*, Vintage Books, New York.

Borden, S. 2008, 'The Moral Justification for Journalism', *Center for the Study of Ethics in Society Papers*, 84, <https://scholarworks.wmich.edu/ethics_papers/84>.

Burch, G., Burch, J., Bradley, T. and Heller, N. 2015, 'Identifying and overcoming threshold concepts and conceptions: Introducing a conception-focused curriculum to course design', *Journal of Management Education*, 39, 476–496.

Bzowyckyj, A.S., Brommelsiek, M., Lofgreen, M., Gotham, H.J., and Lindsey, C.C. 2017, 'Reflecting on care: Using reflective journaling to evaluate interprofessional education and clinical practicum experiences in two urban primary care clinics', *Journal of Interprofessional Education & Practice*, 8, 6–9.

Christians, C.G., Fackler, M., Richardson, K.B., Kreshel, P.J., and Woods, R.H. 2012, *Media Ethics: Cases and Moral Reasoning*, 9th edn, Taylor & Francis Group, NY.

Crane, A. and Ruebottom, T. 2011, 'Stakeholder theory and social identity: Rethinking stakeholder identification', *J Bus Ethics*, 102, 77–87.

Drumwright, M. and Murphy, P. 2013, 'How advertising practitioners view ethics: Moral muteness, moral myopia, and moral imagination', *Journal of Advertising*, 33 (2), 7–24.

Faizer, M. 2017, 'Bringing Buddha to the newsroom: Media with mindfulness', *Columbia Journalism Review*, <www.cjr.org/innovations/mindfulness-media-buddha.php>.

Feinstein, A. and Storm, H. 2017, *The Emotional Toll on Journalists Covering The Refugee Crisis*, Reuters Institute for the Study of Journalism, Oxford.

Grantham, S. and Pearson, M. 2022, *Social Media Risk and the Law: A Guide for Global Communicators*, Routledge, London and New York.

Kottler, J.A. 2012, *The Therapist's Workbook: Self-Assessment, Self-Care, and Self-Improvement Exercises for Mental Health Professionals*, 2nd edn, John Wiley & Sons, NY.

Litz, B.T., Stein, N., Delaney, E., Lebowitz, L., Nash, W. P., Silva, C. and Maguen, S. 2009, 'Moral injury and moral repair in war veterans: A preliminary model and intervention strategy', *Clinical Psychology Review*, 29 (8), 695–706. <https://doi.org/10.1016/j.cpr.2009.07.003>.

Locke, J. 1959, *An Essay Concerning Human Understanding*, Dover Publications, NY.

May, R. 1981, *Freedom and Destiny*, W.W. Norton & Co, New York and London.

Patching, R. Hirst, M. 2021, *Journalism Ethics at the Crossroads: Democracy, Fake News, and the News Crisis*, Routledge, London and New York.

Patterson, P. and Wilkins, L. 1997, *Media Ethics: Issues and Cases*, 5th edn, McGraw Hill, Boston, MA.

Pearson, M., McMahon, C., O'Donovan, A., and O'Shannessy, D. 2021, 'Building journalists' resilience through mindfulness strategies', *Journalism*, 22 (7), 1647–1664, <https://doi.org/10.1177/1464884919833253>.

Potter, R.B. 1972, 'The Logic of Moral Argument', *Toward a Discipline of Social Ethics*, Deats, P. ed., Boston University Press, Boston, 93–114.

Riskin, L.L. and Wohl, R.A. 2015, 'Mindfulness in the Heat of Conflict: Taking STOCK, University of Florida Levin College of Law Research Paper No. 16–12', *Harvard Negotiation Law Review*, 20, 12.

Schön, D. 1987, *Educating the Reflective Practitioner: Toward a New Design for Teaching and Learning the Professions*, Jossey-Bass, San Francisco.

Shay J. 2014. 'Moral injury'. *Psychoanalytic Psychology*, 31 (2), 182–191.

Sister True Dedication. 2015, *Presentation to Workshop Mindfulness Training for Journalists*, Dart Center for Journalism and Trauma, Columbia University, 21

September, New York, <https://dartcenter.org/event/training-mindfulness-for-jour nalists>.
Swain, K. 1994, *Beyond the Potter Box: A Decision Model Based on Moral Development Theory*. AEJMC conference paper.
Tarricone, P. 2011, *The Taxonomy of Metacognition*, Psychology Press, East Sussex.
Trammel, R.C. 2015, 'Mindfulness as Enhancing Ethical Decision-Making and the Christian Integration of Mindful Practice', *Social Work & Christianity*, 42 (2), 165–177.
Weil, S. 2015a, 'What Is Sacred in Every Human Being? (La Personne et le sacré)', *Simone Weil: Late Philosophical Writings*, Springsted, E.O. ed., University of Notre Dame, Indiana, 96–117.
Weil, S. 2015b, 'The First Condition for the Work of a Free Person (Condition première d'un travail non servile)', *Simone Weil: Late Philosophical Writings*, Springsted, E.O. ed., University of Notre Dame, Indiana, 119–130.

Cases cited

Court reporter's case: *The Age Company Limited v YZ (a Pseudonym)* [2019] VSCA 313 (19 December 2019), <www.austlii.edu.au/cgi-bin/viewdoc/au/cases/vic/VSCA/ 2019/313.html>.

4 Law and ethics across communication careers

Truth and deception in action

Key concepts

Truth: 'Actuality, or the property of being in accord with fact or reality' (Merriam-Webster, 2022).

Deception: 'The act of causing someone to accept as true or valid what is false or invalid: the act of deceiving' (Merriam-Webster, 2022).

Misinformation: False information published inadvertently with no harm intended.

Disinformation: 'False information that is intended to manipulate, cause damage, or guide people, organisations, and countries in the wrong direction'. (Canadian Centre for Cybersecurity, 2022).

Malinformation: Information that might be rooted in fact but has been exaggerated or underplayed to mislead or cause harm or alarm.

Fake news: A politicised term, originally referring to disinformation published on websites and social media for political purposes or to drive web traffic, but then applied during the Trump Presidency (2017–2021) to almost anything reported in the mainstream media with which the president disagreed.

Third party comments: Comments by other people on a host's social media site. In some places, you might be held legally responsible for the comments of third parties on your site.

Jurisdiction: The 'reach' of a particular state or country's legal powers. It can also apply to the power of a particular type of court to hear a civil or criminal case or other dispute.

Introduction

When singer and songwriter Johnny Cash performed his anti-Vietnam war protest song 'What is Truth?' to US President Richard Nixon in the White House in 1970 he was questioning the fundamental principle that underscores the intersection between philosophy, ethics, law and media. It was a question that had been asked by the great thinkers of the world for millennia. Cash sang about a young man who was asked to swear on the Bible to tell the truth in the witness stand but wasn't believed because of the clothes he was wearing and his

DOI: 10.4324/9781003372752-5

long hair – prompting Cash to sing that the 'lonely voice of youth cries 'What is truth?'. It is a question that is central to the practice of society generally and professional communication in particular.

Dictionary definitions of 'truth' appear relatively straightforward, and usually equate it with 'actuality' or 'the property of being in accord with fact or reality' (Merriam-Webster, 2022). However, as philosophers over the centuries have explained – and communicators come to learn – people have different versions of actuality and reality and their ideas of truth might be founded on different sets of facts that may or may not be provable. Similarly, the 'act of causing someone to accept as true or valid what is false or invalid' (Merriam-Webster, 2022) – a basic definition of 'deception' – can come in a host of guises through to the modern variations of 'disinformation' and 'malinformation' explained in this chapter.

Ethical foundations – philosophical and religious thinking on truth and deception

> When regard for truth has been broken down or even slightly weakened, all things will remain doubtful. – St Augustine (354–430).

From the Ancient Greeks starting with Aristotle, via the Christian philosopher St Augustine through to modern moral philosophers starting with Immanuel Kant in the 18th century and Sissela Bok in the 20th century, truth-telling has been lauded as a virtue that is essential to the proper functioning of society. Three of the four main philosophical schools praise truth-telling and admonish deception in almost all circumstances. The deontologists argue society depends on the universal obligation to tell the truth and ask the key question: if deception were universally tolerated, then how could we ever trust what anyone told us? Contractualists see truth-telling as part of our social contract – an obligation of each of us to our fellow citizens. And virtue ethicists see honesty as one of the key character traits to which we should all aspire. Kant – the most famous of the deontologists – spoke of the virtue of truthfulness when he wrote: 'By a lie a man throws away and, as it were, annihilates his dignity as a man' (Kant, 1964: 93). William Shakespeare (1564–1616) summed up the virtue ethicist's stance when he scripted the flawed character Polonius stating:

> To thine own self be true, And it must follow, as the night the day, Thou canst not then be false to any man.
> (Shakespeare, Hamlet, Act 1, Scene 3)

Truth-telling appears more complicated for consequentialists and some media practitioners, who might excuse strategic lying in special circumstances where the end justifies the means – perhaps where a journalist has operated under a false identity to get information about corruption or drug-dealing, using the greater public benefit of the exposure of a heinous crime as the excuse for the lesser vice of deception.

Philosophers who worked against the moral and rationalist grain on matters of truth and deception included Renaissance Italian Niccolò Machiavelli (1469–1527), German-Swiss philosopher Friedrich Nietzsche (1844–1900) and the 20th century postmodernists. In *The Prince* and other works, Machiavelli proposed deception as a legitimate tool in Renaissance politics:

> For some time I have never said what I believed and never believed what I said, and if I do sometimes happen to say what I think, I always hide it among so many lies that it is hard to recover.
> (Machiavelli cited in Dietz, 1986: 777)

While his view was strategic and devious, his intent was pragmatic – to overthrow the Medici dictatorial rule and establish a republic true to his libertarian ideals (Dietz, 1986: 778). In other words, his willingness to operate with falsities to mislead acknowledged the acceptance of provable truths that he then manipulated or denied to meet his ends. The idea of truths being provable was in accord with later notions of realism, rationality and objectivity that were championed by the key philosophical figures of the Enlightenment period and informed the key democratic institutions of the modern era.

However, the postmodernist movement in the 20th century – led by the thinking and writing of French philosopher Michel Foucault (1926–1984) and compatriot philosopher and literary theorist Jacques Derrida (1930–2004) – worked on the assumption that notions of truth were social constructs, as were principles of morality. Even important institutions like science and social tools like language were questionable for their political ends and historical and social contexts. In other words, there were no universal, absolute and objective truths – truth was always contestable because it was dependent on power relationships and societal structures.

Many attribute the foundations of postmodern versions of truth to Nietzsche who rejected the notion of objective truth as an illusion. Rather, he believed even our observations were just part of 'perspectivism' – creations of our own minds:

> What then is truth? A movable host of metaphors, metonymies, and anthropomorphisms: in short, a sum of human relations which have been poetically and rhetorically intensified, transferred, and embellished, and which, after long usage, seem to a people to be fixed, canonical, and binding. Truths are illusions which we have forgotten are illusions – they are metaphors that have become worn out and have been drained of sensuous force, coins which have lost their embossing and are now considered as metal and no longer as coins.
> (Nietzsche, 1873)

Foucault refined this idea of subjective truths in the 1960s by arguing all knowledge is dependent on power relations which might be apparent in varying degrees of complexity and subject to interpretations. He was a contemporary of Derrida, who applied the 'deconstruction' approach to his critique of literary texts – essentially proposing they be revisited in light of the social, cultural and historical contexts of their time.

Religious notions of truth and deception

All the world's religions require truth-telling of their followers, but also equate truth with spiritual belief. Christianity puts truth on a pedestal – with Christ having proclaimed to his followers 'I am the way, the truth and the life' (John 14:6). Via that statement, Christians saw Jesus as the embodiment of truth.

Judaism and Christianity share the Ten Commandments, which include at number nine 'Thou shalt not bear false witness against thy neighbour' (Exodus 20:16) which both Christians and Jews interpret as God's command that they not lie, particularly about another person. This was reinforced in Christianity's *New Testament* at Ephesians 4:25: 'Therefore each of you must put off falsehood and speak truthfully to your neighbour, for we are all members of one body'.

In Buddhism, the path of Right Speech including truth-telling is one of eight interdependent steps in the Buddha's path to enlightenment. Its foundational Five Precepts require Buddhists to abstain from false speech, which can impact upon both one's self and others through the principle of karma. Truthfulness is also described as the seventh perfection in the list of ten 'Paramis' – Buddhism's key virtues.

Islam also counsels against being untruthful. The Muslim mystic Al-Ghazali suggested a liar should put themselves in the position of those who are being lied to:

> If you want to know the foulness of lying for yourself, consider the lying of someone else and how you shun it and despise the man who lies and regard his communication as foul.
>
> (cited in Bok, 1978: 29)

This echoes the Golden Rule of Christianity examined in Chapter 1 – doing to others what you would want them do to you. The promotion of truth-telling and the disapproval of deception in all religions underscores the importance of honesty and integrity as a spiritual and moral foundation and also reinforces the societal need for truth-telling in any rule-based community.

Reflect – Research – Review:

Philosophy and religion offer various interpretations of the importance of truth and the problems of deception. Think of three examples of lying or deception that have arisen in your own life and explain how you rationalised them at the time and how you might approach them now after reading the chapter. For example, perhaps as a teenager you lied to your parents that you were going to a friend's house when you were actually sneaking out to go a party. Was that just a 'fib' or a 'white lie'? What might be a comparable situation today in a professional communication workplace?

Modern conceptions of truth and deception

Against this philosophical and religious backdrop in recent times there have been modern manifestations of dishonesty in a digital context. Terms such as 'fake news' 'misinformation', 'disinformation', 'malinformation' and 'astroturfing' all point to deviations from factuality and honesty in Internet and social media content.

The campaign and presidency of US President Donald Trump coincided with the coining of two new expressions: 'fake news' – disinformation published on websites and social media for political purposes or to drive web traffic – and 'post truth' – where objective facts are less influential in shaping public opinion than appeals to emotion and personal belief (Flood, 2016; Hunt, 2017). The linguistic evolution of 'fake news', when used in its politicised form, resulted in its meaning being converted from intentional disinformation to drive Internet traffic ('clickbait') to almost anything reported in the mainstream media with which then President Trump disagreed. The January 6, 2021 riots and attack on the US Capitol could be at least partly blamed on false information and conspiracy theories. According to the Canadian Centre for Cybersecurity (2022), the three main types of false or misleading information online are:

Misinformation: False information that is not intended to cause harm.
Disinformation: False information that is intended to manipulate, cause damage, or guide people, organisations, and countries in the wrong direction.
Malinformation: Information that stems from the truth but is often exaggerated in a way that misleads and causes potential harm.

Professional communicators need to be adept at distinguishing verified facts from myths, rumours and opinions to avoid contributing to the spread of false information in these categories. After all, truthful facts are the foundation stones for reasoned opinions in the media, politics, law and scholarship. While some might speak of 'alternative facts', what they really mean is falsity. It does not become true simply because it has been repeated by others, no matter how influential or powerful they might be. Professional communicators might not have much time available for verification, but they can at least look to the URLs of credible sites such as those from government agencies or academic institutions to check on accuracy. Social media does not function well for verification unless you are speaking directly to an authoritative source – and you know it is actually them you are communicating with. On social media, we are too often communicating with those with similar world views and prejudices – the 'bubble' or 'echo chamber' effect. It behoves all professional communicators to use verification to stop misinformation, disinformation and malinformation in its tracks by verifying before sharing or publishing to avoid becoming a cog in the wheel of falsity in society.

> **Reflect – Research – Review:**
>
> Find an article about cybersecurity from an authoritative source (.gov or .edu or .ac) and make a list of 10 corporate strategies to deal with 'fake news' (false news), misinformation, disinformation and malinformation.

Communication careers – different needs, different values

Philosopher Sissela Bok used numerous examples from various professions in her seminal work *Lying – Moral Choice in Public and Private Life* (1978). She wrote that many people justify lying because we never really know the truth or falsity of something anyway:

> Some have used this argument to explain why they and their entire profession must regretfully forego the virtue of veracity in dealing with clients.
>
> (Bok, 1978: 12)

Bok applied this line of thinking to those working in law, advertising, public relations and journalism:

> Lawyers manipulate the truth in court on behalf of their clients. Those in selling, advertising, or any form of advocacy may mislead the public and their competitors in order to achieve their goals. ... And journalists ... often have little compunction in using falsehoods to gain the knowledge they seek.
>
> (Bok, 1978: xvii)

Here we consider how the ethics and law of three types of professional communication careers manage the issues of truth and deception.

Career in focus – the journalist

Journalism in Western democracies is grounded in the libertarian tradition emanating from the Enlightenment, embodied in the pro-press freedom attitudes of historical figures like John Milton, Jeremy Bentham, John Stuart

Mill and Thomas Jefferson, as explained in Chapters 1 and 2. Journalists have traditionally placed free expression, the public interest and the public's right to know above other rights and interests when pursuing the news. Their role as a crucial pillar of society was summed up by the expression the 'Fourth Estate'. That term is said to have been coined by the English statesman Edmund Burke in 1790 when there were three 'estates of the realm' in Parliament – the Lords Spiritual, the Lords Temporal and the Lords Common. It is said that Burke pointed to the press gallery in parliament and said, 'There are three estates in Parliament but in the reporters' gallery yonder sits a fourth estate more important far than they all' (Inglebart, 1987: 143). Only in the later 20th century with the rise of a social responsibility approach to journalism – along with new forms of journalism respecting the rights and needs of others – did the brazen 'publish and be damned' approach to the news become somewhat moderated. The Enlightenment origin of journalism values traditionally assumed an objective truth that news professionals were reporting – rather than an agenda or position that they needed to identify and disclose. Journalists working in mainstream media effectively serve two masters – their employers (and their associated demands for circulation, ratings, page views and advertising) and 'the public' (their large and diverse audiences of citizens who consume their news products). Public trust in news products – particularly in a digital era with so many alternatives for audiences – depends on journalists reporting truths based on verified and attributed facts.

Key ethical codes for journalists underscore the importance of truth and the public's right to information and counsel against the various forms of deception. For example, many such codes are modelled on the US journalism code – the *Society of Professional Journalists (SPJ) Code of Ethics* – which calls upon members to 'seek truth and report it' as one of its four core principles (SPJ, 2014). It encourages journalists to strive for the 'free exchange of information that is accurate, fair and thorough'. To minimise deception, they are advised to verify information before releasing it, to never deliberately distort facts or context, and to 'avoid undercover or other surreptitious methods of gathering information unless traditional, open methods will not yield information vital to the public'. That latter clause demonstrates that journalists are not absolutists in the realm of lying and deception. It is a good example of a consequentialist approach – where the end (yielding vital information) justifies the means (undercover or surreptitious methods). Some have even questioned the very basis of the journalistic interview as an exercise in a reporter's deception of a source to meet their ends. *New Yorker* writer Janet Malcolm famously suggested this in her book *The Journalist and the Murderer* – the account of the explicit and implied undertakings of a writer to his source on Death Row. Malcolm wrote:

> Every journalist who is not too stupid or too full of himself to notice what is going on knows that what he does is morally indefensible.
>
> (Malcolm, 1990)

84 *Foundational approaches*

The deception of interviewees (and often of themselves) is evident when journalists undertake the exercise of the 'death knock' (see Chapter 7), using spurious arguments to invade the privacy of people who are grieving the loss of family members killed in tragic and newsworthy circumstances.

Case example:

Princess Diana interview: A classic example of a journalist using deception to obtain a story of major public interest was the 1995 interview of Princess Diana by BBC journalist Martin Bashir where the princess famously stated 'there were three of us in this marriage' referring to the ongoing affair between her husband and Camilla Parker-Bowles (now King Charles and Queen Consort). A 2021 BBC inquiry into the episode found Bashir had mocked up fake bank statements to gain access to the princess and persuade her to do the interview (Gillett, 2021).

In their search for truth, journalists should approach the claims of their sources with a healthy scepticism. If someone makes a bold or questionable claim in an interview, they should quiz the source on its factual basis and then check it independently. These processes of verification and attribution underscore many of the media law defences covered in this book. Part of a journalist's check on the bona fides of a source requires them to consider the motivations and allegiances of those giving them information and other factors that could be influencing their opinion or the quality of information they are providing.

Career in focus – the corporate communicator and PR consultant

Surprising as it might seem to some journalists, most codes of ethics for public relations place a strong emphasis on truth and counsel against deceit. For example, the Public Relations Society of America (PRSA) *Code of Ethics* begins by acknowledging its advocacy role and providing 'a voice in the marketplace of ideas, facts, and viewpoints to aid informed public debate' (PRSA, 2023). It proceeds to proclaim members 'adhere to the highest standards of accuracy and truth' before reinforcing this with a section on 'Honesty'. There, it requires it members to:

- Be honest and accurate in all communications.
- Act promptly to correct erroneous communications for which the member is responsible.
- Investigate the truthfulness and accuracy of information released on behalf of those represented.
- Reveal the sponsors for causes and interests represented.
- Disclose financial interest (such as stock ownership) in a client's organisation.
- Avoid deceptive practices (PRSA, 2023).

In fact, it has a greater level of specificity on matters of truth and deception than some journalism codes. It proceeds to offer examples of improper conduct that might show dishonesty or deception:

- Front groups: A member implements 'grass roots' campaigns or letter-writing campaigns to legislators on behalf of undisclosed interest groups.
- Lying by omission: A practitioner for a corporation knowingly fails to release financial information, giving a misleading impression of the corporation's performance.
- A member discovers inaccurate information disseminated via a website or media kit and does not correct the information.
- A member deceives the public by employing people to pose as volunteers to speak at public hearings and participate in 'grass roots' campaigns (PRSA, 2023).

Unlike the journalist whose ultimate allegiances are owed to their employers and the public, the communicator working in a corporate context has a clear duty to their client. That would typically be either the company that employs them to perform a public relations role or the client for whom their public relations consultancy has been contracted to conduct a campaign. While moral duties regarding truth and deception might not change in such a situation, it does create alternative paths to reaching an ethical position. In the first instance, if the overall brief is to lie or deceive then the communicator can opt out of taking the position or the client's brief. Due diligence on the product or service prior to accepting the job or the contract will often sound alarm bells, particularly if the organisation has a history of socially irresponsible practices. In matters of crisis communication affecting the corporation, there is also the option to say nothing at all as an alternative to lying and deception. Of course, most sound crisis communication practices involve being frank, frequent and transparent in public communications around a crisis so there is much scope for truth-telling when all seems to be going wrong. Opaque messaging and deception by corporations in the public eye for the wrong reasons usually just adds to the problem.

Case example:

The MH370 disappearance: Crisis communication expert Hamish McLean outlined the best approach for Malaysian Airlines when its flight MH370 disappeared with all 227 passengers and four crew in 2014. He explained how important accurate, timely and trusted information was to an effective response to a crisis. Reliable facts can help address the key issues in the hours after a disaster. He said the airline could learn from the communication model of New York Mayor Rudolph Giuliani in the days following the 9/11 terror attacks on the US: 'This is what we know. This is what we don't know. This is what we are doing. This is what you can do' (McLean, 2014).

86 *Foundational approaches*

Further, the corporate context demands public relations practitioners abide by the principles of both corporate social responsibility (CSR) and stakeholder theory. As we explained in Grantham and Pearson (2022: 12), CSR is an ethical approach imbuing organisations to integrate social concerns into their operations to generate interaction with stakeholders – groups of people who can be impacted by an organisation's decisions and announcements due to the stake they have in the situation. Both concepts imply a high level of honesty and integrity in communications with all stakeholders – even those without a direct financial stake in the corporation. In summary, it is perfectly feasible to aspire to truthful communications and avoid deceptive practices while serving as a public relations practitioner in a corporate context. In fact, the dominant ethical approaches, industry codes and the law require you to do so.

Career in focus – the government or NGO communications officer

Other dynamics and obligations apply to the government or non-government organisation (NGO) communication or media officer. As a public servant or as an advocate for an important not-for-profit international or national cause, this communication professional has a duty to the broader public via their employer. In the moral and ethical realm of truth and deception, they have commonalities with the responsibilities of the journalist and the corporate communicator. Effective communication by government agencies and NGOs can be crucial to public health and safety and the good governance of society generally. Communication officers in these roles therefore serve an important function in a democracy. It can be their communication that tells us the truth about the building of important roads and bridges, announcements by government officers or the key points of protest against government policies. Their behaviour on truth and deception will be controlled by the public service code of conduct of their government employer or by the mission statements, employment contracts and social media policies of their NGO. In some countries, the so-called 'separation of powers' applies, where the elected legislature, the judiciary and the public service ('executive') are meant to be at arms length from each other. However, in others, including the US, many senior officials are either partisan political appointees or are in elected positions – essentially making the administrator subject to political influences.

Truth, deception and politics crossed paths in the US during the Trump Administration in 2017–2021. Kellyanne Conway, senior counsellor to former President Trump, coined a new euphemism to describe falsities in political speech in 2017. She was trying to explain why the White House press secretary had falsified the size of the crowd attending Trump's swearing-in ceremony as 'the largest audience to ever witness an inauguration, period, both in person and around the globe'. Defending Sean Spicer's account, Conway said his untrue statements were simply 'alternative facts' (Gajanan, 2017. By the end of Spicer's term as Trump's press secretary, *Politico* summed his performance up this way:

> Spicer never failed to fib when a fib would serve the president. ... Had his nose grown with every Pinocchio he uttered, it would have reached the moon.
> (Shafer, 2017)

The reality is that many professionals who work in government or NGO communications or media relations roles – unlike Spicer who was a political careerist – are in fact former journalists. They should bring with them the ethics and values of journalism and combine them with a democratic public service ethos and the principle of corporate social responsibility to uphold standards of truth-telling and transparency.

Truth and deception in media law

Truth-telling is central to the law of most societies. In jurisdictions that have evolved from the English system of law, a witness in court is expected to swear by God (or solemnly declare and affirm) that their evidence 'will be the truth, the whole truth and nothing but the truth'. Of course, such a guarantee can only be aspirational because no individual could ever claim to know the 'whole truth' of a matter or to be able to verify everything to ensure it is 'nothing but the truth'. Nevertheless, proven deception in court can lead to the serious criminal charge of perjury – lying while under oath.

Truth and deception also arise in various areas of media law, and we will examine them in more detail in the ensuing chapters. For example, we learn in Chapter 5 that in defamation – the law available to those whose reputations have been damaged by a publication – truth is approached differently in the US from how it functions in the UK and its former colonies including Australia, New Zealand and Canada. In the US, the libertarian notion of freedom of the press enshrined in the First Amendment to the Constitution has influenced defamation law so much that even false statements that damage the reputations of public figures are not considered defamatory unless they are also malicious (see Key Case 2.1: Sullivan's case (1964)). However, in the UK, Australia, New Zealand and Canada, the defamatory material is assumed to be false and if the defendant publisher wants to use the truth defence, they must prove the defamatory material and its meanings ('imputations') were true. The result is that public figures – including politicians, actors, sports people and celebrities – find it much harder to win a defamation case in the US than in those other countries.

Other media laws engaging notions of truth or deception include some corporate laws of advertising and marketing which prohibit false representations or misleading or deceptive conduct, an action for 'injurious' or 'malicious' falsehood, and intellectual property laws where people misrepresent the work of others as their own.

88 *Foundational approaches*

Communicating via the Internet, social media and artificial intelligence (AI)

All professional communication careers now involve the use of the Internet and social media (and the growing use of AI) – while some are fully imbued in a digital role, such as the position of social media producer or moderator. Special considerations apply to the ethics, law and regulation of dealing in this space, particularly with regard to matters of truth and falsity or deception. No organisation has zero legal risk, but one of the basic strategies that can be used to minimise legal action over the outputs of professional communicators is to be able to prove their truth and factuality and to eliminate any basis for an accusation of deception. Grantham and Pearson (2022: 48–53) list a series of strategies you can use to assess your general legal risk for social media communications, which can be adapted to apply to the legal ramifications of falsities and deception. Worthy of special mention with regards to truth and deception on the Internet and in the social media space are the following special issues.

The law of publication

Each time you post something you may be subject to the laws of more than 600 nations, provinces, states and territories. You can never quite be sure where your words, sounds and images might end up and what the legal consequences might be. As professional communicators, we need to at least be aware of those risks and work to minimise them. Depending on its seriousness, you might be sued in another place (jurisdiction) or perhaps even prosecuted criminally over something you have published – even if it is true. Australia's High Court has decided publishers are liable for defamation wherever their material is downloaded (Gutnick's case, 2002). Even the bastion of democracy, the US, went to extraordinary lengths in the UK courts in the 2019–2023 period to win the extradition of Wikileaks founder Julian Assange over true and factual material he had published back in 2010 that they claimed was an act of espionage (Holden, 2022).

Your responsibility for publishing the comments of others

Media organisations have long been aware that they are legally responsible for the comments of other people they quote in their news stories – particularly in the law of defamation. It is not enough just to put quotation marks around somebody's words and think you will be immune – your republication of the statement or allegation can make you jointly responsible for any damage to their reputation. With the advent of social media some jurisdictions have also made publishers responsible for comments posted by other people (third parties) to their social media sites (see Voller's case, 2021 in Chapter 5). This does not apply in the US, however, where s230 of the *Communications Decency Act* of 1996 gives immunity to social media and Internet hosts over false, deceptive, defamatory or malicious postings by third parties on their platforms. Legal responsibility for publication of material created by artificial intelligence is still being determined, but falsities and unverified assertions abound.

Terms of use

In Chapter 2 we considered the terms of use (or 'terms of service') of some of the major social media platforms in respect to human rights breaches. They also have various terms of use, protocols and complaints mechanisms for matters related to falsity and deception in posts. Meta's Facebook policies appear under headings for both 'False news' and 'Misinformation' in its Transparency Center. At those locations Meta claims to take seriously its responsibility to reduce the spread of false news but acknowledges the balance between helping people to stay informed and not stifling public discourse, satire or opinion. Its strategy is to demote false news to the lower end of its Facebook news feed. Meta also claimed to be disrupting the economic incentives for the propagation of misinformation, including the development of a machine learning AI model to predict false stories and the use of independent fact-checkers (Meta, 2022a). It prohibits outright advertising debunked by such third-party fact-checkers and places restrictions on advertisers who habitually post false information (Meta, 2022b). Twitter and various other platforms (Facebook, Instagram and YouTube) took the extreme measure of suspending the account of former US President Donald Trump in January 2021 soon after the riots at the Capitol building because of his false claims of widespread election fraud. He later launched his own platform Truth Social. Twitter (now X) reinstated his account in 2022 after its new owner Elon Musk conducted a poll of users on the issue (Milmo, 2022). The suspension was one of numerous such actions against prominent people for incitement of violence or spreading misinformation of a political nature or false news about health during the COVID-19 pandemic.

Bots and cookies

We deal in more detail with the collection of personal data in Chapter 7 when we consider privacy and data protection. However, the surreptitious use of cookies and bots to collect an individual's data, habits and viewing preferences raises the use of deception in marketing and advertising and is controlled by various data protection laws internationally, led by the European Union's tough General Data Protection Regulation (GDPR) introduced in 2018. While HTTP cookies can serve useful purposes when placed on a device during an Internet session, such as adding items to shopping carts and saving time by helping pre-fill data fields, so-called 'tracking cookies' can be used in a deceptive fashion by compiling long-term records of users' browsing histories. Social media bots can also be used dishonestly to engage in social media to mimic human users. Such malicious bots are a form of malware that can infect an organisation's system, steal data and engage in other fraud. Ethical communication professionals obviously should not engage in such practices. You should undertake your organisation's cybersecurity training courses so you can learn to detect and report such practices and avoid being entrapped.

Basic Australian legal principles on truth and deception

This section summarises some of the Australian laws and regulations related to truth and deception we have covered at an international level earlier in this chapter, under key topic headings.

Defamation

Chapter 5 goes into more detail on defamation, but several aspects of the Australian law relate to the issues of truth, factuality and deception. The defendant has the onus of proving the substantial truth of a defamatory imputation (meaning) contained in a publication (*Defamation Act 2005 NSW*, s25). A defence of 'contextual truth' at s26 excuses defendants who have already established the substantial truth of an imputation also having to prove other, lesser, imputations going to that same character attribute. (Both were used effectively in the War Hero case in 2023, when media outlets and journalists successfully defended allegations that Victoria Cross winner Ben Roberts-Smith had murdered innocent civilians while serving in Afghanistan. That decision was being appealed.) Further, defamatory opinions will fail to meet the requirements of the 'honest opinion' or 'fair comment' defence unless they are built upon a platform of 'proper material' – including provable facts stated in the material (s31). Reports of important public occasions like parliamentary and court proceedings will normally earn the frequently used defamation defence of 'fair report' but this requires the material to be a 'fair and accurate' account of such proceedings (s29). The 'public interest' defence to defamation (s29A) – introduced to most Australian jurisdictions in 2021 – does not require proof of truth but suggests courts might take into account a range of factors including the extent to which the matter published distinguishes between suspicions, allegations and proven facts; the sources and their integrity; the plaintiff's side of the story; and other steps to verify the information. All of these factors encourage truth-telling and work against possible deception being used under the guise of the public interest.

Intellectual property

There is provision within intellectual property laws for actions over untrue or deceptive claims about creative material, explained in Chapter 9. A basic copyright principle is that copyright is owned by the creator of the material, so any representation that it is the work of someone else can be a breach. For example, the 'cut and paste' business model of some media organisations to simply appropriate the news of others and republish it as their own can breach

Law and ethics across communication careers 91

the 'moral rights' of creators to have their works attributed to them (*Copyright Act 1968*, s195AC). The separate action of 'passing off' is the wrongful appropriation of the reputation of another or that of their goods (see Chapter 9).

Commercial laws

Truth and deception are also prominent in Australian commercial and consumer law. An example is 'injurious falsehood' available to individuals and corporations who can prove someone maliciously published a false statement about them, resulting in actual damage, as explained in Chapter 5. In addition, there are provisions in the Australian Consumer Law (*Competition and Consumer Act 2010*) concerning the making of 'false and misleading representations' (s29) and 'misleading and deceptive conduct' (s18) in the course of trade or commerce (explained in Chapter 12).

Surveillance laws

In Chapter 7 we look at the deceptive conduct of recording – and perhaps publishing – conversations secretly without the knowledge of a party to the conversation and the placement of bugging devices to secretly record audio and images. Various laws in all Australian jurisdictions prohibit deception of this kind (see Key Case 4.1).

Regulatory processes

Depending upon the medium in which false or deceptive news is published, its creation might also invoke complaints to the various self-regulation and co-regulation bodies in control of the ethics and licence conditions of broadcasters in Australia (the Australian Communications and Media Authority), the MEAA's National Ethics Committee or the Australian Press Council. For example, a broad definition of 'fake news' might include the royal prank call from Sydney radio station 2DAY-FM, the subject of Key Case 4.1.

Key Case 4.1: Lying in action, the 2DAY-FM royal prank call

2DAYFM Case: *Today FM (Sydney) Pty Ltd v Australian Communications and Media Authority* [2013] FCA 1157; *Australian Communications and Media Authority v Today FM (Sydney) Pty Ltd* [2015] HCA 7, 4 March 2015 S225/2014.

Facts

A surreptitious prank call recording by radio disc jockeys Mel Greig and Michael (MC) Christian on Sydney's 2DAYFM in 2012 made

---

international news when they managed to get connected through to a nurse in a London hospital who was caring for the Duchess of Cambridge who was suffering morning sickness during her pregnancy with Prince George. The DJs put on voices purporting to be the then Queen and Prince Charles. The global prank turned sour when the duty nurse who had connected the call through to the ward committed suicide and left a note blaming the humiliation of the episode for her despair. (Mental health warning: if this issue causes you concern, please contact your preferred crisis and support agency.)

Legal and ethical principles

The Australian Communications and Media Authority (ACMA) launched an investigation into whether the radio station had breached a condition of its license prohibiting it from breaking the law, in this case the *Surveillance Devices Act 2007* (NSW). The ACMA's authority to make such a ruling was questioned in a High Court appeal, which found it did indeed have the power to rule that a station's behaviour had been criminal even though this had not been proven in a court.

Lessons for professional communicators

The basic premise of the prank call is to lie or mislead to exploit the naivety, trust and vulnerability of the target for the entertainment of the listener. A prank call typically involves a family member, friend or work colleague contacting the radio station to set the target up with some information about something they know has upset them and will likely trigger a reaction. By definition, the targeted individual is already vulnerable in some way – frustrated by bureaucracy, upset over a relationship, feeling guilty about some trivial misdemeanour, or just known to be gullible and an easy target.

Indeed, the prank call concept is premised on the introductory guise being untrue and, while one could find benefits in bringing the humour of laughing at the expense of others to some members of the audience, it is an unwelcome experience for the target. In this case it had tragic consequences. Given the topic of the prank was the royal family, it also raised the issue of the extent to which celebrity gossip-style journalism is sustainable given the requirements of truth in both ethics and the law. Professional communicators are counselled against both celebrity gossip and prank calls. They are a legal and ethical minefield.

Law and ethics of specialist fields

Most laws encountered by communication professionals are the same laws any citizen would encounter if they went about the same tasks. However, in some specialist reporting and public relations domains, there are particular laws applying to false or misleading communication about certain topics. In the finance domain, the Australian Securities and Investment Corporation (ASIC) polices the *Corporations Act 2001*, which has strict requirements about untruths or deception to do with financial and corporate matters, such as company floats, initial public offering (IPO) announcements and investment advice. The Therapeutic Goods Administration (TGA) also has powers to police and issue fines over false and misleading claims about health products and services under the *Therapeutic Goods Act 1989*. Both are explained in Chapter 12.

Truth and deception in action – applying reflection-in-action techniques

Truth and deception constitute such fundamental moral decisions that it is difficult for some to imagine professional communicators not pausing to reflect on their 'common sense', 'intuition' or 'gut feeling' when they are doing anything other than truth telling or when they are about to engage in some form of deception. However, as we have learned in this chapter there are many actions that fall short of truth-telling – including evasion or avoidance or selective fact sharing. There might also be many ways to rationalise the withholding of truth, lying or deception: perhaps for the perceived need to protect someone else, loyalties to an organisation, or even for the greater public interest. Each of the reflective techniques introduced in Chapter 3 could hold value for a professional in this situation, depending on the situational facts and the occupational dilemma.

Mindful reflection, journaling and mindmapping

Each of these strategies for reflection-in-action can be applied to the truth/deception situation as it arises, at the very least as a means of acknowledging the feelings and relationships involved in such a foundational ethical dilemma.

Bok's model

Sissela Bok's three steps of consulting your conscience, consulting others, then consulting widely and publicly (even hypothetically) is a good starting point for fathoming the ethics of truth and deception (Bok, 1978: 94–103).

Stakeholder mapping

The potential impacts of falsity or deception upon stakeholders using this technique might give further insight into potential financial and brand damage (Grantham and Pearson, 2022: 18).

The Potter Box

The quadrant of Facts/Values/Loyalties/Principles is a useful aid. The 'Facts' quarter can apply to the situation but also to the truth of the matter – whether facts have been verified and attributed. 'Values' points to the fundamental moral and religious values with regard to truth and deception drawn from one's own moral compass and the various ethical codes we considered earlier. 'Loyalties' is the area where the temptation to lie or deceive can gain traction because of a perceived loyalty to one's employer, family, other vested interest or oneself. Of course, a fundamental loyalty to the public interest and society generally can be at play. 'Principles' invokes the application of the various philosophical approaches like the rules-based deontological position, the end-justifying-the-means consequentialist approach, the contractualist's notion of mutual obligations and the virtue ethicist's question about what the decision might do in terms of your professional reputation and character. Consultation with others can be particularly fruitful.

The TARES test

If it is a situation of communication persuasion that might be in a PR, marketing or advertising context, then the TARES test (Truthfulness, Authenticity, Respect, Equity and Social Responsibility) is useful (Baker and Martinson, 2001). It features truthfulness and authenticity as its first two planks, indicating the moral difficulty of lying or deceiving for persuasion. The truthfulness requirement goes beyond mere literal truth because of the wide and imaginative possibilities of deception. It is also useful to engage with Bok's higher level of 'public justification' of any tendency to hide the truth or deceive to serve a self-interest or the moral myopia of the so-called 'persuasion professions'.

Specific Legal Risk Analysis Approach

The Grantham and Pearson (2022) five-point checklist can be used to tease out the potential legal issues arising from a proposed act of falsity or deception. Identifying the key legal principles would draw on the communication professional's knowledge of the main problems that can arise such as the loss of key defamation defences and liability under consumer or corporate laws. Those issues can be revised in more detail to shore up verification and attribution. Upward referral to supervisors and/or the seeking of legal advice would be wise if the untruth or deception was proposed as the likely course of action. Finally, a decision would be made to publish, amend, delete, correct, apologise or even compensate based on the course of action and on expert legal advice.

> **Reflect – Research – Review:**
>
> Use three different ethical analysis tools from the selections above to work through your proposed course of action in each of the following professional communication scenarios:
>
> - A senior politician is suspected of corruption. You have nobody willing to go on the record to speak against her and have no official documents as evidence to support the claim. However, you think the politician will agree to be interviewed if you lie by telling her you have three close colleagues who have given you publishable comments and that you have in your possession correspondence proving the allegations.
> - Your public relations consultancy has been asked to tender for a major government transport account worth several million dollars. However, it requires evidence of a track record in that field. Your boss wants to embellish a small media release job once done for a local bus company to sound like it was a major transport project.
> - You are the media relations officer for the Minister for Justice. Journalists don't normally attend your media conferences unless a major announcement is being made. Your department head says to tell them a major news story will be revealed at the event, when he is really only announcing the appointment of a new magistrate to a lower court.

In a nutshell

- Questions around truth and deception have occupied the minds of philosophers for more than two millennia, with proponents of truth-telling as a virtue including Aristotle in Ancient Greece, St Augustine in medieval times, Immanuel Kant in the 18th century and Sissela Bok in recent decades.
- Of the key approaches to moral philosophy, only the consequentialist might excuse some level of falsity or deception if the so-called end – perhaps the greater public interest – justifies the means of lying or misleading.
- Philosophers who worked against the moral and rationalist grain on matters of truth and deception included Machiavelli, Neitzche and the 20th century postmodernists from Foucault and Derrida through to Habermas.
- All of the world's major religions have truth-telling as a foundational principle and either counsel against deception or view lying as a sin.
- The 21st century has been marked by the emergence of the concepts of 'fake news' (false news), misinformation, disinformation and malinformation, leading some to postulate that we are now living in a 'post-truth' society.

- Professional communicators need to be adept at distinguishing verified facts from myths, rumours and opinions to avoid contributing to the spread of false information.
- While key media careers in journalism, corporate communication and government (or NGO) media relations have different goals and allegiances, all major professional codes of ethics across journalism and public relations stress honesty and truth-telling.
- Truth and deception feature prominently in key areas of media law, most notably in defamation, intellectual property and commercial laws.
- Professional communicators may also fall under the jurisdiction of other regulators when they lie or mislead.
- The Internet and social media present numerous challenges to professional communicators with regards to truth and deception, including jurisdictional differences, the potential responsibility for the lies of others, the operation of social media platforms' terms of use, and the potential for data-stealing via malware bots and tracking cookies. AI raises even more issues.

References and further reading

Baker, S. and Martinson, D.L. 2001, 'The TARES Test: Five Principles for Ethical Persuasion', *Journal of Mass Media Ethics*, 16 (2-3), 148–175.

Bok, S. 1978, *Lying: Moral Choice in Public and Private Life*, Pantheon Books, New York.

Canadian Centre for Cybersecurity. 2022, *How to Identify Misinformation, Disinformation, and Malinformation* (ITSAP.00.300), Government of Canada, <https://cyber.gc.ca/en/guidance/how-identify-misinformation-disinformation-and-malinformation-itsap00300>.

Dietz, M.G. 1986, 'Trapping the prince: Machiavelli and the politics of deception', *American Political Science Review*, 80 (3), 777–799.

Flood, Alison. 2016, ''Post-truth' named word of the year by Oxford Dictionaries', *The Guardian*, 16 November, <www.theguardian.com/books/2016/nov/15/post-truth-named-word-of-the-year-by-oxford-dictionaries>.

Gajanan, M. 2017, 'Kellyanne Conway Defends White House's Falsehoods as 'Alternative Facts'', *Time*, 22 January, <https://time.com/4642689/kellyanne-conway-sean-spicer-donald-trump-alternative-facts/>.

Gillett, F. 2021, 'Martin Bashir: Inquiry criticises BBC over "deceitful" Diana interview', *BBC News*, 20 May, <www.bbc.com/news/uk-57189371>.

Grantham, S. and Pearson, M. 2022, *Social Media Risk and the Law: A Guide for Global Communicators*, Routledge, London and New York.

Holden, M. 2022, 'Julian Assange appeals to European court over U.S. extradition', *Reuters*, 3 December, <www.reuters.com/world/julian-assange-appeals-european-court-over-us-extradition-2022-12-02/>.

Hunt, E. 2017, ''Fake news' named word of the year by Macquarie Dictionary', *The Guardian*. (Australian edition), 25 January, <www.theguardian.com/australia-news/2017/jan/25/fake-news-named-word-of-the-year-by-macquarie-dictionary>.

Inglebart, L.E. 1987, *Press Freedoms: A Descriptive Calendar of Concepts, Interpretations, Events, and Court Actions, from 4000 BC to the Present*, Greenwood Press, New York.

Kant, I. 1964, 'The Doctrine of Virtue', *Part II of the Metaphysic of Morals*, Harper & Row, New York.
Malcolm, J. 1990, *The Journalist and the Murderer*, Knopf, New York.
McLean, H. 2014, 'Clock is ticking on Malaysia Airlines in crisis management', *The Conversation*. 10 March, <https://theconversation.com/clock-is-ticking-on-malaysia-airlines-in-crisis-management-24160>.
Merriam-Webster.com, 2022. <www.merriam-webster.com/dictionary>.
Meta. 2022a, 'False News', *Meta Transparency Center – Facebook Community Standards*, <https://transparency.fb.com/en-gb/policies/community-standards/false-news/>.
Meta. 2022b, 'Misinformation', *Meta Transparency Center – Advertising Standards*, <https://transparency.fb.com/en-gb/policies/ad-standards/unacceptable-content/misinformation/>.
Milmo, D. 2022, 'Elon Musk reinstates Donald Trump's Twitter account after taking poll', *The Guardian*, 21 November, <www.theguardian.com/us-news/2022/nov/20/twitter-lifts-donald-trump-ban-after-elon-musks-poll>.
Nietzsche, F. 1873, *On Truth and Lies in a Nonmoral Sense*, <www.austincc.edu/adechene/Nietzsche%20on%20truth%20and%20lies.pdf>.
Public Relations Society of America (PRSA). 2023, *PRSA Code of Ethics*, <www.prsa.org/about/ethics/prsa-code-of-ethics>.
Shafer, J. 2017, 'Should You Feel Sorry for Sean Spicer? Nope. Absolutely not', *Politico*, 21 July, <www.politico.com/magazine/story/2017/07/21/should-you-feel-sorry-for-sean-spicer-215406/>.
Society of Professional Journalists (SPJ). 2014, *Society of Professional Journalists (SPJ) Code of Ethics*, <www.spj.org/ethicscode.asp>.

Cases cited

2DAYFM Case: *Today FM (Sydney) Pty Ltd v Australian Communications and Media Authority* [2013] FCA 1157 (7 November 2013), <www.austlii.edu.au/cgi-bin/viewdoc/au/cases/cth/FCA/2013/1157.html> *Australian Communications and Media Authority v Today FM (Sydney) Pty Ltd* [2015] HCA 7, S225/2014., 4 March, <www.austlii.edu.au/cgi-bin/viewdoc/au/cases/cth/HCA/2015/7.html>.
Gutnick's case: *Dow Jones & Company Inc. v Gutnick* [2002] HCA 56; 210 CLR 575 (10 December 2002), <www.austlii.edu.au//cgi-bin/disp.pl/au/cases/cth/HCA/2002/56.html>.
Sullivan's case: *New York Times v Sullivan* [1964] 376 US 254 (9 March 1964), <https://supreme.justia.com/cases/federal/us/376/254/>.
Voller case: *Fairfax Media Publications Pty Ltd v Voller; Nationwide News Pty Limited v Voller; Australian News Channel Pty Ltd v Voller* [2021] HCA 27 (8 September 2021), <www.austlii.edu.au/cgi-bin/viewdoc/au/cases/cth/HCA/2021/27.html>.
War Hero case: *Roberts-Smith v Fairfax Media Publications Pty Limited* (No 41) [2023] FCA 555, <www.judgments.fedcourt.gov.au/judgments/Judgments/fca/single/2023/2023fca0555>.

Part 2
Key topics in media law and ethics

5 Reputation and defamation

Key Concepts

Defamation: The wrong of injuring another's reputation without good reason or justification.
Imputation: The defamatory meaning conveyed by published material.
Criminal libel: A rare version of defamation, prosecuted as a crime. Sometimes misused as a form of censorship.
Honest opinion: Also known as 'fair comment', the main defence for expressions of opinion published on a matter of public interest and based upon true facts.
Public interest: A matter of genuine public concern related to something of importance in the public domain. It constitutes a defence to defamation in several jurisdictions.
Fair and accurate report: A reasonably balanced and substantially accurate report of a public proceeding like court or parliament, or a summary of an official public document.
Serious harm: An element of defamation requiring the plaintiff to first prove that the material published stands to cause serious damage to their reputation.
Malice: An ulterior purpose or lack of good faith in publishing defamatory material. A crucial factor that can defeat some defences.

Reputation and defamation

> The purest treasure mortal times afford is spotless reputation ... Mine honour is my life; both grow in one; Take honour from me, and my life is done.
> – William Shakespeare, *Richard II*, Act I, Scene I

As Shakespeare noted, our reputation – our honour or our good name – is something we work hard to establish but can be stolen from us with a mere turn of phrase, a raised eyebrow or even an emoji on social media. Defamation is the legal action available to those who have suffered reputational damage resulting from a publication. It is among the most important areas of media

DOI: 10.4324/9781003372752-7

law and is an area of substantial risk for all communicators. As we shall see, it also has a strong ethical dimension rooted in the moral wrong of speaking ill of others, a recurrent theme in religious teachings and cultural practices and a topic of philosophical debate. This chapter considers that background before looking at international legal principles of defamation and then moving to how it operates in Australia, with cases and examples.

The religious origins of reputational ethics and defamation

The ethical and religious pedigree of defamation law runs deep in teachings and commentary across several cultures for more than two millennia. In fact, it is hard to separate the religious and philosophical teachings on gossip and reputational damage from the legal evolution of defamation. As Rolph (2008: 38–43) notes, defamation as a legal action has a strong theological background. As I have written previously (Pearson, 2015), the action arose in England in 1222 in the ecclesiastical (church) courts where it remained a spiritual offence for about four centuries. Damage to a reputation was seen as an offence to the target's soul – a right that only God should possess – to be judged only by God's earthly adjudicators, the clergy. There was even recourse for appeals from English ecclesiastical court judgments to the Pope (Rolph, 2008: 45). From around the 16th century, defamation actions were brought in the English common law courts, with judges dealing with a list of allegations without needing proof of actual damage being caused by the defamation (Morison and Sappideen 1989: 173). The religious link with reputational damage persists. Even today the *Catechism of the Catholic Church* lists 'detraction' (essentially gossip – or disclosing 'another's faults and failings to persons who did not know them') as a sin – or an 'offense against truth' (Vatican Library, 1993, para 2477). Thus, there is a long Christian genealogy to the moral wrong of reputational damage which worked its way into defamation law.

Yet, while Christianity informed the development of defamation law in the West, it did not have a monopoly on the sanctity of reputation and the admonishment of unkind speech or gossip. In Buddhism, the path of Right (or Wise) Speech was one of eight interdependent steps to enlightenment. Right Speech forms part of its ethical conduct dimension. A fundamental Buddhist tenet is that one's actions such as speech have an impact upon both one's self and others (Pearson, 2015). Dissanayake (2003) described Right Speech as 'One of the cardinal tenets guiding the moral life of a Buddhist'. The Buddha is said to have outlined key criteria of Wise Speech, essentially that it must be truthful, beneficial, kind and timely. This is sensible advice, even to modern communicators working to 24/7 digital deadlines that threaten traditional instincts to pause, check and reflect. However, there is scope for critical or confronting speech in Buddhism as long as it is timed appropriately (Thanissaro, 1997).

Islam – via the Quran and Sharia law – also forbids defamation, 'exposing someone to the public by virtue of an act, attribute or vice that might disgrace him', for which the Arabic term is *tashhīr*. There are few justifiable exceptions, even if an allegation is true (Al-Azhar, 2020). Judaism distinguishes *moẓi' shem ra* (one who invents an evil reputation) from *mesapper leshon ha-ra* (one who speaks with an evil tongue making malicious but true statements, with the intention of exposing the subject of them to public hatred, contempt, or ridicule). Both are prohibited (Bacher and Eisenstein, 1906). In Sikkhism, both false and true defamation are forbidden. The words *ninda* and *nindeya* in Punjabi mean to slander, slur, backbite or smear. Sikh teachings even have admonition for those who listen to slander: 'False are the ears which listen to the slander of others' (SikhiWiki, 2022).

Reputation in moral philosophy

Philosophers have long discussed the moral status of gossip and lying about others. Virtue ethicist Sissela Bok turned her attention to social gossip in her treatise on lying. She concluded:

> Silence and discretion, respect for the privacy and for the feelings of others must naturally govern what is spoken. The gossip one conveys and the malicious reports one spreads may be true without therefore being excusable. And the truth told in such a way as to wound may be unforgivably cruel.
> (Bok, 1978: 72)

This question of the truth or falsity of communication that damages someone's reputation has arisen in both religion and in philosophy. It is also a key principle in defamation law and is treated differently in various jurisdictions.

Traditionalist philosopher David Oderberg has described a good reputation as 'a highly valuable good for its bearer, akin to a property right'. For this analogy he draws on Aristotle's description of property as an 'external good' contributing to happiness. Oderberg argues a good reputation constitutes a 'psychic or spiritual' means to the end of happiness, in that it spurs people on to a standard of continued good behaviour. He describes the rash judgement about another's character, involving a lack of evidence and charity, as potentially a seriously immoral act. He even proposes that 'it is always wrong to think badly of someone, even if they are bad' (Oderberg, 2013). Benziman (2020: 110) took issue with Oderberg's comparison of a reputation with a property right, pointing out that property is a tangible thing that people choose to own, whereas a reputation is intangible, relies upon the views of others and the owner has limited control over it. He also reviewed the philosophical literature on gossip to conclude that it was focussed too much on the interests of those doing the gossiping rather than on the reputation of the person who is its target (Benziman, 2020: 113). This dichotomy of interests arises again in the legal context of defamation – where the commercial benefits to a publisher and the so-called 'public interest' in defamatory material are pitched against the reputational damage suffered by those defamed.

> **Reflect – Research – Review:**
>
> Reflect on a situation where someone has spoken ill of you (or where you have portrayed someone else in a bad light) and analyse it from moral, religious and philosophical angles. Return to this later and consider the same situation from a legal perspective.

Reputations and human rights

The right to reputation for all citizens of the world is coupled with their right to privacy at the United Nations level, with the two key human rights documents enshrining it with similar wording. At Article 12, the *Universal Declaration of Human Rights* (United Nations, 1948) gives all citizens the right against

> arbitrary interference with his privacy, family, home or correspondence, nor to attacks upon his honour and reputation. Everyone has the right to the protection of the law against such interference or attacks.

The *International Covenant on Civil and Political Rights* (UN Human Rights Office, 1966) uses similar wording at Article 17, but qualifies its protection by prohibiting only '*unlawful* attacks' on honour and reputation. Defamation law is all about determining which attacks on honour and reputation might be excusable in various jurisdictions because they are deemed lawful. The *European Convention on Human Rights* protects free expression at Article 10, but states that it is qualified by 'the protection of the reputation or the rights of others' (Council of Europe, 1950, art. 10.2).

> **Reflect – Research – Review:**
>
> To what extent are defamation laws and free expression compatible? Explain how other human rights compete with free expression in this space.

Basics of defamation law internationally

Defamation is the most common area of litigation for writers of all kinds across new and old media. The *Macquarie Concise Dictionary* (Butler, 2006) defines defamation as 'the wrong of injuring another's reputation without good reason or justification'. Just by using a standard dictionary, we learn two crucial things about defamation:

- It consists of injury to another person's reputation.
- In some circumstances it may be justifiable.

Professional communicators need to work from the understanding that anything published that damages the public perception of the character of any individual (and sometimes companies) might form the basis of a defamation action. You might also see this area of the law referred to as 'libel' (its permanently published form) or 'slander' (when the words are spoken). Mass media products, websites, blogs and social media postings fall into the 'libel' category in countries that use these terms. Australia did away with that distinction in 2005. Now all types are simply called 'defamation'.

When the actor Johnny Depp sued his ex-wife Amber Heard for defamation in a celebrity trial in the US in 2022, there were many lessons for professional communicators. Firstly, some individuals will go to any lengths to defend their reputations, while others will act just as staunchly to defend their right to make allegations. (Depp had sued Heard over comments she had made in an opinion piece in the *Washington Post* in 2018 alleging she was the victim of domestic abuse in their marriage.) Secondly, it showed the scale of costs and damages at stake in a major defamation trial. (While they reached a settlement in late 2022, the court had awarded Depp $10 million in damages and Heard had won $2 million in her countersuit. Legal costs would have also been in their millions for the six-week trial.) Thirdly, the case demonstrated how differently the US and British legal systems operate in defamation cases. In 2020 Depp had lost a defamation case against the *Sun* newspaper in the UK over an article labelling him a 'wife beater' because the judge found the material was 'substantially true' (Salam, 2022).

The primary mechanism used by the courts when defamation is proven is to award money to compensate for damage to reputation and for any related hurt and financial loss, but also to provide an element of vindication. Sometimes a court order ('injunction') will be granted, requiring the publisher to stop making certain allegations or to take material down from the Internet. But once the notion has been planted in people's minds that someone is a liar, a cheat, sexually promiscuous, unfaithful, corrupt, incompetent or otherwise disreputable, it is difficult to erase. Of course, sometimes hard truths need to be told about people for the greater good of society. Deciding whether or not to do so needs to involve an informed ethical and legal decision by the professional communicator, preferably after legal advice.

It is important to understand that defamation is almost a daily occurrence. We defame someone whenever we say, write or post something that damages their reputation. It might be an unendearing photo of a friend on Facebook, a nasty statement in a job reference, a scathing review of an actor's performance or an allegation about a politician on talkback radio. In each situation there is real potential for someone's reputation to be damaged. Yet, depending on the circumstances, there could be a defence available. The key to navigating defamation is being able to identify both the elements of defamation and the most straightforward defences. The most any professional communicator can hope for is to know when to sound the alarm bells and ask for expert legal advice. In deciding whether injury to a person's reputation was justified or excusable, courts ask whether the harm caused was serious and, if so, whether there is enough legally admissible evidence to establish a defence.

Defamation language and laws vary between countries – and cultural and societal factors can influence interpretations of what might be damaging to someone's reputation. Defamation is categorised by lawyers as a 'tort' – a legal term describing a civil wrong incurring legal liability, where a person's action causes someone else to suffer loss or harm. Another tort is negligence.

You can still be jailed or fined in some places for 'criminal defamation'. In both Britain and its colonies, a common weapon for silencing the press had been the crime of 'seditious libel' (defamation of the state) – any serious criticism of government or the Crown, whether or not the criticism was truthful. William Murray, Lord Chief Justice and Earl of Mansfield (1704–1793), coined the expression 'the greater the truth, the greater the libel', ensuring that truth would not stand up as a defence. In some countries, criminal defamation and seditious libel are still used as tools of censorship against the media and dissidents by corrupt politicians, business leaders and government officials. Criminal defamation still exists in many liberal democracies, including the US and Australia, but in general prosecutions are rare and are usually reserved for poisonous, malicious attacks on someone's character by someone who lacks the money to pay damages – the kind of person the courts have called a 'man of straw'. Given professional communicators are not in the business of making such false and malicious attacks, we do not deal further with criminal defamation in this book.

Defamation law everywhere requires proof that your publication has been made to at least one other person. It must go to this third person before anyone's reputation can be damaged, because reputation is a person's standing in the eyes of others. In other words, if you insult someone in a direct message to them alone on social media you have not defamed them. But if you repeat the slur to just one other social media follower your victim might then have an action in defamation.

Courts can award substantial damages to someone who has been injured because of your defamatory publication (whether that is in a public forum, print, broadcast, on the internet or in social media). The fact that you did not mean to defame them will not protect you. Under the principle of 'strict liability', only your act of publication needs to be intentional, even if you did not intend to damage a person's reputation or to identify an actual person.

The guiding principles of defamation remain similar across most places in the world formerly governed by the British. Most draw upon English case law for the elements of defamation: *defamatory meaning, identification, publication to another person* and (more recently legislated in some countries) the *potential for serious harm* to reputation. Most Commonwealth countries also offer the basic defences of truth, fair reporting on protected occasions, fair comment, qualified privilege and public interest. Note that in these countries the defendant is left to prove the truth of the material.

In the US, the key elements of a defamation action are somewhat different, and require *publication to someone other than the person defamed* of a *false statement of fact* that is understood as being *of and concerning the plaintiff*, and *tending to harm their reputation*. If the plaintiff is a public figure, they must also prove '*actual malice*' by the publisher.

Two important differences between the US and British-Commonwealth law (including Australia) are that in the US the burden falls on the plaintiff to prove that what was published about them was false (as distinct from the defendant having to prove its truth elsewhere) and that US public figures are required to prove that the publication was malicious. This is because, in the US, free expression and a free press are protected in law via the First Amendment. The US courts have interpreted this via a series of significant decisions, the most notable being Sullivan's case in 1964, which established that plaintiffs who were 'public officials' had to prove a media defendant had acted with 'actual malice' if they were to win a defamation action, even if the defamatory allegation was untrue (see Key Case 2.1). The test has since been expanded to apply to any 'public figure' – essentially anyone who has a public profile. As a result, the US media have been free to publish criticism of virtually anyone in the public domain, even if the allegations prove to be unfounded, so long as they have not acted maliciously or in 'reckless disregard' of the truth.

The defences to defamation vary considerably between nations and jurisdictions within them, often dependent upon the level of free expression tolerated. The proven truth of an allegation is not necessarily a defence to defamation in some places.

Australian law – identifying defamation

Australian actor Rebel Wilson was the toast of Hollywood after her success with the 2015 screen hit *Pitch Perfect 2*. But the jubilation evaporated after allegations in the top-selling magazine *Woman's Day* and on associated websites that portrayed her as a serial liar went viral. She sued for defamation over the reputational harm she had suffered and the Victorian Supreme Court compensated her with a record $4.75 million damages, later reduced on appeal to $600,000 (Rebel's case, 2017 and 2018) (see Key Case 5.1). The case showed why defamation law is of special concern to journalists and other communicators who are in the business of publishing news and information about people and their activities.

Defamation law in Australia is drawn from legislation and the precedents from superior court cases decided over centuries ('common law'). The legislation is known as the *Defamation Act 2005*, other than in the Australian Capital Territory (ACT), where it forms Chapter 9 of the *Civil Law (Wrongs) Act 2002* and in the Northern Territory, where it is the *Defamation Act 2006*. Sections are also numbered differently in some jurisdictions. Where the legislation is mentioned in this book, it will be referred to as the *Defamation Act* and the NSW section numbers referenced. Despite reforms that made defamation law almost uniform across Australia in 2005, a few notable differences remain between jurisdictions, partly because some states had not yet introduced some 2021 reforms as this book was going to press in 2023.

When assessing defamation risk, professional communicators need to analyse material in a three-step process, just as the courts do. The key questions they need to ask are:

- Is the material I am about to publish defamatory?
- Is potential serious harm being caused to someone's reputation here?
- If so, is there a defence available?

Here we offer some basic tools to help answer these questions, but defamation can be a complex topic and the expert advice of lawyers is often needed. The classic definitions of defamatory material are that it:

- damages a person's reputation by exposing them to 'hatred, contempt or ridicule' (Parmiter's case, 1840, at 342);
- 'tend[s] to lower the plaintiff in the estimation of right-thinking members of society generally' (Sim's case, 1936, at 671);
- 'cause[s] him [the plaintiff] to be shunned or avoided' (Youssoupoff's case, 1934, at 587).

The High Court summed up in simple terms the modern definition of defamation in the 2UE case in 2009 when it stated:

> A person's reputation may therefore be said to be injured when the esteem in which that person is held by the community is diminished in some respect.
>
> (at para. 3, emphasis added)

In that case, it was also decided that the concept of 'reputation' in defamation law included all aspects of a person's standing in the community, including someone's business or professional reputation in addition to their moral, ethical or social standing (paras 42–48).

Matter can still be defamatory if it holds someone up to 'ridicule' – that is, prompts others to make fun of them, but only if it does so in such a way that their reputation is seriously damaged.

Case examples:

ET's case (1991): A magazine photograph of a football player damaged his reputation and exposed him to ridicule by portraying his genitals.

Hanson-Young's case (2013): A politician's head was superimposed on to the body of a young woman in lingerie, seen posing in the open doorway of a motel room. This was held to be capable of damaging her reputation by holding her up to ridicule.

The courts tell jurors to use a 'reasonable person' test to decide whether something is defamatory. That is, they must decide whether a 'right-thinking' person of 'average intelligence' would think the person's reputation was harmed seriously by the publication.

Key Case 5.1: Rebel's case

Wilson v Bauer Media Pty Ltd [2017] VSC 521
Bauer Media Pty Ltd v Wilson [No.2] [2018] VSCA 154

Facts

A few days after the world premiere of *Pitch Perfect 2* in May 2015, the magazine *Woman's Day* published the print article 'Just Who is the REAL Rebel', asserting that the Australian lead actor Rebel Wilson was a serial liar who had concocted her name, age and other aspects of her personal life and background. The parent company Bauer Media published similar stories and follow-ups on its websites, which were available online for a further year.

Law

Wilson sued Bauer Media in Victoria, alleging she had suffered injury to her feelings, credit and reputation, and had been humiliated, embarrassed and suffered loss and damage, including special damages. The jury of six accepted her contention that the articles were defamatory and rejected the publisher's defences of justification, triviality and qualified privilege. They accepted that several imputations arose from the original article (and online versions) and were defamatory because they portrayed Wilson as a 'serial liar'.

Beyond the basic issues of whether the imputations were capable of being defamatory, legal argument centred upon:

- whether the defences would apply, including justification (truth) and qualified privilege; and

- various issues to do with Wilson's compensation for film roles she might have lost because of the publication and whether the damages were aggravated by the publisher's actions.

Wilson was awarded $650,000 in damages and $3,917,472 in special damages for those lost opportunities (plus interest). In 2018 the Court of Appeal found there was no basis in the evidence for making any award of damages for economic loss and substituted damages of $600,000 for non-economic loss. The High Court refused to hear a further appeal.

Lessons for professional communicators

As an introductory case in defamation, Rebel's case serves to illustrate several aspects of defamation law:

- The court looks at the defamatory meaning (imputation) that comes from the publication. Several meanings damaging someone's reputation may emanate from a single publication, while similar publications might contain different imputations.
- Some defences are defeated if the publisher shows malice or an 'improper motive' in publishing the defamatory material.
- Courts can award very high damages in defamation cases, despite the fact that non-economic damages are capped.
- The amount of damages awarded can be affected by evidence of the impact on the victim financially and in hurt feelings.
- Appeal courts can sometimes disagree with a trial judge's reasoning, resulting in major changes to the outcome and amount of damages awarded.

Elements of the action

To establish a case for defamation in Australia a plaintiff must prove the publication (in any medium): *conveys a defamatory imputation* (a meaning lowering the plaintiff in the eyes of others); *identifies (without necessarily naming) the plaintiff*; is *published to at least one person other than the plaintiff*; and, since 2021 in most jurisdictions, has *caused or threatened 'serious harm'* (*Defamation Act*, s10A). Some essential definitions appear in s4. The key definition describes defamatory 'matter', which includes material as diverse as an article, programme, report or advertisement in a newspaper or magazine or communicated via television, radio, the internet or any other electronic form including social media; other writing including letters or notes; pictures, gestures or oral utterances; or any other thing communicable to a person. Electronic communication includes data, text, images or sound (or any combination). This definition is important because it means any possible material professional communicators might produce as part of their work in traditional or new media could contain defamatory material.

The imputation

To establish this first element, a plaintiff must prove that the published words conveyed a meaning (in defamation, called the 'imputation') that would make others think less of them, or perhaps ridicule them, shun them or avoid them.

Case example:

Steeplechaser case (1936): A photograph of a jockey made his hanging saddle girth appear as if it was an intimate part of his anatomy, holding him up to ridicule.

What the communicator intended to say is almost irrelevant: jurors are required to judge the meaning of the defamatory material on its own, without any evidence of its intended meaning. They are asked: 'What do you think an ordinary person would understand this to mean?' A single publication can contain several different defamatory imputations about the one person, each of which might have to be defended in court. Communicators need to ensure the precision of their language to avoid hidden meanings that others might see.

An imputation can be conveyed by:

- The natural and ordinary meaning of the words (or material) – the 'sting' might be stated quite explicitly.
- A 'false innuendo' – a secondary meaning derived from 'reading between the lines'. For example, an article might say that money has gone missing from the local bank, and that the chief teller has not been seen for a week. The reader infers that the chief teller is a thief.
- A 'true innuendo' – relying on other facts known to some of those receiving the publication (special background knowledge about the plaintiff).

In short, it is a mistake for communicators to think they can send a defamatory message about someone simply by using clever wording. The court will see the imputation despite such strategies.

That said, media organisations often publish things that upset, offend or inconvenience individuals. What they publish may sometimes also be wrong, but that does not make the material defamatory. For example, an inaccurate item in a real estate gossip column, saying that a property is no longer for sale, might cause inconvenience but would not be defamatory because it does not damage a reputation. (A different action called 'injurious falsehood' could, however, be available, as explained later.)

Reference to (or identification of) the plaintiff

To establish the second essential element of a defamation action, plaintiffs must prove that the publication referred to them (or could reasonably be interpreted as referring to them). If the publication does not name them, they need to prove that at least one person understood it as referring to them. In some cases, professional communicators have not taken care to identify narrowly enough the individual who is targeted, and 'hidden plaintiffs' have come out of the woodwork. Some identification scenarios have been:

- *A person has been named. Another person (or more than one other person) with the same name has sued.*

Case examples:

Lee's case (1934): A Melbourne newspaper reported a magistrate's inquiry in which a 'Detective Lee' was said to be corrupt. In fact it was a Constable Lee to whom the allegation referred. Two Detective Lees sued successfully, after showing acquaintances thought it referred to them.

Tailor's case (2017): An elderly tailor named Tony Zoef sued over an imputation that he was a dangerous gun runner when the article had confused him with his son, also named Tony Zoef, who lived at the same address.

- *No one has been named, but someone meets the description of the defamed person.*

Case example:

Butler's case (1994): The *Sun-Herald* newspaper published an article titled 'Backpack Murders: Police Quiz Socialite', which described a suspect police were questioning in relation to serial killings. A man sued the newspaper, claiming friends and relatives had identified him (incorrectly) as the suspect on the basis of identifying factors listed in the article. (Ivan Milat later received a life sentence for those murders and died in jail.)

- *No individual has been named, but the defamatory article refers to a small group of people.* Courts usually decide such cases by looking at the size of the group being defamed, the generality of the charge made and the seriousness of the accusation. The test is whether ordinary, reasonable individuals would believe the defamatory statements referred to the plaintiffs.

Case example:

Mount Druitt case (1999): The whole Year 12 class of 1996 at Mount Druitt High School in Sydney was defamed by a front-page photograph and story in the *Daily Telegraph* headed 'Class We Failed'. Twenty-eight members of the class – who were not identified beyond the class photograph and the mention of their school year group – won the defamation action and a confidential damages settlement.

- *A fictitious character has been named. A real person meeting the fictitious person's description sues, claiming people thought the publication referred to them.*

Case example:

Artemus Jones case (1910): A barrister names Artemus Jones sued successfully after showing that people thought a fictitious immoral lawyer by the same unusual name featured in a newspaper story was him.

- *The wrong person has been named or depicted.* Mistaken identity cases have often happened when a photograph of the wrong individual is accidentally added to a defamatory story.

Case example:

Finn's case (2002): Brisbane's *Courier-Mail* newspaper was ordered to pay $12,500 in damages to a John Finn, whose photograph was published accidentally next to a story about a conman who shared his name.

Publication to at least a third person

The third element the plaintiff has to show is that the defamatory material was published to at least one person other than the plaintiff. In other words, you can write an email to a person criticising them but they cannot establish a case in defamation. If they then show it to a friend, you still cannot be sued: in such a case, it is they who are doing the publishing. But if you as the publisher share the same email with just one other person you have then defamed the plaintiff to that person.

Case example:

HotCopper case (2016): A defamation claim was dismissed when a plaintiff failed to establish that anyone other than he had ever actually seen the defamatory imputations posted to an internet forum. (See also Massarani's case (2022)).

Serious harm

The 2021 reforms introduced a requirement that a publication must have caused, or is likely to cause, 'serious harm' in order to be actionable for defamation (s10A). Two jurisdictions – Western Australia and the Northern Territory – had yet to introduce this added element at the time of publication. For not-for-profit entities or corporations with fewer than 10 employees the serious harm test relates to actual or potential serious financial loss as a result of the defamation. The test is meant to act as a disincentive to trivial defamation claims and adds an extra hurdle for the plaintiff to establish their case, potentially adding time and cost for both parties.

Case example:

Rescue Children case (2022): In Australia's first superior court application of the new serious harm test, a NSW Supreme Court judge ruled out several matters in a defamation claim by a family dispute resolution practitioner against the head of an international child rescue organisation over online posts in which she claimed he had defamed her. The judge drew upon UK case law on a similar provision to decide the plaintiff needed to show evidence of serious harm.

Key aspects of Australian defamation law

Internet publication

The Australian High Court was the first to decide in an international dispute that online publications could be actionable wherever defamatory material was downloaded if the person has a reputation there (Gutnick's case, 2002). The case involved Australian businessman Joseph Gutnick who was then permitted to sue US-based publisher Dow Jones in his home city of Melbourne over the internet version of its weekly financial magazine *Barron's* – published out of New Jersey – which had 550,000 subscribers internationally, of whom only 1700 had Australia-based credit cards. In cases of multiple publications of material across Australian jurisdictions, s11 of the *Defamation Act* now applies the law of the jurisdiction where the plaintiff has the closest connection.

Case example:

Treasurer case (2015): Former federal treasurer Joe Hockey won $200,000 in damages over imputations conveyed in newspaper posters and tweets, stating 'Treasurer for Sale' and 'Treasurer Hockey for Sale'. It was the first major Australian case involving publication on Twitter. The stories explained that Hockey had provided 'privileged access' to a 'select group' in return for donations to his Liberal Party via the 'secretive' fundraising body, the North Sydney Forum – but the court held that some readers might deduce an imputation of corruption by reading the tweets or posters only without the deeper context of the full articles.

Defamation limitation period

Plaintiffs have only one year from the date of publication within which to launch their defamation action. If they can convince the court that it was not 'reasonable in the circumstances' that they should have been expected to do so, that time limit can be extended by up to three years. Prior to the 2021 reforms, the clock restarted for the one-year limitation period every time material was downloaded and read – effectively meaning there was no time limit while the material remained online. Now the 12 months starts from the moment the material is first uploaded by the publisher in a reform known as the 'single publication rule'.

Legal standing in defamation

Any living person or legal entity (except large corporations and government bodies) can bring an action for defamation. Section 9 of the Act states that corporations cannot sue for defamation unless they are not-for-profit, or have fewer than ten employees and are not related to another corporation. Corporations can, however, choose other actions, such as injurious (malicious) falsehood or breach of confidence (both of which we consider later), and their directors and officers can still sue in defamation if the story affects their reputation. Section 9 of the Act also prevents 'public bodies' – government authorities and local councils – from suing for defamation, although their officers can still sue if they can prove the publication defames them as individuals. Non-profit bodies, such as unions and charities, have to show that the defamation caused them financial harm. People must in general be alive in order to sue or be sued for defamation, except in Tasmania (s10). However, communicators should be cautious in their reportage of people after their death: aspersions about the dead can sometimes reflect on the living. Anyone responsible for the publication can be sued, including the person who created the material, the editor and the official publisher.

Publishing the comments of others

It is a common misconception that you are protected from defamation action if you are just quoting someone else. If you quote someone who is making a defamatory statement or if you publish a letter or online comment from someone that contains defamatory material, your re-publication of the material leaves you and your organisation, often as well as the person you have quoted, liable for defamation unless you have a defence available. Professional communicators also need to be aware their organisation can bear the responsibility for the untrue or deceptive comments other people (third parties) post to their corporate social media site, as explained in Chapter 4. A line of Australian cases has led to this extension of a body of case law dating back to early in the 20th century in the UK when a defamatory statement was pinned to a golf club notice board and a court held the club could be held responsible because they had not removed the defamatory material after it had been brought to their attention (Golf Club case, 1937). In 2011 the Federal Court found this applied in the context of consumer law in the Allergy Pathway case unless a host removed the comments within a 'reasonable time' of being notified of them. The High Court ruled in the Voller Case (2021) that news outlets could be held responsible for defamatory comments posted by other people about items they had posted to their corporate Facebook pages – from the instant the third parties posted the comments. In the words of the majority decision, the news outlets had 'facilitated, encouraged and thereby assisted the publication of comments from third-party Facebook users' and were therefore publishers of the comments. The case was settled in 2022 and publishers then lobbied to have the law changed to more favourable requirements from 2024 where an innocent dissemination defence would apply if the social media host removed the defamatory comments within seven days of a written complaint (Meade, 2022).

> **Reflect – Research – Review:**
>
> Take the top ten stories on a major news website today and identify how many of them defame someone. List the defamatory meanings – 'imputations'. (There should be several published examples because much defamation is actually defensible.)

Defending defamation in Australia

Despite there being considerable material meeting the basic test for defamation, the reality is that much defamatory material is published every day without any legal consequences. Some of it is published safely because the publisher cannot be identified or is beyond the legal reach of the victim. Sometimes it is because the plaintiff already has such a damaged reputation that the publication does no additional harm. Sometimes the potential plaintiff lacks the resources or emotional resilience for a court battle against a wealthy opponent. And often there is a defence available to the publisher. Defences are the key to working with defamation. The professional communicator needs to know how to make otherwise defamatory material publishable by ensuring – so far as possible – that a defence is available. This chapter focuses on the five defences of greatest benefit to professional communicators in their daily publishing.

There is then a short summary of what we call the 'lawyers' defences' – those technical and unusual defences that would require high level legal advice. The *Defamation Act 2005* legislated certain defences but also preserved the common law defences that had existed over hundreds of years. Each is identified below where necessary.

The five key defences for professional communicators

1. Truth/Justification

Truth as a defence is based on the foundational premise in Rofe's case (1924, at 21–2) that 'by telling the truth about a man, his reputation is not lowered beyond its proper level, but is merely brought down to it'. Truth (also called 'justification') is shackled by two conditions:

- The publication is presumed to be false, and its truth must be proven in court, using evidence which is relevant and which complies with strict admissibility rules. A belief in its truth is not enough.
- Proving truth is only half the battle: a defendant is required to prove the truth of the imputations (defamatory meanings) that a judge or jury find arises from the material.

The Act deals with the defence of justification in s25:

It is a defence to the publication of defamatory matter if the defendant proves that the defamatory imputations carried by the matter of which the plaintiff complains are substantially true.

If a media organisation has enough legally admissible evidence to prove the substantial truth of the imputations that the jury finds were conveyed, it has an excellent defence. But if so much evidence is readily available, it is unlikely the plaintiff would have sued in the first place. Confidential sources are problematic because courts usually don't allow 'hearsay' evidence (something someone told them) and whistleblowers are unlikely to be willing to appear to testify. Other complications about the admissibility of evidence include recordings (for example, audio or video files that may have been illegally recorded or edited), photocopied or scanned documents (which themselves may contain hearsay, and may have been 'doctored'), journalists' notebooks (which may not have been filed efficiently, and may contain illegible notes or identify sources), previous drafts of articles, email and social media communications with sources and colleagues, witnesses who disappear overseas or die, and contested signatures. Many a defamation defendant has been left high and dry, convinced of the truth of what they wrote but unable to produce enough evidence to convince a judge or jury.

If such difficulties can be overcome the defendant will succeed with a truth defence, so long as the evidence establishes that all the imputations that the jury accepts an ordinary reasonable reader would draw from the publication were substantially true on the 'balance of probabilities' (the civil burden of proof). While professional communicators should strive to ensure every aspect of every story is true, the 'substantially true' element excuses minor errors. Legal advice is usually needed for all but the clearest cases, and always for serious allegations.

Case examples:

War Hero case (2023): A Federal Court judge upheld the defences of truth and contextual truth (see below) used by investigative journalists and their publishers to justify their claims that Australian war hero, Victoria Cross recipient Ben Roberts-Smith, had committed murder and other acts of violence while serving in Afghanistan and had tried to cover them up. This decision was under appeal at the time of printing.

Vocational Education case (2018): The Victorian Supreme Court upheld the *Australian* newspaper's use of the 'substantial' truth defence in a story alleging unscrupulous conduct and non-compliance with quality standards by an education businessman despite a factual error.

Actor case (2018–2020): The Federal Court struck out the entire truth defence relied upon by Sydney's *Daily Telegraph* defending its defamation of actor Geoffrey Rush on the basis that it was hopelessly bad and imprecise.

Section 42 of the *Defamation Act* allows proof that a person was convicted of an offence in an Australian court as conclusive evidence that the person did actually commit that offence. However, importantly, an allegation made by a senior investigating detective that someone had behaved so that they might reasonably be suspected of being a murderer is not protected.

Case example:

Barrister's Wife case (2017): A West Australian barrister won $2.623 million in damages from the state government after a detective described him as the 'prime' and 'only' suspect in widely broadcast press conferences about the investigation into his wife's 2007 death. After he was acquitted on the murder charge he sued for defamation.

2. Absolute privilege, public documents and fair report

Even if defamatory material is untrue, it might still be protected on certain occasions where there is an overriding occasion of public importance. The highest level of protection from defamation is 'absolute privilege' – which is available to anyone who defames another while addressing court or parliament. Professional communicators will only be able to avail themselves of this if they are appearing as a witness in court or before a parliamentary hearing (or equivalent proceedings). Absolute privilege is covered by s27 of the Act. Section 28 of the Act allows a defence for the publication of public documents of the kind listed in the Act and its schedules. This can be the actual document itself or a 'fair summary of, or a fair extract', which is the avenue of most use to journalists and other communicators.

Case example:

Racehorse Cruelty case (2017): The s28 defence was used effectively by the business journalist Kate Lahey in 2017 when she drew upon court documents from the preliminary processes of a civil action to list various allegations of cruelty against a trainer from a prominent racehorse family.

Fair report

Under s29, journalists and others are free to report upon certain public proceedings (regardless of the truth of the statements made in those proceedings) as long as any defamatory matter 'was contained in a fair report of any proceedings of public concern'. This protection stems from the notion that there are certain social institutions that are so important to the democratic or judicial process that the public deserves access to fair reports of their proceedings – regardless of whether people happened to be defamed in the process, and that reporting of such occasions encourages public confidence in their integrity. This is a lesser, derivative protection from the 'absolute privilege' explained above, known as a 'fair report'. The report must be both 'fair' and 'accurate'. Other public proceedings such as local government meetings and public meetings offer a rich source of protected material (but note that there is usually an additional 'public interest' requirement for protection of reports of such gatherings).

Case examples:

Eye Surgeon case (2003): A newspaper failed in its fair reporting defence when it inaccurately implied a doctor's eye surgery had blinded a patient when he had actually failed to warn the patient of the risks involved in the operation. The reporter had relied upon another judge's inaccurate summary of the case.

Tailor's case (2017): Misidentifying the accused as his father (who shared the same name) constituted a substantial inaccuracy, thus losing the fair report defence.

> **Reflect – Research – Review:**
>
> Search <www.austlii.edu.au> for a recent defamation case using the defences of truth or fair report. Write a case note about it following the format of the key cases in this book: 'Facts/Law/Lessons for Communicators'.

3. Honest opinion / fair comment

The defence of 'honest opinion' (known as 'fair comment' in its common law version) is the standard defence used for all defamatory opinion and commentary in the news media. Using this defence quite harsh criticism can be published in various review formats of everything from sports and theatre performances through to restaurant meals and films. Of course, criticism is the opinion of the commentator or reviewer. It is impossible to prove the truth of your opinion – only that it was fairly based and honestly held.

The common law 'fair comment' defence will succeed in Australia only where the defamatory material is clearly in the form of an opinion rather than a statement of fact. It must be based on true (provable) facts, or privileged material (for example, a protected court report), which is either set out or adequately referred to in the publication. It must be honestly held, the subject to which it relates must be in the public domain or a matter of public interest, and the comment must be fair (not necessarily balanced, but an opinion that could reasonably be held, based on the stated facts). Finally, the opinion held must be congruent with the imputations conveyed.

Let's look at the legislative version of the 'honest opinion' defence as detailed in s31 of the Act. First, sub-section 1 offers the three basic planks of the honest opinion defence:

(a) the matter was an expression of opinion of the defendant rather than a statement of fact, and
(b) the opinion related to a matter of public interest, and
(c) the opinion is based on proper material.

The defamatory statement must be one of opinion, not fact

Fact dressed up as opinion will not satisfy the defence. The test is how others would interpret the material. If a sports blogger wrote: 'Memo to Referees Association: Fred Whistleblower is unfit to umpire first grade', that would almost certainly be held to convey that the referee was incompetent and unfit to be a first-grade referee, as a statement of fact. If the writer referred to previous errors, and then said: 'Based on yet another sorry performance last night, surely it's time someone showed Whistleblower the red card', the item conveys much the same defamatory meanings, but this time it is an expression of opinion, likely covered by the defence.

Case example:

Archbishop's case (2017): A parishioner defamed the Archbishop of the Assyrian Church of the East on his publicly open Facebook page (in Arabic) where he had more than 260 'friends'. His defence of honest opinion failed because the parishioner's opinion alleging the archbishop's hypocrisy and incompetence was 'indistinguishably mixed up with the (alleged) facts upon which it might be based'.

The opinion must relate to a matter of public interest

The kinds of topics the courts have found to be matters of public interest upon which a defamatory opinion might be expressed have included court, parliament, public meetings, public conduct of officials, books, accommodation, performances, compositions, public entertainment, sports or people's role in the public domain (among others).

Case example:

ZGeek case (2015): The Supreme Court of the ACT found defamatory comments about a lawyer on an internet forum that related to the existing legal proceedings between the lawyer and the publisher of the website not to be on a matter of broader public interest, and defences of honest opinion and fair comment were lost.

The opinion must be based on proper material

Section 31(5) defines 'proper material' as material that is substantially true (provable facts), or was published under the absolute privilege, qualified privilege or fair report provisions. All the facts or privileged material on which the opinion is based need to appear – or be adequately referred to – in the publication, so that the audience can clearly see the basis for the opinion and judge for themselves whether they agree or disagree. In the classic Lobster case (1989), a restaurant reviewer failed in the fair comment defence for a scathing review of a seafood restaurant in the *Sydney Morning Herald* because he had made some errors of fact but had also effectively 'eaten the evidence'.

Case examples:

Media Watch cases (2002 and 2017): Journalists also sue sometimes. In Carleton's case (2002), the ABC programme Media Watch used the fair comment defence successfully when it accused a *60 Minutes* reporter of plagiarising a BBC documentary. In the Toxic Playground case (2017), the NSW Court of Appeal upheld both the fair comment and honest opinion defences used to defend *Media Watch*'s criticism of a journalist's newspaper story about the alleged discovery of toxic substances on land near an industrial site and a children's playground. The court held the imputations of irresponsible journalism and trickery were expressions of opinion, which were based on facts truly stated or sufficiently identified in the programme, that the opinions were expressed on a matter of public interest and that they were objectively fair. (See also the Football Hormone case (2016).)

Whose opinion?

The Act allows for situations where the published opinion is not that of the actual defendant, but of someone else such as an employee or agent of the defendant or of a third party, such as a letter writer or social media commenter.

The opinion must be 'honestly held'

A defendant will lose the defence if the communicator (or the company) did not honestly hold the opinion at the time it was published. If the defendant was publishing material by an employee such as a journalist (or agent) or a third-party contributor, then the plaintiff has to prove the publisher knew the author did not honestly hold the defamatory opinion – a difficult hurdle. The opinion must be fair, but not necessarily perfectly balanced. Extreme opinions are acceptable if the court finds a reasonable person looking at the facts could form such an opinion. Both honest opinion and fair comment are defeated by evidence of malice.

The opinion must fit the imputation

To satisfy this aspect of the defence, the commentator must foresee the imputation claimed by the plaintiff to be conveyed by the defamatory material, and found by the judge or jury to arise.

Case example:

Lloyd's case (1985): *The Age* newspaper ran a column alleging the West Indies cricket team had 'thrown' the second match in a World Series final. Team captain Clive Lloyd sued for defamation and the newspaper lost its fair comment defence because the writer had stated on oath that he did not intend to convey the imputations that were claimed to arise. The court held that if the author had not intended to convey this meaning, then it could not be his 'honest opinion' for the purposes of the fair comment defence.

All this necessitates strict protocols for commentary pieces alleging wrongdoing, letters to the editor and moderated comments. They need to be checked for their accuracy and authenticity, with editorial changes approved and signed off by the author. Further, anyone defamed in a letter or comment must get a right of reply. All these letter and comment protocols need to be vetted by lawyers to ensure compliance.

A warning on satire

While cartoonists appear to enjoy a great deal of freedom to satirise and comment, the courts have frowned upon other forms of satire.

Case examples:

Hanson's case (1999): The High Court refused the ABC leave to appeal against a Queensland Court of Appeal decision to uphold an injunction against the broadcast of a satirical song about the politician Pauline Hanson, titled 'I'm a Backdoor Man', which used digitised sound grabs of her voice to make her sound ridiculous and hypocritical.

Friendlyjordies case (2022): Satire was costly for the commentator Jordan Shanks-Markovina – aka 'Friendlyjordies' – and for Google after his YouTube channel accused former NSW deputy premier John Barilaro of corruption. Shanks settled out of court and apologised but the Federal Court ordered Google to pay Barilaro $715,000 after what the judge described as a 'relentless, racist, vilificatory, abusive and defamatory campaign'. Google had refused to take down the video and had withdrawn its honest opinion defence after the judge found it was not based on proper material.

> **Reflect – Research – Review:**
>
> Research the elements of the honest opinion (fair comment) defence and then use it to write a highly critical review of a song by your least-favourite artist. Explain how you would defend the review.

4. Public interest

The public interest defence was introduced at s29A in five Australian jurisdictions in 2021, with WA and the NT committed to follow. It was based partly on the UK public interest defence introduced in 2013. To earn this defence, the defendant has to show the defamatory matter concerned an issue of public interest and that they 'reasonably believed' that publication of the matter was in the public interest. Courts are directed to consider all circumstances of the case, but are offered the following as possible considerations:

a. the seriousness of any defamatory imputation;
b. the extent to which the publication distinguishes between suspicions, allegations and proven facts;
c. the extent to which it relates to the public functions or activities of the person;
d. whether it was in the public interest in the circumstances for it to be published expeditiously;
e. the sources of the information and their integrity;
f. if a source is confidential, whether there is good reason for their identity to be kept confidential (including, for example, to comply with a journalism ethical code);
g. whether the publication contains the person's side of the story and, if not, whether a reasonable attempt was made by the defendant to obtain and publish their response;
h. any other steps taken to verify the allegations; and
i. the importance of freedom of expression in the discussion of issues of public interest.

Given the new defence had only recently been introduced at the time of this book's publication, there is little Australian case law as guidance. However, there was a precedent for the factors related to the integrity of sources and the need for a right of reply because there were similar requirements under the previous s30 qualified privilege defence. (See the Club Rawhide case (2015) for a reporter's investigations being found 'not reasonable in the circumstances'. Whether this impacts the new requirement of 'reasonable belief' by the publisher remains to be seen.) However, the UK version of the defence has been used successfully in its ten years of operation, with some instructive precedents.

Case examples:

UK domestic abuse allegation case (2021): Two newspapers published allegations against a Dubai-based man by his ex-wife that he had engaged in domestic abuse and had abducted their son. The UK version of the public interest defence failed because the newspapers were unable to demonstrate they had a reasonable belief publication was in the public interest. They had failed to take proper steps to verify the allegations prior to publishing or to include his side of the story. The court took into account industry ethical codes of practice in reaching its decision.

UK rape allegation case (2016): A man used the public interest defence successfully to defend a press release and contributed newspaper articles alleging his daughter's claims a shipping tycoon's son had drugged and raped her were not fabricated. (The mentally ill daughter had committed suicide on the eve of her trial for perverting the course of justice by making false claims.) The decision suggested journalists and media organisations might be held to a higher standard than private citizens on factors like seeking a right of reply.

> **Reflect – Research – Review:**
>
> Think of a matter that is of such overwhelming public importance that the media might be able to argue the public interest defence. Explain how you would defend it and the steps you would need to take in your journalism to establish it. Why not just go for the truth defence?

5. Qualified Privilege

This defence covers important social or public situations where the publisher might not have enough evidence available to prove truth, and other defences might not apply.

Qualified privilege as a defence in Australia takes three forms:

- qualified privilege at common law;
- qualified privilege as it was incorporated into s30 of the *Defamation Act 2005* and further amended in 2021; and,
- the extended political qualified privilege defence (the Lange defence) – covered in the next section on lawyers' defences.

Common law qualified privilege

The common law defence of qualified privilege excuses people who are legally, socially or morally obliged to give defamatory information to others, even if they cannot prove the truth of the material, provided those to whom they publish have a correspondingly strong legal, social or moral interest in receiving that information (Adam's case, 1917). Such protection is necessary for the normal working of society, particularly for communicators operating in the corporate and professional spheres. The defence hinges on there being a reciprocal duty–interest relationship between the publisher of the defamatory material and the person receiving it. Defamatory material in a job reference is a classic example earning the qualified privilege defence. In the professional communication context, public relations practitioners working in a small consultancy need to be able to discuss their clients frankly with managers and perhaps write emails about their attitudes, circumstances, personalities or difficulties. Anything defamatory in such communications – even if unwittingly false – would be protected as long as it was deemed necessary that it be stated and that it was only circulated to those with a direct interest in knowing it.

The defence has traditionally not been accessible for mass-media publishers, because the courts do not regard the media as having a duty to publish defamatory material to the world at large: not every member of the audience would have a legitimate stake in receiving the defamatory material. The common law defence has been extended to the media for defamation that occurs during discussion of political matters (treated below as a separate defence of extended Lange qualified privilege) and also when it publishes a reply to a public attack directed at it (or someone else's reply to an attack upon them), when the first attack was also itself published in the media.

Case example:

South Sydney rugby league case (2012): Businessman Peter Holmes à Court and actor Russell Crowe were making a $3 million bid for a controlling interest in the flailing South Sydney rugby league club, which was to be put to the board for a vote. A director was strongly opposed to the bid. Mr Holmes à Court wrote to the director's employer – a major industrial union – alleging he was spreading misinformation about the bid and was suspected of corruptly channelling funds to himself and the union. The High Court upheld Holmes à Court's common law qualified privilege defence, finding the letter met the reciprocal duty-interest requirement.

Statutory qualified privilege

Under s30 of the Act, a publisher will be protected for publishing defamatory material if the publisher can prove three things:

- the recipient has an interest or apparent interest in having information on some subject, and
- the matter is published to the recipient in the course of giving to the recipient information on that subject, and
- the conduct of the defendant in publishing that matter is reasonable in the circumstances (at sub-section 1).

Section 30(3) sets out a number of factors that the court may take into account in deciding whether a publisher's behaviour was 'reasonable in the circumstances', including the seriousness of the allegations; the extent to which the material distinguishes between suspicions, allegations and proven facts; whether it was in the public interest to publish it expeditiously; the nature of the publisher's business environment; steps taken to verify the information; and other factors a court might consider relevant. News media-specific factors – such as sources, a right of reply and a public interest requirement – were deleted in the 2021 reforms because the new public interest defence was meant to replace this defence for the media. The continued usefulness of the defence to professional communicators in non-news contexts is yet to be seen.

Case example:

Psychic Stalker case (2017): Search engine Google paid $115,000 damages when it failed to establish the statutory qualified privilege defence. Google had been notified that its search engine results on a search of the plaintiff's name generated excerpts of websites where a medical researcher was described as a 'Psychic Stalker' after she had posted negative reviews of psychics' predictions. The Full Court of the Supreme Court of South Australia held it could not win the statutory qualified privilege defence because not all readers who used the search engine had a legitimate 'interest' in seeing the material when they made the searches for 'curiosity alone'. Google's conduct had not been 'reasonable in the circumstances' after she asked it to remove the material, losing its innocent dissemination defence (see below).

All qualified privilege defences are defeated if the plaintiff can show that the publisher was actuated by malice (such as a lack of good faith or an improper motive).

Summary of the technical defences best handled by media lawyers

1. 'Contextual' truth

A news story will often contain several defamatory imputations, but sometimes the plaintiff only complains of one. They might ignore other more serious meanings because they know that the media defendant can prove them true. The defence of 'contextual truth' in s26 allows the defence to point to the missing meanings, prove their truth and argue that their seriousness 'swamps' or outweighs anything about which the plaintiff has complained. It was used successfully to defend media imputations made against Victoria Cross recipient Ben Roberts-Smith over his actions in the Australian Special Armed Services (SAS) in Afghanistan between 2009-2012. Once imputations of murder and attempted cover-up had been found against him, the court found lesser allegations of violence and bullying to be proven contextually as they did not further harm his reputation (War hero case, 2023) – under appeal at time of printing.

2. Extended Lange qualified privilege defence for political discussion

In a series of decisions through the 1990s, the High Court held that common law qualified privilege applied to defamatory material published in the course of political discussion. Australia has no written guarantee of free expression in its Constitution. The court decided that implied in the Constitution was a freedom to communicate on matters of politics and government for all citizens, which laws should not burden unreasonably (ACTV case and Wills' case, 1992). In ensuing years, this notion was developed further into a defamation defence (Theophanous's case, 1994). While this development initially suggested a more liberal approach, it fell far short of the US First Amendment-based defence, because the onus remained upon the media to satisfy a high standard of 'reasonableness'. In 1997, the High Court reaffirmed the existence of the implied guarantee of political free speech in Lange's case, and explained how a qualified privilege defence to defamation should apply when it occurred during the discussion of matters of politics or government. The defence required the publisher to demonstrate that it had acted reasonably, which meant proving:

- it had reasonable grounds for believing each imputation was true
- there was an absence of belief that they were untrue
- proper steps were taken to verify the material, and
- normally a response had been sought and published from the person defamed.

It is certainly not a defence that journalists should rely upon without legal advice. An important consideration for Australian communicators is whether the Lange defence is now less attractive to media defendants in the light of the new public interest defence introduced in 2021.

3. Offer of amends

Sometimes we just make a serious mistake and want to make up for it immediately. You should get legal advice the instant someone issues you with a concerns notice alleging defamation – or even if they just make a verbal complaint threatening action. Some disputes can be resolved without litigation, as outlined in ss12–19 of the Act, offering a mechanism for a publisher to make an 'offer of amends' to an aggrieved person. An offer of amends is a defence for those who have made a reasonable, speedy and carefully worded offer to remedy a defamatory publication. Section 18 makes it a complete defence to any future defamation action, provided you are prepared to perform it at any time up to trial. Section 20 encourages apologies by preventing their use as an admission of fault or liability. All offers are best handled by a lawyer. Rash or poorly worded apologies can sometimes go wrong and escalate a matter or erode your chance of arguing one of the defences. Most defamation cases are settled out of court. Out-of-court settlements might include financial compensation, correction notices and other agreements between parties.

4. Innocent dissemination

Section 32 provides a defence of 'innocent dissemination' which excuses publication by 'subordinate distributors' who did not know the defamatory material was there, did not write or produce it, and did not have the capacity to exercise editorial control. The only individuals who have an excuse by arguing 'innocent dissemination' under s32 of the Act are distributors, such as newsagents, librarians, booksellers and, in some circumstances, Internet service providers (ISPs) and content hosts like Google and Facebook, who lose the defence if it is shown that they knew the publication contained the defamatory material or if they did not remove the material within a reasonable time of being notified. Reforms agreed between states in 2022 recommended extending the innocent dissemination defence to social media page hosts from 2024 under certain conditions, countering the High Court's Voller case (2021) ruling making hosts responsible for defamatory comments by third parties from the instant they were posted.

Case examples:

Search Engine cases (2012–2018): Melbourne man Michael Trkulja won $200,000 in damages from Google and $225,000 from Yahoo! after his image and name appeared in search results for underworld criminal figures and the multinational outlets refused to remove them when asked, thus forfeiting their innocent dissemination defence. After a separate action over further instances of search results for Melbourne underworld figures showing images of him, and autocomplete predictions on a search for his name prompting an association with criminal identities, in 2018 the High Court unanimously held that search engine results had the capacity to convey defamatory imputations and that Internet platforms like Google could be held responsible for those results.

Underworld lawyer's case (2022): The High Court decided Google could not be held responsible for a search engine result providing a link to defamatory material when the text of the result (containing the title of a webpage, a snippet of the content found on that webpage and a hyperlink) was itself not defamatory and they did not entice the searcher to open it.

Psychic Stalker case (2017): A delay of 16 months after notification of defamatory material to a search engine before removing it was unreasonable, meaning Google lost any claim to an innocent dissemination defence.

Remedies

There are two main remedies available to plaintiffs in defamation cases: damages and injunctions.

Damages

The most common remedy for defamation is an award of damages to compensate the plaintiff for their emotional hurt and any financial loss they might have suffered from a defamatory publication. Compensatory damages are awarded for non-economic loss (general damages) – capped under the Act at $443,000 in 2022 – as well as for economic loss (special damages) suffered by the plaintiff as a result of the defamation (no limit). Aggravated damages are also unlimited and can be awarded for the publisher's behaviour exacerbating any reputational damage. Damages can range from a pittance (even just $100) through to $4.75 million in Rebel's case (2017) (reduced on appeal), $2.9 million to Geoffrey Rush in the Actor's case (2020) and $2.623 million in the Barrister's Wife case (2017).

Injunctions

Judges also have the power to issue injunctions – court orders – preventing the publication of defamatory material or insisting that already published items be removed. Courts are generally reluctant to issue injunctions before publication because of the centuries-old principle against 'prior restraint' (see Chapter 2). Under that principle, it is felt that free expression is better served by dealing with defamatory material through the courts post-publication so there is minimal censorship pre-publication. For examples of interlocutory injunctions ('gag orders'), see Hanson's case (1998) and the Security case (2016).

Court costs

Most people could not afford to bring a defamation action if they had to pay for it themselves. Apart from damages awards, the costs of a defamation action for both parties (including legal fees and court costs) can be prohibitive for both plaintiffs and defendants. In both 2019/2020 and 2020/2021, the ABC reported spending about $7 million on legal functions (Elsworth, 2021). The protracted legal proceedings against the ABC by former Commonwealth attorney-general Christian Porter in 2021 – eventually settled in mediation with no apology – was estimated to cost the ABC at least $780,000 (Norman, 2021). In the Vocational Education case (2018), the 35-day trial was reported to have cost both sides more than $3.5 million in legal fees (Duke and Vedelago, 2018). The War hero case in 2023 was deemed to have broken all records with an estimated $25 million spent on the proceedings, with an appeal pending (Pelly, 2023).

> **Reflect – Research – Review:**
>
> If someone wins $1 million in defamation damages, to what extent will that be likely to restore their reputation? Draw a mind-map illustrating the points you generate from your thinking about this issue.

The alternative action of injurious falsehood

Included in any study of defamation must be a brief account of the civil action for injurious falsehood (also known as 'malicious falsehood'), which provides an alternative for larger corporations who are excluded from suing under the *Defamation Act* s9. It is of particular interest to corporate communicators. The threshold of proof is much higher than for defamation because the plaintiff needs to prove the statement:

- was false (as opposed to the defamation defendant having to prove its truth);
- caused actual financial loss (as opposed to defamation, where damages can compensate for non-economic loss); and
- was actuated by malice (not a requirement for defamation, although it can negate some defences).

It does not deal directly with damage to reputation, but rather to false and malicious statements disparaging someone's goods (known as 'slander of goods'), implying a person does not have title to property (known as 'slander of title'), or some other 'malicious falsehood' that can cause financial loss. A false statement – for example, that a commercial operator had ceased business – might well cause financial loss and will sometimes be made with malice – perhaps by a competitor or a vengeful former employee.

Case examples:

See the Go Daddy case (2005), the ReGroup case (2016), and the Toll Uniform case (2017).

Reflect – Research – Review:

Go online or to a law library and find out more about injurious or malicious falsehood. Write a two-page summary and present it to your colleagues or fellow students.

Defamation in action – applying reflection in action techniques

Much defamation action could be avoided – along with its associated pain and cost – if professional communicators first reflected upon the potential reputational damage using one of the basic moral and ethical frameworks. With reputational damage, we recommend a three-step process of reflection to think through the dilemma and then to map out a course of action. The three steps are

a. mindful reflection (pausing to breath and reflect on the situation and your own emotions using meditation, journaling or mindmapping);
b. applying a more systematic moral lens to the situation as outlined in Chapter 3 (Applied Ethics Matrix, Bok Model, Potter Box or TARES test);
c. deciding on the legal course of action, use the specific legal risk analysis (Grantham and Pearson, 2022: 51–53).

> **Reflect – Research – Review:**
>
> Here we apply the techniques to the example of a speech writer for an opposition politician accusing a government member of serious wrongdoing.
>
> 1. Pause for a few minutes to breath and reflect upon the situation and your emotions using mindful reflection (meditation), journaling or mindmapping. This stabilises your state of mind and crystallises your concentration. It helps you to identify your moral gut feeling about the situation (which could be well founded or a false alarm) and helps the key issues and intentions bubble to the surface, ready for more systematic analysis.
> 2. Assess the basic morality and ethics of the situation. Here we have chosen the Applied Ethics Matrix to break it down. Also experiment with one or more of the alternative ethical analysis tools from Chapter 3 and decide which best suits you. When considering the allegation of wrongdoing against the opposition member, the Applied Ethics Matrix suggests you ask the following:
>   - What if everyone acted this way? Should this approach become the rule? What duties do I owe to others? (deontological) – *Political allegations are part of the workings of democracies. On the one hand, it is the duty of the political opposition to raise important allegations against governments. But it is also their duty to have enough evidence to substantiate them. They must be more than mere gossip.*
>   - Does my proposed action lead to the greatest benefit for most stakeholders? (consequentialist) – *There is clearly benefit for the opposition in applying pressure to the government, but more broadly are there benefits for all citizens (accountability/informed vote/ justice for all) that outweigh the character damage to the government member and the erosion of confidence in the government?*
>   - How do the rights and interests of various stakeholders get affected by this action? (contractualist) – *A thorough stakeholder analysis might be justified here. At the very least, the government member has a right to an untarnished reputation if that is deserved, while the*

citizens have a right to know of proven wrongdoing. The opposition has a right to raise well founded allegations.
- What virtues or vices are evident in this action? How does it shape my character? (virtue ethicist): *Key virtues that could be at play for the speech writer as a professional communicator might be (in Aristotlean terms): wisdom, prudence, justice, fortitude, courage, proper ambition, magnanimity, patience, righteous indignation and truthfulness. Vices through wrong action might be gossip-mongering, rashness, self-indulgence, vanity, shamelessness or spitefulness (Aristotle, 1955: 104).*
- What clauses from a professional communication ethical code apply to this situation and what guidance is given? – *Both the PRIA and journalists' codes of ethics respect honesty and truth-telling and discourage the dissemination of misleading information. Journalists strive for the public's right to information while respecting the rights of others.*
- How does the action sit with the laws of society? – *See the specific legal risk analysis below.*
- How does the dilemma sit with a theoretical perspective you have adopted, such as feminism, environmentalism or Marxism? – *Assess this individually according to your own perspective.*
- What self-interests are this decision serving as opposed to, or in combination with, the interests of others? – *Clearly there are self-interests at stake here, including the career ambition of the speech writer and the politician. Balancing this is the self interest in preserving their own reputations and brands by not getting it wrong by making false allegations with possible legal repercussions.*
- What does your unique moral compass contribute to your deliberations? That is, how does your culture, family values, religion or political persuasion factor into it? Does a potential bias need consideration or disclosure? – *Clearly, political persuasions are at play with politicians and their staff, which is a clear bias. However, other factors like religious teachings against speaking ill of others can be influential.*
3. Apply the specific legal risk analysis (Grantham and Pearson, 2022: 51–53) – see Table 5.1 over.

In a nutshell

- All major religions and most moral philosophers have viewed poorly the practice of speaking unkindly or gossiping about others to cause damage to their reputations.
- Most major human rights instruments state that all people have the right to a reputation that has not been subjected to unlawful attacks.

Table 5.1 Sample specific legal risk analysis for a speech making allegations against a political opponent. Based on approach detailed in Grantham and Pearson (2022: 51–53)

Specific legal risk analysis	Status	Action required
Identifying the potential (or existing) legal problem	You are a speech writer for an opposition politician and the speech you are drafting accuses a government member of wrongdoing.	You know from your media law studies that allegations of wrongdoing are likely to cause reputational damage – requiring deeper consideration of potential defamation.
Reviewing the areas of the law involved	You review the basics of defamation law and its defences.	You find the proposed speech meets the basic elements of defamation – material that will be published to at least one other person that identifies the politician and stands to cause her serious harm via an allegation of wrongdoing. You also assess the prospects of one of the key defences – truth or public interest – depending upon key elements like provable facts and whether the opponent has been given a right of reply. Given the political context, you also consider whether you would attract absolute privilege if the speech was delivered in Parliament – and consider prospects for a Lange qualified privilege defence given its political context.
Projecting the possible consequences for stakeholders	Given the potential range of stakeholders, a full stakeholder mapping process is required to determine consequences.	Consequences for key stakeholders: *Self (speech writer)* – professional accolades if handled well versus reputational damage if handled poorly. *Speech maker* – political mileage if correct and defensible versus political damage and defamation damages if wrong. *Opposition party* – political mileage if correct and defensible versus political damage if wrong *Government member* – reputational and political damage whether correct or not; possible damages award in defamation case *Citizens* – Better informed vote if allegations are correct versus misguided vote if wrong

Seeking advice/ referring upward	Given the potential legal and regulatory implications, further advice is absolutely essential.	First show the draft speech to close colleagues and discuss the various implications and potential legal problems with your politician boss. Engage lawyers to advise on all but the most clear-cut defences. Keep a diary note of all communications at this stage to help protect you if trouble arises later.
Publishing/ amending/ deleting/ correcting/ apologizing/ compensating	Pre-publication there are opportunities to verify the allegations with evidence, give the politician a right of reply, or perhaps make changes or delete the allegation. If evidence is short you can always wait before making this allegation. Once the speech has been given any retractions or apologies must be handled carefully, after advice.	Supervisors and lawyers must be consulted if strategic legal risks are being taken that could have political or reputational consequences. Any changes, deletions or delays need to be analysed in turn for their own implications. If the material is communicated and then legal demands are made, then lawyers must be engaged to assist with any corrections, apologies or offers of amends.

- Damaging someone's reputation can trigger lawsuits for defamation, and even fines and jail in some places as 'criminal libel'.
- To establish a case, plaintiffs need to show that the material was published to at least one other person, that it was defamatory (made others think less of them), that they were identified and that it caused serious harm to their reputation.
- Someone can sue for defamation if they are identifiable, even if you haven't named them.
- Blogs, tweets/posts, Facebook entries, hyperlinks, email messages and even re-posts or 'likes' can make you liable for defamation action, depending on their contents and your status as a publisher.
- Defamation law in Australia is a combination of legislation in the states and territories and the case law (common law) dating back centuries.
- Anyone involved in a publication can be sued, including the communicator who writes or edits the material.
- The defamatory meaning ('imputation') can come from the natural ordinary meaning of published material or from 'reading between the lines' ('innuendo').
- The internet, social media and AI present special dangers for defamation. An important feature of the internet is that publication occurs wherever someone downloads defamatory material.
- Much more defamatory material can be published by media organisations in the US because of First Amendment protections and a forgiving 'public figure' test.
- If the plaintiff has established the material is defamatory, professional communicators have several possible defences available: truth (or 'justification'); fair report (of a public document or proceedings); honest opinion (or 'fair comment'); public interest; qualified privilege; and its political discussion ('Lange') version.
- Truth (justification) as a defence requires the publisher to prove that the defamatory imputation was substantially true.
- Fair report protects fair and accurate reports of public documents and proceedings such as court, parliament, council and public meetings.
- Honest opinion or fair comment defences are useful for publishing defamatory criticism in reviews and commentary but several essential elements must be satisfied.
- The public interest defence requires the defamatory material to be in the public interest and the publisher to reasonably believe the material is in the public interest. Other factors are suggested for the court's consideration.
- Qualified privilege requires the publisher to prove there is a reciprocal duty–interest relationship that excuses a defamatory publication. It is a useful defence for public relations consultants and news managers for the derogatory references they might write about former staff, as long as they are written in good faith.

- The remedies available to defamation plaintiffs include the award of damages (compensatory and aggravated) and injunctions.

> **Reflect – Research – Review:**
>
> Take a situation from your chosen field of professional communication that might involve a publication damaging someone's reputation. Use the steps of moral, ethical and legal analysis to undertake reflection and proposed strategy.

References and further reading

Al-Azhar. 2020, 'Evils of the Tongue (4): Defamation', *Al-Azhar Observatory for Combating Extremism*, 11 October, <www.azhar.eg/observer-en/details/ArtMID/1153/ArticleID/52198/Evils-of-the-Tongue-4-Defamation>.

Aristotle. 1955, *The Ethics of Aristotle: The Nichomachaen Ethics*, rev. edn, Thomson, J.K. trans., Viking, New York.

Bacher, W. and Eisenstein, J.D. 1906, 'Slander', *Jewish Encyclopedia*, <www.jewishencyclopedia.com/articles/9943-libel-and-slander>.

Benziman, Y. 2020, 'Reputation and morality', *Human Affairs*, 30 (1), 109–119.

Bok, S. 1978, *Lying: Moral Choice in Public and Private Life*, Pantheon Books, New York.

Butler, S. ed. 2006, *Macquarie Concise Dictionary*, 4th edn, Macquarie Dictionary, Sydney.

Council of Europe. 1950, 'Convention for the Protection of Human Rights and Fundamental Freedoms', *Council of Europe Treaty Series 005*, Council of Europe, <www.coe.int/en/web/conventions/full-list?module=treaty-detail&treatynum=005>.

Dissanayake, W. 2003, 'Asian approaches to human communication: Retrospect and prospect', *Intercultural Communication Studies*, 12 (4), 17–37.

Duke, J. and Vedelago, C. 2018, 'Education boss found to be dishonest in losing defamation case', *Sydney Morning Herald*, 25 January, <www.smh.com.au/business/media-and-marketing/education-boss-found-to-be-dishonest-in-losing-defamation-case-20180125-p4yyvb.html>.

Elsworth, S. 2021. 'ABC Spent about $2.6 Million in the 2020–21 Financial Year on External Legal Costs', *The Australian*, 19 December, <https://protect-au.mimecast.com/s/nIkNCp8ArRHn2BPNZUPN0je?domain=amp.theaustralian.com.au>.

Grantham, S. and Pearson, M. 2022, *Social Media Risk and the Law: A Guide for Global Communicators*, Routledge, London and New York.

Meade, A. 2022, 'Defamation reforms: Australian media may not be liable for Facebook comments in future', *The Guardian*, 14 December, <www.theguardian.com/media/2022/dec/14/defamation-reforms-australian-media-may-not-be-liable-for-facebook-comments-in-future>.

Morison, W.L. and Sappideen, C. 1989, *Torts: Commentary and Materials*, 7th edn, Sydney: Law Book Company.

Norman, J. 2021, 'Christian Porter Defamation Case has cost ABC about $780,000, Says Managing Director David Anderson', *ABC News*, 7 June, <www.abc.net.au/news/2021-06-07/david-anderson-abc-senate-estimates-christian-porter/100194822>.

Oderberg, D.S. 2013, 'The Morality of Reputation and the Judgment of Others', *Journal of Practical Ethics*, 1 (2), 3–33, <www.jpe.ox.ac.uk/papers/the-morality-of-reputation-and-the-judgment-of-others-2/>.

Pearson, M. 2015, 'Enlightening communication analysis in Asia-Pacific: Media studies, ethics and law using a Buddhist perspective', *International Communication Gazette*, 77 (5), 456–470.

Pelly, M. 2023. 'At $25m, Ben Roberts-Smith case still cheaper than C7. *Financial Review*. 28 July. <https://www.afr.com/companies/professional-services/at-25m-ben-roberts-smith-case-still-cheaper-than-c7-20220712-p5b148>.

Rolph, D. 2008, *Reputation, Celebrity and Defamation Law*, Aldershot, Ashgate, UK.

Salam, E. 2022, 'Amber Heard settles defamation case with Johnny Depp', *The Guardian*, 20 December, <www.theguardian.com/film/2022/dec/19/amber-heard-johnny-depp-legal-settlement>.

SikhiWiki. 2022, 'Ninda', *SikhiWiki – Encyclomedia of the Sikhs*, <www.sikhiwiki.org/index.php/Ninda>.

Thanissaro, B. trans. 1997, 'Abhaya Sutta: To Prince Abhaya (On Right Speech) (MN 58)', *Access to Insight (Legacy Edition)*, <www.accesstoinsight.org/tipitaka/mn/mn.058.than.html>.

United Nations (UN). 1948, *Universal Declaration of Human Rights*, <www.un.org/en/about-us/universal-declaration-of-human-rights>.

United Nations (UN) Human Rights Office. 1966, 'UN General Assembly resolution 2200A (XXI)', *International Covenant on Civil and Political Rights*, <www.ohchr.org/en/instruments-mechanisms/instruments/international-covenant-civil-and-political-rights>.

Vatican Library. 1993, *Catechism of the Catholic Church* (1993), Libreria Editrice Vaticana, Citta del Vaticano, <www.vatican.va/archive/ENG0015/__P8K.HTM >.

Cases cited

Actor case: *Rush v Nationwide News Pty Ltd* [2018] FCA 357 (20 March 2018), <www.austlii.edu.au/cgi-bin/viewdoc/au/cases/cth/FCA/2018/357.html>; *Nationwide News Pty Limited v Rush* [2020] FCAFC 115 (2 July 2020), <www.austlii.edu.au/cgi-bin/viewdoc/au/cases/cth/FCAFC/2020/115.html>.

ACTV case: *Australian Capital Television Pty Ltd v Commonwealth* [1992] 177 CLR 106 (30 September 1992), <www.austlii.edu.au/cgi-bin/viewdoc/au/cases/cth/HCA/1992/45.html>.

Adam's case: *Adam v Ward* [1917] AC 309 (HL)

Allergy Pathway case: *Australian Competition and Consumer Commission (ACCC) v Allergy Pathway Pty Ltd and Anor (No 2)* [2011] FCA 74 (10 February 2011), <www.austlii.edu.au/au/cases/cth/FCA/2011/74.html>.

Archbishop's case: *Zaia v Eshow* [2017] NSWSC 1540 (15 November), <www.austlii.edu.au/cgi-bin/viewdoc/au/cases/nsw/NSWSC/2017/1540.html>.

Artemus Jones case: *E. Hulton & Co. v Jones* [1910] AC 20.

Barrister's Wife case: *Rayney v the State of Western Australia [No. 9]* [2017] WASC 367 (15 December 2017), <www.austlii.edu.au/cgi-bin/viewdoc/au/cases/wa/WASC/2017/367.html>.

Butler's case: *Butler v John Fairfax Pty Ltd* (1994) 1 MLR 106.

Reputation and defamation 139

Carleton's case: *Carleton v ABC* [2002] ACTSC 127 (18 December 2002), <www.austlii.edu.au/au/cases/act/ACTSC/2002/127.html>; *Carleton v ABC* [2003] ACTSC 28 (2 May 2003), <www.austlii.edu.au/au/cases/act/ACTSC/2003/28.html>.

Club Rawhide case: *Hardie v The Herald and Weekly Times Pty Ltd* [2015] VSC 364 (27 July 2015), <www.austlii.edu.au/cgi-bin/viewdoc/au/cases/vic/VSC/2015/364.html>.

Cricketer's case: *Gayle v Fairfax Media Publications Pty Ltd; Gayle v The Age Company Pty Ltd; Gayle v The Federal Capital Press of Australia Pty Ltd [2017] NSWSC 1261*, <www8.austlii.edu.au/cgi-bin/viewdoc/au/cases/nsw/NSWSC/2017/1261.html>.

ET's case: *Ettingshausen v Australian Consolidated Press Ltd* (1991) 23 NSWLR 443 (25 June 1991), <https://nswlr.com.au/view/23-NSWLR-443>.

Eye Surgeon case: *Rogers v Nationwide News Pty Ltd* [2003] HCA 52 (11 September 2003).

Finn's case: *Finn v Queensland Newspapers Pty Ltd*, Qld District Court (Townsville), 20 May 2002, no. D63 of 2000, unreported.

Football Hormone case: *Carolan v Fairfax Media Publications Pty Ltd (No. 6)* [2016] NSWSC 1091 (9 August 2016), <www.austlii.edu.au/cgi-bin/viewdoc/au/cases/nsw/NSWSC/2016/1091.html>.

Friendlyjordies case (2022): *Barilaro v Google LLC* [2022] FCA 650 (6 June 2022), <www.austlii.edu.au/cgi-bin/viewdoc/au/cases/cth/FCA/2022/650.html>.

Go Daddy case: *Kaplan v Go Daddy Group & 2 Ors* [2005] NSWSC 636 (24 June 2005), <www.austlii.edu.au/cgi-bin/sinodisp/au/cases/nsw/NSWSC/2005/636.html>.

Golf club case: *Byrne v Deane* [1937] 1 K.B. 818.

Gutnick's case: *Dow Jones & Company Inc. v Gutnick* [2002] HCA 56; (2002) 210 CLR 575 (10 December 2002), <www.austlii.edu.au//cgi-bin/disp.pl/au/cases/cth/HCA/2002/56.html>.

Hanson's case: *ABC v Hanson* [1998] QCA 306. Appeal no. 8716 of 1997 (28 September 1998), <www.austlii.edu.au/cgi-bin/viewdoc/au/cases/qld/QCA/1998/306.html>; *Australian Broadcasting Corporation v Hanson*, B40/1998 [1999] HCATrans 211 (24 June 1999), <www.austlii.edu.au/cgi-bin/viewdoc/au/cases/cth/HCATrans/1999/211.html>.

Hanson-Young's case: *Hanson-Young v Bauer Media Limited* [2013] NSWSC 1306 (11 September 2013), <www.austlii.edu.au/cgi-bin/sinodisp/au/cases/nsw/NSWSC/2013/1306.html>.

HotCopper case: *Sims v Jooste [No. 2]* [2016] WASCA 83 (20 May 2016), <www.austlii.edu.au/cgi-bin/viewdoc/au/cases/wa/WASCA/2016/83.html#fnB14>; *Sims v Jooste [No. 2]* [2014] WASC 373 (5 November 2014), <www.austlii.edu.au/cgi-bin/viewdoc/au/cases/wa/WASC/2014/373.html>.

Lange's case: *Lange v Australian Broadcasting Corporation* [1997] 189 CLR 520 (8 July 1997), <www.austlii.edu.au/cgi-bin/viewdoc/au/cases/cth/HCA/1997/25.html>.

Lee's case: *Lee v Wilson & Mackinnon* (1934) 51 CLR 276 (19 December 1934), <www.austlii.edu.au/au/cases/cth/high_ct/51clr276.html>.

Lobster case: *Blue Angel Restaurant v John Fairfax and Sons Ltd* (1989) 11 *Gazette of Law and Journalism* 13.

Massarani's case: *Massarani v Kriz* [2022] FCA 80 (9 February 2022), <www.austlii.edu.au/cgi-bin/viewdoc/au/cases/cth/FCA/2022/80.html>.

Media Watch cases (2002 and 2017): See Carleton's case and the Toxic Playground case.

Mount Druitt case: *Bryant & Ors v Nationwide News Pty Limited* [1999] NSWSC 360 (21 April 1999), <www.austlii.edu.au/cgi-bin/sinodisp/au/cases/nsw/NSWSC/1999/360.html>; *Carroll v Nationwide News Pty Limited* [1999] NSWSC 856

(3 September 1999), <www.austlii.edu.au/cgi-bin/sinodisp/au/cases/nsw/NSWSC/1999/856.html>.

Parmiter's case: *Parmiter v Coupland* (1840) 151 ER 340.

Psychic Stalker case: *Google Inc. v Duffy* [2017] SASCFC 130 (4 October 2017), <www.austlii.edu.au/cgi-bin/viewdoc/au/cases/sa/SASCFC/2017/130.html>.

Racehorse Cruelty case: *Cummings v Fairfax Digital Australia & New Zealand Pty Limited; Cummings v Fairfax Media Publications Pty Ltd* [2017] NSWSC 657 (26 May 2017), <www.austlii.edu.au/cgi-bin/viewdoc/au/cases/nsw/NSWSC/2017/657.html>.

Rebel's case: *Wilson v Bauer Media Pty Ltd* [2017] VSC 521 (13 September 2017), <www.austlii.edu.au/cgi-bin/viewdoc/au/cases/vic/VSC/2017/521.html>; *Bauer Media Pty Ltd v Wilson [No. 2]* [2018] VSCA 154 (14 June 2018), <www.austlii.edu.au/cgi-bin/viewdoc/au/cases/vic/VSCA//2018/154.html>.

ReGroup case: *ReGroup Pty Ltd v Kazal* [2016] FCA 1485 (6 December 2016), <www.austlii.edu.au/cgi-bin/viewdoc/au/cases/cth/FCA/2016/1485.html>.

Rescue Children case: *Newman v Whittington* [2022] NSWSC 249 (24 February 2022), <www.caselaw.nsw.gov.au/decision/17f3d3d4957fb557929853f2>.

Rofe's case: *Rofe v Smith's Newspapers Ltd* [1924] SR (NSW) 4.

Security case: *Sydney Security Services Pty Ltd v iGuard Australia Pty Ltd* [2016] NSWSC 1808 (7 December 2016), <www.austlii.edu.au/cgi-bin/viewdoc/au/cases/nsw/NSWSC/2016/1808.html>.

Sim's case: *Sim v Stretch* (1936) 52 TLR 669.

South Sydney rugby league case: *Papaconstuntinos v Holmes a Court* [2012] HCA 53; 249 CLR 534 (5 December 2012), <www.austlii.edu.au/cgi-bin/viewdoc/au/cases/cth/HCA/2012/53.html>.

Steeplechaser case: *Burton v Crowell Publishing Company*, 82 F2d 154, CA 2, NY, (10 February 1936), <https://casetext.com/case/burton-v-crowell-pub-co#.U4l_zq21Zlc>.

Sullivan's case: *New York Times v Sullivan* [1964] 376 US 254 (9 March 1964), <https://supreme.justia.com/cases/federal/us/376/254/>.

Tailor's case: *Zoef v Nationwide News Pty Ltd (No. 2)* [2017] NSWCA 2 (27 January 2017), <www.austlii.edu.au/cgi-bin/viewdoc/au/cases/nsw/NSWCA/2017/2.html>; *Zoef v Nationwide News Pty Ltd* [2016] NSWCA 283 (18 October 2016), <www.austlii.edu.au/cgi-bin/viewdoc/au/cases/nsw/NSWCA/2016/283.html>; *Zoef v Nationwide News Pty Ltd* [2015] NSWDC 232 (16 October 2015), <www.austlii.edu.au/cgi-bin/viewdoc/au/cases/nsw/NSWDC/2015/232.html>.

Theophanous's case: *Theophanous v Herald and Weekly Times Ltd* [1994] 182 CLR 104 (12 October 1994), <www.austlii.edu.au/cgi-bin/viewdoc/au/cases/cth/HCA/1994/46.html>.

Toll Uniform case: *Toll Transport Pty Ltd & Ors v Erikson* [2017] FCCA 3120 (7 December 2017), <www.austlii.edu.au/cgi-bin/viewdoc/au/cases/cth/FCCA/2017/3120.html>.

Toxic Playground case: *O'Brien v Australian Broadcasting Corporation* [2017] NSWCA 338 (18 December 2012), <www.austlii.edu.au/cgi-bin/viewdoc/au/cases/nsw/NSWCA/2017/338.html>; *O'Brien v Australian Broadcasting Corporation* [2016] NSWSC 1289 (15 September 2016), <www.austlii.edu.au/cgi-bin/viewdoc/au/cases/nsw/NSWSC/2016/1289.html>.

Treasurer case: *Hockey v Fairfax Media Publications Pty Limited* [2015] FCA 652 (30 June 2015), <www.austlii.edu.au/cgi-bin/sinodisp/au/cases/cth/FCA/2015/652.html>.

UK domestic abuse allegation case: *Lachaux v Independent Print Ltd & Anor* [2021] EWHC 1797 (QB) (1 July 2021), <www.bailii.org/ew/cases/EWHC/QB/2021/1797.html>.

UK rape allegation case: *Economou v de Freitas* [2016] EWHC 1853 (QB) (27 July 2016), <www.judiciary.uk/wp-content/uploads/2016/07/economou-v-de-freitas-2016-ewhc-1853-qb-28-07.pdf>.

Underworld lawyer's case: *Google v Defteros* [2022] HCA 27 (8 September 2022), <www.austlii.edu.au/cgi-bin/viewdoc/au/cases/cth/HCA/2022/27.html>.

Vocational Education case: *Charan v Nationwide News Pty Ltd* [2018] VSC 3 (31 January 2018), <www.austlii.edu.au/cgi-bin/viewdoc/au/cases/vic/VSC/2018/3.html>.

Voller case: *Fairfax Media Publications Pty Ltd v Voller; Nationwide News Pty Limited v Voller; Australian News Channel Pty Ltd v Voller* [2021] HCA 27, 8 September, <www.austlii.edu.au/cgi-bin/viewdoc/au/cases/cth/HCA/2021/27.html>.

War Hero case: *Roberts-Smith v Fairfax Media Publications Pty Limited* (No 41) [2023] FCA 555, <www.judgments.fedcourt.gov.au/judgments/Judgments/fca/single/2023/2023fca0555>. [Subject to appeal.]

Wills' case: *Nationwide News Pty Ltd v Wills* (1992) 108 ALR 681.

Youssoupoff's case: *Youssoupoff v Metro-Goldwyn Mayer Pictures Ltd* (1934) 50 TLR 581.

6 Confidentiality, secrets, sources and disclosure

Key concepts

Confidentiality: The boundaries around shared secrets and the process of guarding them.

Breach of confidence: A legal cause of action where a litigant can sue to protect private information that has been conveyed in confidence and seek damages by way of remedy for its wrongful release.

Off-the-record: An ill-defined term used to describe a negotiated level of confidentiality about information conveyed by a source ('whistleblower') to a communicator, usually a journalist.

Disobedience contempt: Interference with the administration of justice by refusing to obey an order of a court such as a demand that a journalist identify a source or hand over confidential information.

Shield law: A law offering some level of protection to journalists who would otherwise be required to reveal a confidential source or to hand over confidential materials to government agencies or courts.

Freedom of information: Laws aimed at opening as much government data to public scrutiny as is reasonably possible and in the public interest.

Introduction to confidentiality

Confidentiality is a crucial issue in the law and ethics of professional communication. Different communication occupations come to the issue of confidentiality and secrets from a range of perspectives depending on the nature of their roles and the type of information or secrets involved. The investigative journalist will sometimes rely on a confidential source to provide secret information and will be bound by the journalism ethical code to never reveal that whistleblower's identity – even at risk of jail for refusing to identify them in court. Corporate communicators will sometimes have to deal with 'commercial-in-confidence' material about their clients and will be bound by their ethical codes to honour that confidentiality. Communicators working in government might have to work with classified documents and face stiff penalties and dismissal if they breach that trust. And communicators of all types

DOI: 10.4324/9781003372752-8

might be faced with confidentiality clauses in their employment or severance contracts that prevent them sharing certain details about their workplace or settlement deals.

In Chapter 7 we deal with Privacy and Data Protection – which can overlap with this chapter's topic of confidentiality and secrets, so it is important to set out their parameters before we go further. Even their dictionary definitions share much in common. According to Merriam-Webster (2023), something is 'confidential' if it is 'marked by intimacy or willingness to confide', if it is 'private' or 'secret', if it is someone 'entrusted with confidences' or if it contains 'information whose unauthorised disclosure could be prejudicial to the national interest'. The adjective 'private' has numerous definitions, with the most relevant to our purposes being 'intended for or restricted to the use of a particular person', 'not known or intended to be known publicly (secret)', 'preferring to keep personal affairs to oneself', and 'withdrawn from company or observation'. The overlap is not confined to the dictionary. In common parlance, we might use the terms 'confidential', 'private' and 'secret' almost interchangeably. And so too in media law, where we learn in Chapter 7 that some courts – particularly in the UK – have allowed the action of breach of confidence to morph into a new tort of privacy invasion when secret aspects of celebrities' personal lives have been exposed by the media. For our purposes, we prefer the definition of confidentiality provided by the moral philosopher Sissela Bok: 'The boundaries surrounding shared secrets and the process of guarding such boundaries' (Bok, 1989: 119). Those boundaries of shared secrets go to the relationship between journalists and their confidential sources and allow for consideration of the ethics and laws around the ways various communication professionals handle confidential information in their day-to-day work. The next chapter delves more into the invasion of other people's privacy in the work of professional communication – such as when news reporters might intrude upon the grieving relative of a victim – and with the enacted protocols for dealing with people's private data, known as 'data protection' laws.

Philosophical background and human rights context

> And whatsoever I shall see or hear in the course of my profession, as well as outside my profession in my intercourse with men, if it be what should not be published abroad, I will never divulge, holding such things to be holy secrets. – Hippocrates (460–370BC), cited in Thompson (1979: 57).

The ethical origins of professional confidentiality date back to at least the time of the Greek philosopher and doctor Hippocrates (460–370BC) – who wrote the Hippocratic Oath quoted above. It remains the primary ethical code for medical practitioners internationally, requiring doctors to keep patient information secret. As with both truth and reputational damage, confidentiality has its roots as much in religion as in philosophy.

Confidentiality in the profession of the priesthood can be traced to the 4th century, when Saint Aphrahat, the 'Persian Sage', wrote 'And when [a sinner] has revealed [a sin] to you, do not make it public' (Aquilina, 2019). What is said in the confessional has remained secret ever since, and the priest's refusal to break that seal is even protected by law in some places. The Catholic Church's *Code of Canon Law* reads today: 'The sacramental seal is inviolable. Accordingly, it is absolutely wrong for a confessor in any way to betray the penitent, for any reason whatsoever, whether by word or in any other fashion' (Vatican, 2023; 1983: Can 983.1).

Some leading Western philosophers have thought about confidentiality and secrecy via treatises about its opposite concept – publicity. Gosseries and Parr (2022) trace some of the highlights of this discussion. They cite the great deontologist Immanuel Kant's rule-based approach to publicity in a political context and his hypothetical publicity test:

> All actions relating to the right of other human beings are wrong if their maxim is incompatible with publicity.
> (Kant's *Perpetual Peace*, 1795, cited in Gosseries and Parr, 2022)

They stressed the hypothetical nature of the test which seemed to imply that in an ideal world with a rational public, then secrecy had no place if important principles were being developed that affected the rights of others.

While utilitarians and libertarians like Jeremy Bentham and John Stuart Mill were in favour of publicity over secrecy, Gosseries and Parr (2022) pointed to an argument by the more modern utilitarian philosopher Henry Sidgwick (1838–1900) who defended the notion of secrecy for the purposes of recommending certain actions privately that it might not be wise to generalise to the broader public as wider policy, and that this might not be unjust. The line of thinking was that if an 'enlightened' few were permitted to lie for the greater public benefit, then this lying would be best kept secret to avoid the possibility of the broader public adopting lying as standard practice. While Sidgwick's writing was restricted to the notion of lying about the philosophical intricacies of utilitarianism itself, you can see how that same thought progression might be adopted by the enlightened few in power, purportedly acting in the best interests of society more generally. The purposes of effective public policy might be achieved by the means of keeping things confidential. Top secret, classified documents are one example: publicity about them might damage important relationships or perhaps even endanger lives. This is the rationale used by many a political leader and senior bureaucrat to keep some decisions and reasoning secret – to the chagrin of those calling for openness and transparency in government and freedom of information. It is also what leads to many of the secrets that investigative journalists set out to expose in the greater public interest in the tradition of Fourth Estate journalism. Later in the chapter we look briefly at freedom of information laws, a prime example of the public policy battle between secrecy and transparency. As we shall see, while journalists might be advocates for openness and transparency, they are also the ones arguing on ethical grounds to keep secret their sources who give them examples of its abuse for their stories. This becomes quite the faultline for the professional communicator who, depending on their occupation, might sit on either side of the secrecy-transparency debate.

Gosseries and Parr (2022) also underscored the importance of publicity in the work of the 20th century social contract philosopher John Rawls, particularly in the doctrines of *'public reason'* and *'public rules'*. On 'public reason', Rawls argued that political power should be exercised by appealing publicly to the broader citizenry to endorse leaders' reasoning for their policies. The doctrine of 'public rules' has synergies with the principle of 'open justice' that we examine in Chapter 8. Rawls argued principles of justice that operate as a public standard should be preferred because they are not self-effacing, they are definitive and accessible, and compliance with them is verifiable to other citizens. Openness in access to, and reporting of, the justice system encourages this, whereas confidentiality and secrecy in courts would be counter-productive.

Modern moral philosopher Sissela Bok reviewed many of these issues and even devoted a chapter to investigative journalism in her book *Secrets: On the Ethics of Concealment and Revelation* (Bok, 1989: 249–264). In it, she takes issue with media claims of the 'public's right to know'. She argues that even a public right to know enshrined in law can only really operate as a right to access certain kinds of information (Bok, 1989: 258). She also takes up the important ethical issue of whether it is right for reporters to use disguise and deception to meet a public interest end. It is a topic we dealt with briefly in Chapter 4. Bok concludes that elaborate and concocted media undercover operations designed for a 'Gotcha' end can further damage media brands that are already suffering a loss in public trust (Bok, 1989: 264).

> **Reflect – Research – Review:**
>
> Philosopher Sissela Bok has argued that some matters deserve confidentiality and that arguments for a 'public right to know' are ill-founded. What is your supported view on this?

Professional ethical dilemmas in confidentiality

Professional communication industry bodies and media unions internationally require their members to uphold confidences. To illustrate, we will compare some ethical codes for public relations practitioners and for journalists.

Public relations

Overwhelmingly the emphasis in public relations codes is upon client confidentiality in a business sense. Both UK trade associations for public relations – the Chartered Institute of Public Relations (CIPR) and the Public Relations Consultants Association (PRCA) – mention the need to keep confidences in their ethical codes. The former mentions confidentiality only briefly, as part of a list of 'the highest standards of professional endeavour' that members must uphold, along with integrity, financial propriety and personal conduct (CIPR, 2023). However, it gives more detail in its sector-specific guidance for lobbyists, where it states at item 6:

> Professional lobbyists respect confidentiality – this is more than simply keeping a client's commercial information confidential. Professional lobbyists, who may know politicians and civil servants socially, do not misuse privileged information for commercial gain.
> (CIPR, 2023)

It offers the following practice notes for practitioners:

- Safeguarding confidences – for example, of present and former clients and employers.
- Never using confidential and 'insider' information to the disadvantage or prejudice of others, for example clients and employers, or to self-advantage of any kind.
- Not disclosing confidential information unless specific permission has been granted or if required or covered by law.
(CIPR, 2023)

The PRCA demands it quite simply at Item 2.6 of its Professional Charter: 'Honour confidences received or given in the course of professional activity' (PRCA, 2023).

In the US, the Public Relations Society of America (PRSA) has a section on safeguarding confidences, with the core principle that 'Client trust requires appropriate protection of confidential and private information'. Its guidelines cover similar territory to the UK's CIPR (PRSA, 2023a). The society's website features several resources on ethics, with a position paper on Information Leaks (PRSA, 2023b) explaining that several other ethical provisions come into play in relation to the issue of confidentiality, including clauses on the disclosure of information, the free flow of accurate and truthful information, conflicts of interest and public trust in the profession. It demonstrates the many facets of confidentiality in professional communication. The society recommends practitioners follow these practices:

- Be fully aware of all laws, regulations, standing contracts and business terms that govern the flow of information within and on behalf of the organisations they both represent and with whom they interact.
- Adhere to all contractual and legal obligations to protect confidentiality.
- Never act autonomously by sharing information, observations, anecdotes or other information that was obtained in confidence as part of a trusted business relationship.
- Follow all standing procedures for approving the disclosure of information to both internal and external publics.

(PRSA, 2023b)

In Australia, the Public Relations Institute of Australia (PRIA) Code of Ethics binds all members 'to safeguard the confidences of both present and former employees and clients, including confidential information about employers' or clients' business affairs, technical methods or processes, except upon the order of a court of competent jurisdiction' (PRIA, 2023, Clause 4). As an exception under Clause 9, members are required to be 'prepared to identify the source of funding of any public communication they initiate or for which they act as a conduit'. Thus, for Australian PR practitioners there are two exceptions to keeping confidences – if ordered to reveal them by a court and in the interests of transparency of sponsored communications.

Journalism

Journalists' ethical codes are much more concerned with the reporter-source confidential relationship than the handling of confidential information, although there are privacy provisions in that area that we deal with in the next chapter. In the UK and Ireland, the National Union of Journalists' Code of Conduct focuses squarely on the relationship of confidence between a journalist and a source when it states at Item 7 that a journalist 'Protects the identity of sources who supply information in confidence and material gathered in the course of her/his work' (NUJ, 2018). This is common for journalism ethical codes throughout the world, although some include warnings about the motivations of sources who want to be anonymous. The Australian code is an example, which at Clause 3 precedes the firm obligation of confidence to a source with advice to try to attribute and to consider sources' motives (MEAA, 2016):

> Aim to attribute information to its source. Where a source seeks anonymity, do not agree without first considering the source's motives and any alternative attributable source. Where confidences are accepted, respect them in all circumstances.
>
> (MEAA, 2016)

In the US, the Society of Professional Journalists' (SPJ) Code of Ethics (2014) says journalists should 'Be cautious when making promises, but keep the promises they make'. That document offers advice to journalists around the two SPJ Code of Ethics clauses that refer to anonymous sources:

> Identify sources clearly. The public is entitled to as much information as possible on sources' reliability.
> Consider sources' motives before promising anonymity. Reserve anonymity for sources who may face danger, retribution or other harm, and have information that cannot be obtained elsewhere. Explain why anonymity was granted.
>
> (SPJ, 2014)

In obliging journalists to respect confidences in all circumstances, most journalism codes allow no room for manoeuvre. The ethical rationale is simple: where the only way to obtain the information is to guarantee confidentiality, the source has relied upon the journalist's promise and to betray that promise may expose the source to disadvantage, danger or legal action. There is also a practical reason for upholding such promises: if journalists make a habit of outing confidential sources, their sources will soon dry up.

Journalists' codes are unusual in offering no escape from the confidentiality obligation unless the source waives their right not to be identified. Doctors and accountants have 'escape clauses' similar to those in the PRIA Code of Ethics noted above. For example, Australian accountants are not allowed to betray a professional confidence 'unless there is a legal or professional right or duty to disclose' (APESB, 2010: s 140.1a) and, while the Australian Medical Association's (AMA) Code of Ethics instructs doctors to 'Maintain the confidentiality of the patient's personal information' in line with the Hippocratic Oath, exceptions may include 'as required or authorised by law' (AMA, 2016). The journalist's code is as absolute as the priest's, which leads to legal problems for those who refuse to reveal the identity of their sources when that is demanded of them in court, which we deal with momentarily.

Law, cases and examples internationally in confidentiality and disclosure

Confidentiality and disclosure arise in a range of work and legal contexts for professional communicators. Here we focus on key topics that arise across a range of occupational contexts and might involve the communicator as the person who is trying to keep a secret or perhaps the person endeavouring to disclose it. We look at five of the legal avenues that affect those trying to keep secrets and those trying to disclose them:

a. Breach of confidence
b. Disobedience contempt
c. Shield laws

d. Whistleblower laws
e. Freedom of Information laws

We first consider them in an international context before seeing how they operate with cases and examples closer to home.

Breach of confidence

The law in all major jurisdictions offers 'breach of confidence' as a cause of action to those who have had their secrets betrayed by another. They can sue the transgressor for damages if the information has already been shared or they can obtain a court order (injunction) prohibiting publication of the confidential information. Further, the court can order a journalist to reveal leaked material which may identify its source. The law of breach of confidence can impact professional communicators in a host of situations. They might be the journalist or political operative wanting to share or 'leak' the confidential information, or they might be a corporate communicator doing their best to stop confidential material being made public. Breach of confidence has evolved in the US as a common law tort (a civil wrong) – subject to the usual First Amendment free expression limitations – whereas in the UK and its former colonies it has developed as a so-called 'equitable doctrine'. These are procedural issues that do not need to concern professional communicators and the basic elements of the action are similar. There is a further human rights element to it in the UK, as distinct from other former British colonies. The UK incorporated the European Convention on Human Rights into its law in 1988, which included the Article 8 privacy protection as a right. That article gives all citizens the 'right to respect for his private and family life, his home and his correspondence' (EHRC, 2021). The outcome has been that the UK courts have allowed for the merging of the law of breach of confidence with the law of privacy, as we learn in Chapter 7.

Elements of the action

As mentioned, the basic principles of a breach of confidence action are similar across US and UK-associated jurisdictions. The English version was laid out in the Engineers' cases (1948 and 1969) related to the confidential nature of designs, later extended to a host of confidential contexts. Three elements of the action were developed:

- *The information must have had a necessary 'quality of confidence'*: Confidential information is usually material that is of a sensitive financial, legal or private nature. It can include documents, ideas, verbal secrets, works of art and objects. There must be something inherent in the nature of the information itself that makes it confidential. Merely designating something as 'confidential' is not enough. The 'quality of confidence' may have been lost by being disclosed to the public or by entering the 'public domain'.

- *The information must have been imparted in circumstances giving rise to an obligation of confidence*: The courts look to whether the person who received the information knew, or ought to have known, it was confidential. This may be inferred from the nature of the material itself (such as information about a person's private discussions with their client) or from the circumstances in which the information was disclosed (such as in the course of a job interview). This principle also binds secondary recipients, such as journalists, if they ought to know from the nature of the information or the circumstances in which the source received it that it is confidential.
- *There must have been unauthorised use (or planned use) of that information to the detriment of the party communicating it*: Even accidental disclosure incurs liability. Any use other than that authorised can constitute a breach.

Defences

In the US, there are strong First Amendment free expression arguments that can constitute a defence such as 'public interest' or 'newsworthiness' – most successful when argued by news organisations, particularly in relation to public figures. In the UK, the *Human Rights Act* Article 8 obligation of confidentiality is weighed against its Article 10 free expression considerations. In British Commonwealth jurisdictions, the key defences are: legal compulsion (when ordered by a court to break the confidence) and 'just cause or excuse' (a justified disclosure such as the exposure of a crime or an 'iniquity' – a civil wrong or some serious misdeed of public importance, such as a breach of consumer law, or protecting the community from destruction, damage or harm.) This operates as a de facto 'public interest' defence. Mere public curiosity will not suffice. Confidences revealed as part of a fair report of parliamentary proceedings are also excused. A further public interest protection applies to the revelation of secrets about government. In such cases, the government has to prove the revelation of the secret is contrary to the public interest before it can proceed with an action. Of course, criminal prosecutions can also result from the revelation of government secrets in the form of classified information, as we learn in Chapter 10.

Case example:

Pop stars case (1977): A group of pop stars including the chart-toppers Tom Jones, Engelbert Humperdinck and Gilbert O'Sullivan tried unsuccessfully to use the breach of confidence action to stop their former public relations consultant from publishing a series of 'tell-all' stories about their private lives in the London tabloid the *Daily Mirror*. The court held they could not seek to have favourable publicity about themselves published and then act to prevent unfavourable publicity – a ruling since discarded as explained in Meghan Markle's case (2021, para 101) (see Key Case 7.1).

Professional communicators should note that the actual obligation of confidence can arise in a range of situations, including the terms of a contract (written or verbal, express or implied); the employer–employee relationship and associated trade secrets; the professional–client relationship; the transfer of a secret to a third party if the third party knows (or should know) it is confidential; and under legislation as it applies to secret government information, such as defence documents and tax files. The obligation can also apply to unsolicited information, such as the bundle of documents that 'falls off the back of a truck' and onto a journalist's desk. The test is whether it was received in circumstances suggesting it breached an obligation of confidence.

Remedies

If the unauthorized disclosure of a secret has already occurred, a plaintiff will normally seek damages or an 'account of profits' – a reimbursement to the plaintiff of profits the defendant has made through the use of the confidential information. For example, if it could be shown that a newspaper's circulation increased by 10,000 on a particular day as a result of the unauthorized disclosure of a particular secret, it might be called to account for that profit and ordered to reimburse the plaintiff. Damages are the more common remedy, with the courts attempting to restore the plaintiff to the position he or she would have been in had the disclosure not occurred. If the disclosure has not yet happened, the plaintiff will normally seek a temporary or permanent injunction preventing the disclosure. The courts are reluctant to grant such injunctions against the media as it goes against the doctrine of prior restraint, a principle that aims to give priority to free speech in such situations. This is adhered to much more closely in the US than in Australia.

Digital dimensions

There is no doubt that social media have implications for the law of confidentiality. For example, if you receive a message via WhatsApp from a contact in WikiLeaks directing you to certain information, you would likely be on notice that it is confidential. It also casts the appropriation of people's Facebook photos in a new light, particularly if you have worked via friends of friends or have hacked your way through their privacy settings to get them. If someone has their privacy settings on maximum restriction, or just sends a very private image to a small circle of people, then the sharing of that image might be classified as a 'breach of confidence' or the 'disclosure of embarrassing private facts'.

Courts throughout the world have taken different approaches over whether they will order the 'outing' of the identity of an anonymous internet user. Legal case citations have traditionally used the names 'John Doe' or 'Jane Doe' for anonymous or confidential parties. (Some jurisdictions use 'Joe Bloggs'.) When considering whether to order platforms to reveal anonymous social media account owners, UK and Australian courts draw on a decision made by the

House of Lords two decades before mainstream use of the internet. The 1973 Norwich Pharmacal case centred on a company seeking the identity of those importing goods that infringed their patents. The customs commissioners were ordered to reveal the identity of the importers. The House of Lords ruled that where a third party had become engaged in unlawful conduct, it was under a duty to help whoever had suffered damage by disclosing the identity of any wrongdoers and providing them with full information about the matter. In contrast to the US, disclosure becomes the starting point in Britain.

Case examples:

Wikipedia case (2009): The High Court of Justice applied the Norwich Pharmacal test in the Wikipedia case in 2009, when it ordered Wikipedia to reveal the IP address of an anonymous party who had amended an article about a woman and her young child to include sensitive private information about them. The judge suppressed their names on confidentiality grounds because he believed the entries were part of a blackmail threat against the mother. Even though the owner of Wikipedia (Wikimedia) was based in Florida, the court issued the disclosure order. Wikimedia complied, but insisted it was not legally bound to do so because it was in a different jurisdiction and had immunity under s230 of the US *Communications Decency Act 1996* as a third-party publisher of the comments of others.

Financial Tweets case (2017): The NSW Supreme Court issued a Norwich order against Twitter (now 'X') after an anonymous tweeter had created false 'handles' in the name of the CEO of a company and others and proceeded to release confidential financial information to the detriment of the corporation. Twitter – based in the US and Ireland – did not appear to defend the matter. The court issued injunctions preventing Twitter allowing further publications by the account holders and further orders disclosing their identities.

Disobedience contempt

Sometimes professional communicators find themselves in situations where they do not want to reveal secrets – but are determined to keep certain information confidential even when ordered by a judge to reveal it. This can arise in a range of circumstances, but most notably where a journalist has an ethical obligation to keep a confidential source's identity secret but this clashes with a court's need for that information in its quest to administer justice. We learned earlier that journalists' ethical codes typically do not allow for a judicial exception to the obligation of confidence – unlike most other professional codes. The courts have long insisted that a question must be answered – and confidential documents must be tendered – if it is 'relevant and necessary in the interests of justice'. Except in the case of the lawyer–client relationship, which confers a privilege internationally, the courts have been reluctant to accord an evidentiary privilege (an exemption from having to answer a question in court) to professional relationships. While there is a public interest served by journalists protecting sources to aid the exposure of public wrongdoing, other factors enter the equation in the courtroom. Judges also have to consider the accused person's right to a fair trial, the plaintiff's right to a remedy and the community's expectation that justice will be done. As stated in McGuinness's case (1940), the leading Australian case in the area: 'No such privilege exists according to law. Apart from statutory provisions, the press, in courts of law, has no greater and no less privilege than every subject of the King'.

Case example:

Lundin's case (1982): Watkins LJ held that the revelation of a source would have to have served a 'useful purpose' and, in the absence of other much-needed evidence, 'that which was useless could not conceivably be said to be necessary'. Lundin, an investigative journalist with *Private Eye*, had refused to reveal who had given him a photocopy of a document implicating a policeman in a racket disclosing information about gamblers. But Lundin was held not to have committed contempt by refusing to reveal the source of the photocopy because the disclosure would have been rendered useless by the absence of other essential evidence.

Internationally, journalists have faced heavy fines or jail terms for refusing to reveal their confidential sources in court. In Australia, three journalists were jailed for disobedience contempt for refusing to reveal their sources in the late 1980s and early 1990s. In the US – the home of the First Amendment – 22 journalists were jailed under such laws between 1984 and 2018, including video blogger Josh Wolf, who was released in 2007 after serving 226 days for refusing to hand over a tape of protesters damaging a police car. *The New York Times*' journalist Judith Miller served 86 days in prison in 2005 for refusing to tell a grand jury who leaked the identity of a CIA operative to the media. The US Press Freedom Tracker reported a further ten journalists had faced subpoenas or legal orders to reveal confidential information or sources in the 2019–2023 period (US Press Freedom Tracker, 2023). One – a Massachusetts editor – had been admonished by colleagues for agreeing to reveal the names and contact information of ten confidential sources, along with unpublished notes and emails after a court order in a defamation case (Goggins, 2022).

Reflect – Research – Review:

Journalists in several countries have been jailed or fined for refusing to reveal their sources in recent years. Find an example not detailed here and write a short report.

Shield laws

The US jailings and demands to reveal sources occurred despite the extensive existence of shield laws throughout that country. According to Reporters Committee for Freedom of the Press, by 2021 statutes known has 'shield laws' had been enacted in 40 states and the District of Columbia giving journalists some form of privilege against compelled production of confidential or unpublished information. All but two of the remaining ten states had recognized some form of a privilege, either through case law or court rules (RCFP, 2021). In 2023 an attempt to get a federal shield law through Congress in the form of a *PRESS Act* was abandoned. Among Commonwealth countries, the UK had led the way with its *Contempt of Court Act 1981*, which offered some shield law protection to publishers. By 2023 shield laws existed in all Australian states and at Commonwealth level and there were moves to harmonise them nationally. Shield laws internationally vary widely in their scope, sometimes only applying to material that has already been 'published' and sometimes specifically naming 'journalists' and 'news media' as those protected – but not necessarily bloggers or other contributors.

Case example:

Kiwi Blogger's case (2014): New Zealand's High Court included an environmental blogger in the definition of 'journalist' for the purposes of its shield law, even though he had earlier rejected the notion of being called a journalist.

Whistleblower protections

> Bad men need nothing more to compass their ends, than that good men should look on and do nothing. – Philosopher John Stuart Mill, *Inaugural Address at St Andrews* (1867)

Media relations practitioners and press secretaries have long used the 'leak' as a powerful political technique, currying favour with leading journalists and serving the ends of their masters in the process. In addition, there are the 'whistleblowers' – public service, political or corporate insiders – who reveal their organisations' secrets, sometimes because there is an important matter of social conscience that concerns them and often because their attempts at internal reporting of wrongdoing have gone unanswered. Journalists and public relations operatives could be on either side of the whistleblowing equation – either blowing the whistle or receiving the confidential information from those who are leaking it. It is therefore important for professional communicators to have at least a basic understanding of whistleblowing laws. Unless you are an investigative journalist, you are unlikely to have the training or experience in

Confidentiality, secrets, sources and disclosure 155

handling off-the-record information and covering your trail so that both you and any whistleblower are protected.

The most famous modern whistleblowing examples are Chelsea (formerly Bradley) Manning (a US Army soldier) and former US National Security Agency employee Edward Snowden. The international whistleblowing organisation WikiLeaks became famous for releasing thousands of secret US government files on the Middle East conflicts and broader diplomatic relations throughout 2010 and 2011. It reassured sources that its high security, encrypted submission system using an electronic dropbox protected their identity. However, US soldier Bradley (Chelsea) Manning spent seven years in jail after being detected as the source of that leak. WikiLeaks founder Julian Assange took refuge for several years in the Ecuadorian embassy in London before drawn-out legal battles fighting extradition to the United States over his publication of the leaks. In 2013 Snowden worked with mainstream media organisations to release tranches of classified documents, some showing how the phones of world leaders had been electronically monitored. Snowden fled to Russia, where he sought political asylum. The 2016 film *Snowden* is essential media law viewing.

In some places there are broad 'public interest' protections for whistleblowing about crime and corruption. In jurisdictions where anti-corruption agencies have been established, there is usually immunity from repercussions for witnesses who come forward to reveal wrongdoing. Between 1978 and 2021, 48 countries introduced specific national whistleblower protection laws, with that number predicted to rise to more than 60 in 2023 following the passing of the *European Union Whistleblower Directive* at the end of 2021 (Feinstein and Devine, 2021: 8). That directive offers a good example of the way such public interest disclosure laws are designed to operate. It aims to protect whistleblowers who report work-related breaches of EU law in key policy areas – including unlawful acts, omissions and abusive practices. It covers important areas of potential corruption and public safety breaches including public procurement, financial services, money laundering and environmental protection. Importantly the laws apply to people in both the private and public sectors, during and after employment, and extend to those who assist the whistleblowers. They require all public entities and companies with 50 or more employees to set up internal reporting channels and national authorities to establish external channels, with protocols to protect whistleblowers from retaliation or revelation of their identities (Publications Office of the European Union, 2020).

Few of the laws internationally offer protection to whistleblowers who bypass the official channels and go directly to the media with their allegations or who use online methods to leak confidential information. For example, the European Directive only protects those who go public with their concerns if they first reported it through the appropriate channels internally and externally and no action was taken and they reasonably believe there is clear danger to the public interest, risk of retaliation or little chance of their complaints being addressed (Publications Office of the European Union, 2020).

Even where such public interest disclosure laws do apply there has been criticism for their ineffectiveness because of a lack of transparency over their outcomes, under-use of the laws, poor outcomes for whistleblowers and little compensation for those who win (Feinstein and Devine, 2021: 8). Despite such whistleblower protection laws, confidential sources face lengthy jail terms in most countries if they reveal state secrets because courts may not agree that there is a sufficient ethical or public interest in the material being revealed. Neither Manning nor Snowden would have been protected by US whistleblowing laws as they did not cover national security breaches or leaks of classified material. (See also the classic Pentagon Papers case (1971), featured as Key Case 10.1, where a whistleblower leaked documents revealing the true level of US involvement in Vietnam.)

In the modern era, it is even harder to protect digital communications against detection by the authorities, so you need to take extraordinary steps if you hope to keep your sources truly confidential. Geolocation technologies, phone and internet records, security cameras and metadata access laws are just some of the mechanisms agencies can use to determine who has been talking to the investigative journalist or political media relations operator.

Freedom of information laws

The dangers to whistleblowers, other confidential sources and journalists can sometimes be minimised or avoided by the strategic use of Freedom of Information (FOI) laws – statutory requirements where governments open the vault on large swathes of their correspondence and other files on the application of citizens. FOI – also called 'right to information' (RTI) – is meant to be about maximising the transparency of, and accountability for, government decision-making processes in a modern democracy.

According to Goldberg (2006: 35–36), the practice of FOI might well have existed as early as the Tang Dynasty in China (618–907CE), although formal legislation can be traced back more than 250 years to the 1766 Swedish Edict of the Freedom of the Press, the *Tryckfrihetsförordningen* (TF). Swede Peter Forsskal set the intellectual scene for the Nordic law by writing extensively about the need for free expression, lack of censorship and free knowledge in democratic society. The Finn, Anders Chydenius, was a key figure in crafting the law and negotiating its passage through the parliament. By late 2021, at least 132 countries had adopted constitutional guarantees or enacted access to information laws, including many that also had them in sub-jurisdictions such as states or territories (Jelassi, 2021).

The United Nations acknowledged the vital role of FOI by including the right to 'seek, receive and impart information' along with free expression in Article 19 of the *Universal Declaration of Human Rights* (UN, 1948). In 2000, the UN Special Rapporteur on Freedom of Opinion and Expression, appointed by the UN Commission on Human Rights to monitor and report on the implementation of Article 19 of the *ICCPR*, proposed a set of FOI principles including a goal of maximum disclosure, obligatory transparency, minimal exceptions, rapid processing, independent reviews, reasonable costs, open meetings, repeals of laws countering disclosure and protection of whistleblowers (McMillan, 2011: 8–9). However, the sad reality is that in some countries the cost of FOI applications is prohibitive, the list of exemptions to release is extensive, outright refusals are common, the time taken to process applications is excessive and appeal mechanisms are flawed (Knaus and Bassano, 2019).

Basic Australian legal principles in confidentiality and disclosure

It is important to acknowledge that confidentiality about secrets in Australia pre-dated European settlement in 1788 and the legacy of those tribal laws and protocols impacts the outputs of communicators to this day. Aboriginal and Torres Strait Islander peoples had many and varied laws related to secret stories, artefacts and ceremonies that would fit modern legal definitions of confidentiality. Their specifics varied according to the location and culture of particular communities. For example, indigenous boys of the Anangu culture who live in Uluru-Kata Tjuta country in central Australia are gradually introduced via secret ceremonies, songs and sacred sites to the men's business – known as *Tjukurpa* – part of their rite of passage (Parks Australia, 2023). As Anemaat (1989: 38) noted, there was secrecy 'embedded in much of the traditional folklore' which has translated into ethical and legal obligations on those who wish to store or use the information in modern society.

The areas of media law in modern Australia related to confidentiality, secrets, sources and disclosure represent a combination of case law, legislation and regulations. Here we summarise the Australian law in relation to the five topic areas introduced at international level above.

Breach of confidence in Australia

As a former British colony, Australia has drawn heavily on the case law in the UK for the development of the equitable action for breach of confidence. The three main elements of the action developed in the Engineers cases (1948 and 1969) were adopted in Australia, and well summarised by Gleeson CJ in the Lenah Game Meats case (2001, para 30):

> *first*, that the information is confidential, *secondly*, that it was originally imparted in circumstances importing an obligation of confidence, and *thirdly*, that there has been, or is threatened, an unauthorised use of the information to the detriment of the party communicating it (italics added).

158   *Key topics in media law and ethics*

That case was notable because the High Court stopped short of developing the law of confidentiality into a new tort for the invasion of privacy (see Chapter 7). However, the court did concede that a photograph of something private which has been 'illegally or improperly or surreptitiously obtained' could constitute confidential information for the purposes of the breach of confidence action. Those covering crime and court cases need to be aware that the breach of confidence action is available against anyone who might inadvertently identify sexual assault victims in breach of the special publishing restrictions applying in all jurisdictions, and perhaps other situations like family law cases, as we explain in Chapter 8. In the Jane Doe case (2007), where ABC broadcasts identified a rape victim, she successfully sued the broadcaster for the breach of her confidence and invasion of her privacy among other actions.

Government information and the public interest

The requirement that, in order to win an action of breach of confidence, governments must prove the disclosure was contrary to the public interest, evolved in Australian case law. This additional test is known as the 'Fairfax test', as it was developed by High Court Justice Anthony Mason in the Defence Papers case (1980) involving the newspaper group then owned by the Fairfax family. He ruled: 'Unless disclosure is likely to injure the public interest, it will not be protected'. It applies to information about government and its own workings, but not to information that government holds on private individuals or companies.

Case example:

Maleny Towers case (2016): An environmental engineer had applied under Queensland Right to Information (RTI) laws to the Sunshine Coast Regional Council for correspondence between the council and the National Broadband Network (NBN) about the proposed construction of communications towers. Under Queensland legislation, information is exempt from release if its disclosure would establish an action for breach of confidence. After working through the elements of the action, and considering the Fairfax test, the Information Commissioner decided that the general rollout information in the requested material would not constitute a breach of confidence action and should be released by the council.

Fair report

As noted, the disclosure of otherwise confidential information as part of a fair and accurate report of parliamentary proceedings is a defence to a breach of confidence action.

Case example:

Westpac Letters case (1991): Sydney and Melbourne newspapers obtained copies of letters from a bank's solicitors about serious breaches of foreign exchange regulations by its merchant banking subsidiary. Westpac won injunctions to stop them publishing on breach of confidence grounds. Once the information was released in the South Australian parliament, other media outlets were able to publish the details as a fair report of Parliament, but the newspapers covered by the injunctions were gagged until after the information was disclosed at a parliamentary banking inquiry and the injunctions were discharged. Some media are now hesitant to give warning of publication for fear of triggering an injunction, but there are other pitfalls in such a strategy, such as the loss of some defamation defences.

Key Case 6.1: AFL case

Australian Football League (AFL) & Anor v The Age Company Ltd & Ors [2006] VSC 308 (30 August 2006)

Facts

The AFL had an anti-doping code banning performance-enhancing drugs. In 2005, it struck a deal with the players' association for a second drugs policy, covering illicit substances such as narcotics, aimed at education and rehabilitation. Under it, a player's first and second positive test would be kept confidential. In 2006, two newspapers received information identifying three AFL players as testing positive for illicit drugs. The AFL and the players' association sought injunctions to stop publication of the players' names.

Law

All parties agreed the information had originally been confidential. The newspapers argued it had passed into the public domain, that an injunction would serve no purpose and was futile, that the information disclosed 'iniquitous behaviour' and that protection of the confidential information must give way to the public interest in the identity of the three players being disclosed. Justice Kellam found the names of the players had been publicised to a limited extent, but not sufficiently to destroy confidentiality. One contributor to a discussion forum had said a player 'knows a lot about ice' and another referred to a 'nostril related hamstring' injury. The judge did not accept the 'circumstances of iniquity' argument based on players having committed criminal offences because the media purpose was for increased readership, not the exposure of wrongdoing. Finally, he could see no real 'public interest' being demonstrated by allowing the names to be revealed, as drug testing policies could be debated publicly without identifying particular players. The greater public interest was served by keeping it confidential. Permanent injunctions were granted, restraining the newspapers from identifying any player who had tested positive on one or two occasions under the policy.

Lessons for professional communicators

- Even if confidential material is circulated to many people, it might still be a breach of confidence to reveal it in the media.
- Publication is not excusable just because it reveals a crime. It needs to be a crime affecting the community as a whole, and the person disclosing it needs to have a 'real and direct interest in redressing the alleged crime', not just in building their audience.

Disobedience contempt in Australia

Disobedience contempt – where journalists have refused court orders to reveal their confidential sources or to hand over documents – has arisen numerous times in Australia. Outright disobedience – without any duty to confidential sources involved – occurred in 2017 when blogger Shane Dowling was jailed for four months for refusing to obey court orders to take down from his website the names of women who had allegedly had sexual relationships with a high-profile media executive (Kangaroo Court case, 2017).

Before the advent of shield laws in Australia (covered below), the courts showed little patience with journalists refusing to answer questions on ethical grounds. As one NSW Supreme Court expressed it: 'Litigants cannot be constrained by the private codes of strangers' (Buchanan's case, 1964). Between 1989 and 1994, three Australian journalists were jailed, and a fourth was sentenced to a community service order. Since then, several others have been fined, while yet others remain at risk of such consequences for obeying the section of their ethical code which requires them to respect confidences (MEAA, 2016).

Case examples:

Barrass's case (1989): Perth journalist Tony Barrass served five days of a seven-day sentence in 1989 and was later fined a further $10,000 for again refusing to reveal the same source in a higher court. Barrass was jailed for refusing to tell a Perth magistrate the name of the person who had given him printouts of two tax files.

Budd's case (1992): Brisbane journalist Joe Budd served seven days in prison in 1992 for refusing to reveal his source in a defamation trial. Budd's article contained statements about a prosecutor's treatment of witnesses and his handling of a case against police officers. When he refused to reveal his source, Justice John Dowsett suggested Budd write it on a piece of paper and hand it to the Bar table. Budd refused.

War Veterans case (2006): Journalists Michael Harvey and Gerard McManus received criminal convictions and were fined while their alleged source – whistleblower Desmond Kelly – was acquitted on criminal charges of having communicated confidential information to them. It related to a story about federal government cuts to war veterans' entitlements.

Chinese Businesswoman case (2010–2017): Three Fairfax journalists and *The Age* newspaper lost a second application for special leave to appeal to the High Court over a decision upholding orders that they disclose their sources. Their 2010 story – predating a Victorian 'shield law' partially protecting journalists' confidences – accused a Chinese businesswoman of having bribed a former defence minister (but it was based on copies of allegedly forged documents provided by confidential sources). However, the Senate was told she dropped the defamation action after other evidence surfaced of her connections with Chinese intelligence.

Judicial inquiries and corruption bodies are a minefield for journalists. They have investigative powers that may lead them to the filing cabinets, digital data and notebooks of reporters.

Case examples:

Journalist F case (2021): A Queensland journalist was called to give evidence to the state's Crime and Corruption Commission (CCC) in a corruption inquiry into a confidential police source who had allegedly tipped him off to a police raid on a murder suspect. Queensland's new shield law and its extension to the CCC came too late to protect him. The journalist unsuccessfully claimed a public interest immunity and lost his appeal. As this book went to press, he was facing a potential fine or jail term. In the wake of the case, another journalist – Witness D – came forward to reveal he had faced a similar conviction before the CCC's predecessor body in 2007 (Witness D, 2022).

Cornwall's case (1993): Deborah Cornwall was reporting crime for *The Sydney Morning Herald* when she was ordered to give evidence to the NSW Independent Commission Against Corruption (ICAC) about an unnamed police officer who told her that underworld figure Neddy Smith had been a police informer. Cornwall was given a two-month suspended sentence, including an order to complete 90 hours of community service.

162 *Key topics in media law and ethics*

> **Reflect – Research – Review:**
>
> Why would a journalist refuse to reveal a source in court when they could lie to the court and say, 'There is no source'? Explain which moral and legal issues arise.

Contempt of Parliament

Another field of contempt stems from the powers of parliaments, both state and Commonwealth. Contempt of parliament is aimed at preserving the smooth and fair operation of parliament. There are a number of ways journalists and media advisers might find themselves in contempt of parliament, including a similar situation to disobedience contempt of court. A parliamentary committee could call a journalist as a witness and insist that a confidential source be revealed. If the journalist refuses, they can be found in contempt. More commonly, contempt of parliament involves revealing the confidential inner discussions of a parliamentary committee that is bound to secrecy. Professional communicators who 'leak' recommendations of such a committee have found themselves facing a contempt charge. Contempt charges were threatened in Queensland in 2022 when confidential hearings of a parliamentary committee were posted online (Facer, 2022).

Shield laws in Australia

All Australian jurisdictions now have shield laws offering limited protection to journalists who refuse to answer questions or to hand over documents that might reveal the identity of their confidential sources. The sections are typically inserted into the *Evidence Act* of the respective state or territory and at Commonwealth level and require a court to weigh the importance to society of the relationship of confidentiality against the interests of justice in the particular case. The legislation varies across jurisdictions as to the types of communication professionals who might be covered, with some covering only journalists and others allowing the exemption to anyone actively engaged in the production of news for a news medium. Some apply only to questions asked in courts, while others cover tribunals such as corruption commissions. In late 2022 attorneys-general agreed to take steps towards harmonising shield laws nationally. Meanwhile, professional communicators should examine their local legislation closely – on <www.austlii.edu.au> – if they plan on using information taken 'off-the-record'.

Case examples:

Mafia case (2015): Victoria's shield laws worked to protect the source for journalist Nick McKenzie in the interlocutory stages of a defamation and breach of confidence case over a story alleging the plaintiff was the head of the Calabrian mafia in Melbourne.

Rinehart cases (2013–2014): In a test of Western Australian shield laws, Australia's richest woman, Gina Rinehart, failed to force journalists Steve Pennells and Adele Ferguson to reveal their sources.

Newspaper rule

Prior to the introduction of shield laws, courts sometimes exercised a discretion to excuse journalists from revealing their sources during the preliminary proceedings for defamation cases – known as the 'newspaper rule'. It is drawn upon by media defendants on occasions in jurisdictions in situations where the shield laws do not apply.

Case examples:

Police Press Release case (2005): A South Australian detective superintendent issued a press release and made comments in a press conference about a murder investigation. A journalist used the newspaper rule successfully to protect his notes containing confidential source information from disclosure in the discovery process for a resulting defamation case.

Secret tape case (2022): This defamation case centred upon the identity of a confidential source who secretly recorded a conversation in a hotel. The judge decided the newspaper rule could still apply in preliminary proceedings where the WA shield law was not applicable.

Deep Sleep case (2022): Here the Federal Court of Appeal noted that the newspaper rule had been subsumed by the NSW shield law.

Whistleblowing protection in Australia

The level of protection of whistleblowers has been of ongoing concern in Australia for some decades. Typically, those who take their concerns directly to the media have been pursued for breaches of public service contracts for the release of classified material under Commonwealth or state criminal laws. As noted above in the War Veterans case (2006), occasionally it is the journalists who receive the information who are punished while the alleged whistleblower walks free on a legal technicality. That said, several whistleblowing public servants have lost their jobs and have been dragged through the courts at considerable government expense for raising concerns of legitimate public interest, including Australian espionage against neighbouring Timor-Leste, alleged Afghan War crimes, and aggressive tax debt collection practices. It was reported the government had spent at least $3 million pursuing just four whistleblowers through the courts over those leaks (Knaus, 2020).

Despite calls for a simplified system allowing external whistleblowing on matters of public interest, disclosure to or by the media of wrongdoing may not be considered in the public interest if there are other authorities to whom the disclosure should have been made, such as the police, ombudsman or an anti-corruption body. An example is the NSW whistleblowers legislation, the *Public Interest Disclosures Act 2022*, which at s28 allows for voluntary public interest disclosures to members of Parliament or journalists, but only if the disclosure is 'substantially true' and if the whistleblower has already made the disclosure through the proper channels on a non-anonymous basis and the concern has been considered or the whistleblower has not received a response within a designated period. Other states, territories and the Commonwealth have similar legislation. Corporate communicators should note that in 2019 protections were extended under the *Corporations Act* to whistleblowers inside companies and organisations who go to the financial regulators with reports of potential misconduct or breaches of the law, or who raise concerns through internal avenues. Professional communicators who are considering leaking information, and journalists receiving it, should first research the relevant whistleblowing laws carefully.

Freedom of information laws in Australia

Freedom of Information (FOI) legislation has been used successfully by Australian journalists and political communicators at both state and Commonwealth levels. It was first introduced by the federal government in 1982 and by 2006 all states and territories had their own versions. The Commonwealth legislation is contained in the *Freedom of Information Act 1982*, while in the other jurisdictions FOI is contained in legislation by that name or as a *Right to Information (RTI) Act* in Queensland and Tasmania, *Government Information (Public Access) Act* in NSW or the *Information Act* in the Northern Territory.

FOI is premised on the principle that there is a strong public interest in the administrative decisions of governments and quasi-governmental bodies being as transparent and as open as possible. Nevertheless, there are recognized exceptions to such openness, particularly decisions involving private and commercially sensitive matters and the protection of emergency services and security information. Given the exceptions to the release of information, the cost of filing applications and the time spent applying and appealing against adverse decisions, some cynics have dubbed the legislation 'Freedom *from* Information' instead of 'Freedom *of* Information'. Dissatisfaction with the laws reached high points in 2006 when the High Court upheld the federal government's power to prevent Treasury documents being released to the *Australian*'s FOI editor, Michael McKinnon (Treasury case, 2006) – and again in 2023 when the Information Commissioner resigned citing a lack of review powers and entrenched delays by government agencies (Costin, 2023).

Confidentiality, secrets, sources and disclosure 165

Nevertheless, some media organisations, including *The Australian*, *The Guardian*, Seven Network and the ABC – along with political media officers – have used the FOI laws quite effectively despite their limitations. It is a style of reporting requiring meticulous record-keeping, precise applications, a generous budget and a large serve of patience. While some journalists use the legislation as it is designed, others use it as a protective device to avoid confidentiality binds like those detailed in the sections above. Rather than expose themselves or their sources to disobedience contempt or breach of confidence action, they simply find out from their source as much detail on the document in question so they can file a very specific FOI application seeking its release. For example, a government media relations source might tip the journalist off to the fact that a certain minister had held a meeting with a prominent business leader just before the government passed legislation favouring that businessman. Rather than publishing a story citing 'a government source', the journalist might file an FOI request to see that minister's diary of appointments on that date along with any correspondence from the minister's office to the businessman. Stories based on the resulting documents could then be published without jeopardising the confidential source or facing a disobedience contempt charge.

Each jurisdiction varies in its FOI protocols and fees, and space considerations prevent us going into the detail of costs, time and application protocols. All of these are available by searching for 'freedom of information' or 'right to information' in the relevant jurisdiction.

Typically, an application involves these steps:

- Make the request in writing. (Many agencies have digital forms on their websites.)
- State that it is an application for the purposes of the *Act*,
- Provide information about the documents required, to help the agency or minister identify them,
- Provide an email or postal address so notices can be sent, and
- Send the request by hand delivery, post, email or online submission.

Importantly for journalists and political staffers, the reasons for requesting the information do not have to be provided. While government agencies should respond within a month, they often do not. Further, FOI requests need to be focussed quite narrowly so that the hourly fee for document search, retrieval, decision-making and copying does not become exorbitant.

Case examples:

Remote Housing case (2022): ABC News journalist Kate Ashton won the Walkley Young Australian Journalist of the Year Award for Coverage of Community and Regional Affairs for a portfolio of stories, including one using FOI applications to reveal correspondence between Northern Territory and Commonwealth ministers forecasting they would miss their target to build hundreds of federally-funded homes in remote indigenous communities (Ashton, 2022).

Bleed Them Dry case (2017): The Walkley Award for Investigative Journalism in 2017 – the joint Fairfax-ABC investigation 'Bleed Them Dry Until They Die' – was based partly on documents obtained via freedom of information requests by an aged care resident for records about her own care and file notes by staff about her proposed eviction. The investigative team integrated the supportive documentation into their reportage (Ferguson and Danckert, 2017).

Immigration Documents cases (2013 and 2017): These cases involved FOI applications about the treatment of asylum seekers by the Walkley Award winning journalist Paul Farrell to the Department of Immigration and Border Protection. They involved his successful appeals against the department over its lengthy delays and its long list of exemptions to document release. The cases highlighted the bureaucratic, technical, time-consuming and sometimes politicised side of the FOI application process. Each request took a full year to be filed, rejected and reviewed, and the department still had 28 further days to appeal.

Reflect – Research – Review:

Find the relevant website explaining your state or territory FOI or right to information procedures, and summarise the basic process and costs.

Confidentiality and disclosure in action – Case study 6.1: Applied ethical decision making – the PR source and the reporter

There are so many possible instances of confidentiality and disclosure in the work of professional communicators that it is difficult to offer a single strategy for working through the ethics and law of a dilemma. Instead, to highlight two approaches, for this chapter we view the ethics of the situation through the lens of Bok's Model (1978: 94–103) – premised upon empathy for people and the maintenance of social trust – and we analyse the media law dimensions of the problem using the specific legal risk analysis technique (Grantham and Pearson, 2022: 51–53).

Reflect – Research – Review:

The problem: You are the PR person for a drug company and you find a report stamped 'Confidential' which states the blood pressure treatment pill they are marketing has a high risk of causing brain malformations in the children of pregnant women currently taking the drug. The company wants it kept secret until after further studies. You are alarmed by this and arrange to meet a reporter to hand over the report. [Alternative for journalists: take on the reporter's role here].

A. Applying Bok's Model (1978: 94–103)

Consult your conscience

Engage in the 'soul searching' process about the rightness of your action, perhaps using the technique of mindful reflection, journaling or mindmapping. Try to think through – or map out – the potential implications for the obvious stakeholders – people taking the drug, their children, your employer, the media outlet, their audience and yourself. Are there others? What is your gut feeling on this? Can you separate any nervousness about the potential work implications for you from your concern for the welfare of the patients and children?

Consult others for advice on the course of action that might constitute an ethical breach

You might have a mentor you can talk to – perhaps a family member, wise friend, colleague or former professor in whom you can confide your dilemma to help work through the situation. Their advice can add another dimension to your thinking on the issue. Also review it in terms of the key philosophical positions we have considered. Remember Kant and the great deontologist's maxim – 'All actions relating to the right of other human beings are wrong if their maxim is incompatible with publicity' (Kant's *Perpetual Peace*, 1795, cited in Gosseries and Parr, 2022). Should it be a universal rule that bad corporate decisions that risk harming people's health should be publicised? Should it be a rule that insiders keep their company's secrets unless it is contrary to the public interest to do so? Do the means (breaking a confidence) justify the end (potentially saving lives or harm) in the situation, as a consequentialist approach? Where does it sit with your social contract to honour the human right to health? What virtues might be assigned to you as a professional under either course of action? How does John Stuart Mill's quote apply here?: 'Bad men need nothing more to compass their ends, than that good men should look on and do nothing'.

Consulting widely and publicly among all possible people

Clearly, on a confidential issue you cannot consult too widely, but you can research your professional association's code of ethics to see the extent to which corporate confidences must be upheld, even if there is a greater public interest. Further, there will be publicised cases and examples of whistleblowing in this kind of corporate context – where insiders have exposed wrongdoing that endangers public safety or health. Of course, a crucial point to examine here is whether the media is the best place to take the complaint. Once you have reviewed the legal options, there might be public health and drug authorities or other regulators with whom the issue can be raised, perhaps on an anonymous basis.

B. Applying the specific legal risk analysis technique (Grantham and Pearson, 2022: 51–53).

Identify the potential (or existing) legal problem

A review of this chapter identifies the fact that this matter involves confidential information, which you are considering handing to a reporter, that raises at least these key media law issues: a breach of confidence action against you and perhaps the reporter, and potential disobedience contempt for the journalist if you are a confidential source (with perhaps some shield law protection).

Review the areas of the law involved

Focusing just on the position of the PR practitioner, your primary danger is with a potential action for breach of confidence from your company and possible dismissal. There is also the risk of your identity being revealed by the reporter unless you make it very clear that the information is dependent upon them preserving your anonymity. As for breach of confidence, the basic elements would apply – the information has a quality of confidence about it, you have received it in circumstances requiring confidence (a report stamped 'Confidential') and it will be used to the detriment of the company. However, there is likely a useful public interest defence available to you through the exposure of an iniquity or at least a moral duty to publicise the matter to protect health and perhaps lives. Your work contract and precedents in unfair dismissal laws in your jurisdiction would be useful points of reference. Remember to review public interest disclosure laws in your jurisdiction – particularly in such a corporate or health context. It could be that you have more protection as a whistleblower if you raise your concern through the recommended channels instead of going to the media.

Project the possible consequences for stakeholders

Work through all the potential stakeholders in the situation and consider the legal consequences for them too. We have flagged those related to yourself and the reporter, but others could include negligence actions against your employer from mothers and children affected by the continued manufacture of the drug. The pharmaceutical regulator will also have powers to punish your company for not reporting the matter sooner. Are there other areas of legal exposure?

Seek advice / refer upward

Given the confidentiality and your vulnerability, it is best to get legal advice on what is clearly a litigious situation. Sometimes professional or industry associations have a legal aid service available for such advice.

Publishing / amending / deleting / correcting / apologizing

As this is not a publishing decision but rather an information exchange situation, you need to give it one full review before proceeding with this course of action, particularly on alternative paths to the media approach if that is not protected by corporate whistleblowing laws around disclosure.

In a nutshell

- Communication professionals come to the issues of confidentiality and disclosure from a range of perspectives depending on the nature of their roles and the type of information or secrets involved.
- The philosophical origins of professional confidentiality date back to at least Ancient Greece with the development of the Hippocratic Oath binding doctors to keep secret their conversations with patients.
- Most professional communication ethical codes require members to keep confidences they enter into, but the journalist's obligation to a confidential source does not allow for exceptions when ordered by a court to reveal their identity.
- The courts usually apply a three-point test to determine whether there has been a breach of confidence. The information must have a 'quality of confidence' about it; the circumstances in which the information was imparted must have given rise to an obligation of confidentiality; and the recipient must disclose the information (or threaten to disclose it) or use it to the detriment of someone entitled to prevent its use.

- If the information relates to government or its operations, it must also be proven that its disclosure would be contrary to the public interest for it to amount to a breach.
- Professional communicators may be charged with disobedience contempt for refusing to reveal a source or provide identifying material to a court.
- Journalists get the protection of 'shield laws' in most places, meaning they might not have to reveal their confidential sources of information to the court unless there is an overriding public interest such as the administration of justice.
- Public servants and corporate insiders might get protection for 'blowing the whistle' on corruption and wrongdoing when they go through the appropriate channels, but will usually not earn this immunity if they leak to the media or go online with their secrets. Most jurisdictions have Freedom of Information or equivalent legislation, designed to allow public access to documents held by governments and their agencies, with numerous exemptions.
- Journalists can use FOI requests to reduce their exposure to source identification; however, they are faced with the obstacles of processing delays, application costs and bureaucratic frustrations.

References and further reading

Anemaat, L. 1989, 'Documenting Secret/Sacred (Restricted) Aboriginal History', *Archives and Manuscripts*, 17 (1), May 1989, 37–49, <https://publications.archivists.org.au/index.php/asa/article/download/7995/7989>.

Aquilina, M. 2019, 'A hushed history of Catholic confessions', *Angelus*, 15 May, <https://angelusnews.com/voices/a-hushed-history-of-catholic-confessions/>.

Ashton, K. 2022, 'FOI documents show NT government previously forecast it would not meet target to build 650 remote houses in five years', *ABC News*, 22 April, <www.abc.net.au/news/2022-04-05/remote-housing-nt-government-national-target-foi-documents/100965610>.

Australian Medical Association (AMA). 2016. *AMA Code of Ethics 2004. Editorially Revised 2006. Revised 2016.* <www.ama.com.au/sites/default/files/2021-02/AMA_Code_of_Ethics_2004._Editorially_Revised_2006._Revised_2016_0.pdf>.

Bok, S. 1978, *Lying: Moral Choice in Public and Private Life*, Pantheon Books, New York.

Bok, S. 1989, *Secrets: On the Ethics of Concealment and Revelation*, Vintage Books, New York.

Chartered Institute of Public Relations (CIPR). 2023, *CIPR Code of Conduct*, <www.cipr.co.uk/CIPR/About_Us/Governance_/CIPR_Code_of_Conduct.aspx>.

Costin, L. 2023, 'FOI commissioner quits, citing lack of power and delays', *Australian Financial Review*, 6 March, <www.afr.com/politics/federal/foi-commissioner-quits-citing-lack-of-power-and-delays-20230306-p5cpwj>.

Equality and Human Rights Commission (EHRC). 2021, *Article 8: Respect for your private and family life*, <www.equalityhumanrights.com/en/human-rights-act/article-8-respect-your-private-and-family-life>.

Facer, T. 2023, 'Confidential OIA inquiry documents leaked online', *Bundaberg Today*, 12 January, <https://bundabergtoday.com.au/news/2023/01/12/confidential-oia-inquiry-documents-leaked-online/>.

Feinstein, S. and Devine, T. 2021, 'Are whistleblowing laws working? A global study of whistleblower protection litigation', *Government Accountability Project*, <https://whistleblowingnetwork.org/WIN/media/pdfs/Are-whistleblowing-laws-working-report-2021March_1.pdf>.

Ferguson, A. and Danckert, S. 2017, 'Bleed them dry until they die', *Sydney Morning Herald*, <www.smh.com.au/interactive/2017/retirement-racket/bleed-them-dry>.

Goggins, C. 2022, '"Without sources we are nothing": Reporters' privilege must be protected at all costs', *Live Boston 617*, 15 July, <https://liveboston617.org/2022/07/15/without-sources-we-are-nothing-reporters-privilege-must-be-protected-at-all-costs/>.

Goldberg, D. 2006, 'Access to information laws in Scotland and England: Close freedom of information (FOI) encounters of the third kind', *Comparative Media Law Journal*, 8, 33–72, <www.juridicas.unam.mx/publica/librev/rev/comlawj/cont/8/arc/arc2.pdf>.

Gosseries, A. and Parr, T. 2022, 'Publicity', *The Stanford Encyclopedia of Philosophy*, Summer 2022 edn, Zalta, E.N. ed., <https://plato.stanford.edu/archives/sum2022/entries/publicity/>.

Grantham, S. and Pearson, M. 2022, *Social Media Risk and the Law: A Guide for Global Communicators*, Routledge, London and New York.

Jelassi, T. 2021, 'Advancing universal access to information within the 2030 Agenda for Sustainable Development', *UN Chronicle*, 27 September, United Nations, Geneva, <www.un.org/en/un-chronicle/advancing-universal-access-information-within-2030-agenda-sustainable-development>.

Knaus, C. and Bassano, J. 2019, 'How a flawed freedom-of-information regime keeps Australians in the dark', *The Guardian*, 2 January, <www.theguardian.com/australia-news/2019/jan/02/how-a-flawed-freedom-of-information-regime-keeps-australians-in-the-dark>.

Knaus, C. 2020, 'Australian government spends almost $3m waging "war" on whistleblowers in court', *The Guardian*, 13 August, <www.theguardian.com/australia-news/2020/aug/13/australian-government-spends-almost-3m-waging-war-on-whistleblowers-in-court>.

McMillan, J. 2011, *Guide to the Freedom of Information Act 1982: Protecting Information Rights – Advancing Information Policy*, Office of the Australian Information Commissioner, Canberra, <www.oaic.gov.au/images/documents/migrated/oaic/repository/publications/agency_resources/guide_freedom_of_information_act_1982.pdf>.

Media Entertainment and Arts Alliance (MEAA). 2016, *The MEAA Journalist Code of Ethics*, Media Entertainment and Arts Alliance, Sydney, <www.meaa.org/download/faqs-meaa-journalist-code-of-ethics/>.

National Union of Journalists (NUJ). 2018, *Printable Code of Conduct*, NUJ, London, <www.nuj.org.uk/resource/printable-nuj-code-of-conduct.html>.

Parks Australia. 2023, 'Men's and women's business', *Uluru-Kata Tjuta National Park*, <https://parksaustralia.gov.au/uluru/discover/culture/mens-and-womens-business/>.

Public Relations Consultants Association (PRCA). 2023, *Professional Charter and Codes of Conduct*, London, <www.prca.org.uk/about-us/pr-standards/professional-charter-and-codes-conduct>.

172 *Key topics in media law and ethics*

Public Relations Institute of Australia (PRIA). 2009, *Public Relations Institute of Australia (PRIA) Code of Ethics*, PRIA, Sydney, <www.pria.com.au/about-pria/code-of-ethics-privacy/code-of-ethics/>.

Public Relations Society of America (PRSA). 2023a, *PRSA Code of Ethics*, <www.prsa.org/about/ethics/prsa-code-of-ethics>.

Public Relations Society of America (PRSA). 2023b, *Ethics for an Evolving Profession: Information Leaks*, <www.prsa.org/about/ethics>.

Publications Office of the European Union. 2020, 'Protection of persons who report breaches of EU law', *Summary of: Directive (EU) 2019/1937 on the protection of persons who report breaches of EU law*, Directorate-General for Justice and Consumers, Brussels, <https://eur-lex.europa.eu/legal-content/en/LSU/?uri=CELEX:32019L1937>.

Reporters Committee for Freedom of the Press (RCFP). 2021, *Introduction to the Reporter's Privilege Compendium*, <www.rcfp.org/introduction-to-the-reporters-privilege-compendium/>.

Society of Professional Journalists (SPJ). 2014, *Society of Professional Journalists (SPJ) Code of Ethics*, <www.spj.org/ethicscode.asp>.

Thompson, I.E. 1979, 'The nature of confidentiality', *Journal of Medical Ethics*, 5, 57–64.

United Nations (UN). 1948, *Universal Declaration of Human Rights*, <www.un.org/en/about-us/universal-declaration-of-human-rights>.

US Press Freedom Tracker. 2023, *Incident Database – Testimony About Source*, <https://pressfreedomtracker.us/all-incidents/?subpoena_type=TESTIMONY_ABOUT_SOURCE&categories=Subpoena%2FLegal+Order&endpage=2>.

Vatican Library. 1983, *Code of Canon Law*, <www.vatican.va/archive/cod-iuris-canonici/cic_index_en.html>.

Witness D. 2022, 'Landmark court case exposes serious chink in Palaszczuk Government's shield laws', *Medium*, MEAA, 10 August, <https://medium.com/@withMEAA/landmark-court-case-exposes-serious-chink-in-palaszczuk-governments-shield-laws-7f26754d5c6e>.

Cases cited

Barrass's case: *DPP v Luders*, unreported, Court of Petty Sessions of Western Australia, no. 27602 of 1989; *R v Barrass*, unreported, District Court of Western Australia, 7 August 1990, per Kennedy DCJ.

Buchanan's case: *Buchanan, Re* [1964] 65 SR (NSW) 9.

Budd's case: *R v Budd*, unreported, Supreme Court of Queensland, no. 36188 of 1992, Brisbane, (20 March 1992).

Chinese Businesswoman case: *Liu v The Age Company* [2010] NSWSC 1176, (14 October 2010), <www.austlii.edu.au/cgi-bin/viewdoc/au/cases/nsw/NSWSC/2010/1176.html>.; *Liu v The Age Company Ltd* [2011] NSWSC 53, (11 February 2011), <www.austlii.edu.au/cgi-bin/viewdoc/au/cases/nsw/NSWSC/2011/53.html>.; *Liu v The Age Company Limited* [2012] NSWSC 12, (1 February 2012), <www.austlii.edu.au/cgi-bin/viewdoc/au/cases/nsw/NSWSC/2012/12.html>.; *Age Company Limited and Others v Liu and Another* [2013] NSWCA 26 (21 February 2013), <www.austlii.edu.au/cgi-bin/viewdoc/au/cases/nsw/NSWCA/2013/26.html>.; *The Age Company*

Confidentiality, secrets, sources and disclosure 173

Ltd and Ors v Liu and Anor [2013] HCATrans 205, (6 September 2013), <www.austlii.edu.au/cgi-bin/viewdoc/au/cases/cth/HCATrans/2013/205.html>.; *Liu v The Age Company Limited (No. 2)* [2015] NSWSC 276, (23 March 2015), <www.austlii.edu.au/cgi-bin/viewdoc/au/cases/nsw/NSWSC/2015/276.html>.; *Liu v The Age Company Limited* [2016] NSWCA 115, (20 May 2016), <www.austlii.edu.au/cgi-bin/viewdoc/au/cases/nsw/NSWCA/2016/115.html>; *The Age Company Pty Ltd and Ors v Liu* [2016] HCATrans 306, (16 December 2016), <www.austlii.edu.au/cgi-bin/viewdoc/au/cases/cth/HCATrans/2016/306.html>.

Cojuangco's case: *John Fairfax and Sons Ltd v Cojuangco* (1988) 82 ALR 1 (26 October 1988), <www.austlii.edu.au/cgi-bin/viewdoc/au/cases/cth/HCA/1988/54.html>.

Cornwall's case: *ICAC v Cornwall* (1993) 116 ALR 97 (6 July 1993 and 8 September 1993).

Deep Sleep case: *Herron v HarperCollins Publishers Australia Pty Ltd* [2022] FCAFC 68 (19 April 2022), <www.austlii.edu.au/cgi-bin/viewdoc/au/cases/cth/FCAFC/2022/68.html>.

Engineers' cases: *Saltman Engineering Company Limited v Campbell Engineering Company Limited* [1948] 65 RPC 203; *Coco v A.N.Clark (Engineers) Ltd* [1969] RPC 41.

Financial Tweets case: *X v Twitter Inc.* [2017] NSWSC 1300, <www.caselaw.nsw.gov.au/decision/59cadc2be4b074a7c6e18fa3>.

Immigration Documents cases 1 and 2: *Farrell and Department of Immigration and Border Protection* [2013] AICmr 81 (21 November 2013), <www.oaic.gov.au/images/documents/freedom-of-information/ic-review-decicions/2013-AICmr81.pdf>; *Paul Farrell and Department of Immigration and Border Protection (Freedom of information)* [2017] AICmr 116 (15 November 2017).

Journalist F case (2021): *F v Crime and Corruption Commission* [2021] QCA 244 (12 November 2021), <www.austlii.edu.au/cgi-bin/viewdoc/au/cases/qld/QCA/2021/244.html>.; *F v Crime and Corruption Commission* [2020] QSC 245 (12 August 2020), <www.austlii.edu.au/cgi-bin/viewdoc/au/cases/qld/QSC/2020/245.html>.

Lenah Game Meats case: *ABC v Lenah Game Meats Pty Ltd* [2001] HCA 63; 208 CLR 199; 185 ALR 1; 76 ALJR 1 (15 November 2001), <www.austlii.edu.au/au/cases/cth/high_ct/2001/63.html>.

Lundin's case: *Attorney-General v Lundin* [1982] 75 Cr App R 90.

Meghan Markle's case: *Sussex v Associated Newspapers Ltd* [2021] EWHC 273 (Ch) (11 February 2021), <www.bailii.org/ew/cases/EWHC/Ch/2021/273.html>.

McGuinness's case: *McGuinness v Attorney-General of Victoria* [1940] 63 CLR 73.

Mulholland's case: *Attorney-General v Mulholland and Forbes* [1963] 2 QB 489.

Norwich Pharmacal case: *Norwich Pharmacal Company & Ors v Commissioners of Customs and Excise* (1973) U4HL6 (UK).

Pentagon Papers case: *New York Times v US*; *US v Washington Post* [1971] 713 US 403.

Police Press Release case: *Sands v State of South Australia* [2005] SASC 381 (27 September 2005), <www.austlii.edu.au/cgi-bin/viewdoc/au/cases/sa/SASC/2005/381.html>.

Pop stars case (1977): *Woodward v Hutchins* [1977] 1 WLR 760.

Secret tape case (2022). *Poland v Hedley [No 4]* [2022] WASC 144 (29 April 2022), <www.austlii.edu.au/cgi-bin/viewdoc/au/cases/wa/WASC/2022/144.html>.

Treasury case: *McKinnon v Secretary, Department of Treasury* [2006] HCA 45 (6 September 2006), <www.austlii.edu.au/au/cases/cth/HCA/2006/45.html>.

War Veterans case: *Harvey & Anor v County Court of Victoria & Ors* [2006] VSC 293 (23 August 2006), <www.austlii.edu.au/cgi-bin/viewdoc/au/cases/vic/VSC/2006/293.html>. See also *R v Gerard Thomas McManus and Michael Harvey* [2007] VCC 619 (for decision on penalty) and *R v Kelly* [2006] VSCA 221 (17 October 2006), <www.austlii.edu.au/cgi-bin/viewdoc/au/cases/vic/VSCA/2006/221.html>.

Westpac Letters case: *Westpac Banking Corporation v John Fairfax Group Pty Ltd* (1991) 19 IPR 513.

7 Privacy and data protection

Key concepts

Privacy: Seclusion – the state of being alone or not being observed – and the freedom from intrusion by others into one's private affairs.

Invasion of privacy: Intrusion upon an individual's seclusion or a misuse of their private information.

Data protection: Information privacy laws controlling the collection and storage of personally identifiable information.

Surveillance: The monitoring of people's lives or data using human observation or analogue or digital technologies and applications.

Trespass: Entering land or premises without actual or implied permission, staying there after being asked to leave, or placing a recording device on someone's property.

Privacy in a media context

Privacy – the right to be free from intrusion or the misuse of one's personal information – covers a wide span of moral, ethical and legal terrain in professional communication. At a moral level, it can involve that gut feeling that you should avert your eyes if you stumble upon someone's secluded or private situation. That moral dimension of privacy can vary between cultures and situations. At a professional ethical level, privacy considerations can necessitate important decisions on whether to intrude into someone's grief or publish personal information about them. In media law, it involves important legal actions and crimes across the range of invasion of privacy, data protection and trespass. At the same time, it invokes an attempt to balance two key human rights – the right to privacy and the right to free expression. Privacy does overlap to some extent with other topics covered in this textbook – most notably with defamation (Chapter 6), confidentiality and secrets (Chapter 7), private revelations in crime and court (Chapter 8) and cyberbullying, harassment and discrimination (Chapter 11). Here we focus mainly on the philosophical, ethical and human rights dimensions of privacy and how media laws

DOI: 10.4324/9781003372752-9

operate in the form of a right to privacy and via data protection, both at home and abroad.

Philosophical background and human rights context of privacy

Privacy is a relatively modern legal concept in Western nations, but has a long cultural tradition in most societies. Anthropologists recorded indigenous peoples holding certain rituals and ceremonies in private, often on a gender-selected basis. An example was the indigenous Australian 'secret women's business' covering matters of reproduction and childbirth where men would be 'shamed' if they intruded (Maher, 2002). Notions of privacy in cultures also varied across time and place. English explorer Captain James Cook was said to be shocked by the nudity of Hawai'ians in 1773 (Diamond, 2004) but within two centuries people of his own culture were wearing next to nothing on the beach.

Among the earliest records of philosophical consideration of privacy was Aristotle's distinction between the public sphere of politics – the *polis* – and the family or private – the *oikos* – perhaps the first acknowledgment of a 'private domain' (DeCew, 2018). Utilitarians including John Stuart Mill and John Locke continued this distinction between the public sphere of government and the personal sphere of one's own property, body and consciousness. This has extended through to the philosophical concept of 'privileged access', meaning that each of us has access to our own consciousnesses, but none of us has access to the conscious of another (Peterson, 2020). Such a position could be under threat with improvements in artificial intelligence and virtual reality. As we recorded in Chapter 3, the French philosopher Simone Weil saw solitude to be essential to the attainment of actual 'attention' – a further endorsement of the need for privacy for effective reflection (Weil, 2015:100).

Among philosophers there is disagreement about whether privacy is a justifiable moral category. Some reductionists argue that privacy concerns can be more simply expressed in other terms, 'such as infliction of emotional distress or property interests' (DeCew, 2018). As we shall see, this is also reflected in the law around privacy, where varying wrongs are grouped under its umbrella in different international jurisdictions.

Important to communicators, modern moral philosopher Sissela Bok saw the distinction between secrecy and privacy as important – along similar lines to those that allowed us to distinguish confidentiality and secrecy in Chapter 6 from privacy in this chapter. Bok argued that the two concepts were closely linked, but that secrecy was better defined as 'intentional concealment' while privacy was the 'condition of being protected from unwanted access by others – either physical access, personal information, or attention' (Bok, 1989: 10–11). She also took up the issue of the media's claim to 'the public's right to know' – which she said was actually a limited right to access just some information, not all. Journalists' intrusion into lives to 'satisfy curiosity' rather than to fulfill a need for information might be justifiable, 'but requires special attention to individual privacy' (Bok, 1989: 258).

The moral philosophy background to privacy fed into its ultimate inclusion as a human right in most national constitutions and international treaties. Thomas Hobbes (1588–1679) outlined a series of natural rights in the development of social contract theory that were refined by others and developed into key documents like the *American Declaration of Independence* in 1776 and the *Declaration of the Rights of Man and of the Citizen* of 1789. Early formulations of the distinction between the public and the private were evident in Hobbes' writing (Abizadeh, 2013).

> **Reflect – Research – Review:**
>
> Find another modern moral philosopher and research and report their views on privacy.

Today, privacy is acknowledged as a human right at the highest international levels. It is included in the *Universal Declaration of Human Rights* (Article 12) and the *European Convention on Human Rights* (Article 8) among others. The *International Covenant on Civil and Political Rights* (ICCPR) couples it with reputation when it states at Article 17:

1. No-one shall be subjected to arbitrary and unlawful interference with his privacy, family, home or correspondence, nor to unlawful attacks on his honour and reputation.
2. Everyone has the right to protection of the law against such interference or attacks.

These are in turn reflected in professional communicators' various ethical codes and, to varying extents, in the laws of the countries where they practice.

Professional ethical dilemmas, co-regulation and self-regulation

Ethical concerns and constraints around privacy arise in a range of regulatory and self-regulatory contexts controlling the work of professional communicators, albeit in different ways according to their occupations. The field of journalism is more alert to ethical issues around intrusion into people's grief (known as the 'death knock'), revelation of private details about people's lives and the handling of stories involving children and other vulnerable sources or story subjects. While public relations practitioners and corporate communicators might sometimes encounter such dilemmas, most of their privacy concerns relate to the sensitive and legal handling of people's data and the intrusion into their lives in a digital way. That is also the main focus of the privacy-related 'terms of use' of most of the Internet and social media platforms.

Media and privacy ethics

Constraints upon the media in the name of individual privacy have been growing for more than a century, and the pressure has mounted in the digital era. Journalists are being called to account for decisions that intrude into the private lives of citizens, even though they might believe such intrusions are in the 'public interest'. Politicians, judges, regulatory bodies and reform inquiries like the Leveson Inquiry (2012) in the United Kingdom and the Finkelstein (2012) review in Australia demanded news organisations explain their internal processes for decisions that had legal and ethical consequences.

Journalism ethical codes internationally place an onus on practitioners to respect the privacy of sources and news victims and their families. In the US, the Society of Professional Journalists (SPJ) Code of Ethics makes no explicit mention of the word 'privacy' but uses its 'Minimize Harm' clauses to counsel against 'undue intrusiveness'. It also notes the greater right of 'private people' to control information about them compared with 'public figures' and, while not ruling out the death knock, instructs journalists to 'Show compassion for those who may be affected by news coverage. Use heightened sensitivity when dealing with juveniles, victims of sex crimes, and sources or subjects who are inexperienced or unable to give consent'. Each clause in turn links to blogs as guidance from experts on topics like mental health and suicide, dealing with grief and victims, and undue intrusiveness (SPJ, 2014).

The National Union of Journalists (NUJ) Code of Conduct in the UK states at its Clause 6 that a journalist 'Does nothing to intrude into anybody's private life, grief or distress unless justified by overriding consideration of the public interest' (NUJ, 2018). The Independent Press Standards Organisation (IPSO) also has an Editors' Code of Practice (IPSO, 2021) which has numerous references to privacy and related matters, including harassment, intrusion into grief or shock, along with special requirements on reporting suicide, children, child sex victims, other sexual assault victims, clandestine methods and subterfuge. Despite these requirements the IPSO has upheld or mediated numerous complaints about press behaviour on these grounds (IPSO, 2022). The UK broadcast regulator the Office of Communications (Ofcom) lists 22 privacy rules in its Broadcasting Code, covering general expectation of privacy as well as special considerations relating to consent, surreptitious recording, doorstepping, reuse of material, suffering and distress, the young and the vulnerable (Ofcom, 2021). Its complaints system can lead to sanctions which may include directions not to repeat content, corrections or broadcast of findings, financial penalties, or even the shortening, suspension or revocation of a broadcasting licence (Ofcom, 2023).

In Australia, privacy arises in self-regulatory media codes and in the co-regulatory broadcast framework overseen by the Australian Communications and Media Authority (ACMA). The MEAA Journalist Code of Ethics makes it clear and concise at Article 11: 'Respect private grief and personal privacy' (MEAA, 2016). This should make the death knock a rarity, but it continues because the code finishes like the NUJ version by allowing exemptions for 'the substantial advancement of the public interest or risk of substantial harm to people'. In recent times the practice has moved from the physical phoning or knocking on the door of a victim's family to approaching them via social media, known as the 'digital death knock' (Watson, 2022). Importantly, research has shown the death knock interview can exacerbate the trauma of the families of victims of disasters and tragic news events – but also can harm reporters because of the psychological damage of 'moral injury' caused by breaching their moral compass (Backholm and Björkqvist, 2012; Pearson et al., 2021). The Australian Press Council also warns its newspaper and online members to avoid intrusion on a person's reasonable expectation of privacy, causing offence, distress, prejudice, or creating a risk to safety (APC, 2023). The broadcast regulator – the ACMA – offers guidance with its *Privacy Guidelines for Broadcasters* stating that 'not all matters that interest the public are in the public interest' (ACMA, 2016). The guidelines aim to protect the privacy of citizens in the form of both data protection and invasion upon their seclusion, with special attention paid to children, the vulnerable and public figures. The notion of public interest varies across those groups – with public figure privacy intrusion acceptable in relation to their public roles – but is unacceptable if it is 'merely distasteful, socially damaging or embarrassing'. The ACMA offers special advice in relation to the interviewing of children and the vulnerable by adapting consent protocols and giving them the right to withdraw from interviews or stories. The ACMA has registered codes of practice for all broadcasting sectors other than the ABC and SBS, which have their own codes notified to ACMA. Most of the industry codes have special requirements relating to news and current affairs programmes, which in turn address privacy as an issue. The main broadcasting industry codes covering privacy are Free TV Australia's Code of Practice, Commercial Radio Australia's Code of Practice, the ABC's Editorial Policy and its Charter of Editorial Practice, and the SBS Codes of Practice.

The MEAA and APC enforcement regimes are problematic because they are self-regulatory but under the *Broadcasting Services Act 1992* (BSA) the ACMA can place restrictions on broadcast licenses and issue sanctions. (See Key Case 4.1: Lying in action, the 2DAYFM royal prank call.)

PR and corporate communication ethics and privacy

As explained earlier and in Chapter 6, the focus of the PR and corporate communication industries is much more on the area of commercial confidentiality and data protection than upon the privacy challenges practitioners might encounter in their reporting – invasion of privacy through interrupting someone's seclusion, trespass or the publication of private and embarrassing facts. None of the key public relations professional bodies in the UK or Australia mention privacy in their codes of conduct (CIPR, 2023; PRCA, 2023; PRIA, 2009). The Public Relations Society of America (PRSA) does have a section on safeguarding confidences which requires the protection of 'confidential and private information' and 'to protect the privacy rights of clients, organisations and individuals', again skewed towards the confidentiality end of the equation.

Digital platforms and privacy

Social media users can have their accounts suspended or terminated for breach of the privacy requirements stated in the terms of use of the major social media platforms. A litany of privacy rules is typically listed in such terms and conditions. Instagram's is a good example, where it offers a range of guidance at its Privacy and Safety Center (Instagram, 2023) which include community guidelines, data retention information, abuse, blocking policies, parental guidance, tips on safe sharing of images and channels for complaints.

Corporate policies

Corporate communicators also need to be across their organisation's corporate policy framework – particularly privacy policies and social media policies that can cover breaches for intrusions into the privacy of others. Often the corporate privacy policy is written to comply with privacy and data protection laws in your jurisdiction.

Reflect – Research – Review:

Find and discuss an example of a professional communicator in your preferred field being the subject of an ethical complaint about privacy.

Law, cases and examples in privacy internationally

Despite the philosophical debate around privacy and cultural protocols dating back millennia, there was no enforceable legal 'right to privacy' in Western societies until the second half of the 19th century. Until that time, laws in the US, UK and in Commonwealth countries had evolved over centuries to protect the individual's home and reputation in several ways, including via defamation, copyright, trespass, nuisance and confidentiality.

The birthplace of the right to privacy in modern times was in France where it emerged in a 19th century court case involving one of the leading

Privacy and data protection 181

celebrities of the era. The practice of gentlemen duelling to the death over matters of pride was masterfully recorded by the writer Alexandre Dumas in his novel *The Three Musketeers*. As a celebrity author, Dumas lived an extravagant lifestyle in an era when the stars of print were the equivalent of screen idols today. He was besotted with 32-year-old actress Adah Isaacs Menken – the Paris Hilton of her time – regarded by some as the first female cult celebrity. The lovebirds posed for some saucy photographs (she in her underwear and he without the compulsory gentleman's jacket) but the photographer then tried to trade on their celebrity by registering copyright in the images. Dumas felt aggrieved but, as James Q. Whitman (2004: 1175–1176) explained in the *Yale Law Journal*, the court held that his copyright had not been infringed. However, the judge decided Dumas did have a more relevant 'right to privacy'. With that French decision in 1867, privacy was born as a right in the legal world. It also showed both its similarities to, and differences from, copyright law which we examine in Chapter 9. In this section we look at the development of the right to privacy and also introduce at an international level the laws related to trespass and data protection – making up the balance of the key areas of privacy law of concern to professional communicators, having already looked at defamation in Chapter 5 and confidentiality in Chapter 6.

A right to privacy

In a landmark *Harvard Law Review* article in December 1890, the great jurist Samuel D. Warren and future Supreme Court Justice Louis D. Brandeis announced a new US 'right to privacy' in an article by that name. Warren had been angered when a daily newspaper published the guest list of a high society dinner party his family had hosted at his Boston mansion, which he saw as a gross invasion of his privacy. The right to privacy owes its existence to a wealthy lawyer who resented the media prying into his personal life.

Warren and Brandeis wrote, 'The press is overstepping in every direction the obvious bounds of propriety and of decency. Gossip is no longer the resource of the idle and of the vicious, but has become a trade, which is pursued with industry as well as effrontery'. Their words mirror those of the critics of tabloid newspapers and celebrity gossip magazines and websites today (see Key Case 7.1). In the wake of the Warren and Brandeis article, the US Supreme Court developed four types of action for privacy invasion:

- *Intrusion*: including trespass, covert surveillance and misrepresentation; (covered in our Surveillance and Trespass section below)
- *Appropriation*: misappropriating the names or likeness of someone else;
- *False light*: highly offensive portrayal of someone in a false or reckless way; and
- *Public disclosure of embarrassing facts*: revealing private material about someone that is not of public concern where the revelation would be

offensive to the ordinary person (with some overlap with the data protection laws we examine below).

Of course, in the US the free speech protections in the First Amendment to the Constitution moderate the operation of each arm of this right to privacy, whereas in other Western countries and Europe it has much more force.

Continental Europe features systems of civil law with strong privacy protections under the law of 'delict' (similar to the common law of 'torts'), where citizens can seek compensation for infringements of their personality rights. German law divides privacy into the 'intimate', the 'individual' and the 'private'. In France, specific rights of personality are identified, including the 'right to confidentiality of correspondence', the 'right to privacy of domestic life' and the 'right to a person's name'. The guaranteed right to privacy (Article 8) of the *European Convention on Human Rights* has had a strong impact on privacy law throughout Europe.

For several decades, the right to sue over breaches of privacy failed to take hold in the United Kingdom where free expression held sway. A major turning point came in Britain and Europe with the death of Princess Diana in Paris in 1997 after a car chase involving paparazzi. In 1998, the United Kingdom passed its *Human Rights Act*, which incorporated the European Convention into British law. The approach of the UK courts then started to take on the flavour of their continental European neighbours.

Many of the UK judges avoided the words 'right to privacy', preferring to adapt the ancient action of 'breach of confidence' to fit privacy situations. Most of the litigants in major privacy actions the United Kingdom and Europe have come from the ranks of entertainment, sports and royalty. Actors Michael Douglas and Catherine Zeta-Jones convinced the High Court that *Hello!* magazine had breached their confidence by publishing unauthorised photographs of their wedding taken by a paparazzo who posed as a guest (Douglas Wedding case, 2001) – another case showing the close relationship with copyright law. In 2004, the House of Lords found against the *Mirror* for publishing a photo of supermodel Naomi Campbell leaving a drug addiction clinic because, despite being taken in a public place, it revealed confidential information about her medical condition. The court moulded the breach of confidence action into a new 'misuse of private information' – on the basis the user should have known the information was not free to use – even though there was not a pre-existing relationship between the parties (Supermodel case 2004). The European Court of Human Rights went a step further by finding that Princess Caroline of Monaco had a right to privacy when she was photographed via a long lens while holidaying on a public beach, although it ruled public figures could not claim protection of their private lives in the same way as ordinary citizens (Princess cases, 2004 and 2013).

Further privacy cases over private photos followed, including actions by Formula One chief Max Mosley and actors Hugh Grant and Elizabeth Hurley

(Pearson and Polden, 2019: 451). The decisions were reinforced throughout 2010 and 2011 when the UK courts issued at least eighteen non-publication injunctions ordering that the identities of several high-profile people be kept secret when exposés of their private lives were about to be revealed in the media. Some even fell into the category of 'super injunctions' – where it was prohibited to even reveal the fact that an injunction had been issued. Such an injunction was rendered ineffective when the identities of a reality television star and a football player went viral on social media in 2011. Former reality TV contestant Imogen Thomas had allegedly blackmailed Manchester United superstar Ryan Giggs over their affair, so he won the gag order against her and the tabloid media (Thomas's case, 2011). He later withdrew the blackmail allegation. Despite widespread Twitter coverage and a front page in a Scottish newspaper, the court extended the injunction on privacy grounds because Giggs' identity was not yet sufficiently in the 'public domain'. Another injunction remained in place despite widespread publication on the Internet (Three-way case, 2016).

The author JK Rowling won an appeal over photographs taken of her toddler while she and her husband were walking him in his stroller because even though they were public figures they should be able to hold a reasonable expectation of privacy without intrusive media attention (JK Rowling case, 2008). The line of celebrity actions over privacy invasions has continued into the 2020s, as evidenced by the Sussex cases (2021–2022), featured in Key Case 7.1.

On similar facts to the JK Rowling case involving photographs of children of celebrities being walked in a stroller, the New Zealand Court of Appeal ruled on a right to privacy in 2004 in the Hosking Twins case. The Hoskings were media personalities who had adopted twins and later separated. A magazine photographer snapped the mother walking the twins in their stroller in a public place. The court ultimately decided this fact scenario did not meet its new threshold for privacy invasion, but chose to outline the elements of the new tort. It decided two key criteria had to be met:

1 the existence of facts in respect of which there is a reasonable expectation of privacy; and
2 publicity given to those private facts that would be considered highly offensive to an objective reasonable person.

In Australia there was no formal actionable right to privacy in place at the time this book went to press although the Commonwealth Government had proposed a new statutory tort for serious privacy invasion after more than a decade of earlier attempts had not come to fruition. In 2001 in the Lenah Game Meats case and in 2020 in the Search Warrant case, the High Court had flagged the possibility of a new tort for serious invasion of privacy but had held back from creating one.

Key Case 7.1: The Sussex cases (2021–2022)

Meghan Markle's case (2021). *Sussex v Associated Newspapers Ltd* [2021] EWHC 273 (Ch) (11 February 2021), <www.bailii.org/ew/cases/EWHC/Ch/2021/273.html>; HRH the Duchess of Sussex v Associated Newspapers Ltd [2021] EWCA Civ 1810 (2 December 2021), <www.bailii.org/cgi-bin/format.cgi?doc=/ew/cases/EWCA/Civ/2021/1810.html>.

Various claimants cases: *Jefferies & Anor v News Group Newspapers Ltd (Rev1)* [2021] EWHC 2187 (27 July 2021), <www.bailii.org/ew/cases/EWHC/Ch/2021/2187.html>.; *Various Claimants vs. Associated Newspapers Limited:* Galbraith, C. 2022, 'Press release: Various Claimants vs. Associated Newspapers Limited', *Hamlins LLP*, 6 October, <https://hamlins.com/press-release-various-claimants-vs-associated-newspapers-limited/>.

Facts

Prince Harry and Meghan Markle (the Duke and Duchess of Sussex) were among several litigants at the centre of privacy actions against the media throughout 2021 and 2022. In the Meghan Markle case (2021), the duchess sued for breaches of both privacy and copyright over the publication by the *Mail on Sunday* of extended segments of a personal handwritten letter she had written to her estranged father. At the same time, various claimants including Prince Harry, Sir Elton John and Liz Hurley were in the courts pursuing several news groups over 'criminal activity and gross breaches of privacy' including using private investigators for the placement of listening devices in their cars and homes, eavesdropping and recording their phone conversations, payment to police for inside information about them, and using illicit methods to obtain their medical and financial records. Instances dated as far back as 1996.

Law

The Duchess won £1 in Meghan Markle's case (2021) for the invasion of her privacy plus a substantial amount to account for the profits the newspaper made by infringing the copyright in her letters, damages she said would be donated to charity (for the copyright case, see Key Case 9.1). She won a challenge in the Court of Appeal. The Various Claimants cases were still proceeding through the courts at the time of this book's publication.

Lessons for professional communicators

In the UK, a range of legal actions can be pursued under the umbrella invasion of privacy action and can be sought simultaneously with damages for harm suffered by breach of copyright and various criminal activities. Importantly, the publication of someone's private letters can result in litigation for both breach of privacy and breach of copyright.

Reflect – Research – Review:

Search online to find a recent example of an intrusion into privacy that has prompted legal action. Compare and contrast it with one of the cases in this chapter.

Data protection laws

Much privacy law internationally concerns the storage and handling of personal data by governments and corporations – particularly globalised Internet and social media networks in the digital era. There are data protection laws in most countries, typically restricting that government agency's or organisation's use of your private details to a narrow set of circumstances. They need your permission to use the private facts and then must comply with regulations on their secure storage.

The Organisation for Economic Co-operation and Development (OECD) Guidelines on the Protection of Privacy and Transborder Flows of Personal Data set the platform for international requirements for data protection (OECD, 2013). They attempted to bring different national data protection laws into harmony by ensuring consistency in the handling of private citizens' information across the public and corporate sectors. They strive to require organisations to limit the amount of personal data they can collect, ensure collection is lawful and fair, with consent given and the purpose of the collection stated. They also require that data not be used for alternative purposes, that it be protected by reasonable security safeguards, and that data collection policies be relevant, accurate, comprehensive and updated. Individuals should have the right to be informed about data collected about them and avenues of appeal.

The EU General Data Protection Regulation (GDPR) came into law in 2018 and stands as one of the strictest data protection laws in the world. It allows the EU's data protection authorities to impose fines of (whichever is the higher of) up to €20 million – or 4% of the worldwide turnover of an offending corporation– which can amount to large sums for global entities. More than

900 fines were reportedly issued in Europe and the UK in the two years to May 2020.

The regulation also affords a new 'right to erasure' – or 'right to be forgotten' – affording citizens a right to have data about them erased when it is no longer needed for its original purpose and sometimes just if they withdraw consent (Karp, 2023).

Despite the best efforts of international agreements and national regulators, breaches of data protection laws are frequent, either in a physical or digital form. Social media platforms added exponentially to the scale of private data held and traded globally by companies, political organisations and governments. One of the biggest data breaches in history was the Cambridge Analytica breach which came to light in 2018 when an insider revealed tens of millions of Facebook users' data had been collected without their consent for use in political campaigns. It resulted in billions of dollars in government fines and class action settlements across the US, UK and other jurisdictions. It is featured as our Key Case 7.2.

Another was the series of breaches by the ridesharing company Uber in 2016 where it was alleged to have deceived customers over data access by its staff. It had also failed to disclose breaches of driver and rider data, including hundreds of thousands of names and drivers' licence numbers and millions of names, phone numbers and email addresses. It resulted in a settlement with the US Federal Trade Commission (FTC) promising compliance for the next 20 years as well as paying $148 million in civil litigation across all US jurisdictions and agreeing to implement a corporate integrity programme, specific data security safeguards, and incident response and data breach notification plans, along with biennial assessments (FTC, 2018).

While most nations and regional governance bodies agree, at least publicly, that personal data should not be misused by governments, in June 2013, *The Guardian* and *The New York Times* published articles based on information supplied by former US National Security Agency contractor Edward Snowden, exposing widespread warrantless collection and storage of electronic communications by US government agencies. The volumes of private information held on every UK citizen by governments and corporations was highlighted in the 2010 documentary *Erasing David*, where the lead character went into hiding and hired some of Britain's top investigators to try to find him by discovering everything they could about him via public and private files. He found it was impossible to lead a private and anonymous existence in the early 21st century.

Our digital trail extends wherever and whenever we conduct business on the internet. The typical web browser allows countless 'cookies' that track many of our online activities. Search engines, app stores, airlines, travel booking agencies and numerous other online entities hold all sorts of digital information about us that may or may not be secure. The onus is on individual users to become acquainted with the terms of use of the platform they are using and to ensure their privacy settings are fixed at a suitable level.

A range of privacy-related laws also extend to cyberbullying and harassment, which we examine more closely in Chapter 11.

Key Case 7.2: The Cambridge Analytica–Facebook case

In re Facebook Inc., Consumer Privacy User Profile Litigation [2022] U.S. District Court for the Northern District of California, No. 3:18-md-02843, December 22, 2022, <https://s3.documentcloud.org/documents/23529033/facebook-inc-consumer-privacy-user-profile-litigation.pdf>.

Facts

An international backlash against Facebook resulted from the Cambridge Analytica scandal in 2018, when it was revealed by a whistleblower that the data analytics firm had harvested personal information from the social media profiles of more than 50 million people via a personality quiz. They used it to influence elections internationally (including the 2016 US presidential election and the UK Brexit referendum) and to target fake news at the accounts of swinging voters (Hern, 2022).

Law

Litigation over the massive data breach continued into at least late 2022, with the announcement Meta (Facebook's parent company) had agreed to pay out $725 million in a class action representing those who had their data breached. The claim centred on privacy breaches (plus contract, negligence and statutory claims) over Facebook continuing to share users' data with apps even after it had announced it would end friend sharing, sharing sensitive information with business partners without having disclosed this to users or their friends, and failure to restrict or monitor third parties' use of users' sensitive information. In addition to the class action settlement, Meta had to pay a £500,000 fine to the UK data regulator, $100 million to settle a US Securities and Exchange Commission investigation over misleading investors about user data, $5 billion after a US Federal Trade Commission inquiry, and other national and state penalties and settlements.

Lessons for communicators

- Regulators take data breaches seriously. Even at a local jurisdictional level fines can be hefty for corporate communicators who misuse data for marketing or disobey data protection regulations.
- It is important to ensure data is used for the purpose for which it has been collected and authorised by the person from whom it was collected.
- Disclosure of personal and sensitive data to third parties is fraught.

> **Reflect – Research – Review:**
>
> Research and discuss a privacy data breach by a media company in your jurisdiction. How did it come about and how might it be avoided in the future?

Surveillance and trespass

In addition to the journalism ethical restrictions in place covering deception, most Western jurisdictions have laws restricting the use of surveillance, recording and listening devices. These can have implications for reporters and for political communicators wanting to attempt the entrapment of an opponent. In the US, there are both Federal and State laws controlling such recordings, although in some states you are allowed to record without the other person knowing as long as you are a party to the conversation. Australian laws also vary, as detailed below. In the UK, surveillance and phone-tapping were at the centre of the excesses of the British tabloids which led to the closure of Rupert Murdoch's *News of the World* newspaper and the exposure of a litany of unethical and illegal practices by editors and journalists working with private investigators to gather private information about celebrities. In January 2007, the royal editor of the tabloid *News of the World* was jailed for four months under phone-tapping laws for intercepting the mobile phone messages of Prince William (Leveson, 2012). Illicit recording was also at the centre of some of the privacy complaints at the centre of the Sussex cases featured in Key Case 7.1.

Trespass can occur both in a physical or digital sense. Digital trespass and identity theft in the realm of cybersecurity is covered in Chapter 10. Physical trespass – entering someone's property without their permission or refusing to leave once asked to do so – is an area of media law found internationally and of concern to professional communicators, particularly journalists. While many forms of trespass exist across both criminal and civil law, typical to most jurisdictions is the civil action for trespass to land, defined in the US as 'knowingly entering another owner's property or land without permission, which encroaches on the owner's privacy or property interests' (Cornell Law School, 2022). Proof of intent to enter or remain on the land is required, no matter whether the trespasser knows the land is owned by others. Under UK and Australian law, various intricacies in the action have developed through the case law related to whether there is an implied invitation to the media to enter a property, and whether that further implies that they have permission to film on arrival (Pearson and Polden, 2019: 467–470). Under UK and Australian case law, an exclusive occupier of premises may impose a condition, enforceable by injunction, that an entrant not take photographs while the entrant remains on the premises (Our Dogs case, 1916).

Privacy and data protection

UK and Australian law also has a rarely used action for 'nuisance' – which protects an occupier's use or enjoyment of their land from unreasonable interference. It will succeed only where the defendant has interfered with an interest of an occupier recognised by the courts. Essentially, the nuisance has to be persistent and annoying for it to be actionable – such as where a pack of paparazzi lurk noisily outside the home of a celebrity waiting for them to emerge for a photograph.

Australian privacy law – a developing right, data protection, surveillance and trespass

We now zoom in on the specific laws in Australia around what appears to be a developing right to privacy, along with the data protection provisions of the *Privacy Act 1988*, surveillance and recording laws, and the action for trespass.

Development of privacy law

As this book went to press in 2023, there was still no common law right to privacy in Australia, although a number of laws went part-way to protecting the privacy of citizens, and the Commonwealth Government had started the year with a reform process flagging a possible a statutory tort of privacy and a new right to be forgotten – or right of erasure (Karp, 2023).

Complaints about media intrusion date back to the early 19th century (Pearson and Leighton-Jackson, 2020: 388). In 1847, New South Wales became the first Australian state to add 'public benefit' to its defence of truth for libel – essentially a privacy element in defamation law (ALRC, 1979: 117). In the 1937 Victoria Park Racing case, the High Court decided that a radio station broadcasting horse race calls from a platform on a property overlooking the track did not constitute 'nuisance' by unlawfully interfering with the racing club's use of its property. Further, the station had not breached any 'right to privacy'. Over the ensuing 85 years, support for an actionable right to privacy increased as the concept gained currency internationally.

The High Court revisited that 1937 decision when it passed judgment in 2001 in the Lenah Game Meats case (see Key Case 7.3). It rejected the claim of a Tasmanian abattoir that it had a right to privacy that animal liberationists breached when trespassing to film the slaughter of possums, which the ABC planned to broadcast. However, the court refused to rule out the potential for a right to privacy under a different fact scenario. Intermediate court decisions in the early 21st century awarded plaintiffs damages for invasion of privacy. Notable was the Jane Doe case in Victoria in 2007, where a Victorian County Court held that a rape victim's privacy was invaded – and her confidence was breached – after radio news bulletins broadcast her identity, despite state laws banning the identification of sexual assault complainants for which the ABC journalists had been convicted. The victim was awarded $110,000 damages (Jane Doe case, 2007). The decision was not appealed, which left the issue undecided by a superior court (thus not setting a legal precedent). Then in 2008 the Victoria Court of Appeal held that, while a jilted lover's distribution of secretly made sex tapes was a breach of confidence after she was embarrassed by the exposure of private information, it was not a 'breach of privacy' because there was not yet an invasion of privacy tort in Australia (Sex Tapes case, 2008). Despite that, in 2013 a Queensland District Court judge refused to deny a girl an opportunity to sue Yahoo! for breach of privacy after her image was used to post offensive messages ridiculing her disability (Disability case, 2013).

The line of thinking in Australia has been similar to the British approach in the historic celebrity cases mentioned earlier, in adapting the equitable remedy of breach of confidence to invasions of privacy. It was followed again in Western Australia in 2015 when the Supreme Court awarded $48,404 in damages to a woman whose former lover – a co-worker at a mine site – had posted intimate images and videos of her to Facebook in an act of revenge after she ended their relationship (Revenge Porn case, 2015). The case offers a concise summary of the application of the equitable remedy of breach of confidence (explained in Chapter 6) to a privacy matter. Justice Robert Mitchell explained how the act of posting the indecent material constituted a breach of the man's equitable obligation, owed to his ex-partner, to maintain the confidentiality of the images (para 55). The images had the 'necessary quality of confidence about them', the circumstances in which they were obtained conveyed an obligation of confidentiality, and they had been posted on Facebook to the detriment of the plaintiff. Justice Mitchell drew on historical cases where the breach of confidence action had been used to restrain a defendant from publishing private material, including the 1849 case over etchings created by Queen Victoria and Prince Albert for their own use, which had been secretly copied from the original plates and were about to be published by a London printer (Royal Etchings case, 1847: para. 48).

Key Case 7.3: Lenah Game Meats case

ABC v Lenah Game Meats Pty Ltd [2001] HCA 63; 208 CLR 199; 185 ALR 1; 76 ALJR 1 (15 November 2001), <www.austlii.edu.au/au/cases/cth/high_ct/2001/63.html>.

Facts

Unnamed animal rights activists broke into the Lenah Game Meats abattoir in Tasmania and planted secret cameras that recorded the killing of brush-tailed possums for export. There was nothing illegal about the company's operations and it followed best practice standards in its processes. The vision was delivered to the ABC, which proposed to broadcast it on its current affairs programme, *The 7.30 Report*.

Law

The company sought injunctions stopping the ABC from broadcasting the video, requiring the broadcaster to deliver up all copies of the film it held, and also sought damages and costs. The Full Court of the Supreme Court granted an interim injunction to stop the broadcast but in the meantime the ABC had screened some excerpts. The ABC appealed to the High Court to have the injunction lifted. A majority agreed to allow the broadcast, but the five justices varied markedly in their reasons.

The main elements of the judgments relevant to privacy were:

- A separate new tort of invasion of privacy was a possibility. The majority decided it was best left open for a more suitable test case involving a person's privacy rather than a company's.
- It was unlikely that any such action for invasion of privacy would extend to corporations.
- Showing a film of the processes used by the abattoir was not a breach of confidence, because the processes themselves were not sufficiently confidential, despite the film being made on private premises.
- Despite the fact the footage was obtained illegally via trespass by unknown parties, its publication by a third-party broadcaster was not 'unconscionable'.

The majority of the High Court discharged the injunction on the grounds that the lower court did not have authority in equity to grant it, but in the process raised the prospect of developing a form of privacy action. Gleeson CJ and Callinan J favoured the English approach of extending the breach of confidence action to apply to the filming of private activities, an approach reflected in more recent decisions.

Lessons for professional communicators

This case canvasses issues relevant to a range of media law topics. These include:

- the principle of prior restraint and interlocutory injunctions in defamation cases;
- whether Australian law recognises a tort of invasion of privacy;
- whether corporations have a right to privacy;
- relevance to privacy of the implied constitutional freedom of political communication; and
- trespass to land and whether the owner of premises has a right to restrain publication of film gained while a trespass is being committed.

> A key lesson of relevance to this chapter is that the High Court approved the use of material by the media that might have been gained illegally by an unknown third party. If the ABC had been involved in the trespass in any way, the court might have restrained the publication – particularly if the broadcast contained confidential information, such as a secret technique of processing or equipment.

In the 2008–2023 period several law reform commission and government inquiries recommended the enactment of a new tort for the serious invasion of privacy. Such a proposal was again under consideration as this book went to press (Karp, 2023).

> **Reflect – Research – Review:**
>
> Find the latest proposals for the introduction of new privacy laws in Australia and review their recommendations by comparing them with the case law and earlier proposals.

Data protection in Australia

Data is protected in Australia predominantly under the *Commonwealth Privacy Act 1988* and complementary legislation in each state and Territory. When first introduced, the *Privacy Act* applied only to personal information held by Australian government departments and agencies, but it was extended to larger private sector organisations in 2000. Media organisations remain exempted from the provisions for their news operations as long as they ascribe to privacy standards published by their representative bodies, such as the Australian Press Council and the various broadcasting industry associations.

The preamble to the Act stated the law was designed to meet Australia's obligations relating to privacy under the United Nations *International Convention on Civil and Political Rights* (ICCPR) and the Organisation for Economic Co-operation and Development *Guidelines on the Protection of Privacy and Transborder Flows of Personal Data* (OECD Guidelines). Various parliamentary speeches and amendments have linked it to other international privacy treaties and obligations.

The Act includes 13 Australian Privacy Principles applying to Australian government agencies, as well as corporations and not-for-profit organisations with turnovers of more than $3 million per year, plus a narrow range of smaller businesses. The law governs standards, rights and obligations around:

- the collection, use and disclosure of personal information;
- an organisation or agency's governance and accountability;
- integrity and correction of personal information; and
- the rights of individuals to access their personal information.

The Act distinguishes between personal information and sensitive information, with higher standards and requirements for organisations' management of the latter. 'Personal information' includes a range of information, or an opinion, that could identify an individual. It can be:

- someone's name, signature, address, phone number or date of birth
- sensitive information
- credit information
- employee record information
- photographs
- internet protocol (IP) addresses
- voice print and facial recognition biometrics, and
- location information from a mobile device

'Sensitive information' is information related to a person's racial or ethnic origin, political opinions or associations, religious or philosophical beliefs, trade union membership or associations, sexual orientation or practices, criminal record, or health, genetic and some biometric information. Generally, sensitive information has a higher level of privacy protection than other personal information. A breach of an Australian Privacy Principle is an 'interference with the privacy of an individual' and can lead to regulatory action and penalties. Full details of the requirements can be found at the Office of the Australian Information Commissioner's website, <www.oaic.gov.au/privacy>.

Case example:

Clearview AI case (2021): The Australian Information Commissioner and Privacy Commissioner found the US-based Clearview AI, Inc. breached Australians' privacy by scraping their biometric information from the web in a trial for policing agencies and disclosing it through a facial recognition tool. Its breaches of the Act included: collecting Australians' sensitive information without consent and by unfair means, not notifying individuals their personal information was being collected, not ensuring the information was accurate, and not complying with the Australian Privacy Principles.

In late 2022, in the wake of large data compromises after cyber attacks on Optus and Medibank Private, the Commonwealth Government amended the *Privacy Act* at section 13G to increase penalties for data breaches to $2.5 million for individuals and $50 million for corporations, or up to $150 million if they profited from the breach. They also inserted section 52A requiring those involved in data breaches to outline the nature of the breach and the steps they were taking to remedy it and prevent further breaches. The Optus breach resulted in about 10 million customers having personal data stolen, including identification documents such as drivers' licences, card information, dates of birth and contact details. The Medibank breach affected a similar number of customers, but also involved extensive release of their health details (Taylor, 2022).

Trespass

Under the tort of trespass, every person who is in possession of premises has the right to refuse others entry. You are liable for trespass if you:

- enter land or premises without the consent of the occupier
- remain there when permission to be there has been withdrawn, or
- place an object like a listening device or a camera on someone else's land or in their premises (Walker, 2000: 878).

Professional communicators including journalists have no special right of entry to someone else's property beyond that of an ordinary citizen. Essentially, the law of trespass allows you to enter a person's property to seek an interview unless the interviewee has specifically restricted the purpose for which access to the property has been granted or has previously refused to be interviewed. It also allows you to interview, photograph and film people or their property from outside their land. Once the occupier has asked a journalist to leave the premises, the journalist should leave immediately or will be committing a trespass from that moment. If they refuse such a direction, the owner can use reasonable force to remove them.

Courts can award damages against trespassers, and in extremely rare circumstances can issue injunctions to prevent broadcast or publication of film taken by trespassers, and even information gained in interviews conducted while trespassing. Courts will normally issue such injunctions only if they believe publication would be 'unconscionable' and that irreparable harm would result.

Case examples:

A Current Affair case (2002): A reporter and film crew from Channel Nine's *A Current Affair* joined NSW Environment Protection Authority (EPA) staff in a raid on a property to determine whether environmental offences had occurred. The crew had cameras rolling as they entered the property and confronted the owner. He sued for damages to compensate him for his distress and mental trauma, and the trial judge awarded him $100,000, including aggravated and exemplary damages. The Court of Appeal agreed there had been a trespass without licence, but reduced the damages to $25,000. The fact that the owner had not locked the gate to the property did not constitute an 'implied licence' to enter and film. There was an implied licence for journalists to enter the land to request permission to film, but not to film without permission. The judge warned public authorities not to invite journalists on such raids, known in media relations as 'ride-alongs'.

Piggery case, 2011: The NSW Supreme Court awarded $15,000 in general damages (plus special damages) against activists who trespassed into a piggery to film the state of the animals on behalf of the head of Animal Liberation NSW so he could make a cruelty report to the RSPCA. However, the piggery failed in its attempts to win an injunction to get possession of the video and photographs taken because the trespass did not meet the criteria for breach of confidence or unconscionability. (See also Key Case 7.3: Lenah Game Meats case.)

Nuisance

The rights of an occupier do not include a freedom from the view of neighbouring properties. Observation of someone from outside the bounds of their property would not normally be considered nuisance unless the behaviour was such that it was interfering with their enjoyment of that property (Victoria Park Racing case, 1937). For example, constant, systematic surveillance, as might occur in a 'stake-out' by a group of noisy journalists just outside someone's home, with photographers continually filming into that person's premises, could be deemed nuisance. Continuous telephone calls that persist despite requests for them to cease could be considered a nuisance, while a series of phone calls merely seeking an interview for a story would not normally be considered as such (Walker, 2000: 881).

Case example:

Brown Protest case (2017): High Court Justice Stephen Gageler pointed out that a forestry company could succeed in an action for nuisance against protesters whose conduct on business premises interferes with its business activity: 'There must be a material interference, beyond what is reasonable in the circumstances, with the plaintiff's use or enjoyment of the land or of the plaintiff's interest in the land'. He said picketing was not necessarily a nuisance and unlawful unless it became obstruction and besetting.

Professional communicators working internationally also need to be aware of a host of laws that might apply to their reporting methods or publishing procedures in other countries – which sometimes go well beyond the laws of trespass or nuisance. The journalist and three crew of the Nine Network current affairs programme *60 Minutes* were arrested in Lebanon and spent two weeks in jail on kidnapping charges over their involvement in the 2016 abduction in a Beirut street of children who were at the centre of a custody dispute between their Australian mother and Lebanese-Australian father, who was holding them in his care there. Only after extended diplomatic and legal representations did the team manage to return to Australia to face an internal review over the tactics they had used, with the producer losing his job over his role in the story (Ward, 2016).

Surveillance

Commonwealth and state laws affect the use of surveillance and listening devices and place a range of restrictions on the publication of reports gained by their use. Under Commonwealth law, it is an offence to intercept (listen to or record) a communication passing over a 'telecommunications system' without the knowledge of the person making the communication. This is detailed in section 7(1) of the *Telecommunications (Interception and Access) Act 1979*, which states:

> A person shall not: (a) intercept; (b) authorize, suffer or permit another person to intercept; or (c) do any act or thing that will enable him or her or another person to intercept; a communication passing over a telecommunications system.

Each of the states and territories also has legislation restricting the recording of a private conversation without the consent of all parties to the conversation by someone who is not a party. In Victoria, the law allows recording by a party to a conversation, as do the Northern Territory, NSW, South Australia, Tasmania and the ACT, subject to a twofold test: reasonable necessity, and no intention to republish. Northern Territory laws allow a party to record in the case of urgent public interest.

The legislation is called, in the respective states and territories:

- *Surveillance Devices Act* (Vic., WA, NT, NSW, SA)
- *Listening Devices Act* (Tasmania and ACT)
- *Invasion of Privacy Act* (Qld).

Case example:

Dehorning case (2018): The Western Australian Supreme Court of Appeal dismissed the ABC's appeal against a trial judge's refusal to allow the broadcaster to show video footage of cattle being dehorned, secretly recorded by a cattle station employee in contravention of that state's *Surveillance Devices Act*. The court held that even though the footage had been played in open court during the trial of the animal cruelty case, it was open to the trial judge to conclude that publication of the illegally recorded footage would not materially enhance public debate on the issue (see also Key Case 7.3: Lenah Game Meats case).

Whatever recording is done, it is likely to come under close scrutiny and legal advice should be sought before setting up or carrying out any form of phone recording, video surveillance or data-tracking. You should also avoid accessing people's internet and social media accounts without their permission. Hacking into someone's account to bypass their privacy settings can be a simple but illegal process, as explained in Chapter 10 when we look at cybersecurity.

Other Australian privacy laws

Jurisdiction-based human rights instruments in Queensland, Victoria and the Australian Capital Territory (ACT) contain privacy rights along with a host of other rights. Queensland's *Human Rights Act 2019* protects against unlawful or arbitrary interference with a person's privacy. Victoria's *Charter of Human Rights and Responsibilities Act 2006* and the ACT's *Human Rights Act 2004* confer a right not to have anyone's privacy, family, home or correspondence interfered with unlawfully or arbitrarily, in line with international human rights charters.

In addition, various laws protect the privacy of vulnerable people before the law and are designed to protect the integrity of trials. These include identification restrictions in sexual offence cases, juvenile matters, mental health proceedings, state wards and family law matters. They vary across jurisdictions and are covered in more detail in Chapter 8. Privacy is also a factor allowable as an exemption to the release of documents under Freedom of Information and Right to Information laws as explained in Chapter 6.

Reflect – Research – Review:

Privacy and data protection in action – Case Study 7.1: Applied ethical decision making – the celebrity's garbage bin

Occasionally a situation arises that covers a number of important areas of media ethics and law. For this scenario, you are asked to work through the ethical ramifications of the situation using the basic Potter Box technique (Potter, 1972), as explained in Chapter 3, and the legal ramifications of your decision using the specific legal risk analysis technique (Grantham and Pearson, 2022: 51–53).

The problem

You are an investigative reporter for a celebrity gossip magazine – SCOOP!. Your friend lives next door to a successful but reclusive actress who has just won an Oscar for her thrilling performance as the lead in an action movie. Garbage bins are collected on Tuesday nights so your friend has swapped his bin with hers so you can go through all her rubbish to piece together the secret parts of her life. In it you find enough domestic waste to be able to write about her eating and drinking habits (including empty junk food wrappers and tequila bottles). There are also several old credit card statements, medical fund transactions and tax files giving you insights into her health and finances. All this, combined with some long lens photos taken by your friend of her sunbathing topless by her pool, and you have an exclusive cover story for your next edition.

Applying the Potter Box

Remember, the Potter Box (1972) asks you to work with this quadrant of factors to think through the ethics of the scenario, as illustrated by Patterson and Wilkins (1997: 90):

Facts	Loyalties
Values	Principles

Before you engage with the Potter Box, you should set aside 10–15 minutes to engage in mindful reflection upon the overall scenario and the issues involved – using a breathing concentration technique like mindful meditation, journaling or mindmapping. Then turn to the four factors of the Potter Box:

Facts

Take in the facts of the situation. What is really going on here? Even if it was okay to trawl through the celebrity's rubbish, how can you be sure this actually belongs to her? What other facts need to be confirmed and verified in this scenario?

Values

What does your own moral compass say about this situation? What is your gut feeling about the act of snooping through the rubbish looking for someone's secrets? If we are thinking about values from your upbringing reflected in your 'moral compass', what would your parents, grandparents, teachers or mentors think about you doing this? What kinds of values lead to you working for a gossip magazine where this kind of story is your stock in trade? What values can be drawn from fundamental human rights for this situation? Professional ethical obligations are also relevant here – what do those codes say about privacy?

Loyalties

How do you weigh up your obligations to yourself, your employer, the actress, your audience and your colleagues? Where is the power in this situation? It can help to return to your journaling or mindmapping to articulate these loyalties clearly in relation to the various stakeholders.

Principles

Which philosophical principles apply here? Using the consequentialist approach, does the end of entertaining your audience and increasing the circulation of your magazine justify the means of privacy invasion and the resulting emotional distress you are inflicting on the celebrity through this act? Deontological: How does your action sit with the rules of your occupation and society more generally? Contractualist: How does the action treat the rights and interests of the various stakeholders? Does it breach your social contract as a citizen? Virtue ethics: How does this kind of action build your character as a professional and more broadly as a person?

Given the Potter Box should not be a linear, step by step process (Christians et al., 2011: 5), return randomly to each of the earlier categories and reflect on them again until you are satisfied you have given the problem a thorough analysis. You should now be able to reach a more definitive ethical decision about the overall situation.

Applying the specific legal risk analysis technique

Now it is time to turn to the legal dimensions of the problem and to assess your exposure to legal risk, using our basic five steps.

Identifying the potential (or existing) legal problem

At least two key topic areas arise as covered in this chapter – potential invasion of privacy (or breach of confidence as covered in Chapter 6) and a breach of data protection laws.

Reviewing the areas of the law involved

Go over those areas of the law as they apply. How does the situation sit with the elements of breach of confidence? Of invasion or breach of privacy? As a possible breach of other local data protection laws such as the *Privacy Act*? The basic elements of breach of confidence would apply again here – the information has a quality of confidence about it, you have received it in circumstances requiring confidence (via a personal garbage bin stolen by a friend) and it will be used to the detriment of the celebrity. What about the potential breach of privacy action? Would there be any public interest defence available, or is this just a matter of public curiosity as opposed to legitimate public concern? As for data protection laws, what does your jurisdiction say about the publication of someone's health, financial and other personal information without their permission? What legal remedies might apply to these three areas of the law? Are there other laws involved such as trespass to property or theft?

Projecting the possible consequences for stakeholders

What are the potential consequences for all key stakeholders – for you, your friend who is her neighbour, your publisher and the actress herself? What journey lies ahead of you all in adverse publicity, legal costs and damages awards or perhaps criminal sanctions? What level of emotional distress or financial loss could the actress suffer as a result of your publication? If she is traumatized by this, how many millions of dollars in lost salary might you be ordered to pay her in addition to compensatory damages?

Seeking advice/referring upward

Before acting, check with supervisors and lawyers using your company's escalation policy. Given the kind of magazine you are working for, one imagines there is a team of lawyers on hand to advise on all this. Perhaps they have done this all before and are calculating the potential commercial gain against the potential ethical and legal damage. In other words, perhaps it is part of their business model. If so, is this the type of outfit you really want to work for – and have your reputation attached to their dubious actions?

Publishing/amending/deleting/correcting/apologizing

Having considered all of this, you need to make the key decision on whether to proceed to publication with your bin full of salacious secrets. Over to you as a communication professional on that decision – and on the wording of any consequential deletions, corrections or apologies (after legal advice, of course!)

In a nutshell

- The notion of privacy has long been a cultural phenomenon and it has received attention from philosophers, particularly in recent decades.
- Each of the main communication industry bodies has codes or principles that professional communicators and media organisations are expected to follow, and each has a set of privacy requirements and complaint procedures.
- Journalism has more ethical code restrictions in the areas of invasion of privacy, intrusion into grief, and interviewing or photographing the vulnerable, particularly children, while other communication professions are more focused on data protection and commercial confidentiality.
- There is no common law right to privacy in Australia, although a number of laws go part of the way to protecting the privacy of citizens, and there are moves towards establishing such a right, especially in the wake of the 2001 Lenah Game Meats case.
- *The Privacy Act 1988* requires government agencies and larger corporations to abide by 13 Australian Privacy Principles but features some exemptions for journalism.
- The internet and social media raise privacy concerns at an international level, particularly in the realm of data protection.
- A journalist has no special right of entry to someone else's property above that of an ordinary citizen. Under the law of trespass, every person who is in possession of premises has the right to refuse others entry to those premises.
- The basic rule of trespass is that, once the occupier has asked someone to leave their premises, the intruder should do so or they will be committing a trespass.
- In most places it is illegal to record, broadcast or publish a private conversation without the consent of all parties to the conversation, particularly by someone who is not a party to the conversation.

References and further reading

Abizadeh, A. 2013, 'Publicity, privacy and religious toleration in Hobbes's Leviathan', *Modern Intellectual History* 10 (2), 261–291.
Australian Communications and Media Authority (ACMA). 2016, *Privacy Guidelines for Broadcasters*, ACMA, Melbourne, <www.acma.gov.au/publications/2016-09/guide/privacy-guidelines-broadcasters>.
Australian Law Reform Commission (ALRC). 1979, *Unfair Publication: Defamation and Privacy*, ALRC, Canberra, <www.alrc.gov.au/report-11>.
Australian Press Council (APC). 2023, *Statement of Principles*, APC, Sydney, <www.presscouncil.org.au/standards/statement-of-principles>.
Backholm, K. and Björkqvist, K. 2012, 'The mediating effect of depression between exposure to potentially traumatic events and PTSD in news journalists', *European Journal of Psychotraumatology*, 3, 183–188.
Bok, S. 1989, *Secrets: On the Ethics of Concealment and Revelation*, Vintage Books, New York.

Chartered Institute of Public Relations (CIPR). 2023, *CIPR Code of Conduct*, <www.cipr.co.uk/CIPR/About_Us/Governance_/CIPR_Code_of_Conduct.aspx>.

Christians, C.G., Fackler, M., Richardson, K.B., Kreshel, P.J., and Woods, R.H. 2012, *Media Ethics: Cases and Moral Reasoning*, 9th edn, Taylor & Francis Group, NY.

Cornell Law School. 2022, *Trespass*. Legal Information Institute, 22 May, <www.law.cornell.edu/wex/trespass>.

DeCew, J. 2018, 'Privacy', *The Stanford Encyclopedia of Philosophy*, Spring 2018 edn, Zalta, E.N. ed., <https://plato.stanford.edu/archives/spr2018/entries/privacy/>.

Diamond, M. 2004, 'Sexual behavior in pre contact Hawai'i: A sexological ethnography', *Revista Española del Pacífico*, 16, 37–58, <www.hawaii.edu/PCSS/biblio/articles/2000to2004/2004-sexual-behavior-in-pre-contact-hawaii.html>.

Finkelstein, R. 2012, *Report of the Independent Inquiry into the Media and Media Regulation*, Department of Broadband, Communications and the Digital Economy, Canberra, <www.archive.dbcde.gov.au/2013/august/independent_media_inquiry>.

Grantham, S. and Pearson, M. 2022, *Social Media Risk and the Law: A Guide for Global Communicators*, Routledge, London and New York.

Hern, A. 2022, 'Facebook owner to settle class-action suit over Cambridge Analytica scandal', *The Guardian*, 24 December, <www.theguardian.com/business/2022/dec/23/facebook-owner-to-settle-class-action-suit-over-cambridge-analytica-scandal>.

Independent Press Standards Organisation (IPSO). 2021, *Findings*, ISPO, London, <www.ipso.co.uk/rulings-and-resolution-statements/>.

Instagram, 2023, *Keeping Instagram a Safe and Supportive Place*, <https://about.instagram.com/safety>.

Karp, P. 2023, 'Australia to consider European-style right to be forgotten privacy laws', *The Guardian*, 19 January, <www.theguardian.com/australia-news/2023/jan/19/right-to-be-forgotten-australia-europe-gdpr-privacy-laws>.

Leveson, B. 2012, *Report of an Inquiry into the Culture, Practice and Ethics of the Press*, The Stationery Office, London, <www.official-documents.gov.uk/document/hc1213/hc07/0780/0780.asp>.

Maher, P. 2002, 'A review of 'traditional' aboriginal health beliefs'. *The Australian Journal of Rural Health*, 7, 229–236.

Media Entertainment and Arts Alliance (MEAA). 2016, *The MEAA Journalist Code of Ethics*, Media Entertainment and Arts Alliance, Sydney, <www.meaa.org/download/faqs-meaa-journalist-code-of-ethics/>.

National Union of Journalists (NUJ). 2018, *Printable Code of Conduct*, NUJ, London, <www.nuj.org.uk/resource/printable-nuj-code-of-conduct.html>.

Office of Communications (Ofcom). 2021, 'Section 8 – Privacy', *Ofcom Broadcasting Code*, <www.ofcom.org.uk/tv-radio-and-on-demand/broadcast-codes/broadcast-code/section-eight-privacy>.

Office of Communications (Ofcom). 2023, 'Broadcasting and on demand sanction decisions', *Bulletins*, <www.ofcom.org.uk/about-ofcom/latest/bulletins/content-sanctions-adjudications>.

Organisation for Economic Co-operation and Development (OECD). 2013, *OECD Guidelines on the Protection of Privacy and Transborder Flows of Personal Data*, OECD, <www.oecd.org/sti/ieconomy/oecdguidelinesontheprotectionofprivacyandtransborderflowsofpersonaldata.htm>.

Patterson, P and Wilkins, L. (1997). *Media Ethics: Issues and Cases*, 5th edn, McGraw Hill, Boston, MA.

Pearson, M., McMahon, C., O'Donovan, A., and O'Shannessy, D. 2021, 'Building journalists' resilience through mindfulness strategies', *Journalism*, 22 (7), 1647–1664, <https://doi.org/10.1177/1464884919833253>.

Pearson, M. and Polden, M. 2019, *The Journalist's Guide to Media Law*, 6th edn, Allen & Unwin, Sydney.

Pearson, M. and Leighton-Jackson, V. 2020, 'Privacy and defamation in Australia – a post-colonial tango', *Research Handbook on Comparative Privacy and Defamation*, Koltay, A. and Wragg, P. eds, Edward Elgar, UK and MA, 381–398.

Peterson, J. 2021, 'The value of privileged access', *European Journal of Philosophy*, 29 (2), 365–378.

Potter, R.B. (1972). The Logic of Moral Argument. In Deats, P., ed., *Toward a Discipline of Social Ethics*. Boston: Boston University Press, 93–114.

Public Relations Consultants Association (PRCA). 2023, *Professional Charter and Codes of Conduct*, London, <www.prca.org.uk/about-us/pr-standards/professional-charter-and-codes-conduct>.

Public Relations Society of America (PRSA). 2023, *PRSA Code of Ethics*, <www.prsa.org/about/ethics/prsa-code-of-ethics>.

Society of Professional Journalists (SPJ). 2014, *Society of Professional Journalists (SPJ) Code of Ethics*, <www.spj.org/ethicscode.asp>.

Taylor, J. 2022, 'Medibank hackers announce "case closed" and dump huge data file on dark web', *The Guardian*, 1 December, <www.theguardian.com/australia-news/2022/dec/01/medibank-hackers-announce-case-closed-and-dump-huge-data-file-on-dark-web>.

Walker, S. 2000, *Media Law: Commentary and Materials*, Law Book Company, Sydney.

Watson, A. (2022). The 'digital death knock': Australian journalists' use of social media in reporting everyday tragedy. *Australian Journalism Review*, 44 (2), 245–262. doi:10.3316/informit.733686208233540.

Weil, S. 2015, 'What Is Sacred in Every Human Being? (La Personne et le sacré)', *Simone Weil: Late Philosophical Writings*, Springsted, E.O., ed., University of Notre Dame, Indiana, 96–117.

Whitman, J.Q. 2004, 'The two western cultures of privacy: Dignity versus liberty', *Yale Law Journal*, 113, 1151–1221.

Cases cited

Brown Protest case: *Brown v Tasmania* [2017] HCA 43 (18 October 2017), <www.austlii.edu.au/cgi-bin/viewdoc/au/cases/cth/HCA/2017/43.html>.

Cambridge Analytica – Facebook case: *Facebook Inc., Consumer Privacy User Profile Litigation* [2022] U.S. District Court for the Northern District of California, No. 3:18-md-02843. (22 December 2022), <https://s3.documentcloud.org/documents/23529033/facebook-inc-consumer-privacy-user-profile-litigation.pdf>.

Clearview AI case: *Commissioner initiated investigation into Clearview AI, Inc. (Privacy)* [2021] AICmr 54 (14 October 2021), <www.austlii.edu.au/cgi-bin/viewdoc/au/cases/cth/AICmr/2021/54.html>.

Current Affair case: *TCN Channel Nine Pty v Anning* [2002] NSWCA 82 (25 March 2002), <www.austlii.edu.au/au/cases/nsw/NSWCA/2002/82.html>.

Dehorning case: *Australian Broadcasting Corporation v Sawa Pty Ltd* [2018] WASCA 29 (15 March 2018), <www.austlii.edu.au/cgi-bin/viewdoc/au/cases/wa/WASCA/2018/29.html>.

Disability case: *Doe v Yahoo!7 Pty Ltd & Anor; Wright v Pagett and Ors* [2013] QDC 181 (9 August 2013), <www.austlii.edu.au/au/cases/qld/QDC/2013/181.html>.

Douglas Wedding case: *Douglas v Hello! Ltd* [2001] 2 WLR 992; [2001] 2 All ER 289.

Federal Trade Commission case: Federal Trade Commission (FTC). 2018, *Federal Trade Commission gives final approval to settlement with Uber*, Press Releases, 26 October, <www.ftc.gov/news-events/news/press-releases/2018/10/federal-trade-commission-gives-final-approval-settlement-uber>.

Hosking Twins case: *Hosking & Hosking v Simon Runting & Anor* [2004] NZCA 34 (25 March 2004), <www.austlii.edu.au/nz/ cases/NZCA/2004/34.html>.

Jane Doe case: *Jane Doe v Australian Broadcasting Corporation* [2007] VCC 281 (3 April 2007), <www.austlii.edu.au/au/cases/vic/VCC/2007/281.pdf >.

JK Rowling case: *Murray v Big Pictures (UK) Ltd* [2008] EWCA Civ 446 (7 May 2008), <www.bailii.org/ew/cases/EWCA/Civ/2008/446.html>.

Lenah Game Meats case: *ABC v Lenah Game Meats Pty Ltd* [2001] HCA 63; 208 CLR 199; 185 ALR 1; 76 ALJR 1 (15 November 2001), <www.austlii.edu.au/au/cases/cth/high_ct/2001/63.html>.

Our Dogs case: *Sports and General Press Agency Ltd v 'Our Dogs' Publishing Co. Ltd* [1916] 2 KB 880.

Piggery case: *Windridge Farm Pty Ltd v Grassi and Ors* [2011] NSWSC 196 (28 March 2011), <www.austlii.edu.au/cgi-bin/viewdoc/au/cases/nsw/NSWSC/2011/196.html>.

Princess cases: *von Hannover v Germany (Application No. 59320/00)* 2004 ECHR 294 (24 June 2004), <www.worldlii.org/eu/cases/ECHR/2004/294.html>; *von Hannover v Germany (No. 3)* [2013] ECHR 835 (19 September 2013), <www.bailii.org/eu/cases/ECHR/2013/835.html>.

Revenge Porn case: *Wilson v Ferguson* [2015] WASC 15 (16 January 2015), <www.austlii.edu.au/cgi-bin/sinodisp/au/cases/wa/WASC/2015/15.html>.

Royal Etchings case: *Prince Albert v Strange* [1849] EngR 255; (1849) 1 Mac & G 25; 41 ER 1171, <www.worldlii.org/int/cases/EngR/1849/255.pdf>.

Search Warrant case: *Smethurst v Commissioner of Police* [2020] HCA 14 (15 April 2020), <www.austlii.edu.au/cgi-bin/viewdoc/au/cases/cth/HCA/2020/14.html>.

Sex Tapes case: *Giller v Procopets* [2008] VSCA 236 (10 December 2008), <www.austlii.edu.au/cgi-bin/sinodisp/au/cases/vic/VSCA/2008/236.html>.

Supermodel case: *Campbell v MGN Ltd* [2004] UKHL 22 (6 May 2004), <www.bailii.org/uk/cases/UKHL/2004/22.html>.

Sussex cases: *Sussex v Associated Newspapers Ltd* [2021] EWHC 273 (Ch) (11 February 2021), <www.bailii.org/ew/cases/EWHC/Ch/2021/273.html>; HRH the Duchess of Sussex v Associated Newspapers Ltd [2021] EWCA Civ 1810 (2 December 2021), <www.bailii.org/cgi-bin/format.cgi?doc=/ew/cases/EWCA/Civ/2021/1810.html>.;

Thomas's case: *NewsGroup Newspapers Limited v Imogen Thomas* (2011) EWHC 1232 (QB) 2011 HQ11XO1432 (16 May 2011), <www.bailii.org/ew/cases/EWHC/QB/2011/1232.html>.

Three-way case: *PJS v News Group Newspapers Ltd* [2016] UKSC 26 (19 May 2016), <www.supremecourt.uk/cases/docs/uksc-2016-0080-judgment.pdf>.

Various claimants cases: *Jefferies & Anor v News Group Newspapers Ltd (Rev1)* [2021] EWHC 2187 (27 July 2021), <www.bailii.org/ew/cases/EWHC/Ch/2021/2187.html>.; *Various Claimants v Associated Newspapers Limited*: Galbraith, C. 2022,

'Press release: Various Claimants vs. Associated Newspapers Limited', *Hamlins LLP*, 6 October, <https://hamlins.com/press-release-various-claimants-vs-associated-newspapers-limited/>.

Victoria Park Racing case: *Victoria Park Racing and Recreation Grounds Co. Ltd v Taylor* [1937] 58 CLR 479 (26 August 1937), <www.austlii.edu.au/au/cases/cth/HCA/1937/45.html>.

8 Communicating justice

Key concepts

Open justice: The principle that the courts should remain open when feasible to public and media attendance and scrutiny.

Suppression orders: Orders by a judge or magistrate to prevent disclosure or publication about all or part of a case.

Contempt of court: Communications or behaviours that 'interfere with the proper administration of justice' or constitute a 'disregard for the authority of the court'.

Sub judice: From the Latin meaning 'under a judge' this area of contempt restricts the publication of material that is intended to, or has a 'real and definite tendency' to, prejudice an upcoming trial or (more generally) to interfere with the due administration of justice.

Contempt in the face of the court: Improper behaviour (usually in a courtroom) during a hearing that interferes with the administration of justice in the proceedings.

Scandalising the court: The publication of material that tends to undermine public confidence in the administration of justice.

Why examine the communication of crime and justice?

A book on communication law and ethics is incomplete without due consideration of the intersection between the media and the justice system. The news media and the courts have a responsibility to society – recognised in the principle known as 'open justice' – to show the community whether justice is being done. Of course, journalists must know the boundaries of their reportage in this sector. The charging of young journalist Krystal Johnson with contempt of court in Australia and the fine of $300,000 issued against her employer Yahoo! over her story that caused a murder trial to be aborted underscored the importance of knowing the legal limits of covering criminal cases (Krystal's case – see Key Case 8.2).

Public relations practitioners and social media content producers also need to know the terrain. They must understand what they can or cannot say when

DOI: 10.4324/9781003372752-10

a case involves a client or when drafting a media release about a crime. The policing and justice sector is also a common field of employment for public relations practitioners – as communication managers in policing agencies and as court information officers in justice departments. Such roles require expertise in what they might say about crimes or court cases – and how they might interact with journalists who are reporting such topics.

Philosophical background and human rights context of communicating crime and justice

Philosophers have long pondered the issues of crime and justice in society. The notion of justice was at the centre of ancient Western philosophers' thinking, especially in the development of virtue ethics we discussed in Chapter 1. In his *Nicomachean Ethics*, Aristotle saw a concept of universal justice as equating to 'virtue as a whole' because it encapsulated morality in terms of 'what we owe to each other' (Miller, 2021). In Roman times, the 6th century codification of law called the *Institutes of Justinian* defined 'justice' as 'the constant and perpetual will to render to each his due' (Miller, 2021).

To trace the development of philosophical thinking around the intersection between the media, free expression, crime and justice we need to look first to early scholars in jurisprudence (philosophy of law) and then to more recent work across the fields of philosophy, sociology, criminology and communication studies.

Much of the early legal thinking in this space related to the notion of 'open justice' – the principle that, wherever feasible, the courts should remain open to public and media attendance and scrutiny. It is a principle that still holds true in the courts of democratic societies today, with some notable exceptions. English Master of the Rolls, Lord Neuberger (2011), traced the history and modern application of open justice in an important lecture. It stems back to the earliest period of the English courts. Even in Saxon times (the 5th to 11th centuries), courts were constituted by the attendance of the people who gave their verdict, and in Norman times (the 11th and 12th centuries), the idea of a jury of 12 neighbours continued this open tradition. Sir William Holdsworth (1945: 156) recorded that, as early as the 16th century, the Star Chamber (a notorious English court) was routinely open to the public. Sir William Blackstone, in his *Commentaries on the Laws of England* (1765–1769: 373), wrote that the open examination of witnesses 'in the presence of all mankind, is much more conducive to the clearing up of truth'.

The 19th century legal scholar Jeremy Bentham wrote in his 1825 treatise on the need for publicity of the judicial process (at 477):

> In the darkness of secrecy, sinister interest and evil in every shape have full swing. Only in proportion as publicity has place can any of the checks applicable to judicial injustice operate. Where there is no publicity there is

no justice. ... Publicity is the very soul of justice. It is the keenest spur to exertion and the surest of all guards against improbity.

(Scott's case, 1913)

The open justice concept was tied closely to the notion that justice was compromised when conducted behind closed doors, because secrecy gave the impression that perhaps wrongdoing or bias was being allowed to creep into deliberations not subject to the public gaze. Such concern arose in a British case, the Sussex Justices case, in 1924 when Chief Justice Lord Hewart pronounced that 'justice should not only be done, but should manifestly and undoubtedly be seen to be done'.

In the modern era open justice has been enshrined in international human rights. Article 14 of the *International Covenant on Civil and Political Rights* (OHCHR, 1976) states that 'everyone shall be entitled to a fair and public hearing' and the press should only be excluded from trials when 'strictly necessary in the opinion of the court in special circumstances where publicity would prejudice the interests of justice'. Similar wording appears in human rights documents elsewhere, such as in the Victorian Charter of Human Rights and Responsibilities in Australia.

It is important that journalists and other professional communicators are aware of the principles of open justice because, as with freedom of the press, they might be called upon to defend them. Occasionally, judges and – much more frequently – magistrates are tempted to restrict the reportage of controversial or distressing cases. Unless they are reminded of the important role the media play in the administration of justice through the free and fair reporting of court cases, they may be tempted to agree to restrictions, often because the prosecution and defence have reached an agreement to consent to non-publication orders. Here a comment in the judgment of Sir Christopher Staughton in *Ex parte P* (1998) is relevant: 'When both sides agreed that information should be kept from the public that was when the court had to be most vigilant'.

While open justice persists to this day, it was only in more recent decades that scholars have considered the role of the media in the portrayal of crime and violence. Communication academics have considered it through lenses of criminology and sociology. Criminologist and cultural/media studies pioneer Stuart Hall turned his attention to media coverage of crime in his analysis of news reporting of muggings in the UK in the early 1970s. Hall pointed to the central role of the media in creating 'moral panic' – 'when a society enters a sort of self-produced spiral – a moral tail-spin – about a troubling issue' (Hall, 1975: 572). This set the scene for future scholarship on the morality and ethics of media coverage of crime. Ericson, Baranek and Chan (1987) went on to argue that the media's role in reporting crime and justice fulfils a function of social control: by reporting the consequences of deviant behaviour, it sends a message to the broader society that such behaviour is unacceptable. At the same time, it should serve to demonstrate that those falsely charged will be acquitted through the effective working of the justice system. While the media's role might be seen as such an agent of social control, there is no doubt that the legal system is also inherently newsworthy, providing both public-interest and economic reasons for reporting court. Court cases – large and small – help to sell newspapers, generate website traffic and social media sharing, and boost viewing and listening audiences. As Gregory (2005: 12) explained, court reports 'appeal to the voyeur in ordinary citizens'.

It is that notion of commercialised voyeurism that occupied the attention of moral philosopher Sissela Bok in her book *Mayhem – Violence as Public Entertainment* (1998). There, she argued:

While commercial linkages can put a damper on the most probing examination of the media's vested interests in entertainment violence, a desire to attract attention, to reach larger audiences, to break through walls of indifference, whether for reasons of public service or commercial gain, can also lead journalists to sensationalize their own coverage.

(Bok, 1998: 114)

Bok also flagged the potential for the psychological condition of 'vicarious trauma' to arise when children view violence on their home television screens (Bok, 1998: 65) and also perhaps among journalists covering (or editing material from) traumatic events (Bok, 1998: 114–115). Put simply, this means unethical reporting of violence, crime and justice can have detrimental mental health impacts on others, such as children and victims, and also upon the professional communicators themselves. It moots for mindful reflection upon the ethics of decisions in this space – both in the nature and the quantity of the coverage – to enhance the resilience of the practitioner, as foreshadowed in Chapter 3.

Conflict has been widely identified as a core news value (O'Neill and Harcup, 2009). Both crime coverage and the court system are replete with conflict. Violent crime in the form of murder and assault in all its forms is self-explanatory. As for the justice system, the British-based system of law found in the US, UK, Australia, Canada and New Zealand, reflects the medieval justice system it replaced: the duel. This adversarial system, involving two distinct sides to any case, lends itself to a news portrayal as a battle of words and evidence, with clear winners and losers. Of course, this might not be the optimal method of coverage, but it helps to explain how the news ingredient of conflict is often highlighted. Audiences enjoy the theatre of the courtroom and the drama of people's lives that has led them there – theft, arguments, assault, deceit, vice and murder. Court reporting keeps judges under public scrutiny and also helps ratings and circulation. But the media sometimes overstep the mark – and in the modern era it is usually judges and magistrates performing the philosophical role of adjusting the levers of open justice, free expression and the right to a fair trial as they ponder granting suppression orders or contempt charges or close courts to the public or the media.

Ethical codes, regulation of crime and court coverage and a solutions approach

Journalism and public relations ethical codes in most countries do not address the issues of crime and justice directly – however they typically use the words 'fairness' and 'honesty' as expectations of ethical practitioners. This feeds into the work professional communicators do in their reporting or managing the communications in the realm of crime and justice. However, the journalism codes typically balance those requirements of fairness and accuracy with the need to fulfill the 'public's right to know' and to act in the 'public interest'. While the principle of open justice certainly embraces the public's right to know, media coverage of crime too often confuses the 'public interest' with 'public curiosity'. Other clauses counsel journalists against discriminatory language, however discrimination can come at a broader ethical level in crime and court reportage – such as media profiling of 'muggers' as being of a particular racial or demographic class (Hall, 1975: 571–572).

Broadcast regulators in all countries attempt to play a role in limiting the viewing by children of violent news material. For example, in the US the broadcast and cable television industries developed voluntary TV Parental Guidelines to rate violent, sexual and indecent programming, approved by the Federal Communications Commission (FCC) in 1998. From 2000, all television sets were required to carry a 'v-chip' – circuitry detecting programme ratings and blocking channels carrying violent material during certain time periods. However, this does not apply to Internet or social media content.

Violent graphic material broadcast on the Internet and social media is harder to regulate, although governments have tried. For example, the Australian government passed a law in 2019 – the Criminal Code Amendment (Sharing of Abhorrent Violent Material) Bill – requiring major platforms like Facebook and Google to remove live-streamed material, following the use of that technology by the shooter who killed 50 people in a massacre in New Zealand that year.

Change need not only come from ethics and regulation. It can also emanate from new models of reporting. 'Solutions journalism' and 'constructive journalism' – approaches focussing on social policy changes using local voices instead of upon the sensationalised news reporting of crime – promise some answers. A study conducted in the notoriously crime-ridden area of South Los Angeles showed respondents associated typical news stories about their neighbourhood as including violence, death, robbery, crime, drugs, gangs, prostitution and police brutality (Wenzel et al, 2018: 665). They welcomed an alternative type of news story discussing initiatives quoting local voices about a solutions-oriented proposal to convert vacant lots into community parks so students had safe places to play (Wenzel et al., 2018: 657). Similar 'big picture' and policy-driven approaches to stories about crimes and court cases and trends, with suggested policy solutions, can be used as an alternative model to the daily coverage of crime creating fear and moral panic. Sometimes the communication about these topics enters the sensitive domain of mental health and suicide reporting. Professional communicators need to be aware of the appropriate behavioural strategies and language usage in these important areas. For guidance on the reporting of mental health and suicide, communicators should consult Mindframe Guidelines (<https://mindframe.org.au/guidelines >), the result of an Australian project designed to encourage responsible coverage of suicide and mental illness. We look more closely at those guidelines in Chapter 11 in the context of discrimination and cyberbullying.

Reflect – Research – Review:

A local teacher has approached you as a suburban newspaper reporter to tell you that there has been a spike in the number of senior high school students experiencing bipolar disorder and taking their own lives and suggests you do a story to cover it. Consult the Mindframe Guidelines (<https://mindframe.org.au/guidelines>) and write a research plan on how you might approach this assignment from a solutions, constructive or mindful journalism perspective.

Law, cases and examples internationally

The legal restrictions on covering crime and the courts vary considerably across major Western jurisdictions, but the foundations of the law in the English-speaking world are similar. The US has diverged considerably from other jurisdictions in the freedom it allows in its coverage of major criminal trials as a result of the incorporation of the First Amendment enshrining press freedom into its Constitution in 1791 – so much so that some critics coined the expression 'trial by media' to describe the high level of sensationalised coverage. Here is an introduction to some of the key legal constraints on the media reporting of crime and the courts internationally.

Open justice

As mentioned, open justice is the principle under which the judicial process should be transparent and open to public examination, enshrined in international human rights instruments. Ordinary people should be able to sit in court and watch cases as they unfold. The media are the 'eyes and ears' of citizens who cannot be in the courtroom to witness proceedings themselves. While senior judges internationally endorse the principle, they are also quick to apply exceptions to the rule in the interests of justice. The most notable is the issuing of a 'suppression order' (sometimes called a 'gag order', or a 'stop writ') which prevents publication of all or part of a case.

Contempt of court

Those who interfere with the administration of justice – either through their behaviour or their publishing – can face the ancient charge of contempt of court. Contempt has been defined as 'Words or actions which interfere with the proper administration of justice or constitute a disregard for the authority of the court' (Butt and Nygh, 2004). The reason why this area of law is of special concern to the media is that so much of a journalist's work relates in some way to the justice system: reporting crimes, covering court cases, scrutinising the workings of the courts and sometimes even appearing in court as a witness. Public relations consultants occasionally have to navigate the judicial system when a client appears in court. Some professional communicators deal with the courts and contempt restrictions daily – as crime or court reporters, as public information officers (PIO) for the various court systems or by working in a police media branch.

Contempt deals with a range of actions with the potential to impair the administration of justice. The laws of contempt try to balance fundamental rights and freedoms – including freedom of expression (and of the press), an individual's right to a fair trial, the public's right to be informed of the workings of the legal and political process, journalists' interests in maintaining confidentiality – particularly for protected sources – and the general community's need to be assured of the effective administration of justice.

The original purpose of contempt law was to establish and maintain the authority of the court by punishing those whose actions were disrespectful. Arlidge and Eady (1982) report that as early as the 12th century, the *Treatise on the Laws and Customs of the Kingdom of England* (known as 'Glanvill') referred to '*contemptus curiae*', meaning the contempt shown by a party in failing to appear before a court. Contempts recorded through the Middle Ages concerned direct physical or verbal threats to the authority of the court, such as drawing a sword or throwing a brickbat to strike a judge; assaulting clerks, jurors, witnesses or opposing parties; or writing letters deriding judges. Modern contempt law is still premised on an underlying need to preserve the dignified authority of the administration of justice.

There are five key types of contempt that can impact media coverage:

1. *Disobedience contempt:* failure to comply with a court order or undertaking given to a court, such as refusing to answer a question in court or to deliver notes or other materials to a court or quasi-judicial body (we dealt with journalists' refusal to reveal their confidential sources to a court in Chapter 6);
2. *Sub judice contempt:* publishing material that tends to prejudice the right of an accused to a fair trial;
3. *Contempt in the face of the court:* improper behaviour in or near a courtroom during a hearing;

4. *Scandalising the court:* publishing allegations that tend to undermine public confidence in the administration of justice; and
5. *Revealing jury deliberations:* In English-based jurisdictions, the discussions of jurors in reaching their verdicts are strictly confidential. (Some US states allow much more media contact with jurors.)

We deal with each in turn.

Disobedience contempt

This can arise in situations beyond a journalist's refusal to a court to reveal their confidential sources discussed in Chapter 6. It can also happen when a professional communicator disobeys a suppression order, a situation that has resulted in the jailing and fining of journalists in many countries in recent years.

Case example:

Facebook Juror case (2011): Manchester mother of three, Joanne Fraill, 40, was sentenced to eight months in prison by London's High Court in 2011 for exchanging Facebook messages with the accused in a drug trial while she was serving on the jury, against the instructions of the judge to refrain from using the Internet.

Sub judice *contempt*

The legal system enshrines the principle that an accused person should be considered innocent until proven guilty in court on the basis of admissible evidence considered (in the case of serious indictable offences) by a jury of twelve fellow citizens. In 1811, Lord Ellenborough put it this way in Fisher's case:

> If anything is more important than another in the administration of justice, it is that jurymen should come to the trial of those persons on whose guilt or innocence they are to decide, with minds pure and unprejudiced.

The Latin phrase *sub judice* translates as 'under or before a judge or court' (NSWLRC, 2000: 8), and applies to the period during which there are limitations placed on what the media may report about a case. The courts have attempted to balance the competing rights and interests of those involved in court cases and those reporting on them by restricting what may be published about a case while it is before the courts. Adverse or sensational publicity interferes with the usual safeguards on the fair trial of an accused person, with potentially dire consequences for the case at hand and for public confidence in the administration of justice.

The practical concern the courts have here is the potential influence such a media trial might have on current or prospective jurors (and, to a lesser degree, on witnesses or even parties to the case, or their legal representatives). The fear is that their judgement (in the case of jurors) or testimony (in the case of witnesses) might be tainted – or even *be seen* to be tainted – by media coverage of the case which might 'poison the fountain of justice before it begins to flow', as one judge expressed it (Parke's case, 1903).

There are differences across jurisdictions in the handling of prejudicial publicity. In the US, given the strong First Amendment free expression influence, a media report must present a 'clear and present danger' to a trial before there will be proceedings for contempt. Contempt by publication has been prosecuted most often in the United Kingdom and Commonwealth countries, although many other countries have laws against publications that might seriously damage a trial. In the UK, *sub judice* contempt has been covered by legislation since the enactment of the *Contempt of Court Act 1981*, and by the balance of the respective fair trial and free expression rights in the *Human Rights Act 1998*. Australia, South Africa and Canada have been guided by the case law prior to those UK developments, and authorities typically will not move to proceed with a contempt charge unless the publication is *intended* to interfere with the administration of justice or *presents a real and substantial risk* to a trial, or a *real and definite tendency* to prejudice it. Proceedings in Australia are considered *sub judice* from when they are 'pending', whereas in the UK the restrictions start when they are 'imminent', while in Canada the starting point is ambiguous. This can affect a media organisation's responsibility to take down or withdraw prejudicial material they are about to publish the instant an accused has been arrested or charged with a serious crime.

In Australia and the UK there is a public-interest defence to *sub judice* contempt, whereby measured discussion of a pending case is allowed if there is an overriding matter of public interest at issue after balancing free expression and fair trial interests. In New Zealand, contempt was codified in the *Contempt of Court Act 2019*, and only applies if there is a real risk of prejudice to a jury trial of a higher-level offence. Ignorance of the trial and a fair report of court proceedings are defences. Online publishers can claim immunity for offences by third party offenders using their sites if they were unaware of the material. Sossin and Crystal (2013) provide a useful comparison of the sub judice contempt laws across major English-speaking jurisdictions.

In summary, key considerations for professional communicators in the realm of *sub judice* contempt include the following:

- Publicity suggesting the accused is guilty – or even innocent – can be considered prejudicial to the administration of justice.
- A media outlet is liable for *sub judice* contempt even when it is merely reporting the contemptuous comments of others, except as part of a fair and accurate court report.

- The fact that police or other official sources provided the *sub judice* material for publication is no defence.
- It is no excuse that other media organisations had already reported the matter or that it was widely circulated on social media.
- Ignorance is no defence in most places: newspapers and digital media are expected to check for themselves to see whether proceedings are pending and whether relevant orders have been made.
- The fact that the *sub judice* material is later proved to be true is no defence. At issue is the risk of prejudice to the proceedings at the time of publication.

Case example:

***Evening Standard* case (1924)**: The courts are particularly concerned that the media do not become a second-rate, de facto criminal investigative body, making their own inquiries to solve crimes and jeopardising the official criminal investigation. This point was established in this case, where three English newspapers were fined for publishing the results of their independent investigations into a murder when the police had already charged someone. The sensational reports had the tendency to prejudice the trial.

Key Case 8.1: The *Sunday Times* case

Attorney-General v Times Newspapers Ltd [1974] AC 273.

Facts

The British drug company Distillers had manufactured and sold a drug containing thalidomide, which was used by women to prevent morning sickness in the early stages of pregnancy. Between 1959 and 1961 the use of thalidomide resulted in 451 babies being born with deformed limbs or organs. The ensuing legal action by parents against the company dragged on, and in 1972 there were still claims pending. The *Sunday Times* newspaper in London launched a series of articles investigating the saga and compared Distillers' relatively small compensation payouts with its huge profits over the period. The articles were met by complaints from the company but prompted no official action at that stage. Anticipating potential difficulty, the newspaper then warned the Attorney-General it was about to publish a hard-hitting article questioning Distillers' actions prior to putting the drug on the market and putting a case for the victims to get much greater compensation. Distillers obtained an injunction preventing publication of the article on the grounds it was *sub judice*. The appeal process eventually reached the House of Lords.

Law

The House of Lords ordered that the injunction (non-publication order) should stand because the proposed article discussed issues central to the case that the courts had yet to consider. The judges made the following points:

- The media should not be allowed to prejudge a case.
- Issues of public interest will be relevant in deciding whether a publication is in contempt.
- In this case justice was better served by postponing discussion until after the courts had considered the matter.

The International Court of Justice later disagreed with this ruling on free expression grounds, but its decision was not binding. This historic case is at one extreme of the *sub judice* scale. Courts today would place more emphasis on the important issue of public interest which would likely override the *sub judice* concerns.

Lessons for communicators

The lesson is that the courts sometimes have a very different view from the news media about what is in the public interest. Even on an important matter of genuine public concern, such reporting should be approached without attempting to prejudge a case.

Contempt in the face of the court

Almost any behaviour that disrupts the courtroom can be considered a 'contempt in the face of the court'. This branch of contempt law is directed at behaviour in or near the actual courtroom that interferes with the administration of justice. It has been defined as:

> Improper behaviour in court. Anything done to interrupt significantly the smooth and appropriately dignified hearing of a case in a courtroom risks being treated as contempt and punished accordingly.
>
> (ALRC, 1987: 3)

Examples have included outright physical assaults in the courtroom, verbal abuse, inappropriate dress, sleeping and even attempting to release laughing gas into the court building. In recent decades, people have been convicted in India, the US and the UK because their mobile phones rang in court. Judges have a wide discretion in determining what is unacceptable behaviour in court that actually interferes with the administration of justice.

Scandalising the court

This type of contempt can be committed by publishing material that scandalises the courts or judges by abusing them in scurrilous terms, alleging they are corrupt or lack integrity, or that they have bowed to outside influences in reaching their decisions. Historically, the courts have been tolerant of reasonable criticism. Lord Atkin summed the approach up well with this quote in 1936 in Ambard's case: 'Justice is not a cloistered virtue; she must be allowed to suffer the scrutiny and respectful, though outspoken, comments of ordinary men'.

Revealing jury deliberations

In most of the English-speaking world apart from the US, the identification of jurors and coverage of their decision-making processes is prohibited. Numerous laws prohibit identifying or communicating with jurors and legal advice should be sought before publishing any material that may have come from jurors, even if it was unsolicited.

> **Reflect – Research – Review:**
>
> You overhear a juror in a high-profile murder trial explaining to friends at a social gathering that the jury foreman bullied her and the other jurors into deciding on a guilty verdict. What steps will you take as a reporter or news blogger, and what issues arise?

Court reporting privileges and practice

Universally throughout the English-speaking world, journalists are allowed to attend court to write fair and accurate reports about proceedings. In granting the public and journalists access to the courts, society is striking a balance between the right of an accused to a fair trial, their privacy and an untarnished reputation, against the right of the press to report on a case so that the public can see justice taking its course in the tradition of open justice. Accurate reporting of a trial also enhances its 'fairness' by putting every important aspect of the trial on the public record. While in some people's eyes court reporting might be about economics and entertainment, the ethical and mindful journalist or communicator trying to report court is faced with balancing these pressures against a duty to present matters of genuine public interest both fairly and accurately. Covering only selected cases, perhaps only in part, can lead to allegations of unfair reporting from both the public and the judiciary, and possible loss of fair report protection. Professional communicators other than journalists need to be careful when reporting upon cases in which they have some kind of vested interest. For example, the fair reporting defence to both defamation and *sub judice* contempt might be lost if you publish a media release or blog about a court case involving a competitor, perhaps focussed only on the aspects of testimony favourable to your client. Most jurisdictions now allow journalists to use their devices in court, at least for the accurate recording of notes, if not for broadcast or social media dissemination. Rules on both vary markedly across jurisdictions.

Identification restrictions

Restrictions on the publication of the identities of those involved in different types of cases vary markedly between jurisdictions. The ban on the identity of sexual assault victims is almost universal, however even that can vary in terms of whether the accused is also non-identifiable in the early stages of proceedings and whether the victim is allowed to self-identify during or after a trial. The main statutory restrictions a communicator can expect to encounter in most places – and of which every reporter should be aware – concern the identities of parties to sexual offences, children, divorce cases, custody disputes, inquests, mental health proceedings, jurors, some bail hearings, national security cases and official secrets material. Sometimes matters can be reported, but on an anonymised basis. In other situations, it is not just the identity of parties that is suppressed; the court's doors are closed to both the public and the media.

Case examples:

Voyeur case (2018): A Welsh newspaper editor lost his appeal against a conviction for naming a sexual offence victim after various details about the relationship between a victim and defendant were published in the newspaper's report about a man convicted of voyeurism. He had already been convicted of identifying a youth offender in another newspaper and he was ordered to pay the equivalent of more than A$10,000 in court costs and compensation (*BBC News*, 2018).

Facebook streaming case (2019): A far-right activist who live-streamed aggressively outside the public court entrance during a trial of Muslim men for sexual crimes was eventually jailed for nine months after a High Court trial on a range of charges related to interfering with the course of justice by intimidating the accused and breaching a reporting restriction.

Reflect – Research – Review:

Find the legislation for your jurisdiction controlling the reporting of sexual offences, children in court, jurors' deliberations, mental health, family law matters or coronial inquests into suicides, and explain how their operation might affect your communication about a case.

Basic Australian legal principles and cases in crime and court reporting

Peculiarities of Australian law in the realm of crime and court reporting abound. It is important for professional communicators to learn the laws as they apply to their own jurisdictions and those they are publishing into. Legal advice is required for any attempts at pushing the boundaries.

Open justice

As mentioned, open justice is the principle under which the judicial process should be transparent and open to public examination, enshrined in international human rights instruments. Former NSW Chief Justice Jim Spigelman (2005) said that the principle that justice must be seen to be done 'is one of the most pervasive axioms of the administration of common law systems'. The High Court has made several pronouncements on the importance of open justice, including in Zhao's case (2015), where it stated that 'the rationale of the open court principle is that court proceedings should be subjected to public and professional scrutiny, and courts will not act contrary to the principle save in exceptional circumstances'. Chief Justice French stated that the right to publish a report of proceedings is a corollary of the right to attend and observe them (Sex Offenders case, 2011: para. 22). Open justice includes the right to identify parties to court proceedings as part of a report. While the principle may be overridden by statute in certain circumstances, any provision purporting to do so must show a clear intention on the part of parliament to displace the principle.

Case example:

Raybos's case (1985): The defendant, a solicitor named Bernard Patrick Jones, sought a court order suppressing the publication of his name. In refusing the application, Justice Kirby famously stated:

Widespread publicity, through the modern media of communications, may do great harm. Sometimes quite unjustifiable damage can be inflicted on individuals. However that may be, a price must be paid for the open administration, particularly of criminal justice. The alternative, of secret trials, where important public rights may be in competition and individual liberty may be at risk is so unacceptable that courts of our tradition will tend to avoid the consequence.

At common law a court must be satisfied that an order restricting access or reporting is strictly necessary to ensure the administration of justice in the circumstances. In the Idoport case (2001) NSW Supreme Court Justice Einstein identified six limited exceptions to the open justice principle – types of cases where a court might be closed or a suppression order might be issued:

1. Those involving trade secrets, secret documents or communications;
2. Extortion (blackmail) cases, where public disclosure would undermine the whole purpose of the action;
3. Where there is an overriding need to maintain order in the court;
4. Some cases involving national security;
5. Those with administrative actions that may best be dealt with in chambers; and
6. Guardianship cases over wards of the state or mental illness.

While Justice Einstein's list reflects the position at common law, communicators need to bear in mind the forest of statutory restrictions on publication which differ markedly from state to state. In 2009, the Australian Law Reform Commission (ALRC) identified more than 500 secrecy provisions in 176 pieces of primary and subordinate legislation, with hundreds more at the state and territory levels (ALRC, 2009). Sometimes courts will issue a notice to 'take down' certain material from a site or to shut down the whole site. Such orders are sometimes issued to the Internet Service Provider (ISP) or search engine host, but will not usually be ordered if the action would be 'futile', because the material had already been published far and wide.

Case example:

Ibrahim's case (2012): A court can order an internet content host to remove material on the grounds of prejudice to a forthcoming trial, but they must have been made aware of the suppression order and would not be subjected to orders if they were 'futile' – in other words, if the material was readily available and easily searched by prospective jurors beyond the jurisdiction where the suppression order had been issued.

Reflect – Research – Review:

Given the number of exceptions to the open justice principle, do you think it still has force, or has it become mere rhetoric? Explain.

Contempt of court

Powers to charge and adjudicate on the five main areas of contempt of court affecting professional communicators in Australia stem from a combination of case law, legislation and court rules in the various jurisdictions.

Disobedience contempt

Beyond those refusing to reveal their sources mentioned in Chapter 6, many disobedience contempt cases in Australia have related to journalists and other citizens disobeying other orders of the court – such as a suppression order.

Case examples:

Rape Priors case (2013): The Australian journalist and blogger Derryn Hinch was fined $100,000 (and then jailed for 100 days for not paying the fine) for breaching a suppression order by revealing details of the criminal history of a man accused of rape and murder in Melbourne.

Pell suppression case (2021): Twelve of Australia's leading news groups were fined a total of more than $1 million for breaching suppression orders related to the trial of the late Cardinal George Pell on sexual abuse charges (on which he was later acquitted).

Sub judice *contempt*

In Australia, the sub judice period starts when a matter is 'pending' – when the accused has been arrested *or* charged.

Case example:

James' case (1963): The High Court held that an article published while a 'manhunt' was in progress after a double murder was not in contempt because the proceedings were not 'pending', as no warrant had been issued for the suspect's arrest. They were certainly 'imminent', however, as an arrest occurred within a day of the publication and police were on the suspect's trail.

Journalists and police media personnel are best advised to be cautious, and to consider that the restricted period starts from the moment of arrest, as it can be difficult to establish the point at which charges have been laid. That was certainly the message of the NSW Court of Appeal in Mason's case (1990), when it identified the moment of arrest as the starting point 'when the criminal law was set in motion'. Once proceedings are 'pending', and until facts related to a crime are actually mentioned in open court, the media are restricted to reporting just the 'bare facts' of the crime. These were described in Packer's case (1912) as being 'extrinsic ascertained facts to which any eyewitness could bear testimony, such as the finding of a body and its condition, the place in which it is found, the persons by whom it was found, the arrest of a person accused, and so on'. But journalists cannot report on any fact that might be contested in court, and certainly not on facts that might indicate guilt or innocence, most importantly including any prior criminal record or alleged confession. The *sub judice* period ends when the proceedings are no longer considered to be 'under a judge'. This is also a grey area, particularly when cases may be subject to appeal or retrial.

By far the most concern has been about safeguarding the process of criminal trials, and this is where journalists and bloggers need to be particularly careful. If proceedings are pending, it is a contempt to:

- publish material *intending* to prejudice the trial, or
- publish material that *has a tendency* to do so.

The former requires proof of *mens rea* (guilty mind), consisting of an intention to prejudice the proceedings, while for the latter it need only be proven that the act of publication was intentional, regardless of whether the publisher intended to prejudice proceedings.

Just how likely must prejudice be for the courts to deem a publication contemptuous? High Court Justices Gageler and Keane stated in the Crime Commission case (2013) that such a contempt occurs 'only when there is an actual interference with the administration of justice', or 'a real risk, as opposed to a remote possibility', of such an interference. They continued that

> the 'essence' of contempt of that kind is a 'real and definite tendency to prejudice or embarrass pending proceedings' involving 'as a matter of practical reality, a tendency to interfere with the due course of justice in a particular case'.

The courts take into account a number of relevant factors in determining whether there is such a real possibility of prejudice, including the prominence of the item printed or broadcast; the images accompanying it; the time lapse between publication and likely trial; the social prominence of the maker of contemptuous statements; the extent of existing pre-trial publicity; and the extent or area of publication.

Case examples:

Mason's case (1990): The NSW Attorney-General charged two newspapers and four television stations with contempt over their coverage of an alleged murderer's 'walk through' of the crime scene after he had been charged but before his trial. The outlets with the less sensational reports attracted lower fines ($75,000 as against $200,000). Police media personnel should avoid such parades of the accused.

Rape Priors case (2013): While this was used an example of the breach of a suppression order, blogger Derryn Hinch was found not guilty on a *sub judice* contempt charge because his posts did not have a tendency to prejudice potential jurors because of: the small readership of the article; the period of delay between the publication of the article and the likely trial date of the accused; and other prejudicial material about the accused circulating in the media and social media at the time.

Contempt charges are normally not pursued in judge-only trials because it is jurors and witnesses who are seen as most vulnerable to prejudicial publicity. It is now well established that judges and magistrates are not considered susceptible to media influence because of their legal training. *Sub judice* contempt charges are also very rarely pressed in civil matters.

However, witnesses can be influenced, so photographs or drawings of the accused cannot be published if identification may be an issue at the trial, even if it is a judge-only trial. The media routinely 'pixelate' the faces of the accused once they have been arrested, even where there has already been wide publication of identifying material during a 'manhunt' for a suspect.

Case example:

Who Weekly case (1994): The publisher of *Who Weekly* magazine faced contempt charges over its cover photograph of Ivan Milat, later convicted of the 'backpacker serial killings' in the Belanglo State Forest in NSW between 1989 and 1992. Unknown to the publisher, a single identification witness, Paul Onions, had been brought out from England for the trial. The magazine's publisher was fined $100,000 and its editor $10,000 for this error of judgement. The publication came in a crucial time zone – after Milat had been arrested and charged, but before his trial. Identification was going to be crucial. The court ruled that publication of a picture of an accused person would normally be regarded as carrying a risk of interference with the due course of justice, unless the identification were so clear-cut that neither party would dispute it. Milat died in jail in 2019.

There are two possible defences that can be raised against *sub judice* contempt charges in Australia. The first is clear-cut: a fair and accurate report of what has been said in open court – the basis of the court reports you see and hear on the news media. The second is more difficult to establish: that there was some overriding public interest at stake in continuing discussion of some larger public issue, that the *sub judice* report formed part of that discussion, and that any effect on the due administration of justice was an incidental and unintended by-product of that discussion (Bread Manufacturers case, 1937).

Case example:

Hinch's case (1987): Then Melbourne radio journalist Derryn Hinch had made three *sub judice* broadcasts relating to an upcoming trial of a former Catholic priest, Father Michael Glennon, on child molestation charges. In the broadcasts, Hinch named the accused and detailed previous charges Glennon had faced, including some for which he had been jailed. Hinch questioned why a person with such a record should continue in his role as governing director of a youth foundation, particularly when facing further charges. Parts of the broadcast either stated or implied the priest was guilty. The thrust of the broadcasts was, in the words of High Court Chief Justice Mason, to highlight the danger to children and to question why Glennon should continue in his position. The court ruled that although the Bread Manufacturers (1937) public-interest defence could be extended from civil matters to apply to a criminal case, Hinch had overstepped the mark by pre-judging Glennon's guilt. He might have qualified for the defence if he had just called for him to step down from his position. Hinch was jailed for 28 days. Glennon narrowly lost his High Court appeal against his conviction on the grounds of the prejudicial publicity and died in jail in 2014 (Glennon's case, 1992).

Key Case 8.2: Krystal's case (2016–2017)

DPP v Johnson & Yahoo! [2016] VSC 699 (28 November 2016) <www.austlii.edu.au/cgi-bin/viewdoc/au/cases/vic/VSC/2016/699.html>

DPP v Johnson & Yahoo! (No. 2) [2017] VSC 45 (17 February 2017) <www.austlii.edu.au/cgi-bin/viewdoc/au/cases/vic/VSC/2017/45.html>

Facts

Journalist Krystal Johnson uploaded to the Yahoo! website an article titled 'Man Paused to Take "Smoke Break" While Bashing Girlfriend to Death' on the second day of the Melbourne trial of Mataio Aleluia for the murder of Brittany Harvie. Under the sub-heading 'Brittany Harvie predicted her death on Facebook', the article presented social media posts in which the victim had made chilling predictions of her death at the hands of the accused, taken from media coverage after she had been killed. The posts suggested a history of violence against the victim by the accused, even though the highly prejudicial evidence had not been presented to the jury and the prosecutor did not intend to present it. The judge was alerted to the article four days after its publication and decided after submissions that the jury should be discharged.

Law

Victorian Supreme Court Justice John Dixon was satisfied beyond reasonable doubt that the publication 'objectively and as a matter of practical reality, had a real and definite tendency to prejudice the trial of the accused' (Krystal's case 2: para. 1). He reached this conclusion after offering a useful summary of the fifteen key elements of *sub judice* contempt (Krystal's case 1: para. 24). He decided the article still had a 'real and definite tendency to prejudice the trial', despite the fact that the jury had been instructed not to access the internet and to disregard publicity about the case; that the article was only viewed by about 4,000 people; and that other historic articles containing the offending material could still be accessed at the time of the trial. Both Johnson and her employer Yahoo! were found guilty of contempt of court. He fined Yahoo! $300,000 but allowed Johnson to undertake to enter a two-year good behaviour bond which, if she complied, would lead to the dismissal of the charge.

Lessons for professional communicators

Quite apart from the useful summary of the principles of *sub judice* contempt, the case had very important lessons for those covering crime and court. First, it underscored the fundamental principle that reports of criminal cases after a jury has been empanelled should be limited to fair and accurate coverage of the content of each day's proceedings in a trial – and only material that has been presented in open court in the presence of the jury. This demands a reporter's physical attendance at a court case and requires that they do not recycle material from earlier coverage.

Second, the judge found serious flaws in Yahoo!'s editorial checking mechanisms. Resources and deadline pressures meant the inexperienced reporter uploaded the article directly to the website when it should have been checked by a more senior editor. Legal advice had not been sought prior to publication, which the company agreed to make available in future instances when required. Justice Dixon observed, 'Time pressures inherent to the media's work must be balanced against the responsibility to ensure that the appropriate checks are in place' (Krystal's case 2: para. 29).

Contempt in the face of the court

Many a rookie journalist has approached court reporting duties with trepidation worried that some minor breach of court etiquette might land them in jail for contempt in the face of the court at the whim of a belligerent judge or magistrate. Such concern is largely unjustified, as charges for 'contempt in the face of the court' have normally been pressed against those appearing in court or their lawyers, and usually when emotions have been running high.

Case examples:

Indigenous Laughing case (2017): An Aboriginal land rights activist was jailed for two hours after defying a Gympie magistrate by laughing at him in the courtroom. Gary Tomlinson (also known as 'Wit-boooka') had challenged the authority of the court to hear public nuisance and trespass offences related to a protest at Gympie Regional Council.

NT Homeless 'Genius' case (2017): A homeless man, self-described genius and would-be mayoral candidate who continuously insulted court officers, interrupted the judge and disrobed in court was twice jailed for contempt in the face of the court. His appeals failed against his total of five months' contempt sentence and alleged bias against him.

Journalists are warned to show respect in the courtroom. This includes paying attention to the proceedings, remaining clothed and avoiding throwing projectiles at the magistrate.

Scandalising the court

The term 'scandalising the court' was described in the High Court in Dunbabin's case in 1935 as applying to:

> publications which tend to detract from the authority and influence of judicial determinations, publications calculated to impair the confidence of the people in the Court's judgments because the matter published aims at lowering the authority of the Court as a whole or that of its judges and excites misgivings as to the integrity, propriety and impartiality brought to the exercise of the judicial office.

The basic principles have been described as being the upholding of free speech while preserving the administration of justice, but not merely to protect the 'individual person' of the judge (Anissa case, 1999). Instead, magistrates have the right to sue in defamation for assaults on their character (O'Shane's case, 2013). Journalists and media advisers need to ensure that any criticism of the judiciary and the legal system is carefully phrased and measured so it does not unfairly imply any wrongdoing that might erode public confidence. It is a defence to a charge of scandalising the court if you can prove that the substance of your criticisms was true or that they were made in good faith, were honestly held, fairly expressed and did not imply improper motives on the part of the judiciary.

Case examples:

BLF cases (1972 and 1983): The two classic cases in this area in Australia are known as the BLF cases, as both involved trade union leaders from the Builders' Labourers Federation (BLF). In each case, the accused had made comments (which were then published) implying judges had bowed to union pressure in reaching their decisions. In the first, official Jack Mundey was acquitted of contempt despite calling the judge a racist in the context of protests against South Africa's apartheid regime. He had not accused him of racist bias in the case, so it was not scandalising. In the second, union boss Norm Gallagher was sentenced to three months in jail for suggesting a court had bowed to union strike action in reaching its decision.

Liberal Ministers' case (2017): The Victorian Court of Appeal issued a public statement warning of potential *sub judice* and scandalising contempt charges against three Commonwealth ministers who had implied on social media that the Supreme Court would issue a lesser penalty against terrorists because the judges were left-wing appointments and had an ideological agenda. The court asserted the statements were 'calculated to improperly undermine public confidence in the administration of justice'. The comments had been quoted in an article in *The Australian* titled 'Judiciary "Light on Terrorism"'. The charges were not pursued after the newspaper and the ministers eventually apologised.

Talkback case (2006): Veteran Adelaide broadcaster Bob Francis was given a nine-week suspended jail sentence and fined $20,000 over a programme in which he criticised a magistrate for considering granting bail to a man accused of possessing child pornography. Francis told his audience, 'Oh, smash the judge's face in'. The magistrate also settled out of court for a reported $110,000 defamation payout (McGarry, 2006).

While it is technically a different form of contempt, it is also an offence to bring improper pressure upon parties in a proceeding. That was the accusation against the political satirist Jordan Shanks during his defence of a defamation case brought by politician John Barilaro, when the court referred him and Google for possible contempt charges over online materials he published alleged to be pressuring the plaintiff (Friendlyjordies case, 2022).

Revealing jury deliberations

Identification of jurors is prohibited in most jurisdictions in Australia, but there are variations. In Queensland, you cannot publish any information identifying a juror or information about what went on during a jury's deliberations, but jurors can identify themselves (and be identified) as former jurors after proceedings have ended. In NSW, nobody can seek information from jurors, even after a trial has concluded, but a jury's deliberations can be revealed after a trial if the information is volunteered by a juror who does not receive a fee or reward in return. Journalists should seek legal advice before dealing with jurors in any way at all, even if the jurors have approached them.

Case example:

John Laws case (2000): Sydney broadcaster John Laws had his staff phone a former juror on a murder trial so he could interview her. He was given a 15-month suspended sentence as the approach to a juror was in breach of the NSW *Jury Act 1977*. If the former juror had taken the initiative and approached Laws independently, the broadcaster would have been free to broadcast her remarks.

Reflect – Research – Review:

Search online and find a recent example of contempt of court. Compare and contrast it with one of the cases in this chapter.

Covering court cases and performing court communication roles

Australia's states, territories and Commonwealth vary markedly in the privileges they allow the media in reporting court, and the restrictions they place upon them. Journalists and court Public Information Officers (PIOs) are advised to check carefully court rules and legislation in your jurisdiction. Given Internet and social media posts go everywhere, it is safest to work to the most conservative law in operation at any time.

Photography is allowed outside the courthouse on public property, but photographers and camera personnel should approach subjects with care and be aware of the legal risks of identification. All courts prohibit the use of devices to take visual images or footage in the courtroom and courts vary on the extent to which they allow journalists to use social media during a trial. Several courts stream judges' delivery of judgements and sentencing remarks for media use. The advent of streamed court proceedings during the COVID-19 pandemic led to courts developing new rules preventing media from screen-capturing or recording proceedings for publication or broadcast.

Journalists have no special rights in the courtroom, but they *may* be granted some privileges as media representatives, such as priority seating, permission to take notes, carry communication devices and post social media updates from court, and access documents and court personnel. These can help improve the accuracy and fairness of a story. PR personnel might not be afforded the special media privileges given to journalists in the same courtroom. Courts in most jurisdictions now allow accredited media to use their digital devices to record the audio of proceedings for the sake of accuracy, but not for broadcast.

Key court documents that journalists access are the summary and charge sheets, statements of facts, court lists (or 'cause lists' in some places) and, when available, transcripts. Journalists' level of access to court documents will vary. Access is sometimes taken away, as with the Federal Court withdrawing journalists' access to documents filed early in proceedings (Karp, 2023).

The requirement that a court report be fair and accurate to meet defences for defamation and *sub judice* contempt does not mean it must be perfectly balanced. It requires that both sides of the trial be given *appropriate* coverage. If, for example, an allegation is made by the prosecution in a criminal case, the rebuttal of that allegation by the defence must also be reported. Similarly, the requirement of accuracy allows a small amount of leeway. A report may well have some minor errors in it but not lose a defamation defence or contempt immunity, provided the inaccuracy is not 'substantial'.

Reporting identification restrictions

If you are covering crime or courts in Australia, your alarm bells should be ringing and you should be checking for restrictions relating to any of the following:

- preliminary hearings such as bail applications and committal proceedings, and matters conducted in the absence of the jury;
- sexual offences (identification of victim and/or accused, depending on jurisdiction);
- juvenile matters (identification of juvenile offenders, child witnesses, victims, child family members of accused adults, wards of the state, child custody hearings, adoptions and child protection notifications – sometimes even children who have died – or adults who were children at the time of the events alleged);
- family law proceedings (identification of parties);
- mental health tribunal hearings and coroners' inquests into suicides;
- guardianship proceedings (may involve adults who have mental incapacity);
- jurors (approaching them, identifying them or revealing their deliberations);
- disallowed questions;
- lapsed convictions;
- national security (for example, no identification of ASIO officers or people in preventative detention);
- witnesses to investigative bodies (e.g. state crime commissions); and
- interviewing prisoners.

Also note that bail applications cannot be covered in Tasmania. More detail on the key restrictions follows.

Sexual offences

Sexual offence laws in all Australian jurisdictions prohibit the identification of the complainant (victim) in a sexual offence case. This is to protect complainants from further embarrassment and trauma, to encourage others to be prepared to come forward, and in some circumstances to protect them from the fear of threat or abuse during the trial. The no-identification rule means exactly that: nothing can be published that narrows down the individual closely enough that they might be identified. In the Northern Territory, the identification restriction is taken even further by prohibiting the identification of the accused in a sexual offence until they have been committed for trial. In Tasmania, there can be no identification of a person accused of incest, unless authorised by the courts. Breach of such laws is considered a serious offence and publishers can face a hefty fine or jail. Breach can also result in an action for damages. Sometimes the legislation allows for the publication of the name of a sexual offence complainant if there is no charge pending, or if the court or victim agrees to the identification. Laws in some jurisdictions (Tasmania in 2020 and NSW in 2021) changed so that sexual assault survivors could consent to being identified as a result of #LetHerSpeak campaigning by victim and 2021 Australian of the Year, Grace Tame.

Case example:

Jane Doe case (2007): The ABC breached the Victorian *Judicial Proceedings Reports Act 1958* by broadcasting three reports that identified by name and address a husband convicted of raping his wife, and a fourth in which the wife herself was named. The reporters involved were prosecuted for breaching the Act, and the victim then sued the ABC for negligence, breach of its duty not to name her, invasion of privacy and breach of confidence. The case was subsequently settled by the ABC.

Child identification

Most states and territories ban the identification of children charged with criminal offences. Jurisdictions vary in other aspects of reporting cases involving children. People now must be eighteen at the time of the offence to be treated as an adult in all Australian jurisdictions. In some places, the court will allow (or legislation provides for) the media to be present during juvenile cases but will restrict their reportage either totally or on the point of identification of the child. Children who appear as witnesses or complainants, or who are even mentioned in trials, cannot be identified, although this varies somewhat. Some states do not allow mere parental consent for the identification of a child and instead require the permission of the court.

Family law

The Federal Circuit and Family Court of Australia deals with child custody and matrimonial cases. Section 121 of the *Family Law Act 1975* bans publication of a report of proceedings that identifies any party or witness involved in a family law matter. The prohibitions are extensive, covering a person's name, title, pseudonym, alias, home or work address or locality, physical description, style of dress, occupation, official or honorary position, relationship to identified friends, relatives or business acquaintances, recreational interests, political or philosophical or religious beliefs or interests, or any property they might own that might identify them. Needless to say, images of them are banned.

Case example:

Courier-Mail case (2014). The publisher of Brisbane's *Courier-Mail* newspaper pleaded guilty to a breach of the *Family Law Act* after it published on its front page the names and photographs of sisters at the centre of an international custody battle. It was fined $120,000.

Strict laws apply in all jurisdictions banning the identification of parties to adoption and also prohibiting identification by any means of wards of the state and former wards of the state. In some jurisdictions, identification is allowed with the consent of the individuals involved and/or the permission of the court. Journalists should consult with a local lawyer before identifying anyone in these situations.

Absent juries, withdrawn questions and the voir dire

The media are restricted to coverage of proceedings in open court in the presence of a jury. The court can be closed or the jury can be absent for a range of reasons, rendering proceedings unreportable. Anything said in court when the jury is not present cannot be published. Sometimes questions will be put to a witness in the presence of the jury and promptly withdrawn. These cannot be reported because the question is deleted from the court record. Beware the *voir dire* – a mini-hearing where the jury is absent so lawyers can debate the admissibility of evidence. These cannot be reported.

Prisoners

In addition to the restrictions on reporting at the police and court end of the judicial process, there are varying restrictions on reporting at the other end of the process – when prisoners are in custody or released on parole. Journalists have run foul of state and territory-based restrictions in this area.

Suicide and mental health proceedings

The Commonwealth Criminal Code makes it an offence to use a 'carriage service' (the internet, a wire service or a broadcast medium) to publish material that promotes or provides instruction on a method of committing suicide. Some state laws also restrict suicide inquest reports. Refer to the Mindframe guidance on such reporting at <https://mindframe.org.au/guidelines>. There are also restrictions on the reporting of mental health cases in the courts and specially constituted mental health tribunals, and the identification of the mental health patients involved (Pearson et al., 2017).

> **Reflect – Research – Review:**
>
> Find three reports of the same major court case in three different media outlets. Compare and contrast the ways journalists have reported the case.

Crime and court reporting in action – Case Study 8.1: The ethics and law of the activist's court report blog

Occasionally a situation arises encompassing a number of important areas of media ethics and law. For this scenario, you are asked to work through both the ethical ramifications of the situation using the basic TARES test as explained in Chapter 3 (Baker and Martinson 2001; Baker, 2020) and the legal ramifications of your decision using the Table 8.1 Crime reporting time zones chart provided for you below.

The problem

You are the public relations officer for the #YesMeAsWell activist group calling for victims of sexual assault to come forward to tell their stories and to bring justice to their assailants. Tomorrow is Day 1 of the celebrity trial of a prominent film director for the sexual assault of the leading female actor on the set of a film that won an Oscar two years ago. She is a prominent #YesMeAsWell voice who raised her allegation after she named and shamed the accused at your organisation's protest rally. You have an overseas trip planned, so you only have time to blog on the first day of the proceedings – when the prosecution will be presenting its case against the film director.

Let's examine it in terms of both the ethics and law of crime and justice.

Applying the TARES test

Truthfulness (of the message)

Remember Baker and Martinson's advice that your communication must have an 'intention not to deceive, the intention to provide others with the truthful information they legitimately need to make good decisions about their lives' (2001: 160). How honest would such a blog be? Whose truth would you be bringing by reporting only on the first day of a major celebrity trial? What strategies could you use to get the whole truth of the proceedings covered?

Authenticity (of the persuader)

Baker and Martinson (2001, p.161) ask you to examine your 'integrity and personal virtue in action and motivation', along with your loyalty to causes and your 'moral independence and commitment to principle'. What moral independence do you have in the writing of this blog? Can you honestly say it will be fair and accurate?

Respect (for the persuadee)

In an echo of stakeholder mapping, Baker (2020: 155) asks you to assess the interests of others and whether you are giving them complete information. Can your course of action be adjusted so you do this task with such respect for your audience, the jury, for all parties to the case and to the justice system?

Equity (of the persuasive appeal)

Baker (2020: 5) turns to actual fairness and in this case we direct our attention to the prospects of the accused for a fair trial in the light of articles like yours. Baker asks: 'Is it fair to targeted or vulnerable audiences?' raising the issue here of the potential impact of unequal coverage upon both the accused and victims of such assaults. Can this be adjusted?

Social responsibility (for the common good)

The key question in the TARES test here echoes the social responsibility model we examined in Chapter 1: 'Will the cause I am promoting result in benefits or harm to individuals or to society? Is this cause responsible to the best interests of the public?' (Baker, 2020: 155). This can include an assessment of the human rights angle: where does free expression sit with the accused's right to a fair trial and the alleged victim's right to see justice done? What alternative approaches might meet these goals more equitably? Is there a solutions journalism alternative to the actual coverage of the trial?

Table 8.1 Crime reportage time zones

Time zone	Description	Restrictions on reportage
1	After crime, before arrest or charging	No restriction for contempt, but ensure a defamation defence is available. What if the suspect sues for defamation, as happened in WA in the Barrister's Wife's case (2017) after a barrister was named as the prime suspect in his wife's murder and was subsequently found not guilty?
2	After arrest or charging, before first court appearance	Reporting limited to the 'bare facts' of the crime (Packer's case), with no information going to contestable matters, interference with eyewitness identification, such as photographs or 'pen portraits', of the accused, or material that might prejudice a future jury against them such as social media excerpts. Ensure a defamation defence is available. What if no charges are laid, or are withdrawn? The accused could sue you for defamation and you would not yet have the protection of a court-based fair reporting defence. Do not interview potential witnesses. No mention of confessions, previous charges or convictions.
3	After charging, during preliminary appearances and hearings	As for zone 2, however court appearances and committal hearings during this period can be reported with care under the principle that the public interest in open justice usually takes precedence. No photographs or sketches if identification may be an issue. Ensure a defamation defence of fair and accurate report is available. What if charges are dropped? Take special care with state-based laws banning identification, and the ban on bail hearing reportage in Tasmania. Watch for suppression orders on identification or certain evidence. Stay away from witnesses and avoid comment on guilt or innocence.
4	During trial	Restricted to fair and accurate report of trial and description of 'bare facts' of crime. No use of material from preliminary hearings or of anything that takes place in the absence of the jury (as in Krystal's case (2016, 2017)). No photographs or sketches if identification may be an issue. Similar defence applies to defamation. Again, no interviews with witnesses, watch for suppression orders, don't identify children or sex crime victims, and don't imply guilt or innocence.
5	After trial, before appeal expiry date	Report with some care, avoiding anything of an extreme or overly sensational nature that might influence a jury or witness on retrial. No interviewing jurors. Defamation may still be an issue, although fair reporting of a court case is still protected. Beyond that, reportage and comment must be covered by some other defence. Don't imply an acquitted person is guilty.
6	After appeal or acquittal	No *sub judice* restrictions. Defamation still a danger. Ensure a defence is available. Again, don't imply the guilt of someone acquitted.

Applying time reportage time zones table to the scenario

Now it is time to turn to the legal dimensions of the problem and to assess your exposure to legal risk. Work through the time zones featured in Table 8.1 – Crime reportage time zones – to help navigate the legal issues for a publication at this stage of the criminal process.

Know the criminal time zones

What can a journalist or other communicator include in a story at each stage of the criminal process? It is best to pause to reflect upon this in terms of a number of criminal 'time zones'. Each zone involves different limitations on the work of a journalist wanting to report on the judicial system. The restrictions are brought about by the interplay of defamation law (Chapter 5), contempt and reporting identification restrictions outlined above.

In a nutshell

- Moral philosophers from Aristotle in Ancient Greece through to Sissela Bok in the modern era have considered the important issues of justice as a virtue.
- Criminologists and media studies academics have reported on shortcomings in the media portrayal of violence, crime and courts – while solutions journalism experts have suggested creative new ways of approaching it.
- The media report on the courts for a range of reasons, including a duty to society, the newsworthiness of the court list, audience ratings and the sheer convenience of having predictable news occurring at a single location.
- Judges and magistrates have the power to issue suppression and non-publication orders which can be challenged by media organisations.
- Contempt is conduct impairing or threatening to impair the administration of justice.
- Contempt by publication includes:
  - material that tends to prejudice a fair trial (*sub judice* contempt)
  - allegations that tend to undermine public confidence in the administration of justice (scandalising the court)
  - an account of the deliberations of a jury in most jurisdictions.
- Other forms of contempt affecting professional communicators are:
  - improper behaviour in a courtroom during a hearing, which is also known as 'contempt in the face of the court'
  - failure to comply with a court order or undertaking given to a court, which is known as 'disobedience contempt' (applies to journalists who refuse to reveal a source in court, covered in Chapter 6).
- *Sub judice* means 'under a judge' and it applies to the period when proceedings are 'pending'. In criminal matters, it applies from when someone has been arrested or charged.

- Courts are particularly concerned with material that might influence potential jurors or witnesses, such as insinuations that an accused is guilty or even innocent, the mention of potentially inadmissible evidence, publication of an accused person's previous convictions or the publishing of photographs or drawings of the accused, if identification may be an issue at the trial.
- There are two possible defences that can be raised against *sub judice* contempt charges: a fair and accurate report of court or parliament and public interest.
- Visual identification is a particularly sensitive matter, and it can be most difficult to predict whether it will be at issue. Err on the side of caution.
- Judges and magistrates have the power to allow cameras and digital devices – as well as use of social media in court – and are doing so more frequently. However, to do so without permission may be deemed contempt of court.
- Defamation and contempt laws mean that journalists are restricted when reporting a court case to a fair and accurate report of the proceedings conducted in open court while the jury is present.
- The reporter must actually attend the proceedings on which they are reporting rather than rely on second hand information.
- Special restrictions usually apply to reporting of sexual offences, matters involving children, family law and mental health proceedings.
- When publishing reports about crimes and court cases, be aware of the respective criminal time zones and the restrictions on reportage that apply to them. Photocopy the time zone chart (Table 8.1) and have it available for reference when crime stories unfold.
- Ensure that any criticism of the judiciary and the legal system is carefully phrased to avoid contempt by scandalising and defamation action.

References and further reading

Arlidge, A. and Eady, D. 1982, *The Law of Contempt*, Sweet & Maxwell, London.
Australian Law Reform Commission (ALRC). 1987, *Report No. 35 – Contempt*, AGPS, Canberra, <www.austlii.edu.au/au/other/alrc/publications/reports/35>.
Australian Law Reform Commission (ALRC). 2009, *Secrecy Laws and Open Government in Australia*, ALRC, Sydney.
Baker, S. and Martinson, D.L. 2001, 'The TARES Test: Five Principles for Ethical Persuasion', *Journal of Mass Media Ethics*, 16 (2-3), 148–175.
Baker, S. 2020, 'The Ethics of Advocacy: Moral Reasoning in the Practice of Public Relations', *The Routledge Handbook of Mass Media Ethics*, Wilkins, L. and Christians, C.G. eds, Routledge, London and New York, 148–162.
BBC News. 2018, '*Ceredigion Herald* editor Thomas Sinclair loses court appeal', BBC News, 22 January, <www.bbc.com/news/uk-wales-mid-wales-42777235>.
Bentham, J. 1825, *Treatise on Judicial Evidence*, J.W. Paget, London.
Blackstone, W. 1765–1769, *Commentaries on the Laws of England*, Clarendon Press, Oxford.
Bok, S. 1998, *Mayhem – Violence as Public Entertainment*. Addison-Wesley, Reading, Massachusetts.

Butt, P. and Nygh, P. 2004, *Butterworths Encyclopaedic Australian Legal Dictionary*, LexisNexis, Sydney.

Ericson, R.V., Baranek, P.M. and Chan, J.B.L. 1987, *Visualizing Deviance: A Study of News Organisations*, Open University Press, Milton Keynes.

Gregory, P. 2005, *Court Reporting in Australia*, Cambridge University Press, Melbourne.

Hall, S. 1975. 'Mugging: A case study in the media', *The Listener*, 93 (2404), 1 May, 571–572.

Holdsworth, W. 1945, *A History of English Law*, 3rd edn, Methuen, London.

Karp, P. 2023, '"Utterly disgraceful": New federal court rules limiting access to documents criticised by media union', *The Guardian*, 13 January, <www.theguardian.com/media/2023/jan/13/utterly-disgraceful-new-federal-court-rules-limiting-access-to-documents-criticised-by-media-union>.

McGarry, A. 2006, 'Jail for Bob the broadcaster?', *The Australian*, 3 August, 14.

Miller, D. 2021, 'Justice', *The Stanford Encyclopedia of Philosophy*, Fall 2021 edn, Zalta, E.N. ed., <https://plato.stanford.edu/archives/fall2021/entries/justice/>.

Neuberger, Lord of Abbotbury (Master of Rolls). 2011, 'Open justice unbound?', *Judicial Studies Board Annual Lecture*, 16 March, <www.judiciary.gov.uk/Resources/JCO/Documents/Speeches/mr-speech-jsb-lecture-march-2011.pdf>.

NSW Law Reform Commission (NSWLRC). 2000, *Discussion Paper 43: Contempt by Publication*, NSWLRC, Sydney, <www.lawlink.nsw.gov.au/lrc.nsf/pages/dp43toc>.

Office of the High Commissioner for Human Rights (OHCHR). 1976, *International Covenant on Civil and Political Rights*, OHCHR, Geneva, <www.unhchr.ch/html/menu3/b/accpr.htm>.

O'Neill, D. and Harcup, P. 2009, 'News Values and Selectivity', *The Handbook of Journalism Studies*, Wahl-Jorgensen, K. and Hanitzsch, T. eds, Taylor and Francis, Oxford, 161–174.

Pearson, M., Morton, T. and Bennett, H. 2017, 'Mental health and the media: A case study in open justice', *Journal of Media Law* (UK), 9 (2), 232–258.

Sossin, L. and Crystal, V. 2013, 'A Comment on "No Comment": The Sub Judice Rule and the Accountability of Public Officials in the 21st Century', *Dalhousie Law Journal*, 36 (2), 535–580, <https://digitalcommons.osgoode.yorku.ca/cgi/viewcontent.cgi?referer=&httpsredir=1&article=1430&context=scholarly_works>.

Spigelman, J. 2005, 'The principle of open justice: A comparative perspective', address to the Media Law Resource Centre conference, 20 September, London, <www.lawlink.nsw.gov.au/lawlink/Supreme_Court/ll_sc.nsf/pages/SCO_spigelman200905>.

Wenzel, A., Gerson, D., Moreno, E., Son, M., and Morrison Hawkins, B. 2018, 'Engaging stigmatized communities through solutions journalism: Residents of South Los Angeles respond', *Journalism*, 19 (5), 649–667, <https://journals.sagepub.com/doi/abs/10.1177/1464884917703125>.

Cases cited

Ambard's case: *Ambard v Attorney-General of Trinidad and Tobago* [1936] AC 322.

Anissa case: *Anissa Pty Ltd v Simon Harry Parsons on application of the Prothonotary of the Supreme Court of Victoria* [1999] VSC 430 (8 November 1999), <www.austlii.edu.au//cgi-bin/disp.pl/au/cases/vic/VSC/1999/430.html>.

BLF cases: *Attorney-General NSW v Mundey* [1972] 2 NSWLR 887; *Gallagher v Durack* (1983) 152 CLR 238.

Bread Manufacturers case: *Ex parte Bread Manufacturers Ltd; Re Truth and Sportsman Ltd* (1937) 37 SR (NSW) 242.
Courier-Mail case: ABC News. 2014, 'The Courier-Mail fined $120,000 for identifying family involved in custody battle', *ABC News*, 3 March, <www.abc.net.au/news/2014-03-24/courier-mail-fined-for-identifying-family-in-custody-battle/5342034>.
Crime Commission case: *Lee v New South Wales Crime Commission* [2013] HCA 39 (9 October 2013), <www.austlii.edu.au/cgi-bin/viewdoc/au/cases/cth/HCA/2013/39.html>.
Dunbabin's case: *R v Dunbabin; Ex parte Williams* [1935] 53 CLR 419.
Evening Standard case: *R v Evening Standard; Ex parte Director of Public Prosecutions* (1924) 40 TLR 833. Ex parte P: reported in *The Times*, 31 March 1998, <http://swarb.co.uk/ex-parte-p-ca-31-mar-1998>.
Facebook Juror case: *A-G v Fraill [2011] EWCA Crim 1570* (6 June 2011), <www.bailii.org/ew/cases/EWCA/Crim/2011/1570.html>.
Facebook streaming case: *AG v Yaxley-Lennon* [2019] EWHC 1791 (9 July 2019), <www.judiciary.uk/wp-content/uploads/2019/07/ag-v-yaxley-lennon-jmt-190709.pdf>.
Fisher's case: *R v Fisher* [1811] 2 Camp 563.
Friendlyjordies case (2022): *Barilaro v Google LLC* [2022] FCA 650 (6 June 2022), <www.austlii.edu.au/cgi-bin/viewdoc/au/cases/cth/FCA/2022/650.html>.
Glennon's case: *R v Glennon* (1992) 173 CLR 592 (6 May 1992), <www.austlii.edu.au/au/cases/cth/HCA/1992/16.html>.
Hinch's case: *Hinch & Macquarie Broadcasting Holdings Ltd v Attorney-General (Vic)* [1987] HCA 56, 164 CLR 15 (2 December 1987), <www.austlii.edu.au/cgi-bin/viewdoc/au/cases/cth/HCA/1987/56.html>.
Ibrahim's case: *Fairfax Digital Australia & New Zealand Pty Ltd v Ibrahim* [2012] NSWCCA 125 (13 June 2012), <www.austlii.edu.au/cgi-bin/sinodisp/au/cases/nsw/NSWCCA/2012/125.html>.
Idoport case: *Idoport Pty Ltd v National Australia Bank* [47] [2001] NSWSC 1024 (14 November 2001), <www.austlii.edu.au//cgi-bin/disp.pl/au/cases/nsw/supreme_ct/2001/1024.html>.
Indigenous Laughing case: Gorrie, A. 2017, 'Gympie activist serves two hours for contempt', *Courier-Mail*, 18 December, <www.couriermail.com.au/news/queensland/gympie/update-gympie-activist-serves-two-hours-for-contempt/news-story/dad9f3dd47cf88157d4e50aa80ead80c >.
James' case: *James v Robinson* (1963) 109 CLR 593.
Jane Doe case: *Jane Doe v Australian Broadcasting Corporation* [2007] VCC 281 (3 April 2007), <www.austlii.edu.au/au/cases/vic/VCC/2007/281.pdf >.
John Laws case: *R v Laws* [2000] NSWSC 885 (5 September 2000), <www.austlii.edu.au/au/cases/nsw/supreme_ct/2000/885.html>.
Krystal's case: *DPP v Johnson & Yahoo!* [2016] VSC 699 (28 November 2016), <www.austlii.edu.au/cgi-bin/viewdoc/au/cases/vic/VSC/2016/699.html>; *DPP v Johnson & Yahoo! (No. 2)* [2017] VSC 45 (17 February 2017), <www.austlii.edu.au/cgi-bin/viewdoc/au/cases/vic/VSC/2017/45.html>.
Liberal Ministers' case: Supreme Court of Victoria. 2017, 'Statement of the Court of Appeal in terrorism cases', 16 June, <www.supremecourt.vic.gov.au/news/statement-of-the-court-of-appeal-in-terrorism-cases>; Supreme Court of Victoria. 2017, 'Statement of the Court of Appeal in *DPP v MHK* and *DPP v Besim* (23 June 2017)', 23 June, <www.supremecourt.vic.gov.au/court-decisions/judgments-and-sentences/judgment-summaries/statement-of-the-court-of-appeal-in-dpp>.

Mason's case: *Attorney-General (NSW) v TCN Channel Nine Pty Ltd* [1990] 20 NSWLR 368, 5 BR 419.
NT Homeless 'Genius' case: *Jenkins v Whittington* [2017] NTSC 65 (21 August 2017), <www.austlii.edu.au/cgi-bin/viewdoc/au/cases/nt/NTSC/2017/65.html>.
O'Shane's case: *O'Shane v Harbour Radio Pty Ltd [2013] NSWCA 315* (24 September 2013), <www.austlii.edu.au/cgi-bin/sinodisp/au/cases/nsw/NSWCA/2013/315.html>.
Packer's case: *Packer v Peacock* (1912) 13 CLR 577.
Parke's case: *R v Parke* [1903] 2 KB 432.
Pell suppression case, 2021: *The Queen v The Herald & Weekly Times Pty Ltd* [2021] VSC 253 (4 June 2021), <www.austlii.edu.au/cgi-bin/viewdoc/au/cases/vic/VSC/2021/253.html>.
Rape Priors case: *R v Hinch* [2013] VSC 520 (2 October 2013), <www.austlii.edu.au/au/cases/vic/VSC/2013/520.html>; *R v Hinch (No. 2)* [2013] VSC 554 (18 October 2013), <www.austlii.edu.au/cgi-bin/sinodisp/au/cases/vic/VSC/2013/554.html>.
Raybos's case: *Raybos v Jones* (1985) 2 NSWLR 47.
Barrister's Wife's case: *Rayney v The State of Western Australia [No. 9]* [2017] WASC 367 (15 December 2017), <www.austlii.edu.au/cgi-bin/viewdoc/au/cases/wa/WASC/2017/367.html>.
Scott's case: *Scott v Scott* [1913] AC 417.
Sex Offenders case: *Hogan v Hinch* [2011] HCA 4 (10 March 2011), <www.austlii.edu.au/cgi-bin/sinodisp/au/cases/cth/HCA/2011/4.html>.
Sunday Times case (1974): *Attorney-General v Times Newspapers Ltd* [1974] AC 273.
Sussex Justices case: *R v Sussex Justices; Ex parte McCarthy* [1924] 1 KB 256.
Talkback case: *DPP v Francis & Anor (No. 2)* [2006] SASC 261 (25 August 2006), <www.austlii.edu.au/cgi-bin/viewdoc/au/cases/sa/SASC/2006/261.html>.
Voyeur case (2018): *BBC News*. 2018, '*Ceredigion Herald* editor Thomas Sinclair loses court appeal', *BBC News*, 22 January, <www.bbc.com/news/uk-wales-mid-wales-42777235>.
Who Weekly case: *Attorney-General (NSW) v Time Inc. Magazine Co. Pty Ltd* [1994] NSW Court of Appeal, 40331/94, unreported (15 September 1994).
Zhao's case: *Commissioner of the Australian Federal Police v Zhao* [2015] 316 ALR 378 (12 February 2015), <www.austlii.edu.au/cgi-bin/viewdoc/au/cases/cth/HCA/2015/5.html>.

Part 3
Challenges in the digital era

9 The ethics and law of intellectual property

Key concepts

Plagiarism: The ethical breach of appropriating someone else's ideas, words or creations and passing them off as your own without adequate attribution.

Intellectual property (IP): Non-physical (and normally legally protected) property that is originated from the mind of its creators, including literary and artistic works, music, inventions, designs, symbols, names and images.

Copyright: Legal protection of the form of expression of a work such as an article or an image.

Trade mark: A legally enforcable sign used to distinguish goods or services dealt with or provided in the course of trade by a person from goods or services of a similar kind provided by others.

Fair dealing and fair use: Exceptions and defences to copyright infringement (the former narrower and the latter broader) available to those using a copyright work in a fair and attributed way.

Public domain ('commons'): Works in the public domain without exclusive intellectual property rights applying, for a range of possible reasons including that they might not apply under law, or have been waived by the owner or have expired. Moral rights to attribution will still apply.

Moral rights: The residual rights under copyright law requiring users to always attribute the work to its original creator even when they might no longer hold the copyright. It also includes a right against false attribution and derogatory treatment of the work.

Introduction

In the digital era, it has become incredibly easy to incorporate someone else's work – an extract of text, a photograph or a sound grab – into our own. Artificial intelligence applications like ChatGPT, an AI-based text generator released in late 2022, make it possible to parade words as our own when they have come from a computer, raising fundamental ethical issues around creativity in publishing. This chapter looks at the ethics and law of intellectual property for professional communicators – from Ancient Greece through to

DOI: 10.4324/9781003372752-12

artificial intelligence. By the end of it you should have a basic understanding of some of the ethical issues around plagiarism, including the professional codes controlling it, and an introduction to the key laws of intellectual property – with a strong focus on copyright law.

Intellectual property is non-physical property that is originated from the mind of its creators. As a professional communicator – whether a journalist, public relations consultant, or corporate communicator – you can find yourself on either side of the intellectual property fence. If you place a high value on the merit of your professional creativity, you are probably not impressed when you discover someone else has cut and pasted your words or images and pretended they are their own. Yet you will often be tempted to draw upon someone else's work and might even want to reproduce it in full. In ethical terms, you might be suffering a moral wrong by someone else's action, but sometimes you might be the one harming them. In a legal sense, sometimes you might be a plaintiff wanting to stake your own claim to intellectual property rights, while on other occasions you might be a defendant needing to justify your use of someone else's material.

Philosophical background and human rights context of plagiarism and intellectual property

Moore and Himma (2022) outlined the development of philosophical thinking and law around intellectual property. They traced its origins to at least 500BCE in Ancient Greece when chefs were granted monopolies for the creation of dishes to their special recipes. In Alexandria in about 200BCE there was the conviction for breach of copyright of poets who had stolen the literary expressions of others. In Rome in the 1st century CE an orator was accused of reciting the works of a famous epigrammatist without attributing them to the author.

While international law has moved to the protection of intellectual property, there have long been debates over the utility of its control. Important positions were taken by philosophers from the various schools of thought we examined in Chapter 1. There have been debates over whether it is fair to compare the ownership of intellectual property with the ownership of real property, yet the arguments favouring its enforceable rights have generally stemmed from such a comparison. Three main endorsements of intellectual property as a right came from:

- The phenomenologist Georg Hegel (1770–1831) who argued intellectual property was an extension of individual personality and that people have moral claims to their own talents.
- Utilitarians who proposed that there would be no encouragement for authors and inventors to create important intellectual property unless it could be safeguarded legally. Piracy would abound and people would be discouraged from creating.

- Social contract theorist John Locke (1632–1704) saw intellectual property in terms of rights. Under the social contract, creators should be able to control the fruits of their labour and engage in their intellectual outputs confident that others would not steal them (Moore and Himma, 2022).

There were, however, free expression arguments posed against the licensing of intellectual property. These went along the lines that intellectual property rights tied up the free flow of information in society, depriving some citizens of access to words, ideas and designs because they could not afford to pay for the right to access them or because they were kept secret behind a veil of legal protection (Moore and Himma, 2022).

To some extent, that argument is underscored by the fact that Article 19(2) of the *International Covenant on Civil and Political Rights* (ICCPR) (UN Human Rights Office, 1966) states that everyone's right to freedom of expression 'shall include freedom to seek, receive and impart information and ideas of all kinds, regardless of frontiers, either orally, in writing or in print, in the form of art, or through any other media of his choice'. However, a specific right to intellectual property forms part of the *International Covenant on Economic, Social and Cultural Rights* (UN, 1966). It states at Article 15(1c) that everyone has the right 'To benefit from the protection of the moral and material interests resulting from any scientific, literary or artistic production of which he is the author'. Additionally, intellectual property rights are accorded in a range of forms via other specific international treaties and free trade agreements, as detailed in the international law section below.

By far the strongest connection between the morals and laws of intellectual property appears in the hybrid term expressing that nexus in the field of copyright – known as 'moral rights' – which originated in Europe and were incorporated into international law via amendments to Article 11 of the *Berne Convention* in Rome in 1928, stating 'Such conditions shall not in any case prejudice the moral right (*droit moral*) of the author' (WIPO, 1928). Moral rights now form part of the copyright law of most countries and are residual rights that require future users to always attribute a work to its original creator even when they no longer hold the copyright. They also include a right against false attribution and derogatory treatment of the work. See Moore and Himma (2022) for a comprehensive summary of all the main philosophical arguments and counter-arguments about intellectual property.

Plagiarism is the ethical equivalent of the legal wrong of copyright breach. It casts a broader net because, unlike copyright, it is not restricted to the theft of a form of expression. Rather, it extends to the unauthorised or unreferenced appropriation of someone's ideas as well. While plagiarism has long been a misdemeanour in academic circles, it was first defined as official misconduct in the realm of science (along with fabrication and falsification) in the official *US Code of Federal Regulations* in 1989 (Hepburn and Andersen, 2021). Some have gone so far as to categorise it as corruption, at least in a moral sense, despite it not being necessarily economic in character. Miller (2018) used the

246 *Challenges in the digital era*

example of an academic plagiarising the work of another to increase her academic status while not committing a direct economic crime. However, like professional communicators, her reputational fame on the coattails of another's intellectual work would enhance her reputation and pay off financially in indirect ways, such as via promotions and awards of grants.

New technologies create new moral and ethical issues. Miller's (2018) article was written before the advent in 2022 of artificial intelligence (AI) text applications like ChatGPT that create original prose to the user's request and AI image generators which respond to text commands. Neither might involve the theft of another's work from a breach of copyright perspective, but each poses a litany of ethical questions for the professional communicator, starting with: What are the ethics of parading such work as your own? What is the veracity of the material created – particularly the truth of the words and facts used? How does your use of AI impact the livelihoods of the creatives who would have otherwise composed these words and drawn these images? The innovations spark these questions and more as academics and policy makers from a range of fields grapple with the moral, ethical and legal implications of artificial intelligence in professional communication.

Reflect – Research – Review:

You have joined an advertising agency and your creative director has asked you to use an AI text generator and AI drawing app as the starting point for a creative pitch to a new client. Reflect on the scenario using mindful reflection, mindmapping or journaling and then use the Potter Box (1972) to work through the facts, loyalties, values and principles involved in the ethics of the situation.

Ethical guidelines and regulation of intellectual property

Intellectual property rights present an ethical issue. Can we borrow someone else's creative work without owing a moral debt – at the very least, by crediting them? Almost all professional communicators now have a tertiary education, and universities are vigilant about plagiarism. Under their academic integrity policies, they dispense penalties ranging from failing an assignment to expulsion. Yet, even in the academic environment, plagiarism is sometimes hard to pin down. When we move to the professional ethical level, typically the journalism codes of ethics make specific mention of members avoiding plagiarism. For example, the Society of Professional Journalists (SPJ) Code of Ethics in the US states very simply 'Never plagiarize. Always attribute' (SPJ, 2014), and links to various commentaries by academics and explanations from its ethics committee. In Australia, item 10 of the MEAA Journalist Code of Ethics again states concisely, 'Do not plagiarise' (MEAA, 2016). In discussing the code, the MEAA's Ethics Review Committee (1996) explained the risk of plagiarism occurring in a journalist's work:

> Plagiarism offends the values of honesty, fairness, independence and respect for the rights of others. It can occur in many ways, including (but not limited to): when secondary sources are relied on too heavily; when material from wire services is fused with the work of staff reporters; because of the ease with which words can be 'cut' and 'pasted' by computer; and when the words of a public relations copywriter are reproduced from a press release verbatim without attribution to the source.

However, the various public relations codes of conduct do not usually make specific mention of plagiarism but require members to follow honest methods of practice. For example, the Public Relations and Communications Association (UK) Professional Charter states at item 1.1 that a member must deal fairly and honestly with 'other professions, suppliers, intermediaries, the media of communication, colleagues, and above all else the public' (PRCA, 2023). The Australian code has a similar requirement at clause 1 that members deal 'fairly and honestly' with the 'communication media' and the 'general public', with no specific mention of plagiarism (PRIA, 2009).

More worrying than ethical stipulations for most professional communicators might be the prospect of being 'outed' as a plagiarist. Just how deeply affronted journalists feel by such an accusation was illustrated when Australian *60 Minutes* reporter Richard Carleton (now deceased) sued the ABC's *Media Watch* programme for defamation after it implied that he and his team had plagiarised a BBC documentary. Justice Higgins described the allegation of plagiarism as being 'regarded by journalists and, indeed, many others as an accusation of disgraceful and reprehensible conduct' (Carleton's case, 2002: para. 105). While he found the allegations against Carleton and *60 Minutes* untrue, he decided that *Media Watch* had based its defamatory opinion on provable facts, establishing a defence of fair comment.

If plagiarism is considered such an abhorrent practice, why is it that some reporters, public relations practitioners and political speech writers seem ready to steal the words of others? Why do editors and news directors turn a blind eye? Why do those same people take umbrage at others lifting their work? Compared with professors doing academic writing, journalists and other professional writers usually have a fairly 'loose' attribution style, sometimes resorting to expressions as vague as 'sources said' or 'media outlets reported'. Some fall back on 'everybody else steals *our* copy', using the morally weak excuse that their plagiarising today of *The New York Times* or Wikipedia was because yesterday the local radio station had 'ripped and read' the story they had written. Yet it is a huge leap from poor attribution to no attribution at all – parading the intellectual property of others as your own creative work.

The terms and conditions of the major Internet and social media platforms typically require you to give up many of your intellectual property rights and

248 *Challenges in the digital era*

potentially allow the platform to reap profits from your creative work. For example, the Meta Terms of Service (2022) concede the user holds the intellectual property rights in the content like photos and videos that they create and share on Facebook, Instagram, Messenger and so on. However, Meta makes you agree to licence them to 'a non-exclusive, transferable, sub-licensable, royalty-free and worldwide licence to host, use, distribute, modify, run, copy, publicly perform or display, translate and create derivative works of your content'. YouTube warns its users must only upload third party content for which they have legal permission, and claims a similar license to Meta's over original content posted (YouTube, 2022). Professional communicators need to be wary of their legal responsibility in breaching the intellectual property of others when using such services and also of the potential for their own revenue streams to be diminished if their creative work is redistributed or sold to others by the global entities.

> **Reflect – Research – Review:**
>
> What are the consequences of plagiarism at your university or in your newsroom or workplace? Find out what the policy is and summarise it.

Law, cases and examples internationally

Renaissance Italy is commonly regarded as the birthplace of modern intellectual property law, with the Republic of Florence issuing a patent in the form of a statute to the architect Filippo Brunelleschi for the design of his marble-carrying ship in 1421 (Nard and Morris, 2006: 233). This was followed by the first general patent statute being issued by the Venetian Republic in 1474, laying the foundation for the modern versions to follow (Nard and Morris, 2006: 234). US and UK intellectual property laws stemmed from the *English Statute of Monopolies* (1624) and the *Statute of Anne* (1710), which established copyright law by giving authors 14 years of rights to their work with the option for a further 14 years of renewal if they were still alive (Moore and Himma, 2022). Other European countries followed this precedent in ensuing decades, leading eventually to the signing of the first international conventions covering industrial property in Paris in 1883, and literary and artistic works in Berne in 1886 (WIPO, 1886). This, along with the various amendments, treaties and conventions that followed, gave intellectual property law a strong international foundation with some common elements that apply no matter where you are based or where your material is consumed.

IP defined

Professional communicators deal with sound, text, images and computer code – all of them subject to various forms of IP protection. Other types of intellectual property you might encounter include performances and broadcasts, inventions and discoveries, industrial designs, trade marks and commercial names – all listed in the *Convention Establishing the World Intellectual Property Organization* (WIPO) in 1967 (WIPO, 1979a). Put simply, IP comprises 'creations of the mind': inventions, literary and artistic works, and symbols, names, images and designs used in commerce, which have found actual material expression. Intellectual property laws are meant to protect our exclusive right to exploit the array of creative outputs we might produce as human beings. But elements of the law and its level of enforcement vary markedly between nations. IP can be one of the most complex areas of law, with specialists earning their living from advising clients on the intricacies of IP in particular jurisdictions, especially as new technologies spawn an array of new creations and the internet and AI highlight technical differences that result in new interpretations from the courts. It all means that you need to seek expert legal advice if you are considering pushing the boundaries of IP law in your publishing or if you have already been threatened with legal action. You can find information about the IP laws of various countries by browsing the Directory of Intellectual Property Offices (WIPO, 2023). The US Copyright Office, for example, has a useful introduction to that area of IP law and details US requirements at <www.copyright.gov>.

Copyright law internationally

As a professional communicator, the IP area you have most likely heard about is copyright, which covers creative works like writing, music and images, and in many countries also includes works of technology like computer programs and databases. As a creator, you are granted rights over your outputs via your form of expression – although if you are producing them as an employee, these might belong to your employer.

The starting point for understanding copyright is that it does not protect an *idea* alone. (You need to look to industrial property laws for protection of inventions or ideas via patent law.) Copyright will only protect the *form of expression* used to convey your idea. So you might post on social media about a brilliant concept you have for a new television drama series and then feel betrayed when someone beats you to the network to pitch that same idea. The courts will just say 'bad luck' unless you can show that your rival has copied a substantial part of your original treatment. The lesson here is that you shouldn't float ideas you might later want to protect.

The WIPO (2016) booklet *Understanding Copyright and Related Rights* is an excellent entry-point for learning about the basic copyright principles applying globally. It explains that 'copyright' translates into 'author's rights' in many other languages because it is the creator of the work – the 'author' of written works – who holds the right to reproduce their outputs. The word 'copyright' in English refers to that act itself – the 'right' to 'copy' something you have created. As the holder of that right, you have the legal power to license others to do so as well.

Case example:

Monkey case (2018): This is the leading modern international example of the principle that copyright rests with the creator of a work. In 2011, an Indonesian monkey named Naruto – a crested black macaque – took a 'selfie' with camera equipment set up by wildlife photographer David Slater. Monkey see, monkey do. Slater complained to Wikimedia Commons after the images were posted there, but they refused his demand that they take them down, arguing he did not hold copyright in the images because he did not actually take them – the monkey did (Wikimedia Foundation, 2014). The basic principle stood: copyright rests with the human creator of a work. However, the monkey did not get to claim damages for the photographer's use of the work. The US Ninth Circuit Court of Appeals denied an application by animal rights group PETA to have the monkey's copyright in the images formally acknowledged, stating that animals did not have standing. The photographer and the monkey (represented by PETA) negotiated a settlement (Toliver, 2017).

Most countries confer upon you a right to the exclusive use of your literary or artistic work the instant you create it – without the need for any kind of registration of the work as your own. You can use it in any way you like – as long as you do not break other laws in the process – and also have the exclusive right to authorise others to use it and to charge them for that use. You can prohibit or authorise the reproduction of your work in a range of formats, the distribution of copies of your work, its public performance, its broadcast or communication to the public in other ways, its translation into another language or its adaptation from one format to another.

It is important to dispel a common misconception. A work does *not* have to display the copyright symbol '©' to be protected by copyright. Of course, it doesn't hurt to include it alongside your name and the year of creation, because there are still a few countries that are not signatories to the Berne Convention (WIPO, 1886; 1979b), which did away with the need to display it. Inserting '©' at least signals your claim of authorship to anyone who might think that because you posted material on the internet or in social media you are giving up your rights to its use. The copyright symbol is still mandatory in the US for works published before March 1, 1989, when it became a signatory to the Berne Convention. It still serves to prevent a violator claiming they were unaware someone held copyright in a work. Some countries, such as the US, offer you several advantages if you have paid to register your copyright work with a federal government agency. For example, you can't file suit for infringement of your copyright in the US unless you have paid the registration fee.

An important difference between countries' copyright laws is duration. Under international conventions, your communication outputs will remain in copyright until at least 50 years after your death. But some countries – including the United States and Australia, as well as all nations in the European Union – have extended this term to 70 years after the death of the creator. In some countries it is even more, ranging up to 95 years after the author's death. Of course, this rule is more relevant if you want to reproduce the work of a famous writer, artist or musician in your own work. You will need to check whether enough time has passed since the author has died for the work to have entered the public domain or whether the creator has voluntarily waived their rights by assigning a general licence to a copyright-free organisation. Also note that translators of works written in other languages hold copyright in the translation, and that might still apply although the original author is long deceased.

Public domain ('commons'), fair use and fair dealing

The law in most places allows for certain situations where you can copy parts of other creators' material without their authorisation/permission but with appropriate attribution. Works in the public domain are those without exclusive intellectual property rights applying, for a range of possible reasons including that they might not apply under law, or have been relinquished voluntarily by the owner, or have expired. Moral rights will still apply, requiring attribution. The not-for-profit Creative Commons is a good example of the public domain. It offers free copyright licences enabling creators to grant a voluntary 'some rights reserved' approach as an alternative to the traditional 'all rights reserved' default system of copyright law. Its public domain tools allow works that are free of known copyright to be easily searched online and provides a mechanism for rights holders to dedicate their works to the public domain. Wikimedia Commons is similar.

Some countries offer 'fair use' or 'fair dealing' exceptions to copyright requirements for important public or creative purposes. These effectively become a defence to a breach of copyright. Of course, the courts and legislators in different countries vary in the way they interpret your 'fair' means of borrowing such material, especially in relation to the proportion you are copying and its significance in the context of the work as a whole. They also take into account how you have used the material, your purpose in doing so, the type of work you are copying, whether you are doing it for commercial gain and the impact of your use upon the future commercial worth of the material. Fair dealing exceptions can apply to uses such as the reporting of news and current affairs, criticism and review, parody and satire, and education – depending on the jurisdiction and its laws.

There are differences between 'fair use' (broader and more flexible) and 'fair dealing' (narrower and specified). Fair use – used in the US – is a wider definition where the courts will look at the overall use and whether an alleged copyright infringement can be justified on a case-by-case basis. The 'fair dealing' defences (in Australia, for example) are much narrower and are specified for use in those special circumstances.

Almost everything you might include in a work of professional communication is likely to be covered by copyright law – either yours or someone else's. That could include the words you compose, illustrations or cartoons you draw, photographs or moving footage you upload, plans you draft, annotated lists you compile and music you share. Most laws and treaties do not mention multimedia products, but experts agree that their unique arrangement of sound, text and images as they are presented on websites also qualifies for copyright protection as creative works.

A range of new considerations has arisen with the advent of the internet and the unique forms of communication it has facilitated on social media platforms. The reality with breach of copyright law is that most private social media users get away with cutting and pasting the words or images of others into their posts or stream the audio or video of others. The most they might usually face is a 'cease and desist' letter from a corporation or lawyer. But as soon as someone starts doing it on behalf of an organisation, or as a celebrity or influencer, the risk of legal action for breach of copyright rises exponentially. It is always best to seek out and get the permission of the creator and pay them or a syndication agency rather than to risk costly litigation – or else to operate within the requirements of the commons, free use, fair use or fair dealing exceptions using appropriate attribution.

Key Case 9.1: Meghan Markle's case (2021)

HRH the Duchess of Sussex v Associated Newspapers Ltd [2021] EWHC 273 (Ch) (11 February 2021), <www.bailii.org/ew/cases/EWHC/Ch/2021/273.html>.; *HRH the Duchess of Sussex v Associated Newspapers Ltd* [2021] EWCA Civ 1810 (2 December 2021), <www.bailii.org/cgi-bin/format.cgi?doc=/ew/cases/EWCA/Civ/2021/1810.html>.

We looked briefly at the 2021 *Meghan Markle case* for its privacy aspects as part of Key Case 7.1 – The Sussex Cases. Here we examine the copyright elements of the same case – considered in paragraphs 130–171 of the first case cited. The second case cited, the appeal by Associated Newspapers against the lower court decision, was unsuccessful.

Facts

British tabloid newspapers and celebrity magazines were full of speculation about the fractious relationship between the Duchess of Sussex – American actress Meghan Markle – and her father Thomas Markle before and after her wedding to Prince Harry in 2018. After a series of damaging media interviews in which her father made various allegations about her, the Duchess wrote him a personal letter pleading with him to stop, covering her own pain, her attempts to contact him after his heart attack before her wedding and his requests for money. In 2019, a *People* magazine article quoted four of her unnamed friends criticising Mr Markle and referring inaccurately to the private letter his daughter had written him. In response, he provided the *Mail on Sunday* extended extracts of her letter, purportedly to set the record straight, which they published at length on 10 February 2019. The front page featured a photograph of the royal couple and the heading 'Meghan's shattering letter to her father', followed by two double page spreads of coverage including 88 quotations from the letter.

Law

The Duchess sued the newspaper group for the misuse of her private information (see Key Case 7.1) and for infringement of her copyright in the letter, which we consider here. The judge worked through the basic elements of the action, and decided the letter was an 'original literary work' over which the owner (the Duchess) had exclusive reproduction rights from the time it was written. Copyright protected the form of expression she used in the letter, not the ideas conveyed. Merely relaying undisputed historical facts might not qualify. But this involved her 'intellectual creation' rather than merely her 'mechanical effort'. The fact that it was simply an admonishment of her father did not detract from its creative content. 'There must be 50 ways to scold your father, and 100 more in which to explain why you have told him off', the judge said. Truth of its contents was not required for copyright to subsist. Publication of a substantial part like this without permission would constitute an infringement unless a defence was available. Potential UK defences included fair dealing for the purposes of reporting current events, and a 'public interest' defence stemming from free expression rights in the *European Convention on Human Rights*. While it covered matters in the news, the publication was 'irrelevant to any legitimate reporting purpose' and 'disproportionate to any such purpose'. For similar reasons, the Convention right to free expression did not trump the property right in this case. If the work had been co-authored with her communications team, the Duchess would still hold a portion of the copyright. (It was later decided she had sole-authored it, with some editorial assistance.) The Duchess won the case. The newspaper was ordered to pay 90% of her legal costs plus an undisclosed sum as 'an account of profits' made from the coverage. They agreed to publish a front-page statement on the result.

Lessons for professional communicators

The case offers a useful insight into the key elements of the breach of copyright action in the UK, with strong similarities to how it works in

254 *Challenges in the digital era*

other places. Professional communicators should read the trial judgement from para 130 as a concise summary of copyright law. Key lessons are:

- You would hold copyright in all but the shortest of your original professional communications – not just the most literary or artistic ones; and
- Use of a substantial portion of anyone's work for news, commentary or current affairs purposes would require their permission and possible payment.

Reflect – Research – Review:

List three situations where professional communicators might want to use someone else's intellectual property in their work and three situations where communicators might want to defend their own intellectual property against misuse. Explain each.

There are many situations in the 24/7 newsroom or PR consultancy where there is a temptation to just 'grab' material – particularly from social media platforms like Facebook. For example, a crime victim's Facebook page or Twitter profile might feature their photograph – but if it is not a 'selfie' (self-taken), then the copyright in the image rests with another person – the photographer who took the image. While the practice is common, and in some circumstances there will be a fair dealing exception available, your safest course is always to get the permission of the creator to reuse their material or to pay them for it. Often that means some detective work on your part because images in particular are copied so quickly on the internet that it can be difficult to find out who is the original creator or copyright holder. But just because an account holder grants you permission to use an image does not necessarily mean they are the creator and copyright holder. Attribution to the social media platform is insufficient, such as 'Photo – Instagram'. The best advice to those wanting to cut and paste material from the Internet and social media is the formula: Freely viewed $\neq$ Freely used.

Case example:

Earthquake case (2014): Haitian photographer Daniel Morel, who took spectacular photographs of the earthquake in Haiti in 2010 and posted them to social media via Twitpic, won a copyright case in New York in 2013. The images had been re-posted by another Twitter user and then sold by Agence France Presse and Getty Images to mainstream media outlets globally (Balasubramani, 2013).

The enforcement of intellectual property laws varies markedly throughout the world. For some creators, there is little that can be done to preserve the creative value of their work once it has been reproduced brazenly online. As a professional communicator, it is often as much a moral obligation you have to your fellow creators to only draw upon their work within the defences and with full and thorough acknowledgement of their original authorship.

Technology advances have complicated copyright law. Courts throughout the world have turned their attention to whether you are breaching copyright by linking to copyright material. Most of the cases have centred on large-scale linking to commercially valuable material within competitors' websites, particularly when it involves the 'mining' of other people's information for new business purposes in the form of inline linking, thumbnailing or framing where the material appears on the linker's page in breach of copyright. 'Deep links' to specific pages or audio-visual material within a larger website is usually acceptable if it then comes under the architecture of the copyright owner's or licensed site, with the link only serving as a referral point rather than an appropriation device.

Artificial intelligence copyright cases started to emerge in the 2020s. For example, the US Copyright Office partially cancelled copyright registration granted to Kristina Kashtanova for the registration of copyright in the 'Zarya of the Dawn' comic book because it included 'non-human authorship' of images using the AI program Midjourney that had not been disclosed (Setty, 2023).

Trade marks

In our globalised commercial world, the unauthorised use of a product name is of special concern to multinational corporations. Many company names have become so commonly used that there is often a question of whether they have become a 'generic' description of a type of product or process. The International Trademark Association (INTA, 2018) warns against the misuse of brand names. It gives recommendations – some verging on the ludicrous – including that the phrase 'separable fasteners' should be used in place of the trade mark 'Velcro' and that 'audio data computer software' should be used instead of the generic use of 'iTunes'. Bear in mind that a trade mark does not amount to worldwide literary copyright: it is designed to protect against others applying the same trade mark to goods competing in the same market. For example, in late 2022 the Australian manuka honey industry won a trade mark battle against New Zealand in the UK and European courts. New Zealand's Manuka Honey Appellation Society (MHAS) discontinued its High Court appeal in the UK, leaving in place the UK Intellectual Property Office's rejection of its application to trademark the words 'Manuka honey'. The New Zealanders also withdrew their application for the 'Manuka Honey' certification mark in the European Union.

The law of 'passing off' and personality rights

Many parts of the world, including Australia, have limitations on how you can use the name and image of others – particularly if you are making a profit out of it. In some countries these actions are called 'passing off', while in others they are known as personality rights or rights in publicity. Satirists need to beware of the action in 'passing off', which can be brought against someone who has falsely represented their work or business as that of another – as in the case of a 'spoof' website. In common law countries like Australia and the United Kingdom, such an action can be commenced against you if you have used someone's name or likeness to imply they have entered into a commercial arrangement to endorse your product or service in some way. In its basic form, the passing off action offers simple protection to businesses against those who try to trade off their reputation by pretending to have some connection with them, or endorsement from them. It has been extended in the creative arts to protect newspaper columnists from deceptive parodies of their work being published under their names in competing publications and also to protect the 'pen-names' of authors being used by their former employers after they have moved on to another title. The ingredients of passing off were stated in the Cricketer case (1974):

> First, that the plaintiff has a business; secondly, that it has a reputation in a name or use of a name in the sense that the particular name is distinctive of the plaintiff; and thirdly, that there is a real probability that the plaintiff's clients or prospective clients will be deceived by believing that the defendant's goods are the plaintiff's, causing him damage.

The action can cover the claim of a false connection, as with a celebrity endorsement (Van Caenegem, 2001: 226) and can protect goodwill and reputation (Walker, 2000: 945).

In European and other civil law jurisdictions, there are tough limits on how you can use the likenesses of others – all bundled up in the laws of privacy. You can't just cut and paste someone's photo from the internet and use it – especially if it appears to be endorsing your enterprise in some way. The US offers a property right known as the 'right to publicity', and several states have passed laws to extend its basic common law protections. It gives people the right to protect their name, image and other identifying features against commercial exploitation by others. However, like so many areas of US law, it is limited by the free speech protections given by the First Amendment, so it usually only encompasses blatant cases of exploitation that lack a free expression rationale.

The issue of passing off frequently arises in domain name (www) registration, with some opportunists tempted to exploit the system by registering famous people's and companies' names as website URLs and social media handles. This is sometimes called 'cyber-squatting'. Disputes often end up in the hands of international and national domain name-registration agencies, which engage in arbitration between the parties to try to resolve the argument over who is really entitled to the name. The Internet Corporation for Assigned Names and Numbers (ICANN) will work with national bodies to withdraw a domain name from a cyber-squatter. You never actually 'own' your URL – you are only licensed to use it for a certain period by the registration body. Cyber-squatters keep a close eye on the registration process and pounce once a popular name becomes available. They then might use it to sell advertising or try to sell it back to you at an inflated price. You can't register every possible variation on the spelling of your name so some spyware and phishing operators register common misspellings of the URLs of famous people and corporations – a practice known as 'typo-squatting'. The international dispute-resolution processes for domain names can be expensive. Cases handled by WIPO's Arbitration and Mediation Center – listed at <www.wipo.int/amc/en/domains/casesx/all.html> – make for interesting reading and feature many of the world's leading brands winning their legitimate URL registration back from shysters and spammers from remote corners of the planet (WIPO, 2023).

A word on fan fiction

The phenomenon or art of fan fiction typically involves the creation of works across a range of media (film, literature or even social media) inspired by a successful work and using one or more of the same characters to do so. In some cases, it is a serious work taking the storyline or concept to a new level. In others it is designed more as a parody of the original. A range of intellectual property laws can be used by the original creators to rain on the fan fiction party – with the most prominent being copyright infringement and others being infringement of trademark, passing off and personality/publicity rights. Most experts agree that amateur fan fiction works will normally not attract legal action if they treat the characters with respect, but commercial attempts will be more likely to attract intellectual property litigation.

Case examples:

Rocky case (1989): Scriptwriter Timothy Anderson wrote a treatment for a new film in the Rocky franchise – Rocky IV – using the original characters from the first three movies and involving a boxing showdown between the hero Rocky Balboa and a communist Russian opponent. He pitched his treatment to the Rocky creator Sylvester Stallone and various studio executives. When Rocky IV was released, also using Russian-American rivals, Anderson sued Stallone for breach of copyright. He failed, with the court holding there were insufficient similarities and that Anderson could not hold copyright because his treatment was an unauthorised derivative work where the key characters were the creations of someone else.

JK Rowling case (2008): Harry Potter author JK Rowling won a breach of copyright action against the creator of a successful web-based fan site – 'The Harry Potter Lexicon' – because he was about to publish an encyclopedia based on the enterprise in competition with her own proposed encyclopedia. The court agreed with the author that there was far too much of her original expression in the work. A fair use argument failed partly on that basis. An injunction was awarded to stop the proposed book and damages were awarded.

Basic Australian legal principles in intellectual property

Here we offer Australian law and examples on the key areas of intellectual property law relevant to professional communicators, including copyright, trade marks and the law of passing off.

Copyright in Australia

Australian copyright law is contained in the *Copyright Act 1968* (Cth). It is less fragmented than most other areas of media law. The three parts most relevant to professional communicators are:

- Part III – dealing with copyright in original literary, dramatic, musical and artistic works;
- Part IV – dealing with copyright in subject matter other than works, such as broadcasts; and
- Part IX – stating the enforceable moral rights of authors.

Copyright in original literary, dramatic, musical and artistic works

Even though some news stories, media releases and speeches might appear far from 'literary', print and online communicators' work fits within this category. In section 31, the *Copyright Act* defines copyright as the exclusive right to reproduce literary, dramatic, musical and artistic works as well as compilations such as films, sound recordings, published editions and broadcasts. Because 'literary work' includes compilations, a newspaper or magazine falls under this category, as does a script for radio or television or a podcast. Copyright in a broadcast rests with the creator of the programme as a whole. In the case of literary works, section 31(1)(a) defines copyright as the exclusive right to reproduce, publish, perform, communicate or adapt a work.

The central concept is that copyright does not protect an idea. It protects the form of expression of an idea – for example, in words. So there is nothing in copyright law to prevent professional communicators from gleaning ideas or information from other sources when creating their own work (although plagiarism could be an issue at an ethical level). But when such 'gleaning' becomes replicating another person's work – in part or in whole – the law of copyright comes into play.

Under Australian law, copyright protection is automatic from the instant a work is created. All that is required under section 32 is that the work be published first in Australia or that the creator of the work is Australian, and that the work is 'original' – the result of the author's own efforts and skill. The work is then protected in most countries under a series of international treaties.

Under section 33(2), copyright in a literary work continues until the expiration of 70 years after the author dies. Copyright in photographs normally lasts for 70 years after the photographer's death. Once copyright has expired, the work is in the 'public domain', meaning that permission is no longer required to use it.

If you are a journalist working for a media corporation or selling your work on a freelance basis, you might not qualify for copyright payments. This is because Australia passed amendments to the Act to assign the employer automatic copyright in work done in the scope of your employment. Contracts with major news organisations usually give those rights to the publisher, so it pays to check before signing.

Like other property, copyright can be transferred to others. You can arrange a full transfer of the ownership of copyright (an 'assignment') or a limited transfer for a particular length of time or purpose (a 'licence'). Importantly, however, section 196(3) of the Act provides that an assignment of copyright (whether total or partial) does not have effect unless it is in writing signed by or on behalf of the assignor. This is particularly important for journalists and photographers, because they often make or receive requests to use copyright material.

Case example:

Kokoda Trail case (2005): The issue of assignment of copyright arose here, where Channel Seven won an injunction to stop Channel Nine screening footage of a Kokoda Trail walk by a group of disadvantaged boys. Channel Seven had funded a freelance camera crew to accompany the youths and had paid for some of the equipment. Later, the group's organiser authorised a production company to make a television documentary, to be screened on Nine. The Full Court upheld Seven's appeal on the grounds that Seven had not assigned its share of the joint copyright to the organisation's leader, so he did not have authority to approve Nine's broadcast of the footage.

Reproducing the work of others

Professional communicators often need to draw on the work of others when reporting, commenting on, or creating publications, broadcasts or material for websites. If the work has not been made available through either assignment or licence, and if you plan to use a substantial part of the work, you have to be willing to pay for the use, or be able to work within one of the fair dealing exceptions outlined below. One difficulty is that, when the legislation uses the expression 'substantial part', it does not define what is meant by that term. The courts have interpreted it to mean any significant or important part of the work, no matter how large or small a portion it might represent (Panel cases, 2002–2005). For example, a photograph might depict a celebrity standing at the airport, but the celebrity's face might only occupy 20 per cent of the frame. However, the face is so significant that a reproduction of just the headshot would likely be the use of a 'substantial part'.

Case example:

***The Panel* cases (2002–2005)**: Network Ten screened a weekly programme, *The Panel*, which involved a panel of comedians and guests commenting on recent events and people in a humorous way. It typically contained excerpts of footage from news events and other television stations' programmes, which formed the basis of critique, satire or simply conversation points. The competing network, Nine, claimed Ten had breached its copyright by using excerpts from several of its programmes on *The Panel*. A High Court majority held that copyright law should not be applied by reference to every single, separate image in a broadcast, but in terms of the overall programme. The Full Federal Court then decided the test of substantiality was a matter of quality – whether the excerpt, no matter how small – was a significant or important ingredient of the programme. Broadcast journalists and online editors need to pay heed to finer aspects of the *Panel* decision on substantiality. They should look carefully at the Full Federal Court's 2002 and 2005 decisions for examples of excerpts complying with, and breaching, the requirements.

Using the fair dealing exceptions

If a substantial or significant part of the copyrighted work is going to being used then professional communicators must either get permission or pay for an assignment or licence or use one of the fair dealing exceptions – the defences most commonly relied upon by news organisations – fair dealing for the purposes of criticism or review (s41), fair dealing for the purpose of reporting news (s42) or fair dealing for the purpose of parody or satire (s41A). (There is also fair dealing for the purpose of research or study at s40, which some communicators might use in a university or research situation.)

The first two exceptions – criticism or review and reporting news – require that 'sufficient acknowledgement' be made, which usually requires the author to be named and the title of the work to be stated. This might present a hurdle for some media organisations, who are reluctant to acknowledge the source for commercial reasons (even when they have used a substantial portion of someone else's work) or whose house style minimises the attribution given. An acknowledgement stating 'a news site reported yesterday' would not be enough, whereas 'Caitlin Cassidy reported in *Guardian Australia* yesterday' would acknowledge both the author and the outlet.

FAIR DEALING FOR CRITICISM OR REVIEW

The Act states at s41 (and at s103A for audio-visual work) that a fair dealing defence will apply if the use is for criticism or review and sufficient acknowledgment is made. The key criteria here are that the dealing be 'fair', that a 'sufficient acknowledgement' be made and that the use serves the purpose of criticism or review. A columnist may review a book or a film and reproduce passages or photographic stills, as long as they sufficiently indicate the source and do not use too much of the work in the review. How much is fair? The courts will determine this on a case-by-case basis but will obviously be reluctant to allow large excerpts or whole works to be replicated to attract readers, viewers or listeners.

Case example:

Clippings case (1990): Two newspaper journalists claimed successfully that a press clipping service had photocopied and sold their articles in breach of copyright. The service, Neville Jeffress Pidler, failed to convince the court that it had copied the articles under the fair dealing provisions. The judge drew upon dictionary definitions of 'criticism' and 'review' to decide there had not been a 'critical application of mental faculties'.

A broad range of journalistic tasks fall within the realm of criticism or review, including dining reviews, book reviews and letters to the editor. Most that might earn the 'honest opinion' or 'fair comment' defence in defamation would qualify, as outlined in Chapter 5, so long as the use was 'fair'. However, as the Federal Court decided in the Panel cases (2002–2005) and the Greenpeace case (Key Case 9.2 – 2021), and as we will see later in relation to parody, the primary *purpose* of the use of the copyright material must indeed be the kind of use relied upon.

FAIR DEALING FOR THE PURPOSE OF REPORTING NEWS

The second exception available to journalists is fair dealing for the purpose of reporting news, set out in s42 (s103B for audio-visual items). Under that defence, a work can be used as part of a news report if it is for the purpose of, or associated with, that news report. However, the playing of music in a news report does not qualify if it is not actually part of the news being reported. In other words, news directors cannot dub in the Star Wars theme music to introduce an item about the launch of a space rocket, but if a busker was playing that music incidentally behind the reporter outside the venue then it would qualify. The key elements are again the operation of the words 'fair' and 'sufficient acknowledgement'. Podcasters need caution here.

FAIR DEALING FOR THE PURPOSE OF PARODY OR SATIRE

In 2006 the federal government enacted an additional fair dealing exception for the purpose of 'parody or satire', to redress problems with that genre raised in the *Panel* cases (2002–2005). It said copyright would not be infringed if the use for parody or satire amounted to a special case, did not conflict with the normal exploitation of the work and did not unreasonably prejudice the legitimate interests of the owner of the work. The exception is detailed in s103AA (audio visual works) and s41A (other works). As the Australian Copyright Council (2014: 3) points out, drawing upon dictionary definitions, a parody may be thought to be an imitation of a work that may need to draw upon parts of the original to be effective. The concept of satire is more difficult to define:

> The purpose of satire, on the other hand, is to draw attention to characteristics or actions – such as vice or folly – by using certain forms of expression – such as irony, sarcasm and ridicule. It seems that both elements are required: the object to which attention is drawn (vice or folly, etc.) and the manner in which it is done (irony, ridicule, etc.). It is not clear, for example, that a cartoon which uses irony or ridicule about characteristics or actions other than something like vice or folly would be satirical.

Ensuing cases will determine whether the use of copyright work for parodic or satirical purposes has been 'fair'.

Case examples:

Twisted Sister case (2021): Mining billionaire and politician Clive Palmer used a song titled 'Aussies Not Gonna Cop It' in his United Australia Party (UAP) 2019 election campaign in video, online and social media communications. It was found to breach the copyright in the most famous 1984 song by the band Twisted Sister 'We're Not Gonna Take It'. The party had first tried to negotiate a licence for the use of the song, but then chose to rely on the parody and satire fair dealing defence. The court rejected it, holding that Palmer's use of the song was opportunistic and not fair and that the purpose of using the song was for political criticism rather than for parody or satire. Despite rewriting the lyrics, he breached the copyright in both the musical and literary work of the original track. Palmer was ordered to stop using it and to pay $1.5 million in damages.

Pokémon case (2017): The Federal Court looked at the parody defence when it was raised by a business called Redbubble, which had created an internet marketplace for 'print-on-demand' personalisation services for customers who wanted a product with an image or word that had been created by an artist or designer. Some featured Pokémon characters. The court decided that what must be shown is that the use made of the work was both *fair* and for the *purpose* of parody and satire, and not just that what was produced might in the eyes of some *be* parody or satire. The company that owned the Pokémon rights was awarded nominal damages of $1.

Television format protections

While Australian IP laws do not protect character rights, they do protect rights in formats – an area of particular concern to media professionals working in 'reality' shows on TV or creating their own online 'shows'.

Case example:

MKR case (2015): Channel Seven broadcast a reality television cooking programme called *My Kitchen Rules (MKR)* over six consecutive seasons. Nine began broadcasting a reality television cooking programme called *The Hotplate*. Seven alleged that Nine was infringing Seven's copyright in *MKR*. The court held that the formats of *MKR* and *The Hotplate* were very similar and was also satisfied that Seven had an arguable case that this close similarity was (at least to some extent) the result of copying but did not issue an injunction to stop the broadcast. Nevertheless, broadcast professionals should note that the format itself can be protected.

Moral rights

International conventions and Australian law grant you 'moral rights' over your work in addition to economic rights. The *Copyright Act* grants authors these legally enforceable rights at s189:

(a) a right of attribution of authorship; or
(b) a right not to have authorship falsely attributed; or
(c) a right of integrity of authorship.

Table 9.1 Key questions to ask when using the work of another

Has the copyright period expired? (Has the creator been dead for more than 70 years?)
Is the work in the public domain? (Creative commons, rights waived etc)
Who is the actual creator or legal owner of the copyright?
Has the copyright holder 'assigned' copyright to you? (A full transfer of ownership and proof of assignment.)
Has the copyright holder 'licensed' you to use the material? (A restricted permission to use the material, such as for a certain time or for a particular purpose.)
If none of the above, do you plan to use a 'substantial' or significant or important portion of the work?
If so, does one of the 'fair dealing' exceptions apply, such as the exception for the purpose of criticism or review, reporting news, or 'parody or satire'?
How do I attribute the work to the creator, which is their moral right?

It explains 'integrity of authorship' at s195AI:

(1) The author of a work has a right of integrity of authorship in respect of the work.
(2) The author's right is the right not to have the work subjected to derogatory treatment.

Even if you transfer the copyright in your work to someone else you still retain your moral rights as an author. This means you can take action against those who might put their own names to your work or those who have put your name to the work but have changed it to your disadvantage. It operates in part to protect you from unfair attacks and parodies where your work has been mutilated, distorted beyond recognition or reproduced in a thoroughly inappropriate context that damages your honour. It does not protect 'reasonable' criticism of your work or any critique to which you have agreed. It also does not prevent employers or clients leaving your name off work if you have contracted to allow them to do so. But it sends a warning to others that they shouldn't mess with your work or republish it without giving you due credit. It also means you should be careful when writing parodies pretending to be someone else or denigrating their content and style by chopping and changing it to your satirical ends. Moral rights remain with the creator, or the creator's heirs, for the same period as copyright.

Case examples:

Corby case (2013): Publishers Allen & Unwin reproduced photographs taken by family members of convicted Bali drug smuggler Schapelle Corby in a book *Sins of the Father* without asking their permission. The publisher relied upon the fact that the copyright owners had previously given permission, including in one case to the book's author, allowing publication of the photographs. The court found that the permission was for another purpose, unconnected with production of the book. Allen & Unwin was liable for breach of copyright, and for infringing the moral rights of the members of Corby's family who took the photographs, which were not attributed to them.

PI case (2015): The *Sun-Herald* newspaper published a report on a private investigator that referred to him as a 'liar, cheat and unlicensed private investigator' who was 'again using aliases to scam unsuspecting clients'. The article featured what appeared to be a professionally created photograph of the PI's partner posed on a bed and semi-naked from the waist up. The PI did not sue for defamation but sought damages for infringement of his copyright in the image and a breach of his moral rights because of the misattribution of authorship. The court ruled a person could not be said to have suffered loss for non-attribution where they would not have wished their name to be published in connection with a photograph so there was no breach of his moral rights. He was awarded $10,001 in damages for breach of his copyright in the image.

Digital IP cases

A series of High Court and Federal Court copyright cases have dealt with some of the more complex intellectual property issues in the digital era. The law in this area is developing rapidly.

Case examples:

DABUS AI case (2022): The creator of an artificial intelligence machine failed in a High Court bid to have his computer nominated as the inventor of the inventions it creates using artificial neural networks for patent purposes. The machine is called DABUS, an acronym for 'device for the autonomous bootstrapping of unified sentience'. The result is that under Australian law a non-human artificial intelligence cannot hold a patent for something it invents.

ISP cases (2016): Proceedings were brought by Village Roadshow and other copyright owners against a large number of Australian Internet Service Providers (ISPs,) ordering them to disable access to various online locations, including The Pirate Bay, TorrentHound and isoHunt, which infringed or facilitated the infringement of copyright. The court was satisfied that if the ISP provided access to an online location outside Australia, whose primary purpose was to facilitate the infringement of copyright, it was not necessary for the applicant to establish knowledge or intention on the part of the ISP itself.

Remedies for copyright infringement

There can be civil or criminal consequences for copyright breaches under the Act. Under section 115, remedies available include an injunction, damages or an 'account of profits', the payment by the infringer of any profits made from the copying. Additional damages can be awarded depending upon the flagrancy of the infringement and other factors. If there is a commercial element to the infringement, breach of copyright can also be a criminal offence (s132).

Trade marks in Australia

A trade mark, according to s17 of the *Trade Marks Act 1995* (Cth) is:

> a sign used, or intended to be used, to distinguish goods or services dealt with or provided in the course of trade by a person from goods or services so dealt with or provided by any other person.

Section 120(1) provides that infringement of a trade mark occurs when:

> the person uses as a trade mark a sign that is substantially identical with, or deceptively similar to, the trade mark in relation to goods or services in respect of which the trade mark is registered.

Corporations are very protective of their trade marks. The masthead of a newspaper or the various permutations of a media organisation's name might be registered as a trade mark under the Trade Marks Act. For example, media mogul Rupert Murdoch's News Corporation has had the trade mark 'Newspoll' registered since 1984 to protect a subsidiary business of that name which conducts and reports public opinion polls. The cases in which use of a trademarked expression can amount to infringement will not typically involve professional communicators, as opposed to business competitors.

Case example:

Hells Angels case (2022): The Hells Angels motorcycle club won an injunction and $78,000 in damages from the online merchandise company Redbubble for infringements of its trademarks in images like its winged skull device and its club logo on clothing, face marks, posters and stickers. It was the club's second such victory in three years against Redbubble, which had allowed users to upload the trademarked images despite its attempts at moderation via keyword searches and deletion of infringing items. The court held that infringement can still be made out if the images were uploaded by third parties in an automated process, even if they were outside of Australia, and even in breach of their agreement with the site owner, and regardless of whether the infringing goods were sold.

The ethics and law of intellectual property 267

Reflect – Research – Review:

Some people mistakenly say they are going to 'Xerox' something rather than 'photocopy' it. Give three further examples of sentences where a company's trade mark might mistakenly be used instead of a product or a process. Explain the basis of the confused meaning.

Key Case 9.2: Greenpeace case (2021)

AGL Energy Limited v Greenpeace Australia Pacific Limited [2021] FCA 625 (8 June 2021), <www.austlii.edu.au/cgi-bin/viewdoc/au/cases/cth/FCA/2021/625.html>

Facts

The environmental activist group Greenpeace started a public campaign against the energy company AGL over its carbon emissions and other practices, using the AGL name and logo in material designed to look like AGL's branding but actually using it to criticise the company and its policies. It described AGL (next to its logo) as 'Still Australia's Biggest Climate Polluter' and 'Generating Pollution for Generations' accompanied by the words 'Australia's Greatest Liability'. The campaign – known as 'brand-jamming' – appeared in a range of media formats, including posters, placards, social media posts, online banner ads and a parody website. AGL sued, arguing the use of the name, slogan and logo were infringements of both their trademark and their copyright.

Law

Greenpeace did not deny they were breaching AGL's copyright, but argued their campaign was exempted from the infringements under the fair dealing exceptions – s41 for criticism or review, and s41A for parody or satire. The judge found almost all its uses were excusable under the parody or satire defence, but only some of them met the criticism or review criteria because others were not critiquing the logo artwork itself. Nevertheless, the parody or satire exception was sufficient for most and it was ordered to refrain from using the others. As for the trade mark infringement, the court held AGL failed at the first hurdle because Greenpeace was not using the adapted logo 'as a trade mark' under s120(1) of the Trade Marks Act. Neither was it using the trade mark in relation to AGL's registered services.

Lessons for professional communicators

The parody and satire fair dealing defence to copyright – and even a trademark infringement – can be used effectively in a narrow range of situations, particularly if the criticism is being directed from the high ground and your organisation is not a competitor with the one being satirised. Corporations are often successful defending their trade marks, so communicators should take legal advice before embarking on this type of strategy.

'Passing off' in Australia

Misleading or deceptive use of another's identity or business name can be pursued using the action for 'passing off' or under consumer laws, also known as trade practices or fair-trading legislation (covered in Chapter 12). The High Court has described the tort of passing off as 'the wrongful appropriation of the reputation of another or that of his goods' (Building Centres case, 1978). It is also meant to prevent news organisations publishing material falsely attributing work to an author who has not created it. The action can cover the claim of a false connection, as with a celebrity endorsement (Van Caenegem, 2001: 226) and can protect goodwill and reputation (Walker, 2000: 945). Public relations practitioners and marketers need to be on the alert against making claims about their own products or services – or those of their clients – that might mislead or deceive consumers. Such claims might arise in sponsored content in corporate promotional material, on websites and in social media, in advertisements and in 'advertorials' or 'advertising features' in the mainstream media. Media releases making unverified claims about products or services are a special risk in this category.

Professional communicators who work in PR or advertising, or who use their journalistic talents as researchers or script consultants on docudramas or 'faction' also need to be aware that while 'character rights' do not exist in Australia, to prevent anyone profiting by the publicity attracted by the mere use of or reference to an established fictional character, passing off principles can extend to such use. (See the Constable Wendy case, 2010). Actions for misleading and deceptive conduct and passing off can also arise in the field of public relations.

Case examples:

Penname case (1977): The action for passing off was used in Australia to protect the penname 'Pierpont' after the business journalist who used that *nom de plume* – Trevor Sykes – moved from the *Australian Financial Review* to *The Bulletin* magazine. His column continued for another 40 years, first at *The Bulletin* and then back at the *Australian Financial Review*.

Crocodile Dundee case (1989): An advertisement for Grosby shoes which partially re-created the knife scene from the blockbuster movie *Crocodile Dundee*, using an actor dressed in a costume similar to the one Paul Hogan wore in the 1986 film, was held to have amounted to passing off, on the basis that viewers would have inferred a connection with (or approval from) Hogan, which did not exist.

Reflect – Research – Review:

Intellectual property ethics and law in action – Case study 9.1: The kids' pic for the cereal campaign

In an era of digital copying and artificial intelligence, opportunities abound for plagiarism and breach of intellectual property laws. Here, we return to the Applied Ethics Matrix to explore the ethics of a problem scenario (Chapter 1, Figure 1.2) before analysing the media law dimensions of the problem using the specific legal risk analysis technique (Grantham and Pearson, 2022: 51–53).

The problem

You are a junior consultant in a leading international public relations consultancy tasked with finding an image of a group of happy children to form part of a media campaign for a breakfast cereal manufacturer. You search in your web browser for 'happy children' and find the perfect image of four preschoolers laughing in a circle on lush green grass. You are about to copy this image as the central image to be used in the campaign.

Pausing to reflect

Your first challenge is to pause then use our 'Reflect – Research – Review' techniques. Your media law and ethics knowledge should have you pause at this juncture – just when you are about to use work created by someone else. What initial method of reflection do you propose to use – a mini mindfulness-based meditation on the issue, some mindmapping to generate the key issues, or perhaps some journaling to record your initial thoughts? At that point you will have at least a preliminary view – perhaps a 'gut feeling' about the ethics and morals of your action. Now it's time to get more systematic …

Applying the Applied Ethics Matrix

Consider using the Applied Ethics Matrix introduced in Chapter 1 as Figure 1.2 – combining philosophy, laws and professional codes, theoretical lenses, relative interests and moral compasses to assist in making a communication ethics decision. Let's apply it to this situation, with you filling in your answers to these questions and then discussing them with others, perhaps your colleagues or professor.

- What if everyone acted this way? Should this approach become the rule? What duties do I owe to others? (deontological)
- Does my proposed action lead to the greatest benefit for most stakeholders? (consequentialist)
- How are the rights and interests of various stakeholders affected by this action? (contractualist)
- What virtues or vices are evident in this action? How does it shape my character? (virtue ethicist)
- What clauses from a professional communication ethical code apply to this situation and what guidance is given?
- How does the action sit with the laws of society? (See more formal analysis below.)
- How does the dilemma sit with a theoretical perspective I have adopted, such as feminism, environmentalism or Marxism (or some combination)?
- What self interests is this decision serving as opposed to, or in combination with, the interests of others?
- What does my unique moral compass contribute to my deliberations? (See Figure 1.1). Does a potential bias need consideration or disclosure?

Applying the specific legal risk analysis technique (Grantham and Pearson, 2022: 51–53)

Identifying the potential (or existing) legal problem

Your chapter review gives you the basic answer here. An image is a creative work and is protected internationally by copyright law.

Reviewing the areas of the law involved

This is a hypothetical situation, so there are many possibilities that could apply to this image and its proposed use in a commercial public relations campaign. All images have been created by someone, who is the copyright holder unless they have waived their rights or assigned or licensed them to someone else. Information from your search engine results might give you some indication of who you need to be dealing with for permission and attribution purposes. It might be a Creative Commons image, which might be free to use in even a commercial situation. Whether or not it is free to use, the moral rights of the photographer require you to attribute it to its creator. If it is not free to use, it might have been covered by either the fair use doctrine or a fair dealing defence, depending on your jurisdiction. But none is likely to apply here because your use is purely commercial, and not for some legitimate public function like education, news, review, parody etc. That means that legally you will need to find the copyright holder and negotiate permission and a fee for use.

Projecting the possible consequences for stakeholders

Here you might go through a basic stakeholder mapping process – identifying the key stakeholders in a decision to use the image without permission. You as a junior professional have your career and reputation at stake. So too does your public relations organisation, with its ethical obligations to honour the work of other communicators. Your client has much on the line if a legal or public relations crisis emanates from the theft of someone's intellectual property in their campaign. And clearly the photographer's rights and interests must be weighed as the creator of the image in question. Can you identify and assess other stakeholders?

Seeking advice/referring upward

As long as you have not yet used the image, a simple discussion among colleagues and your supervisors should resolve the correct course of action – finding the ownership and attributing if its use is free – or negotiating a fee to use. If, however, someone is suggesting you take the risk and go ahead with using the image regardless, then advice would be required on the legal, financial and brand risks at stake.

Publishing/amending/deleting/correcting/apologizing

The scenario only has us at the preliminary selection stage. If the image had been published and it was discovered that it was in breach of someone's copyright, then lawyers and senior management would be engaged to negotiate remedial actions such as apologies and making offers of compensation to the creator. This could be expensive, particularly if it results in litigation.

In a nutshell

- Ancient societies and philosophers considered the principles of intellectual property long before the first laws were developed. Some philosophers have opposed intellectual property laws as limitations on free expression.
- Intellectual property comprises 'creations of the mind': inventions, literary and artistic works, and symbols, names, images and designs used in commerce. IP laws are meant to protect our right to the exclusive use of the array of creative outputs we might produce as human beings.
- Professional communicators might encounter IP laws when you reproduce the work of others or if they steal your creative output and thus you might be destined for either the plaintiff's or the defendant's role in a court case.
- New technologies have presented new challenges in intellectual property, with the latest being the implications of works and inventions created by artificial intelligence.
- There are commonalities and differences in intellectual property law internationally, with the most important being the regulation of infringements and in copyright the differences between defences of 'fair use' (broader and more flexible) and 'fair dealing' (narrower and specified).
- International conventions and Australian law grant you 'moral rights' over your work in addition to your actionable economic rights.
- Copyright protects the creator's form of expression used in the work, not the ideas behind it. Plagiarism as an ethical issue can apply to poorly attributed expression and ideas.
- The not-for-profit Creative Commons promotes the 'creative re-use of intellectual and artistic works', whether owned or in the public domain. It offers free copyright licences, enabling creators the option of a voluntary 'some rights reserved' approach.
- The three exceptions to breach of copyright under the Australian *Copyright Act* most commonly cited by news organisations are fair dealing for the purposes of criticism or review (s41); fair dealing for the purpose of reporting news (s42); and fair dealing for the purpose of parody or satire (s41A).
- Corporations are protective of their trade marks – symbols used to distinguish their products, services or corporate regalia from others.
- Litigants might also turn to the law of 'passing off', personality rights or the consumer law 'misleading and deceptive conduct' provisions to pursue an action over the wrongful use of commercial names and materials.

References and further reading

Australian Copyright Council (ACC). 2014, *Parodies, Satire and Jokes*, Australian Copyright Council, Sydney, <www.copyright.org.au/browse/book/ACC-Parody-Satire-and-Comedy-INFO083/>.

Balasubramani, V. 2013, 'AFP v Morel – lawsuit over Haiti photos taken from Twitter/Twitpic goes to trial', *Technology Marketing and Law Blog*, 13 November, <http://blog.ericgoldman.org/archives/2013/11/afp-v-morel-lawsuit-over-haiti-photos-taken-from-twittertwitpic-goes-to-trial.htm>.

Grantham, S. and Pearson, M. 2022, *Social Media Risk and the Law: A Guide for Global Communicators*, Routledge, London and New York.

Hepburn, B. and Andersen, H. 2021, 'Scientific Method', *The Stanford Encyclopedia of Philosophy*, Summer 2021 edn, Zalta, E.N. ed., <https://plato.stanford.edu/archives/sum2021/entries/scientific-method/>.

International Trademark Association (INTA). 2018, 'Overview', <www.inta.org/about/pages/overview.aspx>.

Media Entertainment and Arts Alliance (MEAA). 2016, *The MEAA Journalist Code of Ethics*, Media Entertainment and Arts Alliance, Sydney, <www.meaa.org/download/faqs-meaa-journalist-code-of-ethics/>.

Media Entertainment and Arts Alliance (MEAA). 1996, *Ethics Review Committee Final Report*, MEAA, Sydney.

Meta. 2022, *Terms of Service*, <www.facebook.com/legal/terms>.

Miller, S. 2018, 'Corruption', *The Stanford Encyclopedia of Philosophy*, Winter 2018 edn, Zalta, E.N. ed., <https://plato.stanford.edu/archives/win2018/entries/corruption/>.

Moore, A. and Himma, K. 2022, 'Intellectual Property', *The Stanford Encyclopedia of Philosophy*, Fall 2022 edn, Zalta, E.N. and Nodelman, U. eds, <https://plato.stanford.edu/archives/fall2022/entries/intellectual-property/>.

Nard, C.A. and Morriss, A.P. 2006, 'Constitutionalizing Patents: From Venice to Philadelphia', *Review of Law and Economics*, 2 (2), 223–321. <https://scholarlycommons.law.case.edu/faculty_publications/587>.

Potter, R.B. 1972, 'The Logic of Moral Argument', *Toward a Discipline of Social Ethics*, Deats, P. ed., Boston University Press, Boston, 93–114.

Public Relations Consultants Association (PRCA). 2023, *Professional Charter and Codes of Conduct*, London, <www.prca.org.uk/about-us/pr-standards/professional-charter-and-codes-conduct>.

Public Relations Institute of Australia (PRIA). 2009, *Public Relations Institute of Australia (PRIA) Code of Ethics*, PRIA, Sydney, <www.pria.com.au/about-pria/code-of-ethics-privacy/code-of-ethics/>.

Setty, R., 2023, 'AI-Assisted 'Zarya of the Dawn' Comic Gets Partial Copyright Win' *Bloomberg*, 23 February, <https://news.bloomberglaw.com/ip-law/ai-assisted-zarya-of-the-dawn-comic-gets-partial-copyright-win>.

Society of Professional Journalists (SPJ). 2014, *Society of Professional Journalists (SPJ) Code of Ethics*, <www.spj.org/ethicscode.asp>.

Toliver, Z. 2017. 'Settlement reached: 'Monkey selfie' case broke new ground for animal rights', *PETA*, <www.peta.org/blog/settlement-reached-monkey-selfie-case-broke-new-ground-animal-rights>.

United Nations (UN). 1966, *International Covenant on Economic, Social and Cultural Rights*, Australian Human Rights Commission, <https://humanrights.gov.au/our-work/commission-general/international-covenant-economic-social-and-cultural-rights-human-rights>.

UN Human Rights Office. 1966, 'UN General Assembly resolution 2200A (XXI)', *International Covenant on Civil and Political Rights*, OHCHR, <www.ohchr.org/en/instruments-mechanisms/instruments/international-covenant-civil-and-political-rights>.
Van Caenegem, W. 2001, *Intellectual Property*, Butterworths, Sydney.
Walker, S. 2000, *Media Law: Commentary and Materials*, Law Book Company, Sydney.
Wikimedia Foundation. 2014, 'Monkey selfie', *Wikimedia Foundation Transparency Report*, <https://transparency.wikimedia.org/stories.html>.
World Intellectual Property Organization (WIPO). 1886, *Berne Convention for the Protection of Literary and Artistic Works*, <www.wipo.int/treaties/en/ip/berne>.
World Intellectual Property Organization (WIPO). 1928, *Berne Convention for the Protection of Literary and Artistic Works*, Rome Act 1928, <www.keionline.org/wp-content/uploads/1928_Rome_revisions_Berne.pdf>.
World Intellectual Property Organization (WIPO). 1979a, *Convention Establishing the World Intellectual Property Organization*, <www.wipo.int/treaties/en/text.jsp?file_id=283854#P50_1504>.
World Intellectual Property Organization (WIPO). 1979b, *Berne Convention for the Protection of Literary and Artistic Works*, <www.wipo.int/treaties/en/text.jsp?file_id=283698>.
World Intellectual Property Organization (WIPO). 2016, *Understanding Copyright and Related Rights*, 2nd edn, <www.wipo.int/edocs/pubdocs/en/wipo_pub_909_2016.pdf>.
World Intellectual Property Organization (WIPO). 2023, *Directory of Intellectual Property Offices*, <www.wipo.int/directory/en/urls.jsp>.
YouTube. 2022, *Terms of Service*, <www.youtube.com/static?template=terms&gl=AU>.

Cases cited

Building Centres case: *Hornsby Building Information Centre Pty Ltd v Sydney Building Information Centre Ltd* [1978] HCA 11; (1978) 140 CLR 216 (19 April 1978), <www.austlii.edu.au/cgi-bin/viewdoc/au/cases/cth/HCA/1978/11.html>.
Carleton's case: *Carleton v ABC* [2002] ACTSC 127 (18 December 2002), <www.austlii.edu.au/au/cases/act/ACTSC/2002/127.html>; *Carleton v ABC* [2003] ACTSC 28 (2 May 2003), <www.austlii.edu.au/au/cases/act/ACTSC/2003/28.html>.
Carlovers case: *Carlovers Carwash Ltd v Sahathevan* [2000] NSWSC 947 (13 October 2000), <www.austlii.edu.au/au/cases/nsw/supreme_ct/2000/947.html>.
Clippings case: *Re De Garis and Moore and Neville Jeffress Pidler Pty Ltd*, No. G1319 of 1988 FED No. 352 Copyright 18 IPR 292 (1991) 20 IPR 605 (1990) 37 FCR 99 (6 July 1990), <www.austlii.edu.au/cgi-bin/viewdoc/au/cases/cth/FCA/1990/218.html>.
Constable Wendy case: *Hatfield v TCN Channel Nine Pty Ltd [2010] NSWCA 69* (8 April 2010) at [111], <www.austlii.edu.au/cgi-bin/viewdoc/au/cases/nsw/NSWCA/2010/69.html>.
Corby case: *Corby v Allen & Unwin Pty Limited* [2013] FCA 370 (24 April 2013), <www.austlii.edu.au/cgi-bin/viewdoc/au/cases/cth/FCA/2013/370.html>.
Cricketer case: *The Cricketer Ltd v Newspress Pty Ltd and David Syme & Co Ltd* [1974] VR 477.

Crocodile Dundee case: *Pacific Dunlop Ltd v Hogan* (1989) 23 FCR 553; 87 ALR 14 (25 May 1989), <www.austlii.edu.au/cgi-bin/viewdoc/au/cases/cth/FCA/1989/185.html>.

DABUS AI case: *Thaler v Commissioner of Patents* [2022] HCATrans 199 (11 November 2022), <www.austlii.edu.au/cgi-bin/viewdoc/au/cases/cth/HCATrans/2022/199.html>.; *Commissioner of Patents v Thaler* [2022] FCAFC 62 (13 April 2022), <www.austlii.edu.au/cgi-bin/viewdoc/au/cases/cth/FCAFC/2022/62.html>.

Earthquake case: *Agence France Presse v Morel*, [2014] BL 224351, S.D.N.Y., 1:10-cv-02730-AJN-MHD, 13 August 2014, <www.bloomberglaw.com/public/desktop/document/AGENCE_FRANCE_PRESSE_Plaintiff_v_DANIEL_MOREL_Defendant_v_GETTY_I?1614649274>.

Greenpeace case: *AGL Energy Limited v Greenpeace Australia Pacific Limited* [2021] FCA 625 (8 June 2021), <www.austlii.edu.au/cgi-bin/viewdoc/au/cases/cth/FCA/2021/625.html>.

Hells Angels case: *Hells Angels Motorcycle Corporation (Australia) Pty Limited v Redbubble Ltd (No 5)* [2022] FCA 837 (19 July 2022), <www.austlii.edu.au/cgi-bin/viewdoc/au/cases/cth/FCA/2022/837.html>.

ISP cases: *Roadshow Films Pty Ltd v Telstra Corporation Ltd* [2016] FCA 1503 (15 December 2016), <www.austlii.edu.au/cgi-bin/viewdoc/au/cases/cth/FCA/2016/1503.html>.

JK Rowling case: *Warner Bros. Entertainment Inc. v RDR Books* [2008] 575 F. Supp. 2d 513, S.D.N.Y. (8 September 2008), <https://scholar.google.com/scholar_case?case=13852164224811081270&hl=en&as_sdt=6&as_vis=1&oi=scholarr>.

Kokoda Trail case: *Seven Network (Operations) Ltd v TCN Channel Nine Pty Ltd* [2005] FCAFC 144 (8 August 2005), <www.austlii.edu.au/au/cases/cth/FCAFC/2005/144.html>.

Meghan Markle's case: *HRH the Duchess of Sussex v Associated Newspapers Ltd* [2021] EWHC 273 (Ch) (11 February 2021), <www.bailii.org/ew/cases/EWHC/Ch/2021/273.html>.; *HRH the Duchess of Sussex v Associated Newspapers Ltd* [2021] EWCA Civ 1810 (2 December 2021), <www.bailii.org/cgi-bin/format.cgi?doc=/ew/cases/EWCA/Civ/2021/1810.html>.

Monkey case: *Naruto Monkey PETA v Slater* [2018]CA9 No. 16–15469 D.C. No. 3:15-cv-04324-WHO Opinion (4 April 2018), <www.documentcloud.org/documents/4444209-Naruto-Monkey-PETA-v-Slater-CA9-Opinion-04–23–18.html>.

MKR case: *Seven Network (Operations) Limited v Endemol Australia Pty Limited* [2015] FCA 800 (6 August 2015), <www.austlii.edu.au/cgi-bin/viewdoc/au/cases/cth/FCA/2015/800.html>.

Panel cases: *TCN Channel Nine Pty Ltd v Network Ten Pty Ltd* [2002] FCAFC 146 (22 May 2002), <www.austlii.edu.au/au/cases/cth/FCAFC/2002/146.html>; *Network Ten Pty Ltd v TCN Channel Nine Pty Ltd* (2004) 78 ALJR 585; [2004] HCA 14 (11 March 2004),www.austlii.edu.au/au/cases/cth/high_ct/2004/14.html>; *TCN Channel Nine Pty Ltd v Network Ten Pty Ltd (No. 2)* [2005] FCAFC 53 (26 May 2005), <www.austlii.edu.au/au/cases/cth/FCAFC/2005/53.html>.

Penname case: *Sykes v John Fairfax & Sons Ltd* [1977] 1 NSWLR 415.

PI case: *Monte v Fairfax Media Publications Pty Ltd* [2015] FCCA 1633 (7 August 2015), <www.austlii.edu.au/cgi-bin/viewdoc/au/cases/cth/FCCA/2015/1633.html>.

Pokémon case: *Pokémon Company International, Inc. v Redbubble Ltd* [2017] FCA 1541 (19 December 2017), <www.austlii.edu.au/cgi-bin/viewdoc/au/cases/cth/FCA/2017/1541.html>.

Rocky case: *Anderson v Stallone* [1989]11 U.S.P.Q.2d 1161 C.D. Cal. (26 April 1989), <www.kentlaw.edu/faculty/rwarner/classes/legalaspects_ukraine/copyright/cases/anderson_v_stallone.html>.

Twisted Sister case: *Universal Music Publishing Pty Ltd v Palmer (No 2)* [2021] FCA 434 (30 April 2021), <www.austlii.edu.au/cgi-bin/viewdoc/au/cases/cth/FCA/2021/434.html>.

10 Defence, national security, cyber security and anti-terrorism

Key concepts

Just war theory: A philosophical theory dating back two millennia outlining the conditions under which it might be permissible to go to war.

National security laws: A range of laws – many of which were introduced in the wake of the 9/11 attacks on the US – designed to counter terrorism but often impinging on other rights and liberties.

Peace journalism: The peace-oriented and solutions-driven approach to reportage that cites a variety of sources to offer a constructive alternative to the enhancement of conflict.

Treason: The crime of betrayal of one's country (or monarch) by attempting to overthrow the government or by giving aid to its enemies.

Sedition: The crime of publishing language intended to incite insurrection against the governing authority, falling short of the direct action of treason.

Cyber security: The art and science of protecting computers, networks, mobile devices, and data from unauthorized access or criminal use and the practice of taking steps to enhance the confidentiality, integrity and availability of information to the intended recipients.

Introduction

Professional communication in the areas of war, defence and national security raises several of the media law and ethics fault lines we have already examined in this book – competing human rights like free expression and the right to life and safety; whether lying and deception is justified to save human life; whether whistleblowers should release data in the public interest; and how someone like a war correspondent can possibly produce a balanced story. War, defence and terrorism deal with what we call existential issues – matters fundamental to existence, matters of life and death. As such, the ethical and legal stakes are high. At an ethical level, the communications created by the professional could serve to accelerate conflicts and cause loss of life or instead might just help forge solutions that save lives. The gravity of some situations is so fraught that professional communicators – war and security correspondents, defence public relations personnel and politicians' media advisers – can construct messages that contribute to deaths and injuries. Their ethical decision making needs to be deep and well informed because that can help prevent such tragedy and also offer resilience to a practitioner's own mental health.

Philosophical background to communication about war, defence and national security

Conflict has been present from time immemorial and philosophers have thought and written about it, often in connection with the key positions in moral philosophy we introduced in Chapter 1. You will recall that the list of virtues developed by Aristotle (384–322BC) as part of a 'life well lived' were dominated strongly by military values, given the importance of the army to the city states of Ancient Greece. Even though he wrote that the aim of war should be peace, he still found the preparation for war was character building because it developed leadership (Husby, 2009: 5). For Aristotle, the highest courage could be found within the soldier who faced death to serve his nation for the most selfless of reasons (Beard, 2019). Many war correspondents too have entered a conflict zone and faced the ultimate risk of death – sometimes to serve their nation, but often to fulfil their professional vocation of telling their audiences their best version of the truth about a vital matter of public importance. Yet, as Beard (2019) points out, courage in a military conflict is not necessarily the highest form of bravery. Some would argue speaking truth to power is a greater courage – such as the bravery of a whistleblower revealing (in breach of official secrets laws) sensitive national security data that could save lives.

Communicators should not go blindly into jobs that might place them at risk of physical or mental injury or as purveyors of propaganda to sell arms or deceive their fellow citizens. These are fields of employment that require a considerable amount of moral and ethical reflection, research and review before taking the first step. Helpful in such decisions is a consideration of the different sides of the primary philosophical debates about human involvement in war and defence, attempting to answer the fundamental question: When can the killing of other humans via war be justified? As the Ethics Centre explains, the Catholic moral theologians Augustine of Hippo (St Augustine) (354–430) and Thomas Aquinas (1225–1274) originated the line of thinking around 'just war theory' which outlined the conditions under which it was permissible to go to war (Ethics Centre, 2016). Of course, that assumes that war is sometimes justifiable. Those who oppose war in all its forms are called 'pacifists' – who argue no plausible moral theory could possibly justify war and its implicit horrors (Lazar, 2020). Such theories can be used by professional communicators in deciding whether they themselves want to go to war or be involved in industries associated with war, and also in their communications such as in stories analysing decisions by leaders about entering a war or their actions during one. The Ethics Centre (2016) points out that modern thinking emanating from those original philosophical positions divides just war theory into three categories, based around their Latin expressions, each with associated ethical rules. They are *jus ad bellum* ('justice towards war'), *jus in bello* ('justice in war'), and *jus post bellum* ('justice after war'). Ethical decision making for each stage involves key questions, not dissimilar to those we raised in our Applied Ethics Matrix in Figure 1.2 in Chapter 1. For pre-war decisions, the primary questions are: 'Is it for a just cause?' 'Is it with the right intention?' 'Is it from legitimate authority?' 'Does it have due proportionality?' 'Is it the last resort?' You can see how these can also be avenues for investigation and questioning from the position of a journalist or an opposition communicator. There should be 'ethical restraint' in war, allowing the observer to distinguish between what philosopher-journalist Michael Ignatieff calls the difference between a warrior and a barbarian (Ethics Centre, 2016). The 'justice in war' stage prompts questions around the attacking of only legitimate targets (enemy forces as opposed to civilians or medics), proportionality in the conduct of the war, using only ethical means in combat and weaponry, and not following unethical orders from command. After a war, the transition to peace might involve restoration of the pre-war status quo, punishment for war crimes, compensation of victims and just peace treaties (Ethics Centre, 2016). Every element of a just war has been subject to intense philosophical debate – as Lazar (2020) has chronicled. Before embarking on a communication position taking you to war or writing or reporting about it, you really need to go into the intricacies of the arguments around each category and decide on your position. This might save you from actually taking up the position or might help shore up your mental health and resilience if you choose to do so.

Of course, debates in moral philosophy related to war, defence and national security go beyond the justification for war. Emergency and volatile situations such as wars and terrorism threats bring into sharp focus many of the ethical issues we have already considered in this book. Lying and deception is a prime example. Philosopher Sissela Bok has addressed the intersection with communication by highlighting the suppression or distortion by governments when war is threatened or under way. She warned against the risks of living in a society 'where public officials can resort to deceit and manipulation whenever they decide that an exceptional crisis has arisen' (Bok, 1978: 178–180). She suggested applying her model to such situations and debating the potential for governmental lying in advance to obtain democratic consent as justification for such potential deceptive practices in the future. Bok is essentially calling for public debate around the practice known as 'propaganda' – the conveying of false or biased information to the citizenry and into enemy territory, in favour of a particular nation's war effort. This is essentially what many call 'fake news' or 'false news' in the modern era, as outlined in Chapter 4, but located more in the defence and security domain. The important ethical question for professional communicators considering working in government media relations or public relations in the defence or national security space is: At a time of crisis, am I willing to produce propaganda in favour of my country's war effort? This leads into both the human rights and ethical dimensions of war, defence and national security communication.

Human rights dimensions to war, defence and national security communication

As we learned in Chapter 2, free expression is enshrined in global human rights instruments like the *International Covenant on Civil and Political Rights* (ICCPR) at Article 19, as well as in the constitutions of most Western democracies – including the First Amendment to the *US Constitution*, the UK's *Human Rights Act 1998*, the Canadian *Charter of Rights and Freedoms*, and the New Zealand *Bill of Rights Act 1990*. Australia is an exception with no explicit mention of free expression in its Constitution but an implied freedom to communicate on matters of politics and government applied by its High Court, and other free expression elements trending through its common law.

However, war, defence and national security raise notable exceptions to the right to free expression, because such human rights instruments place a priority on rights to safety and security for all citizens. For example, Article 19(3) of the ICCPR allows nations to restrict free expression 'for the protection of national security or of public order (*ordre public*) or of public health or morals'. In the US, the Pentagon Papers case (Key Case 10.1) and subsequent cases established that the First Amendment would protect media organisations publishing leaked national security information, but would not protect from prosecution the public servants or others who had leaked it to them.

Other Western jurisdictions have been even less forgiving of the media handling leaked classified information. In Australia, the High Court failed to uphold its implied freedom to communicate on matters of politics and government when a journalist appealed against a Federal Police search warrant for materials that would disclose her insider government source (Search Warrant case, 2020 – Key Case 10.2). National security concerns have meant democracies have maintained a rolling 'state of exception' to free expression obligations (Pearson and Fernandez, 2018). Free expression is not the only other human right that can suffer at the hands of national security laws and in times of war. As then president of the Israeli Supreme Court, Justice Aharon Barak, explained: 'Terrorism does not justify the neglect of accepted legal norms. This is how we distinguish ourselves from the terrorists themselves' (Barak, 2003: 131).

Key Case 10.1: Pentagon Papers case

New York Times v US; US v Washington Post [1971] 713 US 403 (26 June 19710), <https://supreme.justia.com/cases/federal/us/403/713/>.

Facts

Military analyst Daniel Ellsberg leaked the sensitive 'Pentagon Papers' to *The New York Times* in 1971, which revealed the scale of US involvement in Vietnam and the lies of four US presidents. Ellsberg secretly extracted sections of it from a safe in his office and carried it to a friend's office to photocopy it in all-night sessions. The full cache of documents was released by the archives office in 2011. Ellsberg became the second most famous whistleblower of the 20th century (after Watergate source 'Deep Throat', later revealed as FBI associate director Mark Felt, who provided the *Washington Post* with information exposing President Richard Nixon's coverup of a hotel break-in by Republican Party operatives). After an initial story was published, the government attempted to win injunctions to stop the newspapers publishing any more of the material. The newspaper appealed to the Supreme Court.

Law

Despite those government efforts to stop the publication of the Pentagon Papers, the Supreme Court allowed *The New York Times* and *The Washington Post* to go ahead with their release. In the leading judgment, Justice Hugo Black indicated the balance between national security interests and free expression should tilt in the direction of the latter: '(E)very moment's continuance of the injunctions against these newspapers amounts to a flagrant, indefensible, and continuing violation of the First Amendment'. The doctrine against prior restraint of publications meant the government faced a heavy burden in justifying a limitation on free expression. However, while publication was allowed, the court did not render void the *Espionage Act* or allow the media to publish classified documents *carte blanche*. The First Amendment thus protected media outlets which were publishing national security information leaked to them, but not the whistleblowers who leaked it. Rather, Ellsberg and a co-accused later faced charges of conspiracy, theft of government property and espionage (carrying a potential jail term of up to 115 years), along with allegations of FBI wiretapping (Cooper and Roberts, 2011). A federal judge later dismissed the serious criminal charges, seen widely as a vindication of whistleblowing on a matter of public interest. The espionage charges were the same as those listed in the indictment for the extradition to the US of Wikileaks founder Julian Assange in 2019, which he was still fighting in the UK courts in 2023. Ellsberg died in 2023.

Lessons for professional communicators

Professional communicators on both sides of the information flow – journalists and public communication personnel who might become whistleblowers – must all understand the stakes are extremely high when dealing with classified information and leaks. Even when the material appears to be of overwhelming public interest, even the government of the country widely regarded as the icon of free expression might pursue journalists and whistleblowers over their breach of national security laws.

Reflect – Research – Review:

Compare and contrast the different ethical considerations and human rights obligations of a communication officer working for the Department of Defence and a war correspondent working for a leading international media outlet.

Professional ethical dilemmas in war, defence and national security

Among the calamities of war may be jointly numbered the diminution of the love of truth, by the falsehoods which interest dictates and credulity encourages – Samuel Johnson (1709–1784), in *The Idler*, 1758.

Just as war, defence and national security can involve the compromise of free expression and other human rights, their communication invokes several elements of journalism and public relations ethical codes. Most codes of ethics in journalism and PR do not mention war, defence or national security but the topics engage fundamental ethical values like truth, deception, harm, bias, confidentiality, invasion of privacy and conflicts of interest. The Society of Professional Journalists (SPJ) has referenced several considerations in its set of resources called *Resolving Ethical Conflicts in Wartime* (Sussman, 2022). There, they note:

> Journalists face unprecedented ethical pressures during times of war. Popular patriotic passions, the demands and strategic interests of the government, cultural and national sensitivities and traditional journalistic responsibilities are often on a collision course.

Fundamental values such as truth-seeking and being accountable are called into conflict in such times, with ethical dilemmas including whether to publish disturbing images, disclose troop positions or to accede to government demands to suppress enemy 'propaganda'. The materials work through a range of ethical conflicts, posing the most important questions along the way. For example, when assessing a government's motivation in seeking to suppress information, a journalist might ask:

> What are the government's reasons for asking us to refrain from disclosure? Will officials discuss the reasons, even confidentially, or are they asking us to take the request on faith? Are their reasons credible, detailed and to the point? Is the action requested the least restrictive means of responding to the government's asserted rationale? Is this a one-time request? Is there a history of cooperating with journalists to keep the public informed, or is this part of a pattern of indiscriminate and inappropriate secrecy? Are government officials willing to negotiate a compromise that would respond to their concerns by other means than those they propose? Do the grounds for requesting suppression appear to be designed to affect public attitudes – for example, to instil patriotism or insulate the American public from 'propaganda' or perception of government mistakes, incompetence or mendacity – or do they have a legitimate basis apart from such attempts to influence public attitudes? (Sussman, 2022)

For each of the dilemmas, the resources offer a list of potential alternative courses of action that might keep the ethical line while respecting the public's right to information.

Public relations practitioners working for government or defence on topics of war or terrorism can also look to a range of topics in their ethical codes for guidance on managing their communications and actions in such contexts. For example, in the UK the Chartered Institute of Public Relations (CIPR) CIPR Code of Conduct (2023) requires members to maintain integrity and confidentiality, deal honestly and fairly, and to respect laws and regulations. Their explanatory notes state members should check the reliability and accuracy of information they disseminate, be transparent and avoid conflicts of interest – all of which can come into play in the high stakes field of war, defence and national security communications.

All communicators face the responsibility of keeping themselves and others safe – by ensuring their words and actions are not going to jeopardise the lives and safety of others. This can include mental health. You will recall from Chapter 3 we introduced the concept of 'moral injury' from the psychological literature on trauma – which can occur when professionals breach their moral compass and ethics without having properly reflected upon their options. Of course, it is not just compromised ethical values that can impact communicators actually witnessing war first hand. Research revealed more than one quarter of an international group of war correspondents (28.6%)

experienced lifetime post-traumatic stress disorder (PTSD) – often because they had witnessed death and injury and had spent long periods in a state of high alert (Feinstein et al., 2002). Journalism and trauma psychologist and researcher Cait McMahon used vivid examples in her doctoral thesis on the topic (McMahon, 2016). One was a Vietnam War correspondent Bob Gassaway who recounted PTSD symptoms including the triggering of memories he could not prevent, depersonalisation and substance abuse (Gassaway, 1989). The other was CNN correspondent Michael Ware, who covered the Iraq War for CNN. He told *Men's Journal* in 2008 that 'you're always hypervigilant, always on alert ... (and) become conditioned to a state of being where everything is a threat and it's hard to turn that off; that becomes your normal'. Its legacy continues into fractured relationships after the tour of duty (Veis, 2008). Ware later told interviewer Larry King there was a long history of war-related PTSD recorded by Homer in his Iliad and by Shakespeare in Henry IV and that he himself suffered because 'there's certain things that can never be unseen'. He said he had 'images – a kaleidoscope of war – that reels through my life'. However, the experience of being able to report it was a privilege, despite the fact that he would 'spend the rest of my life walking with ghosts' (King, 2016). For those working in theatres of war, death is not just a fear – it is a realistic possibility. Reporters Without Borders stated that in the period 2014–2022 inclusive 686 journalists died in the course of their work, 335 of whom were in war zones (RSF, 2022). Some pay the price twice. *Sunday Times* journalist Marie Colvin was killed in the siege of Homs, Syria, in 2012 (alongside French photographer Remi Ochlik) – 11 years after she lost the sight in her left eye when covering the civil war in Sri Lanka in 2001 (BBC, 2019).

The other ethical dilemma facing those in theatres of war is the question of whose 'truth' they are telling. War correspondents have a long history of telling the story of the side their country happens to be on. This can be because their access to enemy sources and positions is untenable, dangerous or impossible. If they are able to enter the front line of battle, it can be because they are 'embedded' with one side's troops and their accounts are naturally tainted by the fact that they too become the target of enemy fire. In some wars throughout history, the war correspondent has been so partisan their accounts have effectively been the propaganda of the political leaders of their country. There have been some notable exceptions whose reportage has been so powerful that it has changed the course of the war and history as a result. An example was the Australian journalist Wilfred Burchett (1911–1983), an anti-imperialist who was the first reporter to arrive in Hiroshima after the US had dropped the atomic bomb in 1945, and who covered both the Korean and Vietnam conflicts in the 1950s and 1960s from the other side. However, even when giving the enemy's perspective, the Samuel Johnson quotation at the start of this section applies – also expressed more simply as 'in war, truth is the first casualty'.

In the realm of national security, a fundamental ethical question for journalists centres upon whether they can ever actually guarantee a source confidentiality in the era of sophisticated digital surveillance. Anti-terror laws introduced internationally and detailed below give intelligence agencies unprecedented powers to monitor the communications of citizens. Global Director of Research at the International Center for Journalists, Dr Julie Posetti, linked the wide net cast by counter terrorism laws with the erosion of the protections for journalists' confidential sources:

> The developments recorded in the past eight years in 69% (84 countries from 121) of States are generally in directions that run counter to robust source protection in the digital era. The legal frameworks that support protection of journalists' sources are under significant strain in the digital era, with this protection unnecessarily subjected to collateral damage in the face of broader security trends which could result in a loss to societies of the benefits of this particular dispensation.
> (Posetti, 2015: 92)

She found that journalists were adapting their methods to strengthen their digital security and return to analogue means of communication with confidential sources to protect them.

Many of the questions around the ethics of communicating about war, defence and terrorism have been addressed via the communication theory literature and have found their way into alternative approaches to agenda setting and framing messages on these topics. 'Peace journalism' stemmed originally from the peace studies and communication research of Galtung and Ruge (1965), whose work identified important gatekeeping decisions in the news selection process, which featured negativity – bad news – as one of five key ingredients. These observations were refined in later work to develop a new model for a peace-oriented journalism with less emphasis on violence and conflict and more focus on an orientation towards truth, people and solutions (Lynch, 2010: 543). Others have proposed extending peace journalism to better incorporate other media and practices (Keeble, 2021) and other cultures (Robie, 2011). The solutions orientation of peace journalism complemented the field of 'solutions journalism' which had its origins in US experiments with 'public journalism' and 'civic journalism' in the latter half of the 20th century (Parisi, 1997; Solutions Journalism Network, 2023) – and 'mindful journalism' (Gunaratne et al., 2015) using Buddhist principles in reporting. Each offers alternative approaches to the communication of war, defence and terrorism, with a purposeful orientation towards peaceful solutions.

Reflect – Research – Review:

Take a current conflict occurring somewhere in the world and explain how a story could be framed drawing upon a peace journalism or a solutions journalism approach.

Law, cases and examples internationally

The First World War (1914–1918) is widely regarded as the first occasion when nation-states created special propaganda organisations to target their enemies, their allies and their own citizens as a tool of war (Badsley, 2014). Western forces including the UK and its former colonies and the US used their various sedition, espionage and official secrets legislation as censorship devices. However, as Badsley (2014) notes, their use was rarely needed because news organisations generally fell into line with the propaganda efforts of their governments. Many books have been written about wartime propaganda efforts, but the focus of this chapter is predominantly on the latter 20th and early 21st centuries – from the Vietnam War through until the post 9/11 terrorism and digital era – when government information about wars was subject to more rigorous scrutiny and stricter measures were taken by governments to control the message about their defence and national security actions.

Media restrictions in the name of national security were in existence long before the attacks on New York's World Trade Center on September 11, 2001. Treason and sedition laws date back to feudal times when governments attempted to enforce allegiance to lords and monarchs (ALRC, 2006: 51). According to *Wex Legal Definitions* (2022), the crime of treason is 'the betrayal of one's own country by attempting to overthrow the government' while sedition is 'language intended to incite insurrection against the governing authority'.

Laws in treason and sedition were the foundation stones for the national security laws of the modern era. The 20th century platform for the US press freedom battle was the issue of seditious libel and the right to criticise the US government. Pember (2001: 60–61) explains that the first sedition laws in the US, the Alien and Sedition Acts, were passed in 1798, just after the First Amendment to the Constitution enshrining a free press. The laws made it a crime to criticise the president and the government, and many editors and politicians were prosecuted. Sedition prosecutions in the early 20th century led to important Supreme Court decisions reading the laws down in light of First Amendment protections. In 1925, the court ruled that the First Amendment offered protection from censorship by all levels of government (Pember, 2001). The Supreme Court also weakened another sedition law in 1957 – the *Smith Act 1940* – which prohibited advocating the violent overthrow of government. In Yates' case the Court said the accused must have proposed 'specific violent or forcible action toward the overthrow of the government'. It did so again in 1969 when it ruled in Brandenburg's case that the Constitution protected advocacy of unlawful conduct unless it was inciting imminent lawless action (Pember, 2001).

The Supreme Court also showed little tolerance for other laws punishing publications criticising government or publishing classified material. The principle was established firmly in the Minnesota case (1931), when that state suspended publication of a small weekly newspaper, the *Saturday Press*, because of its defamatory articles exposing corruption. The Supreme Court overturned the suspension, ruling that censorship in the form of 'prior restraint' is allowable only in extreme circumstances (Pember, 2001: 67). The approach was reiterated in the Pentagon Papers case in 1971 (see Key Case 10.1).

While the US was developing lines of protection for the publication of national security material, anti-terrorism laws were being used in other Western democracies well before 2001. The UK passed special laws to respond to Irish Republican Army (IRA) terrorism throughout the 20th century, while New Zealand introduced new restrictions after the French spy agency's bombing of the Greenpeace boat *Rainbow Warrior* in 1985, in which a photographer drowned.

But the 2001 terrorist attacks on the US prompted all governments to ramp up their national security laws. They faced the difficult policy task of trying to balance national security and citizens' right to life and safety against other important rights and interests – free expression and a free press, the right to a fair and public trial, the right to privacy and the right against discrimination. The result was a tipping of the scales towards laws shoring up national security, resulting in a diminution of the other rights. Even in countries with a high regard for civil liberties and free expression, new powers were handed to security agencies and police to aid in the detection and arrest of suspected terrorists. America led the way with its USA *PATRIOT Act 2001*, in which the letters stood for: 'Uniting (and) Strengthening America (by) Providing Appropriate Tools Required (to) Intercept (and) Obstruct Terrorism' (replaced by the USA *Freedom Act 2015*). Other countries, including the United Kingdom, Canada, Australia and New Zealand, followed by introducing their own anti-terror laws.

The UK had legislation with terrorism acts on home soil dealing with the IRA in its period of 'The Troubles' in Northern Ireland, and had only just overhauled its national security laws in 2000. In response to the 9/11 attacks, it tightened those measures with its *Anti-Terrorism Crime and Security Act 2001* which offered a template for the legislation in other Commonwealth countries including Canada, Australia, and New Zealand. Pressure mounted in Western democracies for even tougher laws after the Bali bombings in 2002 and 2005 murdered 92 Australians in their holiday playground and the 7/7 London attacks in 2005 took 56 lives.

Too many anti-terror laws have been introduced internationally to detail here, but they can impact your work if you are a professional communicator publishing across borders using the internet or social media. Their implications have included:

- increased surveillance powers for spy agencies and police and the seizure of notes and computer archives – exposing confidential sources to identification;
- new detention and questioning regimes;
- closing certain court proceedings so they are unreportable;
- fines and jail if details of certain anti-terror operations are revealed;

- making it an offence to merely 'associate' or 'communicate' with those suspected of national security crimes;
- exposing publishers to criminal charges if they publish anything seen as inciting terrorism; and
- narrowing the range of material accessible under freedom of information laws.

Those working in the national security space need to weigh up their ethical commitments to sources against their duty to society to protect people from terrorist attacks. Even if you do enter into confidential arrangements, the powers of surveillance, search and seizure make your communication records easier for the authorities to monitor and seize.

Since 2010, sensitive document drops have dominated global security news led by WikiLeaks headed by Australian Julian Assange in the period 2010–2022 and then the data dump by former US National Security Agency (NSA) worker Edward Snowden during 2013–2014. These were followed by the release of the Panama Papers (2016), Paradise Papers (2017–2018), Pandora Papers (2021) and the 2022 leak of the draft US Supreme Court opinion overturning the landmark *Roe v Wade* abortion decision (Mangan, 2023).

The alleged source of the most controversial WikiLeaks documents and vision in 2010 exposing US wrongdoing in the Iraq war was US Army private Chelsea (formerly Bradley) Manning, who was sentenced to 35 years in prison in 2013 for the leak, underscoring the gravity of the offence and the dangers of compromising security operations on an international level. Manning was released from jail in 2017 after former US President Barack Obama commuted her sentence. But in 2023 Assange was fighting extradition to the US from the UK on espionage charges. The timing of his document dumps detailing US presidential candidate Hillary Clinton during the 2016 elections led to allegations he was a 'tool of Russian intelligence' (Smiley, 2017). Snowden's leak of classified US documents had international diplomatic repercussions after he worked with mainstream media organisations to release tranches of surveillance records showing how the phones of world leaders had been electronically monitored. In late 2022 Snowden took out Russian citizenship after almost ten years in asylum after his escape from authorities. While the identities of WikiLeaks and NSA whistleblowers were revealed and they were either jailed or forced to flee, the German journalists who broke the Pulitzer Prize-winning 'Panama Papers' story via more than 100 media organisations managed to keep secret (via encryption and other techniques) their 'John Doe' confidential source who had provided them with more than eleven million financial documents linking international figures to secret bank accounts. The revelations forced two prime ministers (Iceland and Pakistan) to resign, while others faced justice and governments recovered more than $1.3 billion in lost tax revenues (Obermaier and Obermayer, 2022).

Often governments go straight to search engines, social media platforms and Internet service providers (ISPs), demanding that they remove material. The Meta Transparency Report (2022a) shows that the US Government made 69,363 requests to the Facebook parent company for data in the first six months of 2022, including 3943 emergency disclosure requests – the category under which national security data is sought. Almost 90% of requests resulted in data being produced. For example, Meta reported acceding to an emergency disclosure request from Colombian law enforcement for data related to a suspected terrorist in June 2022, reportedly preventing a terrorist attack (Meta, 2022b).

> **Reflect – Research – Review:**
>
> Media organisations and industry groups have protested the limitations national security laws place on free expression. Is this a price worth paying in the post-9/11 era of global insecurity? Discuss.

Basic Australian legal principles – elements and case examples

Throughout the two centuries prior to the spate of international terrorism from 2001, Australia had sedition and treason laws and had used them occasionally against journalists. Pullan (1994) chronicled the use of sedition and seditious libel by governments against editors throughout colonial times.

There were also some national security laws in Australia prior to 9/11, with considerable legislative activity from the late 1960s as a result of political reviews of the operations of the Australian Security Intelligence Organisation (ASIO) and some isolated terrorism incidents, mainly against foreign embassies and consulates in Canberra and state capitals including Sydney, Melbourne and Perth. While there was some national security law making over this period, throughout most of the second half of the 20th century the media operated under what Hocking (2004: 82) called a system of 'voluntary restraint', including the 'D-notice' (defence notice) system. This was a mutual agreement – modelled on a British system established in 1912 – between major media outlets and the Australian government where they refrained from reporting sensitive matters. It continued from 1952 through until the mid-1990s, with the last D-notice issued in 1982. D-notices covered matters including intelligence operations, defence information and capabilities, political asylum seekers, atomic testing, signals intelligence and communications security (National Archives, n.d.)

The 9/11 attacks in the US in 2001 brought on what Hocking (2004) called 'the second wave' of legislative activity around national security. As documented by Williams and Hardy (2022), Australia introduced 92 counter terrorism laws in the 20 years to September 2021 at Commonwealth level, in addition to a suite of State and territory laws. The legislation has passed without any explicit constitutional protection for freedom of expression, and with a series of political opposition parties fearing they would be seen as going soft on terrorism if they opposed them – extending beyond the scale of any such laws seen in other Western democracies. In recent years, a number of suspected terrorist plots have been foiled in their planning stages. These events and the ensuing court cases have raised serious questions about the balance between national security and human rights, free expression and the principle of open justice (Renwick, 2017: 16–25). McGarrity (2011) argued that three key factors have limited the media's ability to effectively hold the executive to account on national security issues: the limited provision of and access to information about terrorism-related investigations and court cases; a chilling effect on freedom of speech; and media manipulation by the federal government. She stated that a crucial factor was the media being deprived of intelligence about counter-terror operations and judicial proceedings. Roach (2011: 310) has called this approach 'hyper-legislation'. Gelber (2016) suggested there were many alternative policy measures and laws already in force to achieve the desired national security goals, reducing the need for all this legislation. The key Australian national security laws with the potential to impact professional communicators are explained here, with some case examples, grouped under the type of behaviour or topics that might be impacted.

Treason and 'urging violence' (formerly sedition)

Section 80.1 of the *Criminal Code Act 1995* defines 'treason' as a range of offences relating to violent acts against the 'Sovereign, the Governor-General or the Prime Minister' levying war against the Commonwealth or assisting an enemy at war with Australia. Section 80.2 (formerly 'sedition'), and its subsections (80.2A–D) outline a range of crimes related to 'urging violence' and advocating terrorism or genocide. A 'good faith' defence sits at s80.3, covering anyone who urges violence if that person '(f) publishes in good faith a report or commentary about a matter of public interest'.

Spy agency activities

The *Australian Security Intelligence Organisation Act 1979* has been amended in a number of ways impacting professional communicators. Section 25A focuses on ASIO powers and access to computer networks, with one warrant now able to apply to an entire computer network using third party computers to access target systems. Amendments make it an offence to disclose information about 'questioning' warrants and 'questioning and detention' warrants (and related operational information) for up to two years, 'even if the operation is in violation of international human rights conventions' (MEAA, 2005). There are no public-interest or media exemptions to the requirement, although disclosures of operational information by anyone other than the subject of a warrant or their lawyer requires the discloser to have shown 'recklessness' in doing so (s34ZS (3)). Following the inadvertent publication of an imminent police raid on a cell of terrorists in the Holsworthy Barracks cases (2013), a new s35P was introduced carrying up to five years in jail for 'unauthorised' disclosure of information related to a 'special intelligence operation' – and up to ten years if the disclosure 'endangers the health or safety' of anyone or will 'prejudice the effective conduct of a special intelligence operation'. Amendments partially exempting 'outsiders' (journalists) were enacted in 2016, but grave concerns remained over the impacts on journalists for 'reckless' disclosure that might endanger safety and jeopardise an operation and the implications for their sources who faced stricter liability and more serious penalties as 'entrusted persons'. Section 92 provides for ten years' imprisonment for anyone who identifies an ASIO officer or affiliate (or anyone connected with them), other than any who have been identified in parliament (such as the director-general). Former ASIO employees and affiliates can be identified if they have consented in writing or have generally made that fact be known.

Case example:

Holsworthy Barracks cases (2013): A plot by terrorists to attack the Holsworthy Army Barracks in Sydney was foiled by the AFP's 'Operation Neath' with a raid on a cell of conspirators in Melbourne. *The Australian* newspaper used a police source – later proven to be Victorian detective Simon Artz – to get details of the raid prior to the arrests of the suspects. It even published some copies of the newspaper including a story about the raids in the hours prior. Artz pleaded guilty to a charge of unauthorised disclosure of information and was given a four-month suspended sentence in the Victorian County Court (Artz's case, 2013). In the wake of the episode, the new Section 35P was introduced (explained above).

Closure of courts and suppression of proceedings

The *National Security Information (Criminal and Civil Proceedings) Act 2004* (NSI Act) and subsequent amendments impacted on media coverage of court cases involving national security or terrorism matters. Division 3 of the Act authorises prosecutors and courts to use national security information in criminal proceedings while preventing the broader disclosure of such information, sometimes even to the defendant. Section 22 allows for courts to make orders regarding the disclosure of national security information. Section 29 permits the closure of courts for national security reasons, with potential delays to the release of the record of those proceedings.

Case examples:

Witness J case (2019): Witness J – also known by the pseudonym 'Alan Johns' – who we later learned was former diplomat and intelligence officer – pleaded guilty to undisclosed Commonwealth offences over his disclosure of confidential information that 'could endanger the lives or safety of others'. He was prosecuted in the Magistrates Court, continuing to the ACT Supreme Court. During the hearing the court was closed and all details were suppressed under s22 of the NSI Act. Johns had already served time for a year with sexual offenders (when he was not one) in a Canberra jail when the secret case came to public attention via obscure remarks by a prison witness during his civil appeal against the refusal to allow him email access to write a book about his prison experiences – subsequently published as *Here, There Are Dragons* (Lulu Press, 2020). Reporters' curiosity was twigged about his secret trial and their inquiries led to the Commonwealth Attorney-General issuing a statement stating some of these details stated above. Only a further inquiry and report from the Independent National Security Legislation Monitor (INSLM) (Donaldson, 2022) brought to light more information about this secret trial. He commented:

> Alan Johns shows how s22 can be used to conduct a federal criminal prosecution in 'secret' from start to finish and to maintain this secrecy, seemingly, indefinitely. This should not have happened in Alan Johns and it should never happen again.

He recommended the government introduce a range of mechanisms to better balance national security and open justice. In January 2023 the Government agreed to his recommendations.

Haneef case (2007): This case sounded a clear warning of the potential for closed courts, secret processes and minimised media access to information in alleged terrorism matters, along with the potential for injustice to occur in the absence of open justice. Gold Coast Hospital registrar (and Indian citizen) Dr Mohamed Haneef was arrested over suspected UK terrorism connections on 2 July 2007 and became the first suspect to undergo special extended detention for investigation purposes under the amended Crimes Act. The charges claimed he recklessly provided resources to a terrorist organisation by providing his cousins in the UK with a telephone SIM card but the charges were withdrawn later that month due to 'no reasonable prospect of conviction'. A 2008 inquiry found the AFP had managed the case poorly. Dr Haneef was reportedly awarded $1 million in compensation by the Australian government. The hearings extending Dr Haneef's initial detention were closed to the media, and only the bold move by his lawyer to release a police transcript to journalists brought his plight to public attention.

Espionage and secrets

Amendments in 2018 to the *Criminal Code 1995* introduced a broader range of offences than those previously featuring in the *Crimes Act*. Part 5.2 of the Code in Division 90 deals with espionage and related offences. Unless a professional communicator is actually a spy, they need to be more concerned about the potential 'reckless' dealing with information at s91.1, where information has a security classification or concerns Australia's national security or benefits another country's national security and is recklessly handled so it results in it being communicated to a foreign principal. It carries a prison term of 25 years. Lesser prison terms apply to offences where the information might or might not carry a security classification but relates to Australia's national security and is communicated to a foreign principal. Each would apply to situations like the WikiLeaks or Snowden document dumps, but Hardy and Williams (2022: 66) suggest even normal journalistic processes could become liable for sharing Australia's political, economic or military relations with other countries. No public interest defence applies. Part 5.6 of the *Criminal Code* deals with secrecy of information – the topic most likely to encompass public servants who communicate secret government information (either as whistleblowers or for another purpose) and journalists who want to publish it. Sections 122.1 and 122.2 carry a seven-year jail penalty for current or former Commonwealth officers who communicate 'inherently harmful information' or information that harms Australia's interests. They also apply if the person does not communicate the information but stores it in the wrong place or deals with it inappropriately. Offences are aggravated for dealing with five or more records with security classifications, if the records carry a classification of 'for Australian eyes only', if the security classification has been altered or removed, or if the offender has a high level of security clearance. Section 122.4 carries an offence simply for unauthorised disclosure of information, regardless of its nature or security clearance, if they are under a duty not to disclose it as a Commonwealth officer. Defences apply in a range of circumstances, including disclosure of information that is already public, to intelligence and integrity agencies, and under the provisions of protected disclosure (whistleblowing) laws – but importantly not to the media. Section 122.4A makes it an offence for others to deal with information disclosed by a Commonwealth officer if:

(i) the information has a 'secret' or 'top secret' security classification;
(ii) the communication of the information damages Australian security or defence;
(iii) the communication interferes with or prejudices the prevention, detection, investigation, prosecution or punishment of a Commonwealth criminal offence; or
(iv) it harms or prejudices the health or safety of the Australian public or a section of the public.

It applies whether or not the whistleblower who gave the information can be identified, and includes any information, even an opinion or a report of a conversation. This is the section that will have the most impact on investigative journalists working on stories exposing wrongdoing by government or

294 Challenges in the digital era

its agencies. However, a limited public interest defence is available for news media workers under section 122.5 unless the information reveals the identity of an ASIO officer, it breaches a witness protection program or it is intended to assist a foreign intelligence or military agency. Under s123.2 a sketch, article, record or document made or possessed in contravention of these laws is forfeited to the Commonwealth – essentially meaning journalists' notes, recordings and draft articles could be seized and never returned. The new suite of offences goes beyond what was previously covered by sections 70 and 79 of the *Crimes Act* which they replaced, and under which the home of journalist Annika Smethurst was searched under a warrant in 2019 (see Key Case 10.2). For extended further reading on these important provisions, see Williams and Hardy (2022), Ananian-Welsh et al. (2022), and Hardy et al. (2021).

Case examples:

Search warrant case (2020): see Key Case 10.2.

Afghan Files case (2019–2023): The day after the Australian Federal Police raid on the home of journalist Annika Smethurst in 2019 (see Key Case 10.2), police raided the Australian Broadcasting Corporation headquarters in Sydney in relation to stories aired on the program *7.30* in 2017 about the activities of Australian special forces in Afghanistan, based on 'hundreds of pages of secret defence force documents leaked to the ABC'. They seized numerous documents in an eight hour search, with the search warrant alleging offences of 'dishonestly receiving stolen property' contrary to s132.1 of the *Criminal Code* and 'unlawfully obtaining military information' under s73A(2) of the *Defence Act 1903*; in relation to several charges placed against the alleged whistleblower, Major David McBride, including theft of Commonwealth property. (He was also charged with unlawfully communicating military information contrary to s73A(1) of the *Defence Act 1903*, and unlawfully disclosing a Commonwealth document contrary to s70(1) of the *Crimes Act 1914*.) After a Senate inquiry and media and ministerial representations, the AFP announced in 2020 it would not pursue charges against the journalist involved, Dan Oakes. As this book went to press, the trial against the alleged whistleblower McBride was proceeding, although there were vocal calls for it to be discontinued. The case is significant to professional communicators in a range of ways, but importantly because a leak of documents could be framed as a theft of property offence against the whistleblower and a 'receiving stolen property' charge against the journalist, with a potential ten-year jail term and no public interest defence available.

Key Case 10.2: Search Warrant case

Smethurst v Commissioner of Police [2020] HCA 14 (15 April 2020), <www.austlii.edu.au/cgi-bin/viewdoc/au/cases/cth/HCA/2020/14.html>.

Facts

In April 2018 the *Sunday Telegraph* newspaper and its website published articles by journalist Annika Smethurst revealing that proposed amendments would extend the powers of the defence spy agency, the Australian Signals Directorate (ASD), so it would be able to access the data of Australian citizens. Two of the articles contained images of top-secret documents. In mid-2019 AFP officers raided Smethurst's home with a warrant to search for evidence related to a charge that she had communicated official secrets in breach of then section 79(3) of the *Crimes Act 1914*, punishable by two years in jail. They retrieved data from her computer and searched her mobile phone and downloaded data onto a memory stick which they took as evidence. It was alleged in the High Court that the whistleblower was an ASD staff member, Cameron Gill, who was being investigated for breaching s40 of the *Intelligence Services Act 2001* related to unlawful communication of information carrying a ten-year penalty.

Law

Smethurst appealed against the legality of the warrant to the High Court, which quashed the warrant retrospectively on technical grounds. Importantly, the court declined to rule on the issue of whether her implied freedom to communicate on matters of politics and government had been breached by the warrant and raid. Her lawyers asked that the court not decide whether her right to privacy had been breached, although in the leading judgment the court flagged that possibility with respect to the searching of her home and her mobile phone, while not ruling on it, indicating the court might still be open to a new judge-made right to privacy as suggested in Chapter 7. In 2020 the AFP announced it had closed its investigation into the leak and that no charges would be laid (McCartney, 2020). Alleged whistleblower Gill denied the allegations throughout the process. The episode prompted a parliamentary inquiry (Parliamentary Joint Committee on Intelligence and Security, 2020).

> *Lessons for professional communicators*
>
> Key take-home messages are:
>
> - The stakes are high in investigative journalism and whistleblowing when dealing with sensitive government information. Legal advice needs to be obtained at every juncture.
> - While charges against the journalist were possible, the target appeared to be the confidential source. Source confidentiality can be compromised when authorities seize computer and phone data. Extreme measures need to be taken to protect their identity.
> - While the law used as the pretext for the Smethurst raid has been superseded, the laws that have replaced it at Part 5.6 of the *Criminal Code* are even more far-reaching, and the theft of Commonwealth property charges used in the related Afghan Files case (2019–23) do not even have a public interest defence.

Discussing terrorism

Under the *Crimes Act 1914*, s3ZQT makes it an offence to disclose the fact that someone has been given notice by the Australian Federal Police (AFP) to produce documents related to a serious terrorism offence under section 3ZQN or a serious offence under section 3ZQO. Journalists could face up to two years in prison for reporting that they have been issued with such a notice related to a story they are covering – perhaps involving their communications with, or contact details for, sources (s3ZQP). 'Control orders' were introduced, banning terror suspects' communications with 'specified individuals' under section 104.5(3)(e) of the *Criminal Code Act 1995*, which could impact journalist–source communications. Similar bans on communication apply to the regime of 'preventative detention orders' (PDOs) under Division 105. A ban on 'associating' at least twice with a person who is a member of, or promotes or directs the activities of, a terrorist organisation under s102.8(1), potentially impacts journalists' coverage of national and international security issues, although required elements of knowledge and intent on the part of the journalist would minimise that likelihood.

Surveillance, data retention and source protection

Journalists' confidential source records are under continuous threat. Section 46 of the *Telecommunications (Interception and Access) Act 1979* allows agencies to intercept the communications of terrorism suspects and those 'with whom the person is likely to communicate' which could involve journalists. Part 5–1A covering Data Retention requires telecommunications providers to retain

Defence, national security, cyber security and anti-terrorism 297

customers' phone and computer metadata for two years so they can be accessed by criminal law enforcement agencies possessing a warrant. Information required to be stored includes: subscriber/account information, the source and destination of a communication, and the date, time and duration of a communication or connection to a service. A 'journalist information warrant' scheme was later introduced to prohibit the disclosure of journalists' confidential sources without special precautions (Division 4C – Journalist information warrants). These require approval of the minister, who may act on the advice of an appointed 'Public Interest Advocate' (s180X), although the processes are secret and disclosure of the details of any warrant for telecommunications data can incur imprisonment for two years (s182A and B). The protocols were breached in 2017 when the Australian Federal Police admitted a journalist's call records had been accessed without following the procedures (Royes, 2017). In his 2020–2021 report, the Commonwealth Ombudsman noted only one authorisation of a journalist information warrant being issued in the previous year (by the Crime and Corruption Commission in Queensland) and several shortcomings in police and corruption agencies' implementation of the scheme and record keeping (Commonwealth Ombudsman, 2022). A loophole in the scheme is that government agencies seeking a journalist's sources do not need to obtain such a warrant if they start their investigations with the source rather than the journalist, thus bypassing the requirement. This aspect was being reviewed in 2023. The Australian Federal Police reported in 2020 that they typically received 12–15 referrals to investigate unauthorised disclosure each year. In the period January 2013 to June 2019 there were nine search warrants issued involving journalists or news organisations (AFP, 2020: 21). A suite of laws known as the 'encryption laws' supplement these. Under the *Telecommunications and Other Legislation Amendment (Assistance and Access) Act 2018* (Cth) (TOLA) agencies can request or require the assistance of technology companies globally. Encryption can be removed from apps like WhatsApp and Telegram as part of the process. As Hardy and Williams explain (2022: 65) judicial warrants are not required and there are no exemptions for journalists. Further, it is an offence to disclose the process has been used.

Case example:

'Jihad Jack' cases (2006–2008): Alleged terrorist 'sleeper' 'Jihad' Jack Thomas became the first Australian to be convicted using the anti-terrorism laws introduced into Australia after 2001. An Appeal Court quashed his conviction for receiving funds from a terrorist organisation on the basis of the inadmissibility of the police record of interview. He was later retried, with the case based partly on admissions Thomas had made in interviews with the ABC's *Four Corners* reporter Sally Neighbour (*Four Corners*, 2006) and to *The Age*'s Ian Munro – admissions similar to those he had made in the excluded police interview – but he was eventually found not guilty of terrorism charges. Both *Four Corners* and *The Age* cooperated with the police, defusing a situation where police would have been tempted to use seizure powers. In *R v Thomas (No. 4)* (2008), the appeal court detailed the extent to which telephone conversations between ABC reporter Sally Neighbour and Thomas had been monitored by an ASIO agent – up to 20 times throughout 2005 on his mobile phone or landline.

Reflect – Research – Review:

Use the <www.austlii.edu.au> database to do an advanced search for a case, report or inquiry using the words 'terrorism', 'media' and 'suppression'. Write a summary covering the key issues and implications for professional communicators.

A word on cyber security

An important topic related to national security and the media is the area of cyber security – and the measures professional communicators must take to secure their data when it can be in the interest of others – perhaps foreign actors – to steal it or to frustrate your use of it. Australian media organisations have experienced so-called 'denial of service' attacks, where international criminals or government agents flood sites with connection requests which can cause a whole server to slow or crash. Other common cybersecurity threats include 'data breaches', malicious software (malware), scam emails (phishing) and ransomware. All are illegal and most organisations now have extensive training in this space – essential for the professional communicator. If you do not have access to such training, an excellent starting point for learning more is the Australian Cyber Security Centre – part of the Australian Government's Australian Signals Directorate (ASD) – which has information, resources and advice at <www.cyber.gov.au/> for individuals, businesses and government. It covers basic strategies like methods of detection of suspicious activity, routinely changing passphrases and using encryption and multi-factor authentication through to more complex security strategies for network managers. Those working in government with special security clearances are required by law to pay special heed to cyber security of their data and work information. Even just sharing job description information on social media platforms like LinkedIn can be a security risk in some communication jobs. The Australian Security Intelligence Agency (ASIO) launched an advertising campaign in 2020 to deter employees from mentioning their security clearance on such sites (ASIO, 2020).

> **Reflect – Research – Review:**
>
> Research the three main cyber security concerns facing professional communicators and explain the best practice strategies for minimising risk.

National security ethics and law in action – Case study 10.1: The government insider and the journalist

The law and ethics of war, defence and national security raise many issues for professional communicators on both sides of the fence – the government communications officer and the news journalist. For the three processes involved in addressing this problem scenario, we draw upon Riskin and Wohl's (2015) 'STOPS and Take STOCK' tool as a reflection process, and Grantham and Pearson's (2022) stakeholder mapping approach and their specific legal risk analysis technique.

The problem

An investigative reporter for a major news network has kept in touch with a good friend from her university days who has worked his way through media relations into a senior government policy role in defence. One morning a large bundle of photocopied documents arrive addressed to the reporter via the media organisation's internal mail system, marked 'Classified' but with no information on who has sent it. The documents include an alarming intelligence briefing to high level defence officials on the cities targeted by a foreign government's nuclear missiles. The journalist shows her news director who instructs her to publish the information as part of a major exclusive news report because it is overwhelmingly in the public interest. What ethical and legal issues arise?

Pausing to reflect:

Remember in Chapter 3 we introduced Riskin and Wohl's (2015) use of mindfulness meditation approaches in their conflict management courses in law schools? Here we ask you to apply an adaptation of it that really extends the 'Reflect-Research-Review' approach we have adopted throughout the text. First, find somewhere quiet and sit to try to focus on your breathing and then on your body sensations, emotions and thoughts (2015: 136–137). This allows you to 'stop and take stock'. Then think through the above problem using their method as described – Stop; Take a breath; Observe your body sensations, emotions, thoughts; Consider the dynamics of this problem situation and your intention with it; Keep going with your further strategies for analysis ('STOCK') (Riskin and Wohl, 2015: 137).

Conduct a stakeholder mapping exercise

This problem requires you to think very carefully through the implications for all the key stakeholders in the situation because the stakes are indeed high with people perhaps facing the loss of their jobs and reputations as well as large fines or jail for security breaches. As Grantham and Pearson (2022: 18) explain, the process of stakeholder mapping involves weighing the relative power and stake in such a vital decision. Yet, power for power's sake might not be appropriate when some who might have minimal power could have a high stake in a communication decision, such as the citizens who would face death or injury in a nuclear war. Stakeholder mapping is quite consequentialist from a moral philosophy perspective – it tends towards decisions favouring the most benefit for the most people. But in this situation some could have much to lose while the populace has a great deal to gain. Such decisions are not easy. Here is a start. Amend and extend the table as you see fit.

Stakeholder	*Power*	*Stake*	*Consequences*
Journalist	High	High	Legal prosecution, fines, jail, potential reputational enhancement for raising issue in the public interest or damage for sensationalising and scaremongering.
Media outlet	High	Medium	Legal prosecution, fines, enhanced ratings, praise for public interest reporting but condemnation for breach of security and causing panic.
Source/s	High	High	Legal prosecution if discovered, then dismissal, fines, jail, perhaps accolades, humiliation.
Citizens	Low	High	Public's right to know. Their ignorance of being targeted by nuclear missiles can result in death or injury. They lose the choice to relocate.
Intelligence services	High	High	Public confidence can be eroded if leaks occur, and enemies can be alerted to their intelligence. Leaks must be stopped by all measures available.
Audience	Low	Medium	Being informed and educated, but also perhaps alarmed unnecessarily if they are not in the target zones.

Working through this mapping process helps raise the ethical considerations but also links them to the legal analysis in the next step.

Applying the specific legal risk analysis technique (Grantham and Pearson, 2022: 51–53)

Identifying the potential (or existing) legal problem

Review the chapter for the areas of law that might apply. How do laws related to the communication of classified and defence documents impact the situation for both the journalist and the whistleblower? What might data retention laws reveal about the possible source of the leak?

Reviewing the areas of the law involved

Of course the hypothetical nature of the scenario leaves many questions unanswered, but work through the various laws and cases in the final section of this chapter to find elements of each law that could apply here, and map out the possible legal risks and balancing rationale for publishing. Are public interest or media defences available to the various laws you have identified?

Projecting the possible consequences for stakeholders

Go back to the stakeholder mapping exercise above and revisit it in terms of legal risks for all stakeholders. Who faces prosecutions or civil suits and what alternative avenues might be available to each player to minimize the legal ramifications?

Seeking advice/referring upward

All defence and national security decisions need expert legal advice – both for the potential whistleblower and for the journalist and media outlet. Public disclosure protections can apply to whistleblowers in some public interest situations, but rarely in security matters.

Publishing/amending/deleting/correcting/apologizing

This is not the kind of story where there are likely to be corrections and apologies – unless of course the documents are published without any verification and prove to be fake. A crucial decision along the way is for the media outlet to decide how much verification can be done without tipping off authorities to their knowledge of the story and facing injunctions banning publication. Legal advice is crucial throughout.

In a nutshell

- Philosophers have debated issues around the ethics of war and its communication for many hundreds of years. Notions of whether there can be a 'just war' have dominated philosophical discourse.

- Philosopher Sissela Bok has addressed the intersection with communication by highlighting the suppression or distortion by governments when war is threatened or under way.
- War, defence and national security raise notable exceptions to the right to free expression, because such human rights instruments place a priority on rights to safety and security for all citizens.
- Peace journalism offers a framework for discussing and approaching the coverage of war, defence, conflict and national security with a focus on solutions, drawing upon interviews with a full range of stakeholders, not just official or political sources.
- Trauma can be an issue for communicators who witness conflict. War correspondents commonly experience lifetime post-traumatic stress disorder (PTSD) because they have witnessed death and injury and have spent long periods on high alert.
- Media restrictions in the name of national security were in existence long before the terrorism attacks upon the US in September 2001. Sedition and treason laws date back to feudal times.
- The 9/11 attacks on the US prompted all governments to ramp up their national security laws, many of which impacted journalists in their reporting.
- National security laws affect journalism in a range of ways, including increased surveillance powers for spy agencies and police, exposing confidential sources to identification, closing courts, restrictions on reporting, and creating exceptions to freedom of information releases.
- There were 92 new anti terror laws passed by the Australian parliament between September 2001 and September 2021.
- Beyond laws against urging violence, key Australian national security laws restrict coverage of intelligence agency activities, terrorism cases in the courts, communicating sensitive documents and discussing terrorism; and increase governments' powers of surveillance and metadata access.

References and further reading

Ananian-Welsh, R., Kendall, S. and Murray, R. 2021, 'Risk and Uncertainty in Public Interest Journalism: The Impact of Espionage Law on Press Freedom', *Melbourne University Law Review*, 44, 764, <https://classic.austlii.edu.au/cgi-bin/sinodisp/au/journals/MelbULawRw/2021/1.html>.

ASIO. 2021, 'Think before you link', *Australian Security Intelligence Organisation*, Canberra, <https://www.asio.gov.au/TBYL.html>.

Australian Federal Police (AFP). 2020, 'AFP Freedom of Information Disclosure Log 15–2020 – FOI – CRM 2020/356', *Senate Environment and Communications References Committee*, <www.afp.gov.au/sites/default/files/PDF/Disclosure-Log/15-2020.pdf>.

Australian Law Reform Commission (ALRC). 2006, *Review of Sedition Laws: Discussion Paper*, Commonwealth Government, Canberra, <www.austlii.edu.au/au/other/alrc/publications/dp/71>.

Badsley, S. 2014, 'Propaganda: Media in War Politics', *International Encyclopedia of the First World War*, Daniel, U., Gatrell, P., Janz, O., Jones, H., Keene, J., Kramer, A. and Nasson, B. eds, Freie Universität Berlin, Berlin.

Barak, A. 2003, 'The Role of a Supreme Court in a Democracy, and the Fight Against Terrorism', *University of Miami Law Review*, 58 (1), 125, <https://repository.law.miami.edu/umlr/vol58/iss1/12>.

BBC. 2019, 'Marie Colvin: Syrian government found liable for US reporter's death', *BBC News*, 31 January, <www.bbc.com/news/world-us-canada-47082088>.

Beard, M. 2019, 'Courage isn't about facing our fears, it's about facing ourselves', *The Ethics Centre*, <https://ethics.org.au/courage-isnt-about-facing-our-fears-its-about-facing-ourselves/>.

Bok, S. 1978, *Lying: Moral Choice in Public and Private Life*, Pantheon Books, New York.

Chartered Institute of Public Relations (CIPR). 2023, *CIPR Code of Conduct*, <www.cipr.co.uk/CIPR/About_Us/Governance_/CIPR_Code_of_Conduct.aspx>.

Commonwealth Ombudsman. 2022, *Commonwealth Ombudsman's annual report - Monitoring agency access to stored communications and telecommunications data under Chapters 3 and 4 of the Telecommunications (Interception and Access) Act 1979. For inspections conducted in the period 1 July 2020 to 30 June 2021 covering records from 1 July 2019 to 30 June 2020*, Commonwealth of Australia, Canberra, <www.ombudsman.gov.au/__data/assets/pdf_file/0036/286839/Commonwealth-Ombudsman-2020–21-Annual-Report-Stored-Communications-and-telecommunications-data.pdf>.

Cooper, M. and Roberts, S. 2011, 'After 40 years, the complete Pentagon Papers', *The New York Times*, 7 June, <www.nytimes.com/2011/06/08/us/08pentagon.html>.

Donaldson, G. 2022, *Independent National Security Legislation Monitor (INSLM) Report Review into the operation of Part 3, Division 1 of the National Security Information (Criminal and Civil Proceedings) Act 2004 as it applies in the Alan Johns matter*, Commonwealth of Australia, Canberra, <www.inslm.gov.au/sites/default/files/2022–07/nsi-report-4thinslm-17june-2022.pdf>.

Ethics Centre. 2016, *Ethics Explainer: Just War Theory*, Ethics Centre, Sydney, <https://ethics.org.au/ethics-explainer-just-war/>.

Feinstein, A., Owen, J. and Blair, N. 2002, 'A hazardous profession: War, journalists, and psychopathology', *American Journal of Psychiatry*, 159 (9), 1570–1575, <https://doi.org/10.1176/appi.ajp.159.9.1570>.

Galtung, J. and Ruge, M. 1965, 'The structure of foreign news: the presentation of the Congo, Cuba and Cyprus crises in four foreign newspapers', *Journal of International Peace Research*, 1, 64–90.

Gassaway, B.M. 1989, 'Making Sense of War: An Autobiographical Account of a Vietnam War Correspondent', *The Journal of Applied Behavioral Science*, 25 (4), 327–349, <https://doi.org/10.1177/002188638902500403>.

Gelber, K. 2016, *Free Speech after 9/11*, Oxford University Press, Oxford.

Grantham, S. and Pearson, M. 2022, *Social Media Risk and the Law: A Guide for Global Communicators*, Routledge, London and New York.

Gunaratne, S., Pearson, M. and Senarath, S. 2015, *Mindful Journalism and News Ethics in the Digital Era: A Buddhist Approach*, Routledge, London and New York.

Hardy, K., Ananian-Welsh, R. and McGarrity, N. 2021, *Democracy Dossier: 'Secrecy and Power in Australia's National Security State'*, GetUp!, <https://cdn.getup.org.au/2836-GetUp-Democracy-Dossier.pdf>.

Hocking, J. 2004, *Terror Laws: ASIO, Counter-Terrorism and the Threat to Democracy*, UNSW Press, Sydney.

Husby, T.K. 2009, 'Justice and the Justification of War in Ancient Greece: Four Authors', *Classics Honors Papers*, 1, <http://digitalcommons.conncoll.edu/classicshp/1/>.

Keeble, R.L. 2021, 'Peace Journalism: Alternative Perspectives', *Handbook of Global Media Ethics*, Ward, S.J.A. ed., Springer Verlag, Berlin, 1049–1064.

King, L. 2016, 'Famed War Reporter Details His PTSD and "Walking with Ghosts"', *Larry King Now*, Ora.TV, 25 March, <www.youtube.com/watch?v=4_H2j1FGQCQ>.

Lazar, S. 2020, 'War', *The Stanford Encyclopedia of Philosophy*, Spring 2020 edn, Zalta, E.N. ed., <https://plato.stanford.edu/archives/spr2020/entries/war/>.

Legal Information Institute. 2022, *Wex Legal Definitions*, Cornell Law School, <www.law.cornell.edu/wex>.

Lynch, J. 2010, 'Peace Journalism', *Routledge Companion to News and Journalism*, Allen, S. ed., Routledge, London and New York, 542–554.

Mangan, D. 2023, 'Supreme Court probe fails to find who leaked abortion ruling', *CNBC*, 19 January, <www.cnbc.com/2023/01/19/supreme-court-probe-fails-to-find-abortion-ruling-leaker.html>.

McCartney, I. 2020, *AFP statement on the finalisation of the News Corp investigation*, Press Release, 21 May, <www.afp.gov.au/news-media/media-releases/afp-statement-finalisation-news-corp-investigation>.

McGarrity, N. 2011, 'Fourth estate or government lapdog? The role of the Australian media in the counter-terrorism context', *Continuum*, 25 (2), 273.

McMahon, C. 2016, *An investigation into posttraumatic stress and posttraumatic growth among trauma reporting Australian journalists*, PhD Thesis, Deakin University, Victoria.

Media, Entertainment and Arts Alliance (MEAA). 2005, '*Turning Up the Heat: The Decline of Press Freedom in Australia 2001–2005*', *The Inaugural Media, Entertainment and Arts Alliance Report into the State of Press Freedom in Australia from September 11, 2001–2005*, MEAA, Sydney, <www.meaa.org/download/press-freedom-report-2001-2005/>.

Meta. 2022a, 'Meta Transparency Report', *Meta Transparency Center*, <https://transparency.fb.com/data/government-data-requests/country/US/>.

Meta. 2022b, 'Government Requests for User Data – Case Studies', *Meta Transparency Center*, <https://transparency.fb.com/data/government-data-requests/case-studies/>.

National Archives. (n.d.), *Fact Sheet 49 – D Notices*, National Archives of Australia, Canberra, <www.naa.gov.au/help-your-research/fact-sheets/d-notices>.

Neighbour, S. 2006, 'The convert', *Four Corners*, ABC TV, 27 February, <www.abc.net.au/news/2006-02-27/the-convert/8953558 >.

Obermaier, F. and Obermayer, B. 2022, 'The Russian Government Wants to see me Dead', *Spiegel International*, 22 July, <www.spiegel.de/international/world/the-first-interview-with-the-panama-papers-whistleblower-the-russian-government-wants-to-see-me-dead-a-9f830d70-297a-472a-b0cc-9632ff2f514a>.

Parisi, P. 1997, 'Toward a "Philosophy of Framing": News Narratives for Public Journalism', *Journalism & Mass Communication Quarterly*, 74 (4), 673–686.

Parliamentary Joint Committee on Intelligence and Security. 2020, *Inquiry into the impact of the exercise of law enforcement and intelligence powers on the freedom of the press*, Parliamentary Joint Committee on Intelligence and Security, Canberra,

<www.aph.gov.au/Parliamentary_Business/Committees/Joint/Intelligence_and_Security/FreedomofthePress/Report>.

Pearson, M. and Fernandez, J. 2018, 'Surveillance and national security "hyper-legislation": Calibrating restraints on rights with a freedom of expression threshold', *In the Name of Security – Secrecy, Surveillance and Journalism*, Lidberg, J. and Muller, D. eds, Anthem Press, London, 51–76.

Pember, D.R. 2001, *Mass Media Law*, McGraw Hill, Boston.

Posetti, J. 2015, 'Protecting journalism sources in the digital age', *World Trends in Freedom of Expression and Media Development: Special Digital Focus 2015*, UNESCO Publishing, Paris.

Pullan, R. 1994, *Guilty Secrets: Free Speech and Defamation in Australia*, Pascal Press, Sydney.

Renwick, J. 2017, *Independent National Security Legislation Monitor Annual Report 2016–2017*, Australian Government, Canberra, <www.inslm.gov.au/reviews-reports/annual-reports/independent-national-security-legislation-monitor-annual-report-2017>.

Reporters Without Borders (RSF). 2022, '1,668 journalists killed in past 20 years (2003–2022), average of 80 per year', *Violence Against Journalists – News*, <https://rsf.org/en/1668-journalists-killed-past-20-years-2003-2022-average-80-year>.

Riskin, L.L. and Wohl, R.A. 2015, 'Mindfulness in the Heat of Conflict: Taking STOCK, University of Florida Levin College of Law Research Paper No. 16–12', *Harvard Negotiation Law Review*, 20, 12.

Roach, K. 2011, *The 9/11 Effect: Comparative Counter-Terrorism*, Cambridge University Press, Cambridge.

Robie, D. 2011, 'Conflict reporting in the South Pacific – Why peace journalism has a chance', *The Journal of Pacific Studies*, 31 (2), 221–240, <www.academia.edu/1374720/Conflict_reporting_in_the_South_Pacific_Why_peace_journalism_has_a_chance>.

Royes, L. 2017, 'AFP officer accessed journalist's call records in metadata breach', *ABC News Online*, <www.abc.net.au/news/2017-04-28/afp-officer-accessed-journalists-call-records-in-metadata-breach/8480804>.

Society of Professional Journalists (SPJ). 2014, *Society of Professional Journalists (SPJ) Code of Ethics*, <www.spj.org/ethicscode.asp>.

Solutions Journalism Network. 2023, [Online]. <http://solutionsjournalism.org/>.

Sussman, P. 2022, *War Journalism Resources – Resolving Ethical Conflicts in Wartime*, Society of Professional Journalists, <www.spj.org/ethicswartime.asp>.

Veis, G. 2008, 'CNN's prisoner of war', *Men's Journal*, 11 December, <https://ontd-political.livejournal.com/1813630.html>.

Williams, G. and Hardy, K. 2022, 'Two Decades of Australian Counterterrorism Laws', *Melbourne University Law Review*, 46, 34–81, <https://classic.austlii.edu.au/cgi-bin/sinodisp/au/journals/MelbULawRw/2022/21.html>.

Cases cited

Afghan Files case: Australian Federal Police (AFP). 2020, 'AFP Freedom of Information Disclosure Log 15–2020 – FOI – CRM 2020/356', *Senate Environment and Communications References Committee*, <www.afp.gov.au/sites/default/files/PDF/Disclosure-Log/15-2020.pdf>.; Australian Federal Police (AFP). 2020, *AFP statement on investigation into ABC journalist*, Press Release, 15 October 15, <www.afp.gov.au/news-media/media-releases/afp-statement-investigation-abc-journalist>.; *McBride v Commonwealth Director of Public Prosecutions (No 2)* [2021] ACTSC 201 (27 August 2021), <www.austlii.edu.au/cgi-bin/viewdoc/au/cases/act/ACTSC/2021/201.html>.

Artz's case: *Director of Public Prosecutions v Artz* [2013] VCC 56.

Brandenburg's case: *Brandenburg v Ohio* [1969] 395 US 444 (9 June 1969), <https://supreme.justia.com/cases/federal/us/395/444/>.

Haneef case, 2007: Law Council of Australia. 2016, 'Mohamed Haneef case', Policy Agenda – Anti-terror laws, <www.lawcouncil.asn.au/policy-agenda/criminal-law-and-national-security/anti-terror-laws/mohamed-haneef-case>.; *Haneef v Minister for Immigration and Citizenship* [2007] FCA 1273 (21 August 2007), <www.austlii.edu.au/au/cases/cth/FCA/2007/1273.html>.; *Minister for Immigration and Citizenship v Haneef* [2007] FCAFC 203 (21 December 2007), <www.austlii.edu.au/au/cases/cth/FCAFC/2007/203.html>.

Holsworthy Barracks cases: *R v Fattal & Ors* [2011] VSC 681 (16 December 2011), <www.austlii.edu.au/cgi-bin/sinodisp/au/cases/vic/VSC/2011/681.html>; *Fattal & Ors v The Queen* [2013] VSCA 276 (2 October 2013), <www.austlii.edu.au/cgi-bin/sinodisp/au/cases/vic/VSCA/2013/276.html>.

'Jihad Jack', cases: *R v Thomas (No. 3)* [2006] VSCA 300 (20 December 2006), <www.austlii.edu.au/cgi-bin/sinodisp/au/cases/vic/VSCA/2006/300.html>; *Thomas v Mowbray* [2007] HCA (2 August 2007), <www.austlii.edu.au/au/cases/cth/HCA/2007/33.html>; *R v Thomas (No. 4)* [2008] VSCA 107 (16 June 2008), <www.austlii.edu.au/cgi-bin/sinodisp/au/cases/vic/VSCA/2008/107.html>; *R v Thomas* [2008] VSC 620 (29 October 2008), <www.austlii.edu.au/cgi-bin/sinodisp/au/cases/vic/VSC/2008/620.html>.

Minnesota case: *Near v Minnesota* [1931] 283 US 697 (1 June 1931), <https://supreme.justia.com/cases/federal/us/283/697/>.

Pentagon Papers case: *New York Times v US; US v Washington Post* [1971] 713 US 403 (26 June 1971), <https://supreme.justia.com/cases/federal/us/403/713/>.

Search Warrant case: *Smethurst v Commissioner of Police* [2020] HCA 14 (15 April 2020), <www.austlii.edu.au/cgi-bin/viewdoc/au/cases/cth/HCA/2020/14.html>.

Witness J case: *Johns v Director-General of The ACT Justice and Community Safety Directorate* [2019] ACTSC 311 (8 November 2019), <www.austlii.edu.au/cgi-bin/viewdoc/au/cases/act/ACTSC/2019/311.html>.

Yates' case: *Yates v US* (1957) 354 US 298 (17 June 1957), <https://supreme.justia.com/cases/federal/us/354/298/>.

11 Discrimination, cyberbullying and harassment

Key concepts

Stereotype: To categorise a person or a group in a false or unfair light because of their personal characteristics or beliefs – often encompassing an assumption they will behave in a certain way or display certain features.
Prejudice: Holding a preconceived and unfair negative attitude or bias towards someone or their group based primarily upon their personal characteristics or beliefs – such as race, age, disability, gender or religion.
Discrimination: Acting unfairly towards someone based on their membership of a group with shared characteristics or beliefs.
Racial vilification: The incitement of hatred, serious contempt or severe ridicule of a person or groups of people on the grounds of race, via a public act.
Cyberbullying: Bullying – insults, demeaning comments, harassment and intimidation – using digital communication platforms and devices.

Philosophical background to stereotyping and discrimination

The terms 'stereotype', 'prejudice' and 'discrimination' are often used interchangeably, but social psychologists make the important distinction between them along the lines of our definitions in the Key Concepts section above. The *stereotype* is the cognitive component – the positive or negative beliefs we hold about members of a particular social group. That translates into an unfair negative attitude – a *prejudice* – against someone simply because they are members of that group displaying that kind of characteristic – such as skin colour, physical appearance, age, religion, sexual preference, gender and so on. Prejudice can be displayed via affective states such as dislike, anger, fear or even hatred. When attitudes translate into action in favour of, or against, members of a particular group or the overall group itself then it becomes what we call *discrimination* (Jhangiani and Tarry, 2022, Chapter 11).

Getting to the core of why people stereotype is crucial to understanding how it takes root and converts to prejudice and discrimination. It is vital that professional communicators understand this process so they work to identify and minimise stereotyping in their own minds and outputs as important social

DOI: 10.4324/9781003372752-14

influencers and so that they can use their considerable skills and platforms to educate others and to call out stereotyping (and prejudice, racism, other '-isms' and discrimination). At the very least, they might learn not to perpetuate it like corporate communications senior executive Justine Sacco who tweeted stereotypical comments about native African people and AIDS as she was boarding a flight to Cape Town. Unbeknownst to her, the comments went viral over the duration of her eleven-hour journey and she was then trolled ruthlessly for months afterwards, at enormous cost to her own wellbeing and her career (Ronson, 2015). Of course, that was in addition to any harm she caused those she was stereotyping in her post.

Stereotyping is well explained as a cultural phenomenon by moral philosopher Lawrence Blum. He argues the stereotype does not originate in our own psyche, but rather it is fed to us by our culture and then reinforced by our natural 'fixity and resistance to counterevidence of stereotypes' (Blum, 2004: 260). So, when a person meets a member of the stereotyped group who does not display the negative characteristic, they will discount that as an exception but continue with their view of the stereotype. The psychological term for this is 'confirmation bias':

> the tendency of people to favour information that confirms their existing beliefs or hypotheses. Some academics have argued that confirmation bias on social media is also a major contributor to the perpetuation of false claims, conspiracies, misinformation and stereotyping.
> (Modgil et al., 2021)

The pioneer of public opinion, Walter Lippman, captured the essence of stereotyping in his great work *Public Opinion*, first published in 1922:

> For the most part we do not first see, and then define, we define first and then see. In the great blooming, buzzing confusion of the outer world we pick out what our culture has already defined for us and we tend to perceive that which we have picked out in the form stereotyped for us by our culture.
> (Lippman, 1997: 54–55)

Blum argues there is much that is morally bad about stereotyping – both intrinsically and instrumentally. At a personal level, stereotyping denies the moral worth of the individual and their group and fails to pay due respect to them (Blum, 2004: 282). When particular stereotypes are traced to their historical roots, they are often found to have originated from times when it has been economically or socially convenient for the majority to view a group as the 'other'. Blum gives the example of stereotypes of indigenous people as being uncivilised being 'part of a rationale employed by Europeans for subordinating, enslaving, displacing, destroying their culture, and killing them' (Blum, 2004: 283). At a broader social level, stereotyping can influence public policy and actually result in discriminatory laws and structures. It can even impact the performance of individuals who have absorbed the negative stereotype about the characteristics of their group (Blum, 2004: 285–286).

> **Reflect – Research – Review:**
>
> Think of a situation where you have encountered or experienced stereotyping – from either side of the equation – and write a journal entry to reflect upon the type of stereotype, its historical origins, its potential impact upon that group and its members, and what a professional communicator could do to address it in their work.

Aside from genocide – the killing of a large proportion of people of a particular racial, national or religious group aimed at destroying that group – slavery must rank as one of the most discriminatory human behaviours in history. Yet even that practice (which continues in some forms to the modern day) has been the subject of philosophical debate for thousands of years. While Aristotle was said to have endorsed slavery in his writings, the Ancient Greek philosophers the Stoics wrote of equality between slaves and masters – and between men and women – from the 3rd century BCE (Hill, 2001). Hill (2001: 15) describes the fundamental principles of Stoicism as 'egalitarian and universalistic':

> The Stoics sought to honour and preserve human as opposed to contingent identity; the community of rational beings is based, not on biological qualities, but on the divine and transcendent quality of 'mind'.
>
> (Hill, 2001: 16)

The first acknowledged Stoic, Zeno of Citium (c. 334 – c. 262BCE), proposed a classless society composed of citizens from all genders, ethnicities and social statuses. As a lesson in virtue ethics, Diogenes the Cynic (412–323BCE) argued that virtue was achievable by all people regardless of their gender, class or education – and that everyone could transcend social barriers to become friends. The Stoics distinguished themselves from Aristotle (384–322BCE), who had argued there were differences in the capacities of men and women and that slaves were naturally inferior (Hill, 2001: 16).

Treating all people equally is clearly the opposite of discrimination. Within three hundred years the Stoic notions of equality had been transformed into a Christian philosophy of a soul-based equality of all people (Lakoff, 2017). This became the backbone of the thinking of philosophers including the social contract theorist John Locke (1632–1704) who argued all people were born equal in their natural state. This ultimately fed into key human rights documents like the American Declaration of Independence (penned by Thomas Jefferson) starting with the words 'We hold these truths to be self-evident, that all men are created equal' (United States Declaration of Independence, 1776). The words did not abolish slavery in the United States, however. It took the American Civil War from 1861 –1865 to resolve that issue, but stereotyping, prejudice and racial discrimination continues today in that country. Similar wording found its way into the *Universal Declaration of Human Rights* in its Article 1:

> All human beings are born free and equal in dignity and rights. They are endowed with reason and conscience and should act towards one another in a spirit of brotherhood.
>
> (United Nations, 1948)

(We look more deeply at the human rights aspects of discrimination in the next section.)

As mentioned, New Testament Christian teachings counselled followers towards equality of all before the eyes of God. Scripture examples include Jesus's second commandment 'Thou shalt love thy neighbour as thyself' (Matthew 22:39); 'There is neither Jew nor Greek, there is neither slave nor free, there is no male and female, for you are all one in Christ Jesus'. (Galatians 3:28); and 'Judge not, that you be not judged' (Matthew 7:1). Of course, as noted with the continuation of slavery, such teachings did not stop Christian nations practising discrimination via slavery, apartheid and misogyny. One of the worst examples was the murder of unknown thousands of Jews and Muslims throughout Spain and South America under the auspices of the Catholic Church in the Spanish Inquisition (1478–1834).

Buddhism, too, espouses equality between men and women, between all races and between all sentient beings (animals with feeling), based upon 'our shared suffering and the natural wish to be free from it' (Adam, 2013). The historical Buddha was said to have challenged two important forms of discrimination such as the Indian caste system perpetuated by the elite Brahmans and gender inequality by initiating a female order of nuns (Adam, 2013). Yet governments in Buddhist countries and even monks have departed from the teachings with discriminatory policies in recent decades against Tamils in Sri Lanka and against Rohinga people in Myanmar, drawing upon skewed interpretations of scriptures by radical and politicised extremists (Gunasingham, 2019: 1).

Muslims also point to numerous scriptures in the Koran advocating equality, including 'Stand out firmly for justice, as witness to Allah, even as against yourselves, or your parents, or your kin, and whether it be against rich or poor' (4:135). The Prophet Mohamed is said to have spoken in his final sermon: 'An Arab has no superiority over non-Arab, nor a non-Arab has any superiority over Arab, also white has no superiority over black nor does black have any superiority over white, except by piety and righteousness'. Badawi (1995) cites numerous other scriptures proclaiming equality between genders. Yet, again, extremist groups and political regimes have cited other teachings to excuse their discrimination against women and followers of other religions to the present day, while critics elsewhere have used such practices to stereotype, fuel prejudice and sometimes discriminate against Muslims (Kharroub, 2015).

The debate among moral philosophers in the modern era has largely centred on differences between 'direct' discrimination, 'indirect' discrimination, and 'organisational, institutional and structural' discrimination (Altman, 2020). Direct discrimination involves specifically excluding someone on the grounds of their race, religion or other identification factor, normally intentionally. Indirect discrimination involves an action or policy that incidentally discriminates against a particular group when there might have been no intention to do so, as with a government purchasing train carriages with doors and corridors too narrow to fit wheelchairs. Organisational, institutional and structural discrimination can be either direct or indirect, and intentional or unintentional. It happens when societal or institutional rules create unjust outcomes for certain groups, such as when a state electoral body places polling booths out of reach of public transport and opens them only during business hours, disadvantaging the working poor (often of a particular racial or ethnic group). An example of organisational discrimination in media workplaces has been the paucity of females of diverse backgrounds who win promotion to senior newsroom positions. A 2022 study found women of colour were experiencing a 'culture of exclusion', where they were ignored for top positions in newsrooms in the UK, Nigeria, India, South Africa, Kenya and the US (Davies, 2022).

> Reflect – Research – Review:
>
> Search news sites for an example of prejudice or discrimination and explain how it meets the definitions and classifications mentioned in this section.

Human rights context of discrimination

While there are aspirational statements of equality evident in many international human rights laws and instruments, there are also specific mentions of rights against discrimination. The right to freedom of opinion and expression is enshrined in articles 19 and 20 of the *International Covenant on Civil and Political Rights* (ICCPR), in article 5 of the *Convention on the Elimination of All Forms of Racial Discrimination* (CERD), and in article 21 of the *Convention on the Rights of Persons with Disabilities* (CRPD). However, in relation to the ICCPR freedom of expression has two dimensions: it relates to professional communicators' own freedom of expression in their outputs, but also to the right of others to exercise their freedom of expression to disagree with them – which might include abuse, discrimination, harassment or cyberbullying.

Each of the key human rights instruments tries to strike the crucial balance between free expression and discrimination. For example, the *Universal Declaration of Human Rights* (United Nations, 1948) speaks of the 'inherent dignity' of all people in its Preamble. Articles relevant to discrimination include:

Article 1: 'All human beings are born free and equal in dignity and rights';

Article 2 entitled without 'distinction of any kind, such as race, colour, sex, language, religion, political or other opinion, national or social origin, property, birth or other status';

Article 7 against any discrimination or incitement to discrimination;

Article 12 prohibiting 'arbitrary interference with his privacy, family, home or correspondence, nor to attacks upon his honour and reputation. Everyone has the right to the protection of the law against such interference or attacks';

Article 18 guaranteeing 'freedom of thought, conscience and religion';

Article 19 enshrining 'the right to freedom of opinion and expression; this right includes freedom to hold opinions without interference and to seek, receive and impart information and ideas through any media and regardless of frontiers'; and

Article 27 establishing 'the right freely to participate in the cultural life of the community'.

(United Nations, 1948).

The *International Covenant on Civil and Political Rights* (ICCPR) (UN Human Rights Office, 1966) goes further at Article 20(2) by declaring 'Any advocacy of national, racial or religious hatred that constitutes incitement to discrimination, hostility or violence shall be prohibited by law'. Article 26 states: 'All persons are equal before the law and are entitled without any discrimination to the equal protection of the law' (UN Human Rights Office, 1966).

Other conventions cover specific forms of discrimination, including the *Convention on the Elimination of all Forms of Racial Discrimination* (CERD) (UN Human Rights Office, 1965) and the *Convention on the Rights of Persons with Disabilities* (CRPD) (UN Department of Economic and Social Affairs, 2006).

Special international attention to online harassment of communicators of diverse backgrounds

In addition to being the disseminators of discriminatory or stereotypical material, professional communicators from diverse groups can also find themselves targeted by stereotypes, prejudice and discrimination – particularly online in the form of cyberbullying. Those living with disability, or culturally and linguistically diverse (CALD), or who identify as First Nations or LGBTQI+ are special targets. On citing the UNESCO commissioned report by Julie Posetti et al. (2021), the UN Secretary-General stated: 'Other forms of discrimination, such as racism, homophobia and religious bigotry, intersect with sexism and misogyny, which leads to significantly higher rates of online violence against women journalists from minorities or marginalized communities' (UN General Assembly, 2021: 3). Furthermore, the report links to another finding of the study that shows that 'women journalists identifying as Black, Indigenous, Jewish or Arab experienced the highest rates of online violence and suffered the most severe effects from it. In many cases, the perpetrators were unknown' (UN General Assembly, 2021: 3–4). The UN Secretary-General (2021: 16) concluded: 'National protection mechanisms should be equipped to cover the digital space and cater for the specific needs of women, minority and other categories of journalists'. The UN Secretary-General encouraged nations, organisations and corporations to take steps to improve the online safety of journalists, including legislation and policies that create a 'protective framework for journalists carrying out their work that includes an express recognition of the protection of online expression and protection from attacks aimed at silencing those exercising their right to freedom of expression online or offline' (UN General Assembly, 2021: 17).

The author's extended account of the law and policy related to the online safety of diverse journalists was published in 2023 as Appendix A to the research report *Online Safety of Diverse Journalists* (Vallencia-Forrester et al., 2023).

> **Reflect – Research – Review:**
>
> Review the right to be not discriminated against and the right to free expression in a human rights instrument such as the ICCPR. Write a paragraph about a situation where discrimination in a media communication might be excusable on free expression or public interest grounds.

Professional ethics, discrimination and cyber-safety

Normally, the straight coverage of racial and ethnic issues will not land professional communicators in legal difficulties. However, a professional needs to be mindful about their own potential for stereotyping and, as this can occur at a subconscious level, the need for others to review their work pre-publication. A range of ethical guidelines at a professional level supplement the legal framework on discrimination and harassment.

International ethical regulation

Public relations organisations internationally typically do not feature clauses specifically addressing discrimination. Instead, they usually call upon members to act fairly in their dealings. For example, the Public Relations Society of

America (PRSA) Code of Ethics requires fairness and a respect for diverse opinions:

> We deal fairly with clients, employers, competitors, peers, vendors, the media, and the general public. We respect all opinions and support the right of free expression.
>
> (PRSA, 2023)

Of course, this leaves the way open for a member to excuse discrimination, stereotyping or harassment on the grounds of free speech and diversity of views – essentially a John Stuart Mill-style consequentialist approach, arguing that all opinions should be allowed to contest for space in the marketplace of ideas (Smith, 1988: 31).

In contrast, journalism codes of ethics typically feature anti-discrimination guidance along the lines of Clause 9 of the International Federation of Journalists' (IFJ) Charter of Ethics which states:

> Journalists shall ensure that the dissemination of information or opinion does not contribute to hatred or prejudice and shall do their utmost to avoid facilitating the spread of discrimination on grounds such as geographical, social or ethnic origin, race, gender, sexual orientation, language, religion, disability, political and other opinions.
>
> (IFJ, 2019)

Further advice on hate speech was featured in the IFJ Digital Ethics Report:

> HATE SPEECH. Your words and images can easily be weaponised, and your credibility co-opted. Avoid characterising sources or subjects by demographic attributes. Generalisations can contribute to stereotyping. Stick to reporting an individual's words or actions.
>
> (IFJ, 2020: 7)

However, no disciplinary actions for breaches of the Charter are mentioned publicly on the IFJ's website, likely because membership of the IFJ is open only to journalists' unions rather than to individual journalists. It is left to the national union bodies to police the unethical behaviour of their individual journalists' actions (IFJ, 2022).

International approaches to online safety of communicators

A host of policies and resources has arisen at international level given the extent of cyberbullying and online harassment of media practitioners. The UN has also recommended media employers instil a greater culture of safety of journalists, with particular attention to attacks on female employees and those from diverse backgrounds, premised on their responsibility to protect their staff (UN Human Rights Office, 2017: 8–9). A key finding of a UNESCO research discussion paper on global trends in online violence against women journalists showed that:

> Nearly half (47%) of the women survey respondents identified reporting or commentating on gender issues (e.g. feminism, male-on-female-violence, reproductive rights including abortion, transgender issues) as a top trigger for online attacks, highlighting the function of misogyny in online violence against women journalists.
> (Posetti et al., 2021: 8)

There has been considerable activity on the issue of online safety of journalists at the level of international organisations, including research, guidelines and advice to journalists who have been targeted, particularly females. Journalists can report online abuse to an NGO which might choose to take up their cause and apply pressure to state actors and/or multinational platforms. For example, Media Defence is an international human rights organisation that provides legal help to journalists and independent media around the world. Their lawyers can provide support for communicators and news outlets when they are confronted with legal action as a result of their reporting. They claim to provide legal support for online threats, doxxing, stolen images, deep fakes, blackmail linked to images, discreditation and reputation damage, account takeovers, fake accounts, hacking and surveillance (Media Defence, n.d.).

Case example:

The cause of Muslim journalist Rana Ayyab was taken up by the NGO Reporters Without Borders (RSF) with the Indian government after Hindu nationalist supporters of the prime minister were trolling her and there had been no action from him (RSF, 2018). She was prevented from flying to Europe to deliver an address on intimidation of journalists after numerous online attacks against her – including rape threats – by members of right-wing Hindu groups for her book and other writing, predominantly on the persecution of Muslims (Hassan, 2022).

International organisations – education and guidelines

Numerous international organisations have developed guidelines, resources and referral points for journalists of all types facing online safety issues. Free Press Unlimited and Greenhost developed Totem, an online platform for journalists and activists to learn more about digital safety and privacy tools (Communication Initiative Network, 2022). The US-based Committee to Protect Journalists (CPJ) has developed a series of digital safety resources and advice (CPJ, 2020). Several international media organisations have joined to create the Online Violence Response Hub (2023) – a resource centre run by the

Coalition Against Online Violence predominantly aimed at female journalists facing online abuse.

Social media platform approaches

The terms of use of social media platforms counsel against discrimination and hate speech. YouTube's hate speech policy is an example, and also contains a list of the key kinds of groups that can face discrimination:

> Hate speech is not allowed on YouTube. We remove content promoting violence or hatred against individuals or groups based on any of the following attributes:
>
> - Age
> - Caste
> - Disability
> - Ethnicity
> - Gender Identity and Expression
> - Nationality
> - Race
> - Immigration Status
> - Religion
> - Sex/Gender
> - Sexual Orientation
> - Victims of a major violent event and their kin
> - Veteran Status
>
> If you find content that violates this policy, report it.
>
> (YouTube, 2023)

In 2021 the United Nations General Assembly called upon social media platforms to respect the human rights of journalists, declaring they 'should seek to prevent or mitigate any adverse impact on human rights directly linked to their operations, products or services' (UN General Assembly, 2021: 16). The UN Consultation outcome document on the Plan of Action on the Safety of Journalists and the Issue of Impunity (2017) called upon Internet and social media platforms to recognise, through public statements and internal policy, the risk to society and to their own business models, of online attacks directed against journalists (particularly females), including hacking, Distributed Denial of Service (DDOS) attacks on websites, cyberbullying, trolling, doxxing and illegal surveillance (UN Human Rights Office, 2017: 9–10).

Social media platform complaint mechanisms are too numerous and varied to detail here. However, the eSafety Commissioner's eSafety Guide has links to many reporting mechanisms for social media platforms (eSafety Commissioner,

Discrimination, cyberbullying and harassment 317

n.d.). The site details how to report harmful content for each platform. The usual limits of the platform's powers are the removal of the offending material and the person committing the harassment being banned or suspended. Frustrations with complaints systems offered by the major platforms abound, particularly with regard to Facebook and its parent company Meta. That company provides a useful example of global hate speech self-regulation in practice. Meta's Transparency Center details its policies on Hate Speech. Its policies and enforcement details on Bullying and Harassment are listed separately (Meta Transparency Center, 2022a). Meta divides hate speech into three tiers, with Tier 1 including content targeting a person or group of people on the basis of 'protected characteristics'. Its examples of offensive speech at Tier 1 are graphic and risk offending some simply by being cited as examples. Tier 2 hate speech focuses again on the 'protected characteristics' with particular emphasis on statements of inferiority, including generalisations of physical, mental or moral deficiencies, other statements of inferiority, and expressions of contempt that might be homophobic or racist, or curses related to sexual behaviour or body parts (Meta Transparency Center, 2023). Tier 3 hate speech typically calls for segregation or exclusion on the basis of the protected characteristic. Meta's Oversight Board is its overarching self-regulatory governing body, established in 2020 with 20 members appointed, expanded to 40 by 2022 (Meta Transparency Center, 2022b). The Oversight Board members are from diverse backgrounds and nationalities, with strong representation of journalism, technology, human rights and law academics and NGO heads (Oversight Board, n.d.). It only chooses to hear a handful of appeals from Meta's standard decision-making processes each year – at 13 March, 2023 it had only published 26 decisions overall (Oversight Board, 2023), at least 15 of which related to hate speech, discrimination, violence and incitement or marginalised communities.

Key Case 11.1: Instagram hate speech case

Meta Oversight Board Decision 2022–003-IG-UA Reclaiming Arabic words [June 14, 2022] <https://oversightboard.com/decision/IG-2PJ00L4T/>.

Facts

An Instagram post was removed by Meta for violating its hate speech policy. The Instagram carousel of ten images within a single post showed pictures of Arabic words that could be used in a derogatory way towards men with 'effeminate mannerisms'. According to the person posting it, the intent was 'to reclaim [the] power of such hurtful terms'. The Oversight Board became involved after Meta initially removed the material, then reinstated it after an objection from the poster, then removed it again after a further complaint, and then restored it after a further Meta internal review.

Law

In its decision, the Oversight Board found that removing the content to be an error out of line with Meta's Hate Speech Policy. 'While the post does contain slur terms, the content is covered by an exception for speech "used self-referentially or in an empowering way", as well as an exception which allows the quoting of hate speech to "condemn it or raise awareness"', the decision stated (Oversight Board, 2022, para 4). The Board recommended several policy changes to the creation, translation, enforcement and auditing of its market-specific slur lists (Oversight Board, 2022).

Lessons for communicators

The decision involved a combination of issues relevant to discrimination, including freedom of expression, hate speech, LGBTQI+ identification, marginalised communities and sex/gender equality. It also demonstrated that satire or parody needs to be handled carefully because it is often misunderstood by regulators.

Reflect – Research – Review:

Communicating suicide and mental illness

Discrimination and cyberbullying can have harmful effects on people's mental health. Professional communicators need to be aware of this as part of their own self-care, and also to ensure they do not exacerbate other people's difficulties through their reporting and other communications. One form of stereotyping and discrimination can be against those experiencing mental illnesses or disorders. The Australian government has funded a useful suite of resources in this space (covering the communication about mental health, suicide, alcohol and other drugs) under the Mindframe project (Mindframe, 2023) (see <https://mindframe.org.au/>). The resources counsel professional communicators to follow basic guidelines in their coverage, reporting and interviews to avoid sensationalising these topics or stigmatising those experiencing them. They feature research reports and links to data on the topics to better inform communications about them – all in a bid to demystify negative stereotypes. Go to the Mindframe website at <https://mindframe.org.au/mental-health/communicating-about-mental-ill-health/language> and read about the recommended ways of discussing mental health in your communications. Then do a search for one of the less desirable terms used in a news story and rewrite that story using the Mindframe recommended approaches.

National ethical self-regulation

In Australia, while the Public Relations Institute of Australia (PRIA) Code of Ethics is silent on discrimination, it does call upon its members to act fairly and desist from disseminating false or misleading information (PRIA, 2009). In journalism, various professional and industry codes of practice direct practitioners to avoid discriminatory and hateful communications. The MEAA Journalist Code of Ethics (2016) makes its stance on prejudicial reportage and commentary very clear at Item 2:

> Do not place unnecessary emphasis on personal characteristics, including race, ethnicity, nationality, gender, age, sexual orientation, family relationships, religious belief, or physical or intellectual disability.

Supplementary guidelines issued in 2020 advise all journalists to exercise care and balance when covering race issues and to be mindful not to allow their work to be used to promote extremist views or hate speech (MEAA, 2020). The enforcement of the organisation's self-regulatory regime is, however, problematic, and complaints about discriminatory or prejudicial material produced by journalists are more likely to be directed to the media-specific self-regulator such as the Australian Press Council (APC) or the Australian Communications and Media Authority (ACMA). The Media, Entertainment and Arts Alliance (MEAA) has taken steps to address the cyberbullying of communicators by partnering with Gender Equity Victoria (GEN VIC) and Australian Community Managers (ACM) to launch a pioneering 'Enhancing Online Safety of Women in the Media' project. GEN VIC has developed three critical resources to help media organisations and publications better support women journalists who experience harassment: Australian Media Moderation Guidelines; workplace support on dealing with online harassment; and media cyber safety training (Gender Equity Victoria, 2021b: 7). They recommend the following four actions for dealing with online harassment: self-care by accessing mental health and referral agencies; taking notes and documenting the event; reporting the harassment to the social media platform; and, pursuing the available legal avenues.

At a self-regulatory level, the Australian Press Council (APC, 2001) has made a special effort to educate newspaper and online journalists and journalism students on the avoidance of discrimination and gratuitous emphasis on racial and other factors in reportage. It removed an anti-discrimination provision from its overarching Statement of Principles in a 2014 revision, but has issued special 'Advisory Guidelines' to its members on related issues including the reporting of asylum seekers, people with an intellectual disability, Nazi concentration camps, religious terms in headlines, race, and persons with gender and sexual diversity. They can be viewed at <www.presscouncil.org.au/advisory-guidelines>. The Council may call for specific measures to prevent recurrence when it upholds a complaint about a breach (APC, 2023).

The Australian Communications and Media Authority (ACMA) is responsible for the co-regulation of the broadcast media, with the various broadcasting industry sectors setting their own programming guidelines in the form of codes of practice, which in turn address race and ethnicity issues. An example is the Commercial Television Industry Code of Practice (Free TV Australia, 2018) under the *Broadcasting Services Act 1992* which at Section 123(3)(e) specifically states that the following is to be taken into account when such codes of practice are developed:

> the portrayal in programmes of matter that is likely to incite or perpetuate hatred against, or vilifies, any person or group on the basis of ethnicity, nationality, race, gender, sexual preference, age, religion or physical or mental disability.

ACMA has certain requirements for the handling of complaints about such matters, with mediation between the broadcaster and the complainant being the first mechanism, working through to a determination of the matter by ACMA's own investigators. ACMA also has a range of penalties available to it under the Act, with the ultimate being the suspension of a broadcaster's licence, through to substantial fines, imposition of conditions on the licensee, down to recommendations such as the counselling and training of staff. Similar regulations apply to radio news and current affairs.

Case example:

Cronulla Riots case (2007): A complaint arose when the talkback radio host Alan Jones fuelled the fire of racial and ethnic tension in December 2005, when angry mobs in southern Sydney staged a protest then set upon youths of Middle Eastern appearance in an episode that became known as the 'Cronulla riots'. The role of the media in the lead-up to the riots, particularly that of Jones, was questioned by the ABC's *Media Watch* programme (2006). In the week before the Cronulla riots, Jones described two people who were accused of assaulting some lifeguards as 'Middle Eastern grubs' and two days later continued with:

> My suggestion is to invite one of the biker gangs to be present in numbers at Cronulla railway station when these Lebanese thugs arrive. It would be

worth the price of admission to watch these cowards scurry back onto the train for the return trip to their lairs. ... Australians old and new shouldn't have to put up with this scum.

On ensuing days, Jones agreed with listeners who called for violent retribution against youths of Lebanese origin. In 2007, ACMA formally found that Jones' comments had breached 2GB's radio licence and the Commercial Radio Code of Practice on three separate occasions, as 'likely to incite, encourage or present for its own sake violence and brutality' and material 'likely to incite or perpetuate hatred against or vilify' those of Lebanese and Middle Eastern background on the basis of their 'ethnicity' (ACMA, 2007).

> **Reflect – Research – Review:**
>
> Go to the ACMA website, <www.acma.gov.au> and find some recent investigations and findings on discrimination or vilification breaches. What was the result of the complaint and decision?

The public broadcasters – the Australian Broadcasting Corporation (ABC) and the Special Broadcasting Service (SBS) have cyberbullying processes in place. The ABC has robust procedures, guidance and training for how to deal with online harm. SBS has internal policies on inclusiveness and protocols for dealing with non-inclusive behaviours (SBS 2022–2024: 12).

Case examples:

Anzac Day case (2017): The part-time ABC commentator Yassmin Abdel-Magied famously left Australia following mainstream media haranguing and social media trolling of her over her seven word Tweet on Anzac Day 2017 stating: *'Lest. We. Forget. (Manus, Nauru, Syria, Palestine ...'* (Carmody, 2017). (Anzac Day is a sacred day of remembrance of Australian and New Zealand war heroes, and this satirical comment critiqued the government's policies on asylum seekers.) The ABC initially distanced itself from her comments but did not move to dismiss her. However, it later 'parted ways' with her after the conservative Coalition campaigned for her sacking (Bornstein, 2022). It axed her documentary show *Australia Wide*, but claimed this was not in response to the campaign against her but part of normal programme reviews (Woods, 2017). Trolling and conservative media attacks reached new lows, as Julie Baird (2017) noted:

> Racism, sexism and Islamophobia make a potent brew. Almost 90,000 words, by one estimate, have been written about Abdel-Magied in three

months. She gets daily death threats, has had to change her phone number and move house. Then, when she said she was moving to London, trolls sent songs: 'You are a c---'. Others taunted her 'funny hat' and asked why it took so long, adding 'good bloody riddance'; now 'London will be an Islamic shithole', 'don't f---ing come back', 'hope you never return'.

Abdel-Magied has since written about the episode in *Talking About a Revolution* (2022).

Troll Hunting (2019): Journalist Ginger Gorman identifies with Jewish heritage on her mother's side and is married to a Filipino Australian partner. Her book *Troll Hunting* chronicled her five years of research into the behaviour and psychology of online harassment after being trolled over a story she had written in 2013. She offered some insight into the approaches by her own employer and others to their journalists who have been subjected to cyberhate. She recalled her husband was critical of ABC management for the way they handled her situation when she was being threatened and intimidated by anonymous Internet trolls, including a tweet that stated chillingly 'Your life is over' (Gorman, 2019: 251). Managers simply suggested she call the Employee Assistance Programme for psychological support but offered no security assistance (Gorman, 2019: 250). She quoted lawyer Josh Bornstein saying: 'There has never been a free-for-all on speech and there never should be a free-for-all on speech. If speech causes harm, then there needs to be regulation' (Gorman, 2019: 217).

International legal approaches to discrimination and cyberbullying

Countries have found different points of balance between the right of free speech and media freedom and individuals' rights against discrimination, cyber-bullying and hate speech. In the United States, for example, there is a strong First Amendment protection even for hateful speech, and the Supreme Court has struck down lower court decisions and state legislation attempting to gag free expression. By contrast, Germany and several other European countries have Holocaust denial laws under which several revisionist historians and neo-Nazis have been jailed for expressing their views.

Major incidents this millennium have shown the tension between free expression, discrimination and hate speech. When the Danish newspaper *Jyllands-Posten* printed 12 cartoons depicting the Prophet Mohammed in 2005, its journalists knew there would be a reaction. Visual depictions of Mohammed are offensive to some traditions of Islam. Within months, the Danish newspaper's images had spread via the internet and scores of other newspapers, triggering protests in which more than 100 people died, and prompting the bombing and arson of Danish embassies, flag burning, the declaration of a fatwa by Muslim clerics and an axe attack on one of the cartoonists. The free expression traditions of Denmark clashed directly with an ancient Sunni Muslim prohibition on the visual illustration of Mohammed.

About two decades have passed since the cartoons were published, but the original cartoonists and editors, and those who reproduced them in other newspapers and online, still hold well-founded fears of retribution for their actions. Such fears seemed justified when in January 2015 two extremists forced their way into the offices of the satirical weekly newspaper *Charlie Hebdo* in Paris, killing 12 people and injuring 11 others. The newspaper had republished the Danish cartoons and followed that with satirical articles about Islam. A month later, an attack in Copenhagen targeted an event titled 'Art, Blasphemy and Freedom of Expression' with Swedish artist Lars Vilks – famous for his satirical drawings of the prophet Mohammed – in attendance.

The most famous fatwa was against British author Salman Rushdie in 1989, when Iranian leader Ayatollah Ruhollah Khomeini sentenced him to death for writing the book *The Satanic Verses*. The book was based loosely on the life of the Prophet. The Japanese translator was stabbed to death in 1991 and the Italian translator was also stabbed. In 1993, the Norwegian publisher of the book was shot outside his Oslo home. In 2022, Rushdie endured 15 stab wounds in surviving an attempt on his life by a follower of the Supreme Leader of Iran at a public lecture at the Chautauqua Institution in Western New York state (Remnick, 2023). Of course, no form of communication justifies violent retribution, but there is marked international variation over what level of expression is acceptable – or even legal – when it might involve racial, ethnic or religious critique.

In the eyes of the law, attacks upon others via the internet or social media go under a range of names according to their type, scale and jurisdiction. They include: cyber-bullying, cyber-stalking, online trolling, malicious online content, using carriage services to menace, harassment, hate speech, vilification, discrimination, stalking and even assault. Some are criminal offences where offenders can be fined or jailed, while others are civil wrongs where courts can award damages to victims. Some are litigated under actions we have already considered, such as defamation, privacy and breach of confidentiality. The digital era has also involved a marked increase in the phenomenon of 'revenge pornography' – the 'non-consensual distribution of nude or sexual images online or via mobile phones' (Henry et al., 2017: 3). A 2017 study found one in five Australians – equally divided between men and women – had experienced distressing image-based abuse and that 80 per cent of Australians agreed it should be a crime to share sexual or nude images without permission (Henry et al., 2017: 2).

Major Western democracies have taken a variety of approaches to discrimination, hate speech and cyberbullying law. Here are some highlights:

United States

Under First Amendment protections, even internet communications disclosing personal information about other citizens that might alarm or intimidate them or 'expose them to unwanted attention from others' is protected in the US. The

Supreme Court hate speech judgments have found that all but communications integral to criminal conduct – fighting words, threats and solicitations – have free expression protection in America.

Case example:

The Slants case (2017): The Supreme Court held that the US Trademarks office could not ban the registration of the name of a rock band 'The Slants' – which might seem racist and offensive to Asian Americans – because of the right to free expression under the First Amendment.

Further, s230 of the USA *Communications Decency Act 1996* gives Internet and social media platforms 'intermediary immunity' – absolving them of all responsibility for the communications by third parties using their platforms and sites. This means regulators cannot prosecute the platforms over material of others that they host – including offensive or harassing material. Subsection 230(c)(1) of the Act states quite simply:

> No provider or user of an interactive computer service shall be treated as the publisher or speaker of any information provided by another information content provider.

European Union

Laws and regulations in the European Union are heavily influenced by the human rights regime of the seven-decade old *European Convention on Human Rights*, enforced by a legal and regulatory regime at which the European Court of Human Rights stands at the summit. Free expression (Article 10), privacy (Article 8), thought, conscience and religion (Article 9) and anti-discrimination (Article 14) all compete in the framework. Non-Government Organisations (NGOs) play an active role in this space in Europe. Within that context European nations are often world leaders in the fight against harassment and privacy invasion, and in their efforts to call to account major platforms hosting offensive material. An example is the Network Enforcement Law in Germany that came into force in 2017. It applies to social media platforms with more than two million German users. It requires the platforms to block or remove access to 'manifestly unlawful content' within 24 hours of receiving a complaint, and 'unlawful content' within seven days of receiving a complaint (German Law Archive, 2017). Fines of 50 million euro can be issued against offending platforms.

United Kingdom

The main anti-discrimination legislation in the UK is contained in the *Equality Act 2010*. It replaced and strengthened previous anti-discrimination laws covering sex, racial and disability discrimination. The UK is also a signatory to the European Convention on Human Rights, with appeals to the European Court of Human Rights. The UK has an array of laws available to those who wish to pursue online harassment. Key laws cover harassment, criminal justice and public order, malicious communications, and defamation. A suite of UK criminal offences is also available to deal with cyberbullying and harassment (Crown Prosecution Service, 2018). As this book was going to press, the UK's new Online Safety Bill was under parliamentary consideration, aiming to prevent the spread of illegal content and activity (such as images of child abuse, terrorist material and hate crimes, including racist abuse), protect children from harmful material, and protect adults from legal – but harmful – content. The law leaves it to large platforms like Meta and Google to decide how to comply. It also empowers the communications regulator Ofcom to regulate their attempts. It carries potential fines of up to £18m, or 10% of their annual global turnover (Rhoden-Paul and Whannel, 2022).

Canada

Canadians are protected from discrimination under Part 1 of the Canadian Human Rights Act. Canada has mainly addressed online harassment crimes via its Criminal Code, with a range of provisions covering behaviour like sharing intimate images, criminal harassment, threats, intimidation, identity theft, extortion, incitement of hatred and defamation. In an attempt to alleviate growing concerns about cyberbullying, the Canadian government passed Bill C-13 (the Protecting Canadians from Online Crime Act) in 2015. It amended many of the Criminal Code offences, aimed mainly at shoring up prosecutions against cyberbullying of school children (Parliament of Canada, 2014).

New Zealand

New Zealand has its Bill of Rights Act (BORA) 1990, which enshrines rights of free expression, non-discrimination, privacy, thought and conscience. In addition to the usual criminal offences that can be prosecuted – similar to other Commonwealth countries – New Zealand's legislation aimed specifically at online harassment and cyberbullying was the Harmful Digital Communications Act 2015 (New Zealand) which criminalised the posting of harmful digital content and established the agency NetSafe to resolve complaints about harmful digital communications.

Reflect – Research – Review:

Find a recent example of hate speech that has resulted in legal action. Compare and contrast it with one of the cases in this chapter.

Australian legal approaches to discrimination and cyberbullying

Discrimination

International human rights instruments have had an influence on Australian law. While Australia is signatory to such human rights instruments, and they might inform judicial reasoning, they are not binding unless incorporated into specific Australian legislation, such as the *Racial Discrimination Act 1975*. The *United Nations Convention on the Elimination of all Forms of Racial Discrimination* (CERD) is cited in the preamble to Australia's *Racial Discrimination Act 1975* as its motivation. Australian state and Commonwealth laws address discrimination at its extremities – the actual vilification of people because of their racial, ethnic or religious group and the incitement to racial hatred or violence against such individuals.

The *Racial Discrimination Act 1975*, in Part II, has broad prohibitions on racial discrimination in most walks of life. Of most interest to the media is Section 18C, which makes it unlawful to do any public action that

a. is reasonably likely, in all the circumstances, to offend, insult, humiliate or intimidate another person or a group of people;
b. because of the race, colour or national or ethnic origin of the other person or of some or all of the people in the group.

Section 18D offers exemptions to the operation of 18C, including artistic performance, genuine discussion or debate in the public interest, fair reporting and fair comment.

It was the requirement that a report be fair and accurate to earn the exemption that proved to be the main stumbling block to *Herald Sun* columnist Andrew Bolt, who famously lost an 18C case in 2011 (see Key Case 11.2). The political nature of that loss prompted several proposals to reform Section 18C, including the failed attempt in the Senate to replace the words 'insult', 'offend' and 'humiliate' with the term 'harass' in 2017 (McGhee, 2017).

Section 46P of the *Human Rights and Equal Opportunity Commission Act 1986* allows people to make complaints to the Human Rights and Equal Opportunity Commission (HREOC) about offensive behaviour based on racial hatred. However, while such behaviour may be an 'unlawful act' it is not necessarily a criminal offence under the legislation. Criminal charges for the most extreme forms of discrimination – urging violence against someone on the basis of their membership of a group 'distinguished by race, religion, nationality, national or ethnic origin or political opinion' – are available under the reformed 'sedition' laws of the *Criminal Code Act 1995* at section 80.2B: 'Urging violence against members of groups' with a penalty of up to five or seven years in jail.

Key Case 11.2: The Bolt case

Eatock v Bolt [2011] FCA 1103 (28 September 2011), <www.austlii.edu.au/cgi-bin/viewdoc/au/cases/cth/FCA/2011/1103.html>; *Eatock v Bolt (No. 2)* [2011] FCA 1180 (19 October 2011), <www.austlii.edu.au/cgi-bin/viewdoc/au/cases/cth/FCA/2011/1180.htm>.

Facts

In April 2009, Melbourne's *Herald Sun* newspaper published an article by conservative columnist Andrew Bolt titled 'It's so hip to be black' and also posted it to its website with the heading 'White is the new black'. Four months later, Bolt wrote another column in the newspaper and website titled 'White fellas in the black'. The articles suggested fair-skinned Aboriginal people were not genuinely Aboriginal, but predominantly European in racial origin, yet pretended to be Aboriginal so they could access benefits and career or political advancement available to Aboriginal people. Pat Eatock brought the action under s18C of the *Racial Discrimination Act* against Bolt on behalf of herself and other fair-skinned Aboriginal people.

Law

Federal Court Justice Mordecai Bromberg held that the articles contravened s18C because they were 'reasonably likely to offend, insult, humiliate or intimidate some Aboriginal persons of mixed descent who have a fairer, rather than darker, skin and who by a combination of descent, self-identification and communal recognition are and are recognised as Aboriginal persons'.

Bolt and his newspaper publisher disputed that the articles conveyed those imputations, denied they would cause offence, and claimed race, colour and ethnic origin were not motivating factors in their writing and publishing of the articles. Bolt failed in his defence that the articles were published 'reasonably and in good faith' as fair comment under s18D because the articles contained 'errors of fact, distortions of the truth and inflammatory and provocative language'. Justice Bromberg ruled that beyond the 'hurt and insult' the articles were 'reasonably likely to have an intimidatory effect on some fair-skinned Aboriginal people, particularly young Aboriginal persons or others with vulnerability in relation to their identity'. The articles would embolden those with racially prejudiced views.

Lessons for professional communicators

The ruling was more about the manner in which Bolt had presented his view than the nature of the view itself. It was not unlawful for writers to deal with racial identification, and 'even challenge the genuineness of the identification of a group of people'. The main lesson is to tread carefully when doing so, and to ensure your opinions are well founded upon provable facts and that such commentary is fairly presented. Pat Eatock died in 2015.

Reflect – Research – Review:

Debate the topic: 'The Bolt case shows the laws of racial discrimination go too far. The media should be free to air all views in society – even those that are racist'.

Case examples:

QUT Students' case (2016 and 2017): Three Queensland University of Technology (QUT) students were approached by an administration officer in the indigenous unit and asked to leave because they did not identify as indigenous. One of them found a computer elsewhere and posted to a Facebook page titled 'QUT Stalker Space': 'Just got kicked out of the unsigned Indigenous computer room. QUT stopping segregation with segregation?' There were other posts in reply, including satirical remarks suggesting they could start a new lab for a white supremacist group. The admin officer also alleged that one of the respondents posted an offensive racist term to the page, but that student claimed someone else must have posted it under his name. The officer launched an action seeking $250,000 in damages for a breach of section 18C(1) of the *Racial Discrimination Act 1975*. The court ruled that it was not reasonably likely that a hypothetical person in the position of the admin officer – or a hypothetical member of her group – would feel 'offended, insulted, humiliated or intimidated' by the comments posted by the two students who had admitted authorship. An appeal judge held that, for some of the comments, no reasonably intelligent person would have understood them 'as other than humour or irony'. With regard to the student who allegedly posted the derogative racist term, both the trial judge and the appeal court held there was no evidence tendered that he was responsible for the contents of the document with his name on it, and he had denied authorship. The court dismissed the proceedings.

***Perth Now* case (2012)**: The Federal Court found the *Perth Now* news website was responsible for racially discriminatory comments it allowed to be posted to its site by readers about four Aboriginal youths who died in an accident in a car they had stolen, and ordered it to pay $12,000 to their mother.

Holocaust cases (2002–2009): Founder and director of the Adelaide Institute, Dr Frederick Toben, had already been jailed in Germany in 1999 for publishing Holocaust denial material on the internet. In this Australian case, he was jailed again for three months for contempt of court for refusing to remove similar material in defiance of a court order to do so. Toben had published material on the institute's website casting doubt that the Holocaust – the murder of hundreds of thousands of Jewish people in gas chambers during World War II – actually happened, and claiming some Jewish people had exaggerated facts about it for financial gain. The publication breached the *Racial Discrimination Act 1975*. Toben died in 2020.

There is some debate over whether section 18C applies to Muslim people, given the ethnic and national diversity of that religion. This is because the section requires that the offensive behaviour targets 'race, colour or national or ethnic origin' (not mentioning religion), but it has been held to apply to discriminatory publications about Jewish people as a race (Holocaust cases, 2002–09). However, alternative avenues are sometimes available for pursuing incidents of hate speech, as detailed below. The conservative Morrison Government attempted to pass a new *Religious Discrimination Act* prohibiting discrimination on the basis of a person's religious belief or activity but this lapsed in 2022.

State and territory laws deal with the area in different ways and with varying levels of intensity, with Western Australia focusing on the publication of material intended to incite racial hatred or to harass people of a racial group. The NSW and ACT laws prohibit any public act (not just publication) inciting hatred or even severe ridicule of an individual or a group because of race. The media are protected to some extent by a provision allowing the publication of a fair report of acts of racial vilification. Professional communicators should look to the particular legislation in their state or territory to check its breadth of operation and application to the media.

The laws of all jurisdictions allow for free and open coverage of the immigration and race debate. Defences of public interest, fair comment and privilege vary across jurisdictions, but usually apply in a similar way to the defamation defences. Potential difficulties arise for media outlets when reporting the views – or hosting the comments – of extremists calling for some action to be taken against a particular section of society. Letters editors, hosts of debates between ethnic groups, the editors of political and ethnic newspapers, moderators of social media comments and producers of ethnic or political programmes need to obtain legal advice on how these laws relate to their particular jurisdictions so they can strike a suitable balance between free speech and sensibility.

Case examples:

Alan Jones cases (2000 and 2009–2013): Sydney talkback radio host Alan Jones went to air in 1995 with a rant on a discrimination case that had been decided in favour of a Dubbo woman who had been refused a rental property by an agent on the grounds of her race. He described a potential tenant as 'looking like a skunk and smelling like a skunk, with a sardine can on one foot and sandshoe on the other and a half-drunk bottle of beer under the arm'. He opened the lines for listeners to express their views. The NSW Administrative Decisions Tribunal found he and his station had breached the racial vilification provisions of the NSW *Anti-Discrimination Act 1977.* Listeners would have associated the Aboriginality of the woman with Jones' derogatory remarks and Jones and 2UE had committed a public act (the broadcast) inciting the ordinary, reasonable listener to feel serious contempt for or severe ridicule for Aboriginal people in NSW on the ground of their race. Despite the public interest in the issue of bad tenants, Jones had failed to establish he had acted in good faith or reasonably by linking the tenant's Aboriginality with her tenancy qualities. The concept of 'incitement' did not require any intent on the part of Jones – simply that the broadcast was capable of conveying to the ordinary, reasonable listener that they were being incited to hold the requisite degree of ill-feeling on the ground of race. The tribunal ordered Jones to apologise. He faced a similar complaint after segments on his breakfast radio programme discriminated against Lebanese males and their Muslim religion. The Tribunal found the comments incited serious contempt of Lebanese males, including Lebanese Muslims, in breach of the Act. It took seven years and four court cases before Jones eventually read a negotiated apology on air and paid damages of $10,000 and court costs of more than $180,000.

Gay cases (2004, 2007 and 2018): Discrimination can also centre on an individual or group's sexual orientation, with homosexual activist Garry Burns leading the charge in NSW with scores of anti-vilification actions spanning two decades. In 2004 and again in 2007, Burns took action under the anti-vilification provisions of the *Anti-Discrimination Act 1977* (NSW). In the first case the complaint was sustained against broadcaster 2UE. Host Steve Price's references to 'grubby activities' and 'poofs' verged 'on the contemptuous', while John Laws' references to homosexual partners as 'a couple of old poofs' and 'a couple of young poofs' were found capable of inciting severe ridicule among ordinary reasonable listeners. A second complaint in

2007 over remarks by Laws, included calling the host of *Queer Eye for the Straight Guy*, a 'pompous little pansy', a 'pillow-biting pompous little prig' and a 'precious little pansy' were held to have vilified homosexuals, but to have done so within the good faith and public-interest exception to the Act. By 2018, Burns had lodged an estimated 74 complaints of homosexual vilification against the owner of a website and YouTube account, John Sunol, some of which were upheld.

Islam case (2017): A 2015 article under the headline 'ISLAM MUST CHANGE' appeared in the print edition of the *Herald Sun* newspaper. The article reported the comments and views of a number of federal Coalition politicians on the topic of the link between Islamic teaching and terrorism. Mr Aladdin Sisalem filed a complaint with the Victorian Civil and Administrative Tribunal (VCAT) alleging that publication of the article was a breach of s8 of the *Racial and Religious Tolerance Act 2001* because the article incited, or was likely to incite, hatred against the followers of the religion of Islam. The Tribunal ruled against the complaint, on the basis that the Act does not prohibit a person from saying things about the religious beliefs of persons which are offensive to those persons, or even prohibit a person from saying things about the religious beliefs of one group of persons that would cause another group of persons to despise those beliefs. The Supreme Court of Victoria refused leave to appeal that decision.

The cases demonstrate that professional communicators should be particularly careful when playing the race, religion or sexual preference card in their reporting or commentary. The vilification and discrimination laws do not tolerate the linkage of race (and various other characteristics) with derogatory comments about an individual unless there is some overriding public interest (such as where the person has made this an issue themselves), or where it is protected by the public interest, fair report or fair comment defences similar to those outlined for defamation in Chapter 5.

Cyberbullying

A range of criminal, civil and regulatory mechanisms are available to victims of cyberbullying and online harassment in Australia, at both State and Commonwealth levels. The main criminal charge used by prosecuting authorities is s474.17 of the *Criminal Code Act 1995* (Commonwealth), 'using a carriage service to menace, harass or cause offence'. It carries a maximum penalty of five years' imprisonment. There were 927 charges against 458 defendants found proven under s474.17 between its introduction in 2004 and 2018. The Attorney-General's Department stated numerous cases related to cyberbullying. In addition, these figures did not include prosecutions conducted by state or territory authorities which are also able to prosecute *Commonwealth Criminal Code* offences (Parliament of Australia, 2018, para 3.15). Similar charges include:

- s474.14 (using a telecommunications network with intention to commit a serious offence);
- s474.15 (using a carriage service to make a threat);
- s474.16 (using a carriage service for a hoax threat);
- s474.29A (using a carriage service for suicide related material).

Case example:

Hampson's case (2011): Internet troll Bradley Hampson served 220 days in jail in 2011 after pleading guilty to using a carriage service to menace, harass or cause offence under s474.17 of the *Criminal Code*. He had plastered obscene images and comments on Facebook tribute pages dedicated to the memory of two children who had died in tragic circumstances. Hampson had already been convicted of a similar offence three years earlier.

Cyberbullying victims can turn to civil actions as alternatives. As explained in Chapter 5, in the Voller case (2021) the High Court ruled that corporate media hosts of social media pages could be held responsible for the defamatory comments of third parties on their sites. In that case, the comments were derogatory slurs against an indigenous activist. Invasion of privacy and breach of confidence are other actions that could be available, with examples being the Jane Doe case (2007) in Victoria and the Grosse case (2003) in Queensland.

The *Online Safety Act 2021* started in 2022, strengthening schemes introduced under the *Enhancing Online Safety Act 2015* to keep Australians safe online, including mechanisms to remove seriously abusive and harmful content. The new laws set out to assist the Commonwealth eSafety Commissioner with deleting the worst online content regardless of host, introduce new measures to protect adults from serious abuse online; and strengthen the cyberbullying protections for children. A set of Basic Online Safety Expectations put the onus on platforms to take responsibility for protecting Australians against online abuse. Under the laws, online platforms and individuals will have to take down harmful and illegal content immediately or face fines. The laws also strengthen eSafety's investigative and data gathering powers to reveal anonymous bullies and abusers. Complaints can be directed to <www.esafety.gov.au/report>. Adult Cyber Abuse of the most serious nature can be reported to eSafety for investigation if the service or platform has not removed the content within 48 hours of a complaint being made. The threshold for investigation requires it to be 'severely abusive online content that was sent, posted or shared with the likely intention of harming the person targeted, and the content must be menacing, harassing or offensive' (eSafety Commissioner, 2023). Under the Act, possible outcomes include fines or penalties for services or platforms that don't remove content, fines or penalties for the person responsible if they don't remove the content, and further legal action.

At Commonwealth level, the *Sex Discrimination Act 1984* (SDA) makes it unlawful to discriminate against a person because of their sex, gender identity, intersex status, sexual orientation, marital or relationship status, family responsibilities, because they are pregnant or might become pregnant or because they are breastfeeding. This can include online discrimination such as sexual harassment over social media platforms. Complaints are made to the Australian Human Rights Commission (Gender Equity Victoria, 2021a: 8–9).

The Fair Work Commission can also hear allegations of bullying or sexual harassment in a work context, under s. 789FD of the *Fair Work Act 2009*. Employees can also be dismissed for inappropriate use of social media, particularly if it is bringing their workplace into disrepute.

Case example:

ACTU case (2022): An employee's termination was deemed justifiable based on the employer's concern that the 'social media posts might negatively impact on; the health and safety, including the psycho-social wellbeing, of ACTU staff, workers who called the Support Centre, and Australian workers more broadly; and the reputation of the ACTU, which is a values-driven and progressive organisation'.

Complaints about online harassment can also be made direct to corporations under Advertising Standards Bureau regulations. Professional communicators need to ensure they moderate their social media pages frequently to delete discriminatory or obscene or demeaning comments made there by third parties. As Smith (2012) noted, the Bureau has had to rule on complaints against companies including VB and Smirnoff Vodka for such comments on their sites for promotional campaigns.

A range of measures are available under State laws for people to complain about online abuse. These include personal safety intervention orders, stalking charges, 'Brodie's Law' in Victoria making serious bullying a criminal offence, and various summary offences (Gender Equity Victoria, 2021a; Law Council of Australia, 2017).

There are also complaints mechanisms about unsafe work environments via state-based workplace health and safety agencies. For example, Worksafe Queensland offers guidance on a range of psychosocial workplace hazards and factors including bullying, stress, fatigue and violence (Worksafe Queensland Government, n.d.). with complaints channels via the Queensland Human Rights Commission and the Fair Work Commission.

Although Australia has no Bill of Rights at Commonwealth level, three Australian jurisdictions do feature bills/charters of rights in Queensland, Victoria and the Australian Capital Territory (ACT). For example, the Victorian Equal Opportunity and Human Rights Commission offers complaints channels for employee and workplace rights, aboriginal rights, disability rights, LGBTIQ+ rights, older people's rights, racial and religious rights, youth rights and women's rights, all linked to human rights listed in that state's *Charter of Human Rights and Responsibilities* and other state-based human rights legislation, including the *Equal Opportunity Act 2010*, the *Racial and Religious Tolerance Act 2001*, and the *Change or Suppression (Conversion) Practices Prohibition Act 2021* (Victorian Equal Opportunity and Human Rights Commission, n.d.).

Reflect – Research – Review:

Discrimination and cyberbullying in action – Case study 11.1: Applied ethical and legal decision making – the provocative social media post

In this scenario you are asked to work through both the ethical ramifications of the situation using the basic Potter Box technique (Potter, 1972) as explained in Chapter 3, and the legal ramifications of your decision using the specific legal risk analysis technique (Grantham and Pearson, 2022: 51–53).

The problem

You are a social media moderator for a policy think-tank – 'Grist to the Mill' – which prides itself on airing controversial topics and encouraging the widest range of views from all quarters of society in the spirit of the utilitarian philosopher John Stuart Mill. In fact, the logo for your website features a cartoon of the great philosopher standing on a platform in a crowded marketplace to address listeners in the spirit of 'Speaker's Corner' in London, Sydney and Auckland. A right-wing politician has posted an article calling for Muslim women's head-dress of all types to be outlawed. While the article itself is provocative but well articulated and documented, comments from readers have started streaming in, some calling for violence against Muslims and others using derogative terms to describe them. Some are even making sick threats against other commenters – of a violent and sexual nature. Consider your position as publisher of the article and host of the comments.

Applying the Potter Box

You will recall the Potter Box (1972) has you apply four factors to use to workshop the ethics in a situation, as per Patterson and Wilkins' (1997: 90) quadrant:

Facts	Loyalties
Values	Principles

As usual, prior to executing the Potter Box method, you need to spend 10–15 minutes using one of our reflection techniques to prime yourself to your gut feeling about the situation and to try to recall some basic guidance from the material you have learned. For this purpose, you should choose between mindful meditation or reflection focused on the scenario, or mindmapping or journal writing around the topic. On this occasion, also use some visualisation to put yourself in the position of a person targeted by the article or comments so you can empathise with their feelings. Once that is done, turn your attention to the four Potter Box criteria:

Facts: Read the scenario again so you are clear on the actual facts of the problem. Go to the factual basis of the original article itself. Are there important facts distorted there, or perhaps omitted to substantiate the argument? Perform the same factual analysis of claims and facts used in the various comments.

Values: What are the overriding values in competition in this scenario? Where does the value (and right) of free expression sit in relation to the right not to be discriminated against or to have one's online safety threatened? What are reasonable limits on free expression when discussing such hot button issues? At a virtue ethics level, what does the moderation task and your course of action say about your own values, character and professionalism as a communicator? Where do your personal or religious values sit in this situation?

Loyalties: As a moderator of such a provocative open think-tank, where do your loyalties lie? What professional obligations do you have to your employer, the article's contributor, your audience, and the individuals and groups mentioned in the article and comments? Conduct a basic stakeholder analysis to consider your loyalties to each and the impact of your actions upon them.

Principles: Given the nature of the think tank, the emphasis needs to be upon the consequentialist (utilitarian) approach to ethical decision making, as modelled by John Stuart Mill. What is the end here, and is it justified by the means? Should the 'marketplace of ideas' really allow all manner of material to be posted, regardless of its impact on individuals and groups in society? The US comes closest to such an open approach, but would all this be permitted there? Even if the comments fall short of a direct call to violence against members of a group, how does this sit with the social contract on how we treat others, best encapsulated by human rights instruments? If we look to a rules-based deontological approach, what rules might apply from your professional code of ethics or of society more generally (see the legal analysis below).

Remember, the Potter Box is meant to be used in an iterative, circular fashion (Christians et al., 2011: 5), so keep returning to each criterion in turn until you feel you have saturated all possibilities. This should now allow you to decide upon your course of action, confident that you have assessed and accounted for all ethical dimensions of the problem.

Applying the specific legal risk analysis technique (Grantham and Pearson, 2022: 51–53)

You should now use our five steps to assess the legal risks in this discrimination/online safety situation.

Identifying the potential (or existing) legal problem

The chapter raises legal issues to do with anti-discrimination laws, anti-vilification laws and laws of online safety and cyberbullying. All could arise here.

Reviewing the areas of the law involved

Review these key laws as covered in the chapter and apply them to the situation as if it occurred in your jurisdiction. What national or local laws could apply? What criminal or civil actions could arise? If it was hosted on a social media site, how might the platform's terms of service apply here? Does the discrimination law cover offensive speech about a religion, or just racial, ethnic or nationality slurs? Does a call to violence in a comment trigger other more serious laws mentioned in the chapter?

Projecting the possible consequences for stakeholders

Make your stakeholder analysis more specific with regard to legal ramifications. What legal avenues might be available to those targeted by the article and comments? What actions might the authors of the respective items face? What is your own position as the publisher of the article and secondly as the host of the derogatory or threatening comments?

Seeking advice/referring upward

What is the supervisory structure at your think tank? Do you have the power (and perhaps the duty) to act alone on this matter, or are there senior personnel with whom you can (or must) consult? What legal advice is available and what is the escalation procedure for using it?

Publishing/amending/deleting/correcting/apologizing

Having weighed all this up, and factored in the ethical considerations of the earlier analysis, what is your plan of action for publishing all or part of the material – and what policies apply for any amendments or deletions at this point or corrections or apologies later?

In a nutshell

- You should pause, consider and consult before you post or publish anything highlighting someone's difference. Mindful consideration of the impact of your words upon others is the key to best practice professional communication on such sensitive topics.
- International human rights instruments ban discrimination in all forms in balance against the right to free expression.
- Each journalism regulatory body has anti-discrimination clauses in its codes or principles that journalists and media organisations are expected to follow, and each public relations professional body requires members to act fairly.
- Laws in most jurisdictions specifically address discrimination at its extremities – the domain of actual vilification of a person because of their racial, ethnic or religious group or other characteristic like sexual orientation and the incitement to racial hatred or violence against such individuals.
- Public interest defences to discrimination and vilification will normally protect communicators going about their usual business of fair and accurate reportage and commentary.
- Cyberbullying and online hate speech is policed in a variety of ways internationally, including via the criminal law, platform terms of service, and civil actions including breach of privacy and defamation.
- Reporting topics like mental health and suicide is fraught. Practitioners should consult the Mindframe guidelines at <https://mindframe.org.au/> for advice on reporting or commenting on these issues.

References and further reading

Abdel-Magied, Y. 2022, *Talking About A Revolution*, Vintage, Melbourne.
Adam, M.T. 2013, 'Buddhism, equality, rights'. *Journal of Buddhist Ethics*, 20, 422, <https://go.gale.com/ps/i.do?p=AONE&u=griffith&id=GALE|A365456238&v=2.1&it=r&sid=oclc&asid=325edbe1>.
Altman, A. 2020, 'Discrimination', *The Stanford Encyclopedia of Philosophy* (Winter 2020 Edition), Zalta, E.N. ed., <https://plato.stanford.edu/archives/win2020/entries/discrimination/>.
Australian Communications and Media Authority (ACMA). 2007, *Breakfast with Alan Jones Broadcast by 2GB on 5, 6, 7, 8 and 9 December 2005*, Investigation Report No. 1485, ACMA, Sydney, <https://apo.org.au/node/15216>.
Australian Government Attorney-General's Department. (n.d.), *Right to Freedom of Opinion and Expression*, Canberra, <www.ag.gov.au/rights-and-protections/human-rights-and-anti-discrimination/human-rights-scrutiny/public-sector-guidance-sheets/right-freedom-opinion-and-expression#where-does-the-right-to-freedom-of-opinion-and-expression-come-from>.
Australian Press Council (APC). 2001, 'General Press Release no. 248: Reporting of 'race', *Reporting Guidelines*, <www.presscouncil.org.au/pcsite/activities/guides/gpr248.html>.
Australian Press Council (APC). 2023, *Handling of Complaints*, <www.presscouncil.org.au/complaints/handling-of-complaints>.
Badawi, J.A. 1995, *Gender Equity in Islam*, World Assembly of Muslim Youth, <www.iium.edu.my/deed/articles/genderequityinislam.html>.
Baird, J. 2017, 'Yassmin Abdel-Magied: The latest woman to be roasted on the spit of public life', *The Sydney Morning Herald*, 14 July, <www.smh.com.au/opinion/yassmin-abdelmagied-the-latest-woman-to-be-roasted-on-the-spit-of-public-life-20170714-gxb6qh.html>.
Blum, L. 2004, 'Stereotypes and Stereotyping: A Moral Analysis', *Philosophical Papers*, 33(3), 251–289.
Bornstein, J. 2022, 'What's gone wrong at the ABC', *The Monthly*, August, <www.themonthly.com.au/issue/2022/august/josh-bornstein/what-s-gone-wrong-abc#mtr>.
Carmody, B. 2017, 'ABC stands by Yassmin Abdel-Magied after Facebook post sparks Anzac Day outrage', *The Sydney Morning Herald*, 26 April, <www.smh.com.au/entertainment/tv-and-radio/abc-stands-by-yassmin-abdelmagied-after-facebook-post-sparks-anzac-day-outrage-20170426-gvsehn.html
Committee to Protect Journalists (CPJ). 2020, *Digital Safety: Protecting against Targeted Online Attacks*, 21 May, <https://cpj.org/2020/05/digital-safety-protecting-against-targeted-online-attacks/>.
Crown Prosecution Service. 2018, *Social Media – Guidelines on Prosecuting Cases Involving Communications Sent via Social Media*, 21 August, <www.cps.gov.uk/legal-guidance/social-media-guidelines-prosecuting-cases-involving-communications-sent-social-media>.
Davies, L. 2022, ' "Culture of exclusion" keeps women of colour from top media jobs, report reveals', *The Guardian*, 30 November, <www.theguardian.com/global-development/2022/nov/30/culture-of-exclusion-keeps-women-of-colour-from-top-media-jobs-report-reveals>.
de Vries, R. 2022, 'Totem', *Email to the Communication Initiative Network*, 28 March, <www.comminit.com/global/content/totem>.

Discrimination, cyberbullying and harassment 339

eSafety Commissioner. (n.d.), *The e-Safety Guide*, <www.esafety.gov.au/key-issues/esafety-guide>.

eSafety Commissioner. 2023, *Adult Cyber Abuse*, <www.esafety.gov.au/report/what-you-can-report-to-esafety#adult-cyber-abuse>.

Free TV Australia. 2018, *Commercial Television Industry Code of Practice*, <www.freetv.com.au/wp-content/uploads/2019/07/Free_TV_Commercial_Television_Industry_Code_of_Practice_2018.pdf>.

Gender Equity Victoria (GEN VIC). 2021a, *Cybersmart Women: Your Legal Options when Facing Online Harassment and Gendered Cyberhate*, <www.genvic.org.au/wp-content/uploads/2021/07/Cybersmart-Women_DIGI_v4.pdf>.

Gender Equity Victoria (GEN VIC). 2021b, *Australian Media Moderation Guidelines*, <www.genvic.org.au/wp-content/uploads/2021/02/GV_MEAA_AUMediaModGuidelines.pdf>.

German Law Archive. 2017, *Network Enforcement Act (Netzdurchsetzunggesetz, Netz DG)*, 1 September, <https://germanlawarchive.iuscomp.org/>.

Grantham, S. and Pearson, M. 2022, *Social Media Risk and the Law: A Guide for Global Communicators*, Routledge, London and New York.

Gunasingham, A. 2019, 'Buddhist Extremism in Sri Lanka and Myanmar: An Examination', *Counter Terrorist Trends and Analyses*, *11*(3), 1–6, <www.jstor.org/stable/26617827>.

Hassan, A. 2022, 'Rana Ayyub, journalists and Modi critic, barred from leaving India', *Al Jazeera*, 30 March, <www.aljazeera.com/news/2022/3/30/rana-ayyub-india-journalist-stopped-from-boarding-london>.

Henry, N., Powell, A. and Flynn, A. 2017, *Not just 'Revenge Pornography': Australians', Experiences of Image-Based Abuse. A Summary Report*, RMIT University, Melbourne.

Hill, L. 2001, 'The first wave of feminism: Were the Stoics feminists?', *History of Political Thought*, *22*(1), 13–40, <www.jstor.org/stable/26219818>.

International Federation of Journalists (IFJ). 2019, *Global Charter of Ethics for Journalists*, <www.ifj.org/who/rules-and-policy/global-charter-of-ethics-for-journalists.html>.

International Federation of Journalists (IFJ). 2020, *Digital Journalism: Supplemental Guidance for Global Charter of Ethics for Journalists*, 2 July, <www.ifj.org/fileadmin/user_upload/Digital_Ethics_Report__English_.pdf>.

International Federation of Journalists (IFJ). 2022, *Constitution 2022–2026*, <www.ifj.org/who/rules-and-policy/constitution>.

Jhangiani, R. and Tarry, H. 2022, *Principles of Social Psychology* (1st international H5P edition), BCcampus, <https://opentextbc.ca/socialpsychology/>.

Kharroub, T. 2015, *Five things you need to know about women in Islam: Implications for advancing women's rights in the Middle East*, Arab Center Washington DC, 4 October, <https://arabcenterdc.org/resource/five-things-you-need-to-know-about-women-in-islam-implications-for-advancing-womens-rights-in-the-middle-east/>.

Lakoff, S.A. 2017, 'Christianity and Equality', *Equality*, Pennock, R.J. and Chapman, J.W. eds, Routledge, New York and London, 115–133.

Law Council of Australia. 2017, *The Adequacy of Existing Offences in the Commonwealth Criminal Code and of State and Territory Criminal Laws to Capture Cyberbullying.* Senate Legal and Constitutional Affairs Committee. 20 October, < www.aph.gov.au/Parliamentary_Business/Committees/Senate/Legal_and_Constitutional_Affairs/Cyberbullying>.

Lippmann, W. 1997, *Public Opinion*, (originally published 1922), Free Press, New York.

McGhee, A. 2017, '18C: Proposed changes to *Racial Discrimination Act* defeated in Senate', *ABC News*, 31 March, <www.abc.net.au/news/2017-03-30/18c-racial-dis crimination-act-changes-defeated-in-senate/8402792>.

Media Defence. (n.d.), *Apply for Case Support – Media Defence*, Media Legal Defence Initiative, <www.mediadefence.org/apply-for-case-support/>.

Media Entertainment and Arts Alliance (MEAA). 2016, *The MEAA Journalist Code of Ethics*, Media Entertainment and Arts Alliance, Sydney, <www.meaa.org/download/faqs-meaa-journalist-code-of-ethics/>.

Media, Entertainment and Arts Alliance (MEAA). 2020, *MEAA Guidelines on Reporting Hate Speech and Extremism*, MEAA, Sydney, <www.meaa.org/download/meaa-guidelines-on-reporting-hate-speech-and-extremism/>.

Media Watch. 2006, 'Front Page – Jones and Cronulla', *Media Watch*, ABC TV, 20 February, <www.abc.net.au/mediawatch/episodes/front-page---jones-and-cronulla/9976172>.

Meta. 2022a, 'Bullying and Harassment', *Meta Transparency Center*, <https://transparency.fb.com/data/community-standards-enforcement/bullying-and-harassment/facebook/>.

Meta. 2022b, 'Creating the oversight board', *Meta Transparency Center*, <https://transparency.fb.com/en-gb/oversight/creation-of-oversight-board/>.

Meta. 2023, 'Hate Speech: Policy Rationale', *Meta Transparency Center*, <https://transparency.fb.com/en-gb/policies/community-standards/hate-speech>.

Modgil, S., Singh, R.K., Gupta, S. et al. 2021, 'A Confirmation Bias View on Social Media Induced Polarisation During Covid-19', *Information System Frontiers*, 20 November, <https://doi.org/10.1007/s10796-021-10222-9>.

Online Violence Response Hub. 2023, *About the Coalition Against Online Violence*, <https://onlineviolenceresponsehub.org/about-the-coalition against-online-violence>.

Oversight Board. 2022, 'Board decisions', *Case Decisions and Policy Advisory Opinions*, 5 August, <https://oversightboard.com/decision/>.

Parliament of Australia. 2018, *Adequacy of Existing Offences in the Commonwealth Criminal Code and of State and Territory Criminal Laws to Capture Cyberbullying*, Commonwealth of Australia, 28 March, <www.aph.gov.au/Parliamentary_Business/Committees/Senate/Legal_and_Constitutional_Affairs/Cyberbullying/Report>.

Parliament of Canada. 2014, *Statutes of Canada: Chapter 31, Second Session, Forty-first Parliament,62–63 Elizabeth II, 2013–2014*, 9 December, <www.parl.ca/DocumentViewer/en/41-2/bill/C-13/royal-assent>.

Patterson, P. and Wilkins, L. 1997, *Media Ethics: Issues and Cases*, 5th ed., McGraw Hill, Boston MA.

Posetti, J., Shabbir, N., Maynard, D., Bontcheva, K. and Aboulez, N. 2021, *The Chilling: Global Trends in Online Violence Against Women Journalists*, Research discussion paper, UNESCO, <https://unesdoc.unesco.org/ark:/48223/pf0000377223>.

Potter, R.B. 1972, 'The Logic of Moral Argument', *Toward a Discipline of Social Ethics*, Deats, P. ed., Boston University Press, Boston, 93–114.

Public Relations Institute of Australia (PRIA). 2009, *Public Relations Institute of Australia (PRIA) Code of Ethics*, PRIA, Sydney, <www.pria.com.au/about-pria/code-of-ethics-privacy/code-of-ethics/>.

Public Relations Society of America (PRSA). 2023, *PRSA Code of Ethics*, <www.prsa.org/about/ethics/prsa-code-of-ethics>.

Remnick, D. 2023, 'The defiance of Salman Rushdie', *New Yorker*, 6 February, <www.newyorker.com/magazine/2023/02/13/salman-rushdie-recovery-victory-city>.

Reporters Without Borders (RSF). 2018, 'RSF is urging Indian authorities to protect women journalists', *Reporters Sans Frontiers*, 27 April, <https://rsf.org/en/rsf-urges-indian-authorities-protect-woman-journalist>.

Rhoden-Paul, A. and Whannel, K. 2022, 'Online Safety Bill put on hold until new prime minister in place', *BBC News*, 13 July, <www.bbc.com/news/uk-62158287>.

Riskin, L.L. and Wohl, R.A. 2015, 'Mindfulness in the Heat of Conflict: Taking STOCK, University of Florida Levin College of Law Research Paper No. 16-12', *Harvard Negotiation Law Review*, *20*, 12.

Ronson, J. 2015, 'How one stupid tweet ruined Justine Sacco's life', *The New York Times*, 15 February, <www.nytimes.com/2015/02/15/magazine/how-one-stupid-tweet-ruined-justine-saccos-life.html>.

Smith, J.A. 1988, *Printers and Press Freedom: The Ideology of Early American Journalism*, Oxford University Press, New York.

Smith, D. 2012, 'Social media marketing', *E-Commerce Law Reports*, *12*(4).

United Nations (UN). 1948, *Universal Declaration of Human Rights*, <www.un.org/en/about-us/universal-declaration-of-human-rights>.

UN Department of Economic and Social Affairs. 2006, *Convention on the Rights of Persons with Disabilities*, <www.un.org/development/desa/disabilities/convention-on-the-rights-of-persons-with-disabilities.html>.

United Nations (UN). 2021, *Safety of Journalists and the Issue of Impunity: Report of the Secretary-General (A/76/285) [EN/AR/RU/ZH]*, General Assembly, 12 August, <https://reliefweb.int/report/world/safety-journalists-and-issue-impunity-report-secretary-general-a76285-enarruzh>.

UN Human Rights Office. 2017, *Strengthening the Implementation of the UN Plan of Action on the Safety of Journalists and the Issue of Impunity*, OHCHR, 16 August, <www.ohchr.org/sites/default/files/Documents/Issues/Journalists/OutcomeDocument.pdf>.

UN Human Rights Office. 1966, 'UN General Assembly resolution 2200A (XXI)', *International Covenant on Civil and Political Rights*, OHCHR, <www.ohchr.org/en/instruments-mechanisms/instruments/international-covenant-civil-and-political-rights>.

UN Human Rights Office. 1965, 'UN General Assembly resolution 2016 (XX)', *International Convention on the Elimination of All Forms of Racial Discrimination*, <www.ohchr.org/en/instruments-mechanisms/instruments/international-convention-elimination-all-forms-racial>.

United States Declaration of Independence. 1776, *Declaration of Independence: A Transcription*, US National Archives, <www.archives.gov/founding-docs/declaration-transcript>.

Valencia-Forrester, F., Carlson, B., Forde, S., Day, M., Pearson, M., O'Sullivan, S., de Groot Hoopner, S. and Barnes, D. 2023. *Online Safety of Diverse Journalists. A Report Prepared for Media Diversity Australia*. Media Diversity Australia, Sydney. <www.mediadiversityaustralia.org/online-safety-of-diverse-journalists/>

Victorian Equal Opportunity and Human Rights Commission. (n.d.), *Change or Suppression (Conversion) Practices*, <www.humanrights.vic.gov.au/change-or-suppression-practices/>.

Woods, C. 2017, 'The ABC Has Axed Yassmin Abdel-Magied's Show and The World is Officially Trash', *Junkee*, 24 May, <https://junkee.com/yassmin-abdel-magieds-abc/106249>.

Worksafe. (n.d.), *Psychosocial Hazards and Factors*, Queensland Government, <www.worksafe.qld.gov.au/safety-and-prevention/mental-health/Psychosocial-hazards-and-factors>.

YouTube. 2023, 'Hate speech policy', *Support*, <https://support.google.com/youtube/answer/2801939?hl=en>.

Cases cited

ACTU case: *Mr Conrad John Corry v Australian Council of Trade Unions T/A ACTU* [2022] FWC 288 (15 February 2022), < www.austlii.edu.au/cgi-bin/viewdoc/au/cases/cth/FWC/2022/288.html>.

Alan Jones cases (2000–2013): *Western Aboriginal Legal Service Ltd v Jones and Radio 2UE Sydney Pty Ltd* [2000] NSWADT 102 (31 July 2000), <www.austlii.edu.au/au/cases/nsw/NSWADT/2000/102.html>; *Trad v Jones & Anor (No. 3)* [2009] NSWADT 318 (21 December 2009), <www.austlii.edu.au/cgi-bin/viewdoc/au/cases/nsw/NSWADT/2009/318.html>; *Trad v Jones (No. 4)* [2012] NSWADT 265 (12 December 2012), <www.austlii.edu.au/cgi-bin/sinodisp/au/cases/nsw/NSWADT/2012/265.html>; *Trad v Jones (No. 5)* [2013] NSWADT 127 (5 June 2013), <www.austlii.edu.au/cgi-bin/sinodisp/au/cases/nsw/NSWADT/2013/127.html>.

Bolt cases: *Eatock v Bolt* [2011] FCA 1103 (28 September 2011), <www.austlii.edu.au/cgi-bin/viewdoc/au/cases/cth/FCA/2011/1103.html>.; *Eatock v Bolt (No. 2)* [2011] FCA 1180 (19 October 2011), <www.austlii.edu.au/cgi-bin/viewdoc/au/cases/cth/FCA/2011/1180.htm>.

Cronulla riots case: Australian Communications and Media Authority (ACMA) 2007, *Breakfast with Alan Jones Broadcast by 2GB on 5, 6, 7, 8 and 9 December 2005*, Investigation Report No. 1485, ACMA, Sydney, <https://apo.org.au/node/15216>

Gay cases: *Burns v Radio 2UE Sydney* [2004] NSWADT 267 (22 November 2004), <www.austlii.edu.au/cgi-bin/sinodisp/au/cases/nsw/NSWADT/2004/267.html>; *Administrative Decisions Tribunal Equal Opportunity Division (No. 2)* [2007] NSWADT 47; *Burns v Sunol* [2018] NSWCATAD 10 (10 January 2018), <www.austlii.edu.au/cgi-bin/viewdoc/au/cases/nsw/NSWCATAD/2018/10.html>.

Grosse case: *Grosse v Purvis* [2003] QDC 151 (16 June 2003), <www.austlii.edu.au/cgi-bin/viewdoc/au/cases/qld/QDC/2003/151.html>.

Hampson's case: *R v Hampson* (2011) QCA 132 (21 June 2011), <www.austlii.edu.au/cgi-bin/viewdoc/au/cases/qld/QCA/2011/132.html>.

Holocaust cases: *Jones v Toben* [2002] FCA 1150 (17 September 2002), <www.austlii.edu.au/au/cases/cth/federal_ct/2002/1150.html>; *Toben v Jones* [2003] FCAFC 137 (27 June 2003), <www.austlii.edu.au/cgi-bin/sinodisp/au/cases/cth/FCAFC/2003/137.html>; *Toben v Jones* [2009] FCAFC 104 (13 August 2009), <www.austlii.edu.au/cgi-bin/sinodisp/au/cases/cth/FCAFC/2009/104.html>.

Instagram Hate Speech case: Meta. 2022, *Meta Oversight Board Decision 2022–003-IG-UA: Reclaiming Arabic words*, 14 June, <https://oversightboard.com/decision/IG-2PJ00L4T/>

Islam case: *Sisalem v The Herald & Weekly Times Pty Ltd* [2017] VSC 254 (18 May 2017), <www.austlii.edu.au/cgi-bin/viewdoc/au/cases/vic/VSC/2017/254.html>.

Jane Doe case: *Jane Doe v Australian Broadcasting Corporation* [2007] VCC 281 (3 April 2007), <www.austlii.edu.au/au/cases/vic/VCC/2007/281.pdf >.

Perth Now case. *Clarke v Nationwide News Pty Ltd trading as* The Sunday Times [2012] FCA 307 (27 March 2012), <www8.austlii.edu.au/cgi-bin/viewdoc/au/cases/cth/FCA/2012/307.html>.

QUT Students', case: *Prior v Wood* [2017] FCA 193 (3 March 2017), <www.austlii.edu.au/cgi-bin/viewdoc/au/cases/cth/FCA/2017/193.html>; *Prior v Queensland University of Technology & Ors* [2016] FCCA 2853 (4 November 2016), <www.austlii.edu.au/cgi-bin/viewdoc/au/cases/cth/FCCA/2016/2853.html>.

Voller case: *Fairfax Media Publications Pty Ltd v Voller; Nationwide News Pty Limited v Voller; Australian News Channel Pty Ltd v Voller* [2021] HCA 27, 8 September, <www.austlii.edu.au/cgi-bin/viewdoc/au/cases/cth/HCA/2021/27.html>.

12 Integrity, conflicted interests and the business of communication

Key concepts

Integrity: The moral virtue of being honest and holding fast to strong ethical principles.

Conflict of interests: A situation where someone's personal vested interests – family, friendships, financial, or social factors – stand to compromise their judgment, decisions or actions.

Corruption: Criminal abuse of one's entrusted position for personal gain or to benefit the interests of one's associates.

Corporate social responsibility: An ethical, self-regulatory framework of obligations of a corporation to broader society, extending beyond its traditional financial and fiduciary obligations to shareholders and other stakeholders.

Consumer law: The area of law giving consumers protection against the false, misleading and deceptive claims of businesses and offering them remedies for such misrepresentations along with rights against unsafe, harmful or unserviceable goods and services.

News media bargaining code: A mandatory code of conduct governing the commercial relationships between Australian news businesses and designated digital platforms who benefit from a significant bargaining power imbalance in the news media market.

Securities law: The regulation of products, markets and participants in the financial services industry, extending to the published claims made about their issue and performance of financial products and services.

Introduction

Professional communicators will inevitably encounter situations in their careers where the opportunity for personal financial gain needs to be set aside for ethical or legal reasons. Sometimes the correct moral decision in these circumstances can be costly – to your financial situation, your relationships or to your career advancement – so you need to be prepared with the ethical and

DOI: 10.4324/9781003372752-15

legal knowledge and tools to show wisdom when temptation arises. Situations where your integrity as a professional communicator stands to be compromised by a conflict of interests or even by corruption are many and varied. They can include the journalist who is offered a luxurious overseas travel opportunity in return for the undisclosed promotion of a hotel chain or airline. Or perhaps the government media relations officer who is instructed to write some press releases for the minister's family business. Or even the public relations consultant who shares some inside information about a company's performance with their friend who is a day trader on the share market. Each scenario involves a challenge to the integrity of the communicator – the moral virtue of being honest and holding fast to strong ethical principles.

The more common situation is what we call a 'conflict of interests' – where your personal vested interests might compromise the decisions or actions you take in your work. These might be the prospect of financial gain for you, your client or your employer, or they could be the chance of some advantage (or disadvantage) to others in your circle such as friends, family or sporting group. For example, it would represent a conflict of interest if you were asked to report upon, or to produce publicity about, a structural defect affecting the apartment complex where you reside – when such news will stand to lower the value of your property or damage your opportunity to sell it. At a social level, you would have a conflict of interest if you reported upon complaints about a sporting club if a close family member was serving on its committee.

While basic principles of integrity apply to all professional communicators, different occupations face unique situations and regulations that could trigger conflicts of interest. A conflict of interest becomes the crime of corruption when someone abuses an entrusted position for the personal or financial gain of themselves or their associates. The clearest examples of corruption are where politicians or public servants accept financial payments to make decisions that advantage those paying them – perhaps a property developer or an underworld figure. Professional communicators are unlikely to find themselves in such situations of direct corruption. However, they are more likely to become aware of such obvious instances through their work and will face the ethical and legal decision about whether to blow the whistle or report upon the situation.

Some industries such as the companies and securities sector demand even higher levels of integrity from their communication personnel because laws regulate the promotion of products and markets in the financial services field and this impacts directly the claims public relations personnel and journalists might make about a proposed public float of a company or about its price-affecting performance. Laws are also structured to protect consumers against false and misleading claims about products and services more broadly under a suite of laws known as 'consumer law'. Communicators need to navigate such laws in their own jurisdictions when profiling or reporting upon any goods or services – in traditional or social media.

Integrity in the corporate sector also opens the ethical framework known as 'corporate social responsibility' (CSR) – which is a self-imposed set of social obligations a company aims to meet, often going well beyond its traditional focus on the return of profits to its shareholders. An example might be a mining company sponsoring sporting and community groups and welfare programs in a neighbouring town as a gesture of goodwill and corporate citizenship.

Philosophical background to integrity and conflicts of interest

Integrity is a cornerstone of virtue ethics and political philosophy dating back to Ancient Greece, with Plato (*The Republic*) and Aristotle (*The Politics*) devising political systems that attempted to limit the potential for corruption by leaders (Miller, 2018). However, the ancients were even more concerned with the moral corruption of the citizenry via the 'corrosion of the civic virtues' – essentially a compromised moral integrity. Modern moral philosophers have struggled to agree on the definition of integrity and its place among the virtues. Of value to the professional communicator is the definition of Cox et al. (2021) who say it is 'primarily a matter of keeping the self intact and uncorrupted'. In that way, it stands as an opposite to corruption – the criminal acceptance of bribes by a public official. However, Cox et al. (2021) identify a disconnect between the fundamentally personal construction of integrity as part of the self and the structures and politics of modern liberal democracies that often fail to support those acting with integrity. This can result in people being forced to choose careers that challenge their notion of integrity. An example could be the investigative journalist forced to make a living writing promotional materials. Cox et al. (2021) link the goal of integrity with the social and political context and the ability to reflect upon moral decisions:

> A capacity for reflection and understanding enables one to work toward integrity even if it does not ensure that one achieves an ideal of integrity. ... The kind of society which is likely to be more conducive to integrity is one which enables people to develop and make use of their capacity for critical reflection.

Their conclusion underscores the importance of the reflective techniques in this book. It becomes even more important when there are strong social or cultural processes at play that can facilitate the wrong moral decision when a conflict of interests arises, even leading to corruption. Many societies are imbued with familial and other cultural obligations which run counter to notions of integrity and the ethics of professional communication organisations. Take, for instance, the concept of *wantok* among indigenous peoples of Papua New Guinea. The word means 'same language' or 'one talk' in the national language Tok Pisin and involves 'a reciprocal relationship of favours between kin and community members' (Walton and Jackson, 2020: 3). The system is so entrenched culturally that even the weekly bilingual newspaper established in 1970 used the term as its name – *Wantok Niuspepa*. But such close obligations can have both positive and negative impacts – at one end of the scale providing potentially lifesaving benefits and at the other encouraging corruption (Walton and Jackson, 2020: 25). Those in positions of responsibility are expected to look after their wantoks. The problem for journalists is the perpetual conflict of interests they face between their cultural obligations to their wantoks and their professional obligations to their code of ethics which requires fairness and independence and prohibits undisclosed conflicts of interest (Media Council of PNG, 2016).

While the Papua New Guinea situation sits at the outer boundary of inbuilt societal potential for conflicts of interest, all societies have cultural obligations at least at the immediate family level which stand to influence the professional communicator. This calls for a special ability to reflect in action to apply the types of tools we offered in Chapter 3 – such as pausing for mindful reflection, journaling and mindmapping. The great 20th century Irish-British moral philosopher Iris Murdoch stressed how difficult it was to identify and resist attachments that work counter to moral motivation and behaviour because objectivity and being unselfish are not the natural human way of operating (Blum, 2022).

Philosophers also have contributions to make in the field of corporate social responsibility (CSR) – an ethical, self-regulatory framework of obligations of a corporation to broader society, sometimes involving the sacrifice of profits to make an important social contribution. It is an area of ethical self-regulation particularly relevant to professional communicators working for larger companies (introduced in Chapter 4). Moriarty (2021) wrote the arguments for CSR were predominantly consequentialist (end justifies means) because, given the major problems throughout the world, all entities with the resources, power and knowledge to address them should do so, and that includes corporations. Others argue against it on the grounds that every act of CSR involves the ceding of an important initiative to a private entity (a corporation) when such deeds should be performed by institutions operating in the public sphere for reasons of equity and accountability. Some believe CSR sits well with stakeholder theory given its orientation beyond the immediate interests of corporate profits and shareholder returns. Moriarty (2021) offers the classic example of CSR involving the big pharma company Merck. A drug they developed in the 1970s to treat parasites in livestock proved useful for treating a human disease in developing countries known as 'river blindness'. Despite the expense estimated at hundreds of millions of dollars, Merck proceeded to develop and distribute the drug freely to those who needed it, a CSR project continuing to the present day. Corporate communicators need to be across their organisations' CSR policies if they are to manage their media and public relations effectively.

Philosophers have also turned their minds to integrity systems at institutional and governmental levels designed to combat corruption. Miller (2018) points out they can be reactive (such as inquiries into corrupt acts) or preventative (training in ethics and implementation of transparency mechanisms). Professional communicators need to be well versed in both approaches because their work might require them to abide by integrity guidelines in government or might have them reporting upon corruption and the activities of corruption inquiries and bodies. The latter can have special dangers, as we learned in our chapters on contempt and confidentiality, because such bodies can be deemed with special powers to demand journalists reveal their sources.

> **Reflect – Research – Review:**
>
> Recall a conflict of interest situation that has occurred in your own life or work (or one from the news if you can't think of a personal situation) and use a mindmapping approach to identify the key moral elements of the situation and a morally or ethically justifiable course of action to resolve the conflict.

Human rights and corruption and the foundation of consumer law

The word 'corruption' does not feature in international human rights and freedoms instruments, but the potential for it to run counter to human rights is well acknowledged. The United Nations' Office of the High Commissioner on Human Rights (OHCHR) has noted the devastating effect corruption can have on the access to goods and services that are essential to the provision of basic human rights such as shelter, food and safety. It notes that corruption exists world-wide, in both developed and developing countries and in democractic and other political systems (OHCHR, 2023). Those experiencing disadvantage are more likely to suffer from the human rights impacts of corruption and those attempting to investigate and report it are at heightened risk of breaches of their human rights and freedoms through physical retribution and intimidation, unjust criminal processes and affronts to their right to free expression.

The other area of human rights with international reach is the field of consumer rights. The United Nations Guidelines for Consumer Protection were adopted by the UN General Assembly in 1985 and updated in 1999 and 2015 (UN, 2016). They include the right to safety, to be informed, to choose and to be heard. The guidelines have inspired new legal frameworks in countries like Australia and Brazil, with some even incorporating consumer rights into their constitutions. More than 70 countries now have consumer protection agencies (Benöhr, 2020). As explained below, professional communicators need to be especially aware of consumer protections against misleading or deceptive advertising or promotion, enshrined under the Guidelines' right to be informed and the right to redress (UN, 2016).

> **Reflect – Research – Review:**
>
> Review the UN Guidelines on Consumer Protection at <https://unctad.org/system/files/official-document/ditccplpmisc2016d1_en.pdf> and find a news story from your jurisdiction about the abuse of a consumer's rights. Write a paragraph explaining how your legal system dealt with it.

Professional ethical codes and dilemmas on conflicts of interests and misleading consumers

Avoiding conflicts of interest and showing honesty in communications are central concerns of professional ethical codes for journalists and public relations practitioners internationally.

All major codes make mention of these two important ethical requirements. The Public Relations Society of America features honesty as a core value, requiring members to adhere to the 'highest standards of accuracy and truth'. It lists the avoidance of conflicts of interest as a core principle, including 'real, potential or perceived conflicts of interest'. Its stated intent of this requirement is to earn the trust and mutual respect of clients or employers and to build trust with the public. Members are required to subordinate their personal interests to act in the best interests of their client or employer and to avoid actions or circumstances creating a conflict between personal and professional interests. Prompt disclosure of potential conflicts is required along with consultation with clients or customers over their existence and implications. It offers examples of conflicts of interest as being when a member fails to disclose a strong financial interest in a client's chief competitor and when a member fails to inform a prospective client that they represent a competitor or a conflicting interest. It also encourages the free flow of accurate and truthful information by requiring members to ensure any gifts given or received are 'nominal, legal, and infrequent' (PRSA, 2023). In Australia, the *Public Relations Institute of Australia's Code of Ethics* (PRIA, 2009) addresses the need for fairness and honesty at Clause 1 and counsels against knowingly disseminating false or misleading information at Clause 3. Clause 9 requires members to be prepared to identify the source of funding of any public communication.

Honesty is also central to journalism codes of ethics. In the UK, the *National Union of Journalists Code of Conduct* (NUJ) (2018) at Item 2 requires its members to strive to ensure that information disseminated is honestly conveyed, accurate and fair. Item 8 demands they resist inducements to influence, distort or suppress information, and take no unfair personal advantage of information gained in the course of their duties before it has been made public. Under the *MEAA Journalist Code of Ethics* (MEAA, 2016) the Australian journalists' union features honesty and fairness as core values and it has strong requirements within its 12 key journalists' ethical principles

350 *Challenges in the digital era*

covering fair and accurate reporting (Clause 1), while at least four other clauses address different dimensions of conflicts of interest of both journalists and their sources (MEAA, 2016). These can be overridden only for 'substantial advancement of the public interest' or where there is 'risk of substantial harm to people'.

Industry bodies also instruct their members to avoid conflicts of interest. For example, the Australian Press Council's *Statement of Principles* for print and online newspaper outlets has a section on 'Integrity and Transparency' requiring at clause 7 they avoid publishing material gathered via deceptive or unfair means unless there is an overriding public interest consideration, and at clause 8 to ensure conflicts of interest are avoided or disclosed adequately and that they do not influence published material (APC, 2023).

Many individual news outlets also have their own ethical standards covering potential conflicts of interest. For example, *The New York Times'* ethics handbook offers guidance on a host of situations where its journalists could encounter such dilemmas (NYT, 2019).

Case example:

The PR News Anchor (2015): An investigation by the *Toronto Star* revealed that the news anchor for Canada's Global Television was also secretly a part owner of a public relations firm whose clients were appearing on his show. Journalist Leslie Roberts hosted two Toronto-based news programs while he was also creative director of BuzzPR – a clear conflict of interest that prompted his suspension and then his resignation. A news executive at the station pointed to the network's 'codified principles and practices document that is quite lengthy that clearly articulates the expectations of all of our journalists in terms of maintaining editorial independence' (Smith, 2015).

Reflect – Research – Review:

Review the code of ethics for your profession in your country or organisation and explain in 200 words how it might apply to a conflict of interests or deceptive conduct situation involving one of your colleagues.

Law, cases and examples of conflicts of interest and misleading conduct internationally

All major countries have laws and regulations policing corruption, serious conflicts of interest and false, misleading or deceptive publications. However, nations vary somewhat in the extent to which their society's rules might affect professional communicators and the mechanisms by which they are prosecuted and enforced.

As we have found in many other topic areas in this book, US law is dominated by the influence of the First Amendment to its Constitution – restricting the extent to which laws can impinge the freedom of the press (and free expression more generally). We saw in Chapter 5 that this can protect publishers from legal actions for defamation, particularly over reputational damage to public figures even where the material was false as long as the plaintiff could not prove the publisher had shown malice. This serves to protect many false, misleading and deceptive allegations about others made in the US media. However, the US Supreme Court has held in a series of cases since 1942 that commercial speech can be treated somewhat differently. In the Submarine case (1942), the Supreme Court held a man was not protected by the First Amendment free speech protections when he distributed pamphlets promoting tours of his private submarine on the streets of New York City in breach of a city ordinance banning advertising material. This was despite his attempt to win First Amendment protection by including on the reverse side of the brochure a note of protest against the city over its failure to provide him pier facilities for his exhibition. Over the subsequent three decades the court set out the circumstances where commercial expression might be protected, including the public distribution of religious materials containing advertising and of advertising containing truthful information about social issues (Parker, 2009). Another was the famous Sullivan's case concerning defamation in 1964, detailed in Key Case 2.1, where an advertisement alleging police had been violent in their treatment of civil rights protesters won First Amendment protection and paved the way for the new absence of malice test for untruthful slurs against public figures. The court eventually decided in the Central Hudson case (1980) that free commercial speech was also important to the workings of a democracy and outlined a four-point test of whether governments would be permitted to limit commercial speech under First Amendment principles:

a. it must concern lawful activity and not be misleading;
b. the government interest in limiting it must be substantial;
c. the regulation must advance that government interest; and,
d. it must not be more extensive than necessary.

Case example:

Nike case (2003): Nike used a public relations and advertising campaign to respond to criticism of its exploitation of workers and unsafe factory conditions in its overseas plants. An activist lawyer sued Nike under California's False Advertising Law and Unfair Competition Law for unfair and deceptive practices in their communications. The Supreme Court majority applied the Central Hudson test to find that that 'communication more likely to deceive the public than to inform it' did not meet the requirement for commercial speech to win First Amendment protection. Nike reached an out of court settlement for $1.5 million with commitments to invest in strengthening the monitoring of factories and worker programs.

That line of cases established that professional communicators in the US producing commercial speech can face stricter regulations from authorities than those producing news material who earn more straightforward First Amendment protections. Such regulations can come from the US Federal Trade Commission (FTC) or state consumer protection bodies under laws like California's False Advertising Law and Unfair Competition Law in the Nike case above. The FTC's Division of Advertising Practices (DAP) enforces the nation's 'truth-in-advertising' laws, which require advertisers to tell the truth and to back up their claims with reliable, objective evidence. It pursues corporations over misleading claims to protect consumers' interests. With the advent of social media, it has focused attention on celebrities and social media influencers to ensure their endorsements are truthful and not misleading and that they disclose to their followers any connections with advertisers. It released its 'Disclosures 101 for Social Media Influencers' (FTC, 2019) to educate influencers about the requirements of endorsements. This includes simple advice about what factors trigger the need for a disclosure and gives examples of acceptable and unacceptable disclosures by influencers. It explains the responsibility for disclosure rests with the influencer and that it cannot be assumed audiences or followers know of an influencer's connection to a brand.

In the UK, undisclosed payments for influencers' promotion of products and services is regulated by two authorities. The Advertising Standards Authority (ASA) polices situations where a brand has editorial control over the endorsements by influencers, while the Competition and Markets Authority (CMA) controls situations where the influencers are paid by a brand but the sponsor has no editorial control over the posts (ASA, 2022). In Australia, undisclosed influencer sponsorships fall within the realm of the misleading and deceptive conduct provisions of the Australian Consumer Law, regulated by the Australian Competition and Consumer Commission (ACCC) as explained in the section on that country's laws below.

Corruption can be defined quite broadly internationally and a government communications officer will need to be aware of the regulations around gifts and benefits that might be offered by those they encounter in their work. For example, corruption bodies typically view as corruption the soliciting of any gifts or benefits by public officials that could be perceived as intended to influence them unless they are of only token value. An example would be a communications manager for a government department being flown to an overseas conference on computer security by a company supplying anti-virus software. Depending on the jurisdiction, some compromising situations might be called 'corruption' or a 'conflict of interest', as with the Canadian example in Key Case 12.1.

Key Case 12.1: Minister's friend PR case

Minister's friend PR case (2022): Office of the Conflict of Interest and Ethics Commissioner. 2022, *Ng report*, Canada <https://ciec-ccie.parl.gc.ca/en/investigations-enquetes/Pages/NgReport.aspx>.

Facts

Canadian Minister of International Trade, Export Promotion, Small Business and Economic Development, Mary Ng, had been friends with the owner of public relations agency Pomp & Circumstance, Amanda Alvaro, for more than 20 years. In 2019 she contracted Ms Alvaro's agency to provide media training for a sum of $5,840 – for a 'customised media strategy session for the employees of the Office of the Minister of Small Business and Export Promotions [sic]' and a 'Minister's session' meant to 'focus on the key skills required to communicate effectively in media interviews and with stakeholders'. In 2020, at the start of the COVID-19 outbreak, she issued the agency with a second contract for $16,950 for two media training sessions with the Minister focusing on various types of interviews (broadcast, print, online and social media platforms), questions and answers and the development of materials.

Law

The Canadian Conflict of Interest Act prohibits public office holders from making a decision that would place them in a conflict of interest. The Act states a conflict occurs 'when he or she exercises an official power, duty or function that provides an opportunity to further his or her private interests or those of his or her relatives or friends or to improperly further another person's private interests'. Office holders are required to recuse themselves from any discussion, decision, debate or vote on any such matter. The Conflict of Interest and Ethics Commissioner found the two women's professional relationship had developed into a friendship over many years including meeting each other regularly, vacationing together, and jointly celebrating several special occasions such as birthdays and holidays. The Minister was operating within her official duties when she approved the signing of the contracts. Ms Alvaro's private interests were furthered by the Minister contracting her to do the media training. The Minister had failed to identify a potential conflict involving her friend when she entered public office and had failed to recuse herself or take remedial action to comply with requirements. The Minister apologised for the oversight. The Commissioner found she had contravened the Act.

Lesson for communicators

Both the Minister and her public relations consultant friend suffered reputational damage as a result of the conflict of interests involved, with the Minister also likely to experience political fallout and the PR person's agency suffering brand damage. In short, even the perception of conflicts of interest can have damaging consequences for all parties involved.

Other business laws

There are limits to how many areas of commercial law can be covered in a book about media law, but the reality is that other key areas of business law can be crucial to the work of a professional communicator operating in a small business or corporate context. Two of the key actions they could face are professional negligence and breach of contract. A breach of a *contract* can be devastating to the financial viability of a public relations consultancy or freelance writer or photographer, and it can ruin the prospects of a start-up media venture getting off the ground. While the law of contract can get very complex, the basic concept of a contract is fairly simple: *a contract is a legally enforceable promise.* It is something crucial to the effective operation of a business because our financial system operates on the principle of promises being kept rather than broken, so that there is an element of trust and predictability in our dealings. Contracts play a role in a variety of situations in the public relations and news business. They can cover the terms of employment for a freelance journalist or other staff, the terms of an advertising agreement with a client, the agreed price and timelines for professional services being offered, and the division of royalties that might flow to investors from a creative news product you are bringing to market. Gibson and Fraser (2011: 305–306) list the essential elements of a contract:

- an intention to contract
- an agreement between the parties (including an offer and acceptance)
- 'consideration' – what Gibson and Fraser describe as 'something of value passing from one party to another in return for a promise to do something' (2011: 305–306).

The action for 'breach of contract' arises when one or more terms of the contract have not been met – which might include work not being completed within an agreed timeline. This is usually where lawyers enter the fray, and a contract dispute can involve long and expensive court action, although alternative forms of dispute resolution are becoming more common.

Case example:

Mining PR case (2004): This contract dispute involved a public relations consultant to a South African mining company that was considering buyouts or mergers with other mining companies. The dispute surrounded a 'partly written, partly oral and partly implied' agreement to provide 'public relations, lobbying, consulting, networking, facilitating and co-ordinating' services. The problem was that very little was detailed in the agreement, forcing the judge to look at previous work done by the consultant and to come to an estimate of the number of hours he had worked and their value on this occasion. The consultant was awarded $830 per day for eight weeks, totalling $33,200 plus expenses.

The tort of *negligence* is a legal action available to someone who has suffered damage as a result of a breach of duty to take reasonable care, owed to them by the defendant, who should have been able to foresee that the plaintiff might risk injury (Gibson and Fraser, 2011: 163). The crucial point that the court needs to decide often turns on whether or not a reasonable person might have foreseen that there was a risk of injury in the particular circumstances of the case. It also requires that the risk was not an insignificant one, and that a reasonable person in the defendant's position would have taken precautions (Gibson and Fraser, 2011: 165). Many of the early negligence cases concerned actual physical injury caused to people through the negligence of others, but later the courts began to award damages for economic loss, not just for physical damage to a person or their property. Since the 1960s, the courts have upheld liability for negligent misstatements that result in economic loss (Griggs et al., 2009: 127). This means that public relations consultants can be liable for bad advice if someone acts upon it to their detriment. Special standards and duties of care apply to professionals, by reference to their professional body's standards (Griggs et al., 2009: 127). Those working in a business context are advised to consult one of the numerous business law texts in your jurisdiction for a thorough rundown on these and other laws that could impact you at the commercial level in your work practice. If you are freelancing or running a business you should also take out a professional indemnity insurance policy against risks such as malpractice suits, breach of contract or defamation litigation. These are sometimes available through your professional body.

Reflect – Research – Review:

Identify the government consumer watchdog in your country and explain what impact it might have on the promotion of goods and services by professional communicators.

Basic Australian legal principles in corruption, conflicts of interest and deceptive conduct

Professional communicators in Australia face an array of laws around corruption, conflicts of interests and their misrepresentations to consumers.

As explained above, the average journalist or public relations practitioner would rarely face corruption charges, but they are more likely to face the perils of reporting or commenting upon a corruption matter before the courts or an anti-corruption body. Government communication officers, however, need to be well versed in the kinds of gifts and benefits they can give or receive in the course of their work. These will vary according to public service regulations in the various jurisdictions. An example is the Independent Commission Against Corruption (ICAC) guidelines in NSW, which state:

> Public officials should not solicit or accept any gifts, benefits or hospitality that could be perceived as intended to influence them, or if they are more than token value. Offers of money in any form should never be accepted.
> (ICAC, 2019)

The ICAC gives the example of a public servant who is given a free upgrade to business class by an airline whose contract for her agency's business is about to end with a new tender about to be issued. She has a leadership role within the business unit responsible for that tender, so should refuse the upgrade to avoid a sense of indebtedness and a perception of corruption (ICAC, 2019). The foremost danger facing Australian journalists with these types of corruption bodies is being ordered to reveal their sources for a story which might have triggered a corruption inquiry or be related to evidence being given to one already under way. At least twice in recent decades Australian journalists have faced contempt charges for refusing to reveal their source to corruption bodies. Both were detailed as case examples in Chapter 6 – the Journalist F case (2021) involving an inquiry by Queensland's Crime and Corruption Commission (QCCC) and Cornwall's case (1993) before the ICAC in NSW.

Conflict of interests – the cousin of corruption but not involving public officials – is a more common ethical and legal challenge for professional communicators. A range of laws and regulations can become involved with indiscretions in this domain. We gave the example earlier of the self-regulatory bodies that monitor such conflicts at an ethical level in Australia. Both the journalist's union (the MEAA) and the Public Relations Institute of Australia (PRIA) can take disciplinary action against their members for breaches of these clauses of their ethical codes. So too can the Australian Press Council against member print and online newspaper groups.

Matters become more serious when actual laws are broken – with the Australian Communications and Media Authority (ACMA) having powers under the *Broadcasting Services Act 1992* to place licence conditions and issue other penalties against broadcasters who breach their various industry codes of practice. And then there are harsh penalties available to the Australian Competition and Consumer Commission (ACCC) for breaches of the Australian Consumer Law and the Australian Securities and Investment Commission (ASIC) for infringements of financial and securities laws.

The ACCC polices s18 of the Australian Consumer Law via the *Competition and Consumer Act 2010*. This prohibits corporations from engaging in conduct in trade or commerce that is 'misleading or deceptive or is likely to mislead or deceive'. Professional communicators need to be on the alert against making claims about their own products or services – or those of their clients – that might make false representations or mislead or deceive consumers. Such claims might arise in corporate promotional material, on websites and in social media, in advertisements and in 'advertorials' or 'advertising features' in the mainstream media. They can also occur on social media via posts by media celebrities and social media 'influencers'. Media releases making unverified claims about products or services are a special risk in this category.

Case example:

Essential Media case (2002): The public relations consultancy Essential Media Communications used the state-based Victorian equivalent version of the Commonwealth consumer protection laws to win a Supreme Court injunction to stop another PR firm – EMC2 – from using that abbreviation of their name. Essential Media claimed the use by its competitor of the abbreviation could 'mislead and deceive' clients, some of whom already knew them by that acronym. The court accepted, in addition, that EMC2 might have been 'passing off' its business as that of Essential Media Communications (see Chapter 9).

News organisations have a 'safe harbour' exemption to some of these provisions under the 'prescribed information provider' exception (s19). The exemption acknowledges the fact that news organisations cannot possibly vouch for every claim made by those quoted in their news columns or stories (Applegarth, 2008). Communicators need to consider their business structures and work practices in relation to the media safe harbour exemption, which requires them to establish that they are a 'prescribed information provider' to win the protection.

Case examples:

Bond Diamond case (2007): Entrepreneur the late Alan Bond and mining company Lesotho Diamond Corporation, to which he consulted, tried to use the misleading and deceptive conduct provisions to sue then freelance journalist and Bond biographer Paul Barry (subsequently ABC *Media Watch* host) over an article making serious allegations against them, which they claimed were false. The Federal Court struck out the consumer law action as having no prospects for success because Barry, as a freelance journalist, would qualify for the media safe harbour. On appeal, the Full Court agreed that freelancers would qualify for immunity and went further to say that media organisations should not be held responsible for freelancers' misleading and deceptive conduct unless they knew of that behaviour at time of publication. See also the Carlovers case (2000) where another freelance journalist qualified for the protection.

Sponsored Links case (2013): Google Inc. won an appeal against the ACCC, which had claimed the search engine should be accountable under the misleading and deceptive conduct provisions of consumer law for representations in sponsored links from advertisers highlighted at the top of search results. The High Court held that Google did not create the sponsored links that it displayed. The court decided ordinary and reasonable users of the search engine would have understood that the representations in the links were those of advertisers, not necessarily endorsed by Google.

Reflect – Research – Review:

You are editing an in-flight magazine for a major Australian airline. One of the main stories is about the special offers it is making available to its frequent flyer club members. Work through the Specific Legal Risk Analysis (Grantham and Pearson, 2022: 51–53) to map out how you might address the requirements of consumer law.

Of particular interest to public relations consultants is the question of whether celebrities' and social media influencers' use of social media and blogs without disclosing secret sponsorships or payments can be in breach of laws against misleading and deceptive conduct. In 2012, the ACCC issued a warning to celebrities that their tweets endorsing certain products and services might be prosecuted under the consumer law. The South Australian Tourist Commission had paid celebrities, including singers Kate Ceberano and Shannon Noll, to tweet to their followers that they had visited Kangaroo Island and had a great time. The ACCC said celebrities did not have to disclose they had been paid for such endorsements but should not mislead followers into thinking that they had been somewhere if they had not (von Muenster, 2012). In 2023 the ACCC conducted a social media 'sweep' to identify undisclosed and misleading testimonials and endorsements by influencers. This resulted from tip-offs from the public after the ACCC had made a Facebook call-out for offenders. It specially targeted influencers in posts about fashion, beauty and cosmetics, food and beverage, travel, health fitness and wellbeing, parenting, gaming and technology. The ACCC said it was also examining the role of other commercial parties in aiding misconduct including advertisers, marketers, brands and social media platforms (ACCC, 2023).

The Australian Securities and Investments Commission (ASIC) also polices deceptive conduct within its domain of financial services and has also focused on the activities of social media influencers. ASIC is an independent Commonwealth entity operating as Australia's corporate, markets and financial services regulator. Its role is to ensure Australia's financial markets are fair and transparent, supported by confident and informed investors and consumers. It enforces large sections of the *Corporations Act*. In 2022 ASIC published an information sheet about discussing financial products and services online. In 2021 it had conducted a survey which found about one third of 18 to 21-year-olds followed at least one financial influencer on social media. It warned influencers against providing financial product advice, dealing by arranging for a person to deal in a financial product (such as buying or selling a financial product) or misleading or deceptive conduct in relation to financial products and services (ASIC, 2022).

Case example:

ASX Wolf case (2022): Gold Coast-based share trader and social media 'finfluencer' (financial influencer) Tyson 'ASX Wolf' Scholz was pursued by ASIC over his charging people for share trading advice, giving financial advice seminars and running private online investment forums when he did not hold a licence to be a financial adviser.

ASIC also imposes strict conditions on claims being made in documents associated with company floats in their prospectuses and initial public offering (IPO) announcements. These are known to tread a fine line between marketing, sales and compliance, and ASIC has powers to pursue those who do not ensure statements about future outcomes are reasonably based and that major risks are disclosed in print, broadcast, online and in social media statements. Special concerns in the corporate sector relate to securities law and directors' powers and duties. For example, before a press release is sent out quoting the managing director of a listed company, advisers need to ensure it is not exposing them to legal action over a statement that should have been notified to the stock exchange, or that suggests they should have declared some conflict of interest in relation to the company's dealings. The media release can itself prompt a PR and legal crisis for the firm. A case in which a draft news release and announcement to the Australian Stock Exchange generated significant litigation was the Asbestos case (2010), which related to approval of an announcement of a 'fully funded' trust to meet future asbestos related liabilities.

Other self-regulatory constraints on celebrities and so-called 'influencers' endorsing brands on social media without disclosing any vested interest include those of the Australian Association of National Advertisers (AANA). Its Code of Ethics requires that 'advertising or marketing communication must be clearly distinguishable as such' (AANA, 2021; Canning, 2017). The AANA guidance notes to Clause 2.7 state:

> Influencer and affiliate marketing often appears alongside organic/genuine user generated content and is often less obvious to the audience. Where an influencer or affiliate accepts payment of money or free products or services from a brand in exchange for them to promote that brand's products or services, the relationship must be clear, obvious and upfront to the audience and expressed in a way that is easily understood (e.g. #ad, Advert, Advertising, Branded Content, Paid Partnership, Paid Promotion). Less clear labels such as #sp, Spon, gifted, Affiliate, Collab, thanks to … or merely mentioning the brand name may not be sufficient to clearly distinguish the post as advertising.

Misleading or deceptive comments in the field of health and medicinal products and services is fraught for professional communicators. In addition to the consumer regulator, the Therapeutic Goods Administration (TGA) has regulatory powers to pursue publishers or social media influencers. The TGA is a Commonwealth government agency with the power to regulate therapeutic goods (medicines, medical devices and blood products). Some advertisements directed at consumers require approval before they can be broadcast or published, while advertising prescription-only and some pharmacist-only medicines to the general public is prohibited. The term 'advertisement' is defined broadly in the *Therapeutic Goods Act 1989* to include 'any statement, pictorial representation or design, however made, that is intended, whether directly or indirectly, to promote the use or supply of the goods'. This can cover public relations material and advertorials, in traditional or social media. Health journalists and public relations consultants to pharmaceutical companies need to be well versed in its limitations.

In the field of consumer law, professional communicators also need to be aware of the line of cases establishing that the hosts of Internet and social media pages are responsible for the claims and allegations made by third party commenters on those sites. A consumer law decision was one of the first in this space. In the *Allergy Pathway case* (2011), Justice Ray Finkelstein ruled that a company was responsible for unproven medical claims about a company's allergy treatments made by others on its website and social media pages – after the company had been earlier ordered to desist from making such claims because they were misleading and deceptive under the existing consumer law. While Justice Finkelstein's decision suggests you would need to take reasonable steps to remove any such comments the instant they are brought to your attention, the more recent Voller case (2021) established in a defamation action that a company could be responsible for the claims of others from the instant they were posted – prompting much more conservative approaches to social media comment hosting by news organisations (See Chapter 5). It is important for a communication organisation to commit staff to routine and effective

Integrity, conflicted interests and the business of communication 361

moderation of comments, which can get quite heated and polarised when topics like politics, religion, human rights, the environment and even sport are being debated.

Other laws can contain elements relating to conflicts of interest. In defamation law, the allegation of corruption or a conflict of interest can be defamatory and key defences can be lost because of a lack of good faith or malice if the publisher had some vested interest in publishing the material. For example, see the Treasurer case (2015) in Chapter 5, where it was ruled a defence of qualified privilege would have been disallowed because email communications between an editor and journalists indicated animus towards the plaintiff. In cases of straight-out falsities or deception designed to damage a business, then the legal action of injurious falsehood described in Chapter 5 might apply.

Key Case 12.2: Casino cash for comment case

Casino cash for comment case (2021): Australian Communication and Media Authority (ACMA). 2021, *BI-549 Investigation report and remedial direction*, <www.acma.gov.au/publications/2021–05/report/bi-549-investigation-report-and-remedial-direction>.

Facts

In the 1990s the ABC programme *Media Watch* famously exposed secret payments being made to talkback radio stars for their endorsement of products and services, without the knowledge of listeners. This became known as the 'cash for comment' scandal and was the subject of a major inquiry by the Australian Broadcasting Authority (ABA), now the ACMA (ABA, 2000). One of those who faced the tribunal's wrath was the broadcaster Alan Jones, who again faced allegations of non-disclosure of a casino group's sponsorship in 2021. In various episodes of his talkback radio program on Sydney's radio station 2GB in 2019, Jones discussed the casino group Star Entertainment's development of the Ritz Carlton hotel. Jones failed to disclose that Star sponsored his program.

Law

By not informing listeners that his station had a commercial agreement with Star, Jones had breached the commercial radio disclosure rules of the ACMA, rules put in place after the earlier cash for comment saga 20 years prior. The authority issued a remedial direction to 2GB requiring staff to undertake formal training on its requirements and to report back on its revised processes. Civil penalties were threatened if it did not comply.

Lessons for communicators

The relevant Disclosure Standard obliges broadcasters to make announcements at the time of the broadcast and to publish details of their current commercial agreements on their websites. Both the radio station licence holders and presenters are obliged to let audiences know if a sponsor has a commercial interest in material being broadcast. This is to assist listeners to come to informed views on the sponsor and the topic.

Reflect – Research – Review:

Find mention of social media influencers among the media releases and decisions on the ACCC website. Explain how they might be impacted by consumer law.

A conflict of interests of sorts also can arise when professional communicators misjudge the nature of their social media posts – blurring the firewall between their private and work personas. This can lead to serious consequences, including dismissal from their employment. Employment law – covering workplace relations, human resources and their associated contracts and policies – is an important area of commercial law affecting public relations consultants and journalists. Effective social media policies are now an essential element of employment law in Australia. Corporate employers need to get their social media policies right, check that they are updated, and ensure that their employees are trained in their terms if they expect to be able to rely upon them to discipline or dismiss staff for misuse of their social networking accounts. Decisions by the Fair Work Commission have been very clear about the fact that a clear and reasonable social media policy is essential if a company wishes to dismiss an employee for online misbehaviour.

Employees need to read their employers' social media policies thoroughly and comply with their terms. The wording of a social media policy can be used against you if you are fired for inappropriate use of social media and you have ignored the policy. Comedian and freelance columnist for *The Age*, Catherine Deveny, was dismissed in 2010 for a series of offensive posts from the Logies Awards ceremony about child celebrity Bindi Irwin (Farmer, 2010). This was followed by other episodes involving journalists and their social media posts, including *Sydney Morning Herald* columnist Mike Carlton, who resigned in 2014 following an uproar after he exchanged insults with readers over his position on Israel and Palestine (*ABC News*, 2014). The following year, SBS dismissed sports reporter Scott McIntyre over critical posts he made about Anzac Day, resulting in him settling an unfair dismissal action against his employer (Visentin, 2016). In a different example detailed in Chapter 11, the ABC did not take direct action against social commentator Yassmin Abdel-Magied over her Facebook post criticising government immigration policies on Anzac Day 2017 on the rationale that she was a part-time employee expressing her private views, which were not representative of the national broadcaster. However, her program was not recommissioned (Bornstein, 2022).

The lesson here is that you should endeavour to draw a clear distinction between your private and work social media accounts, carefully adjust your privacy settings to a suitable level for the content you are sharing and only post on the assumption that your colleagues, clients and competitors might well see everything you post, regardless of those precautions. While it sometimes takes an admirable level of self-control, you should practice mindful communication by not getting personal with your comments and responses on your social media account, even if something someone has said really offends or annoys you. This should help minimise the legal risks in your social media use.

Public servants can face consequences under their own code of conduct for their use of social media, particularly if the lines are blurred between private and public accounts. For example, posting your personal opinion about a political issue on your own account or the department's account would usually breach the entity's social media policy, and likely the relevant public service code of conduct. This would leave you subject to disciplinary action, and perhaps personally liable for any damage you have caused some other person or company.

Case example:

Immigration Tweeter case (2013, 2018, 2019): Public affairs officer with the Department of Immigration and Citizenship, Michaela Banerji, failed in her bid in the Federal Circuit Court in 2013 to prevent her employer from dismissing her over anonymous posts on Twitter (now X) she had sent criticising various political figures, employees of the department, the government's immigration policies and an immigration detention centre security company. She failed to convince the High Court that her implied freedom to communicate on matters of politics and government should prevent her dismissal. It ruled that the code of conduct was fair in its purpose of preserving an apolitical public service.

News media bargaining code

The Australian government passed legislation after it decided international Internet and social media platforms were engaging in a conflict of interests of sorts by publishing news articles produced by Australian media outlets and selling advertising that would otherwise have gone to those media companies. The code – officially called the News Media and Digital Platforms

Mandatory Bargaining Code – was designed to help support the sustainability of public interest journalism in Australia by addressing such bargaining power imbalances between digital platforms and Australian news businesses. The code enables eligible news businesses to bargain individually or collectively with digital platforms over payment for the inclusion of their news on their services. The ACMA has the roles of assessing the eligibility of news businesses who want to participate in the code, appointing mediators to assist bargaining parties, and registering and appointing arbitrators if the parties cannot agree (ACMA, 2022). A review by Treasury in December 2022 found the Code had been a success to that point, with more than 30 commercial agreements struck between digital platforms (Google and Meta) and a cross-section of Australian news businesses – agreements that Treasury decided would have been highly unlikely to have been made without the Code (Treasury, 2022).

Reflect – Research – Review:

Integrity and conflict of interests in action – applying reflection-in-action techniques

A host of situations can arise for professional communicators raising red flags around conflicts of interest and consumer law. Here, we turn to a combination of mindful reflection and journal writing for our reflection technique before applying Bok's Model (1978: 94–103) to the situation, followed by a specific legal risk analysis (Grantham and Pearson, 2022: 51–53).

The problem

Shazza and her friend Fatima studied communication together at university. Since then, Shazza has risen to be marketing manager of Fizz Kombucha – one of the fastest growing beverages in the country – which was recently listed as a public company. Fatima finished her professional surfing career a few years ago and she's now a leading social media influencer with millions of followers. They have stayed close over the years and are godparents to each other's children. Shazza has a $3 million social media marketing budget this year, and she suggests to Fatima at a function that she would like to spend $1 million of it on her, in return for her endorsements of Fizz products in her posts and the strategic product placement of the Fizz items in her photos and videos. She will get an extra $500 every time she uses the marketing slogan 'Fizz it Up' in her messaging, up to a maximum of $100,000. The offer is conditional on her not disclosing the arrangement to anyone. You can approach this from the perspective of either Shazza or Fatima.

Applying Bok's Model

Consult your conscience

Use a combination of mindful reflection followed by journal writing to think about the morality of your situation. What is your gut feeling about this scenario and why are you thinking this way? How does it fit with your recollection of the material covered in the chapter? Think about your own moral compass you mapped in Chapter 1 and ponder what could possibly go wrong here.

Consult others for advice on the course of action that might constitute an ethical breach

If you have a boss or a respected family member or friend then consult them to explain the situation and weigh up their suggestions against your own conscience or gut feeling. Stack it up against the main philosophical positions we outlined in Chapter 1 – Kant's deontological position asking you to see how it fits with the universal rule of publicity about your actions (Kant's *Perpetual Peace*, 1795, cited in Gosseries and Parr, 2022). How does it fit with a consequentialist approach – do the ends justify the means? What about the social contract lens – do the actions respect the rights of other stakeholders in the situation? What could be the impact on the influencer's followers? And what about virtue ethics – what does the proposed arrangement say about the character traits of each of you in the situation?

Consulting widely and publicly among all possible people

Bok's rationale for this suggestion was that if you could not publicise your actual decision on this ethical matter, then you could at least project how others might advise or react by searching for similar situations and seeing the response. Further, in line with Kant's Categorical Imperative, Bok would have you project how society would operate if everyone acted this way. How would society function if everyone in powerful positions issued lucrative contracts to their close friends? This is also the opportunity to review the conflict of interests clauses of your professional ethical code and see how this situation stacks up. See an example of how a similar situation played out in Key Case 12.1. This then leads neatly into the legal analysis for your jurisdiction.

Applying the specific legal risk analysis technique

Identifying the potential (or existing) legal problem

After reviewing this chapter's legal material, you'll see there is at least one key area of media law involved here, and perhaps others depending on your jurisdiction. That key area is consumer law.

Reviewing the areas of the law involved

The particulars of the law will vary between jurisdictions. Contracts awarded in the private sector are not subject to the corruption investigations that would occur in the public service, unless of course there is a government agency as a party. That is not the case here but the Australian consumer law would apply to the misleading and deceptive conduct that it is proposed the influencer engage in by not disclosing the financial arrangement with her sponsor. Further, the company is also liable for the deception, given secrecy is a condition of the arrangement. Advertising regulations can also be at play here because the company's marketing manager might well be affiliated with the Australian Association of National Advertisers (AANA) which requires all advertising to be distinguishable as such, with special mention of social media advertising via influencers.

Projecting the possible consequences for stakeholders

If we consider the key stakeholders here as the kombucha company, its shareholders, customers, its marketing manager, the influencer and her audience, then it is fruitful to map out the consequences for all of them, both before and after the secret deal has been exposed. Consumer law breaches can lead to extended litigation, fines and injunctions for the company and the influencer. The advertising regulator can take its own disciplinary action against the marketing manager. The audience is likely to feel duped through the process, losing trust in both the product and the influencer. From a corporate social responsibility (and shareholder) perspective, the company would lose status over the lack of accountability and favouritism shown to an executive's friend with the expenditure.

Seeking advice/referring upward

Under the timing of the scenario, there is still time to cease or pause the arrangement to make it compliant. Making the relationship transparent and using the kinds of terminology recommended by the Australian Association of National Advertisers (AANA) would legitimise the whole arrangement. Advice from supervisors, industry groups and lawyers should confirm this.

Publishing/amending/deleting/correcting/apologizing

The pre-publication amendments outlined above and steps towards the transparency would eliminate the need for corrections and apologies. If the crisis had already occurred and the arrangement had been exposed mid-stream, then any such actions and their wording would need to be negotiated with supervisors and lawyers using the corporate legal escalation process.

In a nutshell

- Moral philosophers have examined integrity, conflicts of interest and corruption from ancient times through until the modern era.
- Breaches of consumer law have a long list of potential human rights repercussions because they involve citizens being misled and deceived about products and services essential to their lives.
- Legal pitfalls in the corporate communication space can be complex, but you will be more likely avert trouble if you are transparent and honest in your communications, avoid conflicts of interest and create a firewall between your private and professional social media use.
- Always disclose any rewards or incentives you might have received from a sponsor and do not pretend you are offering an independent endorsement if you have received anything in return. Label all advertising and sponsorship in line with industry recommendations.
- Reflect upon the ethical standards and professional values of your occupation and consider whether your words and actions honour them, particularly with regard to conflicts of interest.
- Section 18 of the *Competition and Consumer Act 2010* prohibits conduct that is 'misleading or deceptive or is likely to mislead or deceive'. This should be at the forefront of all communications to the public.
- Special industry requirements control public communications about financial securities and drugs and professionals working in this space must know them well.
- Employment law covers workplace relations, human resources and their associated contracts and policies. Misuse of social media can justify a fair dismissal under designated circumstances.

References and further reading

ABC News. 2014, '*Sydney Morning Herald* columnist Mike Carlton resigns following furore over Gaza column', *ABC News*, 7 August, <www.abc.net.au/news/2014-08-06/smh-columnist-mike-carlton-resigns-following-gaza-column-furore/5651470>.

Advertising Standards Authority (ASA). 2022, 'Recognising ads: Social media and influencer marketing', *Advice Online*, <www.asa.org.uk/advice-online/recognising-ads-social-media.html>.

Applegarth, P. 2008, 'How deep is the media safe harbour?', *Gazette of Law and Journalism*, 23, <http://archive.sclqld.org.au/judgepub/2008/How%20deep%20is%20 the%20safe%20media%20harbour.pdf>.

Australian Broadcasting Authority (ABA). 2000, *Commercial radio inquiry: Report of the Australian Broadcasting Authority hearing into Radio 2UE Sydney Pty Limited*, ABA, Sydney, <www.abc.net.au/mediawatch/transcripts/1339_aba.pdf>.

Australian Association of National Advertisers (AANA). 2021, *Code of Ethics*, <https://aana.com.au/self-regulation/codes-guidelines/code-of-ethics/>.

Australian Communications and Media Authority (ACMA). 2022, *News Media Bargaining Code*, <www.acma.gov.au/news-media-bargaining-code>.

Australian Competition and Consumer Commission (ACCC). 2023, 'ACCC social media sweep targets influencers', *Release number 5/23*, 27 January, <www.accc.gov.au/media-release/accc-social-media-sweep-targets-influencers>.

Australian Press Council (APC). 2023, *Statement of Principles*, APC, Sydney, <www.presscouncil.org.au/standards/statement-of-principles>.

Australian Securities and Investment Commission (ASIC). 2022, '22–054MR ASIC issues information for social media influencers and licensees', ASIC, 21 March, <https://asic.gov.au/about-asic/news-centre/find-a-media-release/2022-releases/22-054mr-asic-issues-information-for-social-media-influencers-and-licensees/>.

Benöhr, I. 2020, 'The United Nations Guidelines for Consumer Protection: Legal Implications and New Frontiers', *Journal of Consumer Policy*, 43, 105–124, <https://doi.org/10.1007/s10603-019-09443-y>.

Blum, L. 2022, 'Iris Murdoch', *The Stanford Encyclopedia of Philosophy*, Winter 2022 edn, Zalta, E.N. and Nodelman, U. eds, <https://plato.stanford.edu/archives/win2022/entries/murdoch/>.

Bok, S. 1978, *Lying: Moral Choice in Public and Private Life*, Pantheon Books, New York.

Bornstein, J. 2022, 'What's gone wrong at the ABC', *The Monthly*, August, <www.themonthly.com.au/issue/2022/august/josh-bornstein/what-s-gone-wrong-abc#mtr>.

Canning, S. 2017, 'Influencers must reveal sponsors, but TV shows can keep quiet about product placement, say new advertising rules', *Mumbrella*, 31 January, <https://mumbrella.com.au/asb-aana-influencers-rules-distinguishable-ads-product-placement-423251>.

Cox, D., La Caze, M., and Levine, M. 2021, 'Integrity', *The Stanford Encyclopedia of Philosophy*, Fall 2021 edn, Zalta, E.N. ed., <https://plato.stanford.edu/archives/fall2021/entries/integrity/>.

Farmer, G. 2010, 'Wrong, Deveny, Twitter is not just passing notes', *Sydney Morning Herald*, 5 May, <www.smh.com.au/federal-politics/society-and-culture/wrong-deveny-twitter-is-not-just-passing-notes-20100505-u7nb.html>.

Federal Trade Commission (FTC). 2019, *Disclosures 101 for Social Media Influencers*, Australian Government, <www.ftc.gov/system/files/documents/plain-language/1001a-influencer-guide-508_1.pdf>.

Gibson, A. and Fraser, I. 2011, *Business Law*, 6th edn, Pearson Education, Sydney.

Gosseries, A. and Parr, T. 2022, 'Publicity', *The Stanford Encyclopedia of Philosophy*, Summer 2022 edn, Zalta, E.N. ed., <https://plato.stanford.edu/archives/sum2022/entries/publicity/>.

Grantham, S. and Pearson, M. 2022, *Social Media Risk and the Law: A Guide for Global Communicators*, Routledge, London and New York.

Griggs, L., Clark, E. and Iredale, I. 2009, *Managers and the Law: A Guide for Business Decision Makers*, 3rd edn, Thomson Reuters, Sydney.

Independent Commission Against Corruption (ICAC). 2019, 'Gifts and benefits', *Foundations of Corruption Prevention*, New South Wales Government, <www.icac.nsw.gov.au/prevention/basic-standards/gifts-and-benefits>.

Media Council of Papua New Guinea (MCPNG). 2016, *General Code of Ethics for the News Media*, <https://35f33828c2.cbaul-cdnwnd.com/5e69b4c745dc56af5815f08a6 7706870/200000046-25e6826deb/MCPNG-General%20Code%20of%20Ethics-Revi sed%20Oct2016-8.pdf?ph=35f33828c2>.

Media Entertainment and Arts Alliance (MEAA). 2016, *The MEAA Journalist Code of Ethics*, Media Entertainment and Arts Alliance, Sydney, <www.meaa.org/download/faqs-meaa-journalist-code-of-ethics/>.

Miller, S. 2018, 'Corruption', *The Stanford Encyclopedia of Philosophy*, Winter 2018 edn, Zalta, E.N. ed., <https://plato.stanford.edu/archives/win2018/entries/corrupt ion/>.

Moriarty, J. 2021, 'Business Ethics', *The Stanford Encyclopedia of Philosophy*, Fall 2021 edn, Zalta, E.N. ed., <https://plato.stanford.edu/archives/fall2021/entries/ethics-business/>.

National Union of Journalists (NUJ). 2018, *Printable Code of Conduct*, NUJ, London, <www.nuj.org.uk/resource/printable-nuj-code-of-conduct.html>.

The New York Times (NYT). 2019, *Ethical Journalism – A Handbook of Values and Practices for the News and Opinion Departments*, <www.nytimes.com/editorial-standards/ethical-journalism.html>.

Office of the Conflict of Interest and Ethics Commissioner. 2022, *Ng Report*, Canada <https://ciec-ccie.parl.gc.ca/en/investigations-enquetes/Pages/NgReport.aspx>.

Parker, R. 2009, 'Valentine v Chrestensen (1942*)*', *The First Amendment Encyclopedia*, Free Speech Center, Middle Tennessee State University, <www.mtsu.edu/first-amendment/article/212/valentine-v-chrestensen>

Public Relations Institute of Australia (PRIA). 2009, *Public Relations Institute of Australia (PRIA) Code of Ethics*, PRIA, Sydney, <www.pria.com.au/about-pria/code-of-ethics-privacy/code-of-ethics/>.

Public Relations Society of America (PRSA). 2023, *PRSA Code of Ethics*, <www.prsa.org/about/ethics/prsa-code-of-ethics>.

Smith, S. 2015, 'Canada Global TV knew Leslie Roberts as journalist, NOT PR firm owner', *iMediaEthics*, 22 January, <www.imediaethics.org/canada-global-tv-knew-leslie-roberts-as-journalist-not-pr-firm-owner/>.

Treasury. 2022, *News Media and Digital Platforms Mandatory Bargaining Code – The Code's First Year of Operation*, <https://treasury.gov.au/publication/p2022-343549>.

United Nations Office of the High Commissioner on Human Rights (OHCHR). 2023, *Corruption and Human Rights – OHCHR and Good Governance*, <www.ohchr.org/en/good-governance/corruption-and-human-rights>.

United Nations (UN). 2016, *United Nations Guidelines for Consumer Protection. (UNCTAD/DITC/CPLP/MISC/2016/1)*, United Nations Conference on Trade and Development, July, <https://unctad.org/system/files/official-document/ditccplpmi sc2016d1_en.pdf>.

Visentin, L. 2016, 'Sacked reporter Scott McIntyre and SBS resolve dispute over Anzac Day tweets', *Sydney Morning Herald*, 11 April, <www.smh.com.au/business/compan ies/sacked-reporter-scott-mcintyre-and-sbs-resolve-dispute-over--anzac-day-tweets-20160411-go37vt.html>.

Von Muenster Solicitors & Attorneys. 2012, 'Cash for tweets: What is the price you might pay?', <www.vmsolicitors.com.au/tag/twitter-kangaroo-island-misleading-and-deceptive-conduct-advertising>.

Walton, G. and Jackson, D. 2020, *Reciprocity Networks, Service Delivery, and Corruption: The Wantok System in Papua New Guinea*, U4 Anti-Corruption Resource Centre, Chr. Michelsen Institute, Bergen.

Cases cited

Allergy Pathway case: *Australian Competition and Consumer Commission (ACCC) v Allergy Pathway Pty Ltd and Anor (No 2)* [2011] FCA 74 (10 February 2011), <www.austlii.edu.au/au/cases/cth/FCA/2011/74.html>.

Asbestos case: *Morley & Ors v Australian Securities and Investments Commission* [2010] NSWCA 331 (17 December 2010), <www.austlii.edu.au/cgi-bin/sinodisp/au/cases/nsw/NSWCA/2010/331.html>.

ASX Wolf case: *Australian Securities and Investments Commission (ASIC) v Scholz (No 2)* [2022] FCA 1542 (20 December 2022), <https://download.asic.gov.au/media/rqybwkr3/22–371mr-australian-securities-and-investments-commission-v-scholz-no-2-2022-fca-1542.pdf>.

Bond Diamond case: *Bond v Barry* [2007] FCA 1484 (16 February 2010), <www.austlii.edu.au/au/cases/cth/FCA/2007/1484.html>; *Bond v Barry* [2008] FCAFC 115 (23 June 2008), <www.austlii.edu.au/cgi bin/sinodisp/au/cases/cth/FCAFC/2008/115.html>.

Carlovers case: *Carlovers Carwash Ltd v Sahathevan* [2000] NSWSC 947 (13 October 2000), <www.austlii.edu.au/au/cases/nsw/supreme_ct/2000/947.html>.

Casino cash for comment case (2021): Australian Communication and Media Authority (ACMA). 2021, *BI-549 Investigation report and remedial direction*, <www.acma.gov.au/publications/2021–05/report/bi-549-investigation-report-and-remedial-direction>.

Central Hudson case: *Central Hudson Gas and Electric Corp. v Public Service Commission* [1980] 447 U.S. 557 (20 June 1980), <www.law.cornell.edu/supremecourt/text/447/557>.

Cornwall's case: *ICAC v Cornwall* (1993) 116 ALR 97 (6 July 1993 and 8 September 1993).

Essential Media case: *Essential Media Communications Pty Ltd v EMC2 & Partners* [2002] VSC 554 (10 December 2002), <www.austlii.edu.au/cgi-bin/sinodisp/au/cases/vic/VSC/2002/554.html>.

Immigration Tweeter case: 2013, 2018, 2019. *Banerji v Bowles* [2013] FCCA 1052. <www6.austlii.edu. au/cgi-bin/viewdoc/au/cases/cth/FCCA/2013/1052.html> *Banerji and Comcare (Compensation)* [2018] AATA 892. <>^#www6.austlii.edu.au/cgi-bin/viewdoc/au/cases/cth/AATA/2018/892.html>; *Comcare v Banerji* [2019] HCA 23 7 August. C12/2018. <www6.austlii.edu.au/cgi-bin/viewdoc/au/cases/cth/HCA/2019/23.html>.

Journalist F case (2021): *F v Crime and Corruption Commission* [2021] QCA 244 (12 November 2021), <www.austlii.edu.au/cgi-bin/viewdoc/au/cases/qld/QCA/2021/244.html>; *F v Crime and Corruption Commission* [2020] QSC 245 (12 August 2020), <www.austlii.edu.au/cgi-bin/viewdoc/au/cases/qld/QSC/2020/245.html>.

Mining PR case: *Newshore Nominees Pty Ltd as Trustee for the Commercial and Equities Trust v Durvan Roodepoort Deep, Limited* [2004] WADC 57 (31 March 2004), <www.austlii.edu.au/cgi-bin/sinodisp/au/cases/wa/WADC/2004/57.html>.

Minister's friend PR case (2022): Office of the Conflict of Interest and Ethics Commissioner. 2022, *Ng report*, <https://ciec-ccie.parl.gc.ca/en/investigations-enquetes/Pages/NgReport.aspx>.

Nike case: *Nike v Kasky* [2003] 539 U.S. 654 (26 June2003), <www.law.cornell.edu/supct/html/02-575.ZC.html>.

Sponsored Links case: *Google Inc. v Australian Competition and Consumer Commission* [2013] HCA 1 (6 February 2013), <www.austlii.edu.au/cgi-bin/viewdoc/au/cases/cth/HCA/2013/1.html>.

Submarine Case: *Valentine v Chrestensen* [1942] 316 U.S. 52 (13 April 1942), <www.law.cornell.edu/supremecourt/text/316/52>.

Sullivan's case: *New York Times v Sullivan* [1964] 376 US 254 (9 March 1946), <https://supreme.justia.com/cases/federal/us/376/254/>.

Treasurer case: *Hockey v Fairfax Media Publications Pty Limited* [2015] FCA 652 (30 June 2015), <www.austlii.edu.au/cgi-bin/sinodisp/au/cases/cth/FCA/2015/652.html>.

Voller case: *Fairfax Media Publications Pty Ltd v Voller; Nationwide News Pty Limited v Voller; Australian News Channel Pty Ltd v Voller* [2021] HCA 27, 8 September, <www.austlii.edu.au/cgi-bin/viewdoc/au/cases/cth/HCA/2021/27.html>.

Index

Note: Figures are indicated by *italics*. Tables are indicated by **bold**.

60 Minutes, 121–22, 195–96, 247

Abdel-Magied, Yassmin, 321–22, 363
Aboriginal and Torres Strait Islander peoples, 4, 34–35, 157, 176, 326–30. *See also* Indigenous peoples
absolute privilege, 118–19
accountability, 4, 132, 193, 347, 366
'account of profits,' 151, 253, 265
Administrative Decisions Tribunal (NSW), 330
admissibility rules, 117, 231, 297
advertising, 56, 348, 351–52, 354, 357–60; deception in, 82; TARES test for, 67–69, 74; 'truth-in-advertising' laws, 352
Advertising Standards Authority (ASA), 352
Advertising Standards Bureau regulations, 333
Age (newspaper), 51–52, 161, 362
Agence France Presse, 254–55
AGL (energy company), 267
Al-Ghazali, 80
Alien and *Sedition Acts* (1798, United States), 286
Allen & Unwin, 264
'alternative facts,' 81, 86–87
altruism, 3, 9, 12–13, 20
Alvaro, Amanda, 353
American and French revolutions, 8
analogue broadcasting licences, 28
Anderson, Timothy, 257–58
Anemaat, L., 157
Animal Liberation NSW, 195

anti-corruption agencies, 155
anti-corruption structures, xviii
Anti-Discrimination Act 1977 (NSW), 330–31
Anti-Terrorism Crime and Security Act 2001 (United Kingdom), 287
Anzac Day, 321–22, 362–63
Aphrahat, Saint, 143
apologies, 129
applied ethics, 3–22, 5–6; defined, 5–6; for integrity and conflict of interests, 364–67; key concepts, 3; mapping moral compass, 16, *16*
Applied Ethics Matrix, xiv–xv, **17**, 18, 19, 20, 66; and defamation issues, 132; and intellectual property, 270–71; moving beyond, 53; and problem scenarios, 56; and war decisions, 279
appropriation, 181
Aquinas, Thomas, 278
Areopagitica (Milton), 26
Aristotle, xiv, 3, 11, 103, 207, 278, 346; on privacy, 176; slavery, view of, 309
Arlidge, A., 121
Article 19 (*Universal Declaration of Human Rights*), 29–30, 45
artificial intelligence (AI), xvii, 88, 89, 176; ChatGPT, 243, 246; copyright cases, 265; image generators, 246; and intellectual property, 243–44, 255, 272; Midjourney, 255
Artz, Simon, 291
Ashton, Kate, 165–66
Asia-Pacific region, 28–29
Assange, Julian, 88, 155, 282–83, 288
astroturfing, 81

Athens, 7, 25
Atkin, Lord, 217
'attention,' 59, 176
Augustine of Hippo (St Augustine), 278
Australia: basic legal principles confidentiality, secrets, sources and disclosure, 157–70; basic legal principles in communicating justice, 219–32; basic legal principles in human rights and free expression, 34–36; basic legal principles in intellectual property, 258–71; basic legal principles on integrity, 355–67; basic legal principles on truth and deception, 90–93; Constitution, 35, 37, 39, 128, 280; defamation law, 107–10; immigration and race debate, 329–30; key laws on human rights, 36–39; no common law right to privacy, 183, 189, 201; territories, legislation in, 36. *See also* Aboriginal and Torres Strait Islander peoples
Australian Association of National Advertisers (AANA), 359–60, 366
Australian Broadcasting Authority (ABA), 361
Australian Broadcasting Corporation (ABC), 42, 130, 158, 165; Afghan Files case (2019–2023), 294; cyberbullying processes, 321. *See also* Lenah Game Meats case (2001)
Australian Communications and Media Authority (ACMA), 33, 39–40, 91, 179, 261, 320, 356; and news media bargaining code, 363–64; *Privacy Guidelines for Broadcasters,* 179
Australian Community Managers (ACM), 319
Australian Competition and Consumer Commission (ACCC), 352, 356–57, 358
Australian Consumer Law, 91, 352, 356–57
Australian Copyright Council, 262
Australian Cyber Security Centre, 298
Australian Federal Police (AFP), 296
Australian Human Rights Commission, 333
Australian Law Reform Commission (ALRC), 220
Australian Medical Association's (AMA) Code of Ethics, 148
Australian Press Council (APC), 39, 40, 91, 179, 319–20, 356; Statement of Principles, 320, 350

Australian Privacy Principles, 193–94, 201
Australian Securities and Investments Commission (ASIC), 93, 356, 359
Australian Security Intelligence Organisation (ASIO), 289–91, 298
Australian Signals Directorate (ASD), 298
Australian Stock Exchange, 359
The Australian (news outlet), 164, 227, 291
Australia Wide, 322
authenticity, 67–69
Ayyab, Rana, 315

Badawi, J.A., 310
Baker, S., 67–68, 233
'balance of probabilities,' 118
Banerji, Michaela, 363
Barak, Aharon, 280
Baranek, P.M., 208
Barilaro, John, 123, 227
Barrass, Tony, 160
Barron's, 114
Barry, Paul, 357–58
Bashir, Martin, 84
Basic Online Safety Expectations, 332
Bauer Media, 109–10
Beard, M., 278
Bentham, Jeremy, xiv, 9–10, 20, 144, 207–8
Benziman, Y., 103
Berne Convention (1928), 245, 248, 250
Bhikkhu, Thanissaro, 59
Bill C-13 (the *Protecting Canadians from Online Crime Act,* 2015)
Bill of Rights: absent in Australia, 35, 36, 334; England, 24; United States, 23, 31
Bill of Rights Act 1990 (BORA, New Zealand), 30, 280, 325
Black, Hugo, 281
blackmail, 152, 183, 220, 315
Blackstone, William, 26, 207
Blum, Lawrence, 308–309
Bok, Sissela, 8, 68, 69, 82, 94; commercialised voyeurism, view of, 209; confidentiality, view of, 145, 176–77; on gossip, 103; on secrecy, 143; on secrecy and war, 279, 302
Bok's model, xv, 53, 65–66, 74, 166–69; 'soul searching' process, 57–58, 167; for truth and deception, 93
Bolt, Andrew, 326–28
Bond, Alan, 357–58
Bornstein, Josh, 322

374   Index

bots and cookies, xv, 89–90
Brandeis, Louis D., 181
'brand-jamming,' 267
breach of confidence, xvi, 142, 143, 148, 149–51; in Australia, 157–60; defences, 150–51; elements of the action, 149–50; 'misuse of private information,' 182; and privacy, 182, 190, 191; remedies, 151
breach of contract, 354–55, 367
broadcasting, 28, 39
Broadcasting Code (Office of Communications, United Kingdom), 178
Broadcasting Services Act 1992 (BSA, Australia), 39, 179, 320, 356
'Brodie's Law' (Victoria), 333
Bromberg, Mordecai, 327
Brunelleschi, Filippo, 248
Budd, Joe, 161
Buddha, 59, 80, 102, 310
Buddhism, 11, 15, 59–60, 80, 102, 285, 310
Builders' Labourers Federation (BLF), 227
Burch, G., 62–63
Burchett, Wilfred, 284
burden of proof, 87, 107, 110–12, 117, 118, 131, 158
burdens, reasonable, 37–38
Burke, Edmund, 83
Burns, Garry, 330
BuzzPR, 350

Cambridge Analytica-Facebook personal data breach scandal, xvi, 186, 187
Campbell, Naomi, 182
Canada, 30, 325, 350
Canadian Centre for Cybersecurity, 81
Canadian Charter of Rights and Freedoms, 30, 280
Canadian Conflict of Interest Act, 353
Carleton, Richard, 247
Carlton, Mike, 362
Caroline of Monaco, Princess, 182
cartoonists, 123
case examples: 2DAY-FM prank call, 91–92; Actor case (2018–2020), 118, 130; ACTU case (2022), 333; ACTV case (1992), 37, 128; Afghan Files case (2019–2023), 294–96; AFL case (2006), 159–60; Alan Jones cases (2000 and 2009–2013), 330; Allergy Pathway case (2011), 116; Ambard's case (1936), 217; Animal Cruelty case (2022), 39; Anonymous Tweets case (2019), 38; Anzac Day case (2017), 321–22, 362–63; Artemus Jones case (1910), 113; Asbestos case (2010), 359; ASX Wolf case (2022), 359; Barrass's case (1989), 160; Barrister's Wife case (2017), 118, 130; BLF cases (1972 and 1983), 227; Bolt case (2011), 326–28; Bond Diamond case (2007), 357–58; Brandenburg's case (1969), 286; Bread Manufacturers (1937), 223, 224; Brown Protest case (2017), 195; Budd's case (1992), 161; Butler's case (1994), 112; Cambridge Analytica-Facebook personal data breach scandal, xvi, 186, 187; Carleton's case, 121–22; Casino cash for comment case (2021), 361–62; Central Hudson case (1980), 351; Chinese Businesswoman case (2010–2017), 161; Clearview AI case (2021), 193; Clippings case (1990), 261; Corby case (2013), 264; Cornwall's case (1993), 161; *Courier-Mail* case (2014), 231; Court reporter's case (2019), 51–52; Cricketer case (1974), 256; Crime Commission case (2013), 222; Crocodile Dundee case (1989), 269; Cronulla Riots case (2007), 320–21; DABUS AI case (2022), 265; Deep Sleep case (2022), 163; Defence Papers case (1980), 158; Dehorning case (2018), 196; Disability case (2013), 190; Dunbabin's case (1935), 226; Earthquake case (2014), 254–55; Engineers' cases (1948 and 1969), 149; Essential Media case (2002), 357; ET's case (1991), 109; *Evening Standard* case (1924), 215; Facebook streaming case (2019), 218; Financial Tweets case (2017), 152; Finn's case (2002), 113; flag burning case, 2011, 30; Friendlyjordies case (2022), 123, 227; Gay cases (2004, 2007 and 2018), 330; Golf Club case (1937), 116; Greenpeace case (2021), 261, 267; Grosse case (2003), 332; Gutnick's case (2002), 88, 114; Hampson's case (2011), 332; Haneef case (2007), 292; Hanson's case (1999), 123; Hanson-Young's case (2013), 109; Hells Angels case (2022), 266; Hinch's case (1987), 224; Holocaust cases (2002–2009), 329; Holsworthy

Index 375

Barracks cases (2013), 290–91; Hosking Twins case (2004), 183; Ibrahim's case (2012), 220; Idoport case (2001), 220; Immigration Documents cases (2013 and 2017), 166; Indigenous Laughing case (2017), 226; Instagram hate speech case (2022), 317–18; Islam case (2017), 331; ISP cases (2016), 265; James' case (1963), 221; Jane Doe case (2007), 158, 189, 230, 332; JK Rowling case (2008), 258; John Laws case (2000), 228; Journalist F case (2021), 161, 356; Kiwi Blogger's case (2014), 154; Kokoda Trail case (2005), 259; Krystal's case (2016–2017), 224–25; Lange's case (1997), 37–38; Lee's case (1934), 112; Lenah Game Meats case (2001), xvi, 157–58, 183, 189, 190–92, 201; Liberal Ministers' case (2017), 227; Lloyd's case (1985), 122; Lobster case (1989), 121; Lundin's case (1982), 153; Maleny Towers case (2016), 158; Mall Preachers case (2013), 38; marketing executive and the high roller, 18–19; Mason's case (1990), 221, 222–23; McGuinness's case (1940), 153; *Media Watch* cases (2002 and 2017), 42, 121–22; Meghan Markle's case, 150, 252–54; MH370 disappearance, 85; Mining PR case (2004), 354–55; Minister's friend PR case (2022), 353–54; Minnesota case (1931), 286–87; Monkey case (2018), 250; Mount Druitt case (1999), 113; Nike case (2003), 351; Norwich Pharmacal case (1973), 152; NT Homeless 'Genius' case (2017), 226; Optus and Medibank breaches, 193–94; Palm Island Parole case (2012), 38; *The Panel* cases (2002–2005), 260, 261, 262; Pell suppression case (2021), 221; Penname case (1977), 268–69; Pentagon Papers case (1971), 156, 280, 281–82, 287; PI case (2015), 264–65; Pokémon case (2017), 263; Police Press Release case (2005), 163; Pop stars case (1977), 150; Princess Diana interview, 84; PR News Anchor (2015), 350; Protesters' case (2017), 38; Psychic Stalker case (2017), 127, 129; QUT Students' case (2016 and 2017), 328; Racehorse Cruelty case (2017), 119; Rape Priors case (2013), 221, 223; Raybos's case (1985), 219–20; Rebel's case (2017–2018), 107, 109–10, 130; Remote Housing case (2022), 165–66; Rescue Children case (2022), 114; Revenge Porn case (2015), 190; Rinehart cases (2013–2014), 163; Rocky case (1989), 257–58; Rofe's case (1924), 117; Search Engine cases (2012–2018), 129; Search warrant case (2020), 294–96; Secret tape case (2022), 163; The Slants case (2017), 324; South Sydney rugby league case (2012), 126; Sponsored Links case (2013), 358; Steeplechaser case (1936), 111; Stephens's case (1994), 37; *Sunday Times* case (1974), 215–16; Sussex cases (2021–2022), xvi, 183, 184, 252–54; Sussex Justices case (1924), 208; Tailor's case (2017), 112, 119; Talkback case (2006), 227; Theophanous's case (1994), 37; Toxic Playground case (2017), 122; Treasurer case (2015), 114–15, 361; Troll Hunting (2019), 322; Twisted Sister case (2021), 262–63; UK domestic abuse allegation case (2021), 124; UK rape allegation case (2016), 124–25; Underworld lawyer's case (2022), 129; Various Claimants privacy invasion cases, 184; Victoria Park Racing case (1937), 189, 195; Vocational Education case (2018), 118, 130; Voller Case (2021), 116, 129, 332, 360; Voyeur case (2018), 218; War Hero case (2023), 90, 118, 130; War Veterans case (2006), 161, 163; Westpac Letters case (1991), 159; *Who Weekly* case (1994), 223; Wikipedia case (2009), 152; Witness J case (2019), 291–92; ZGeek case (2015), 121; Zhao's case (2015), 219
Cash, Johnny, 77–78
Catechism of the Catholic Church, 102
Categorical Imperative, 6, 24–25, 365
Ceberano, Kate, 358
celebrities: defamation trials, 105; and privacy, xvi, 143, 181–83; and requirements for truth, 92; and secret sponsorship, 358
censorship, 25–26, 42, 106, 286
Chan, J.B.L., 208
Change or Suppression (Conversion) Practices Prohibition Act 2021 (Victoria), 334
Channel Nine, 259, 263

Channel Seven, 259, 263
Charles III, 84
Charlie Hebdo, 323
Chartered Institute of Public (CIPR) Code of Conduct, 33, 146–47, 283
Charter of Human Rights and Responsibilities (Victoria), 334
Charter of Human Rights and Responsibilities Act 2006 (Victoria), 36, 197, 208
ChatGPT, 243, 246
children, 177–79, 195, 201, 209, 218–19, 229, 236, 325, 332; identification of, 230
Christian perspective, 6–7, 15, 80, 103, 309
Christians, C.G., 65, 66
Chydenius, Anders, 156
Cicero, 24
Civil Law (Wrongs) Act 2002 (ACT), 108
classified documents, 144
'clear and present danger,' 214
Clinton, Hillary, 288
Coalition Against Online Violence, 315–16
Code of Canon Law (Catholic Church), 144
Code of Ethics (Public Relations Institute of Australia), 33
Code of Ethics (Public Relations Society of America), 84
Code of Ethics Administration Procedure Manual (PRIA), 44
codes of ethics and practice, 5, 7, 33, 56–57, 133; and confidentiality, 145–48; and consumers, 349–50; defined, 23; and discrimination, 313–22. *See also specific codes*
Colvin, Marie, 284
Commentaries on the Laws of England (Blackstone), 26, 207
commercial laws, 91, 96, 354, 362
Commercial Radio Australia, 39–40, 179; Commercial Radio Code of Practice (2017), 40, 321
Commercial Television Industry Code of Practice (Free TV Australia, 2015), 39–40, 320
Committee to Protect Journalists (CPJ), 32, 315
common law, 36–37, 219–20, 256, 280; and breach of confidence, 149; and defamation, 102, 107–8, 117, 120, 125–28, 136; European, 182;

and privacy, 189, 201; and qualified privilege, 125–26
Commonwealth Department of Immigration and Citizenship, 38
communication careers. *See* journalism; law and ethics across communication careers; public relations
Communications Decency Act 1996 (United States), 88–89, 152, 324
communications officers, 86–87, 299, 352
Competition and Consumer Act 2010 (Australia), 357, 367
Competition and Markets Authority (CMA), 352
confidentiality, secrets, sources and disclosure, xiv, xvi, 7, 28, 142–74, 296; among Aboriginal and Torres Strait Islander peoples, 157; anonymous sources, 147–48; basic Australian legal principles, 157–70; 'commercial-in-confidence' material, xvi, 142; contempt of Parliament, 162; defined, 142, 143; in digital era, 151–52, 156, 284–85; disobedience contempt, 138, 142, 148, 152–53, 160–62, 170; escape clauses, 148; Hippocratic Oath, 143, 148, 169; in journalism, 147–48, 152–53; key concepts, 142; law, cases and examples internationally, 148–51; lawyer–client relationship, 152; lessons for professional communicators, 160; and national security, 284–88, 291; newspaper rule, 163; obligation of, 150, 151, 169; 'of embarrassing private facts,' 151; off-the-record, xvi, 142, 155, 162; philosophical background and human rights context, 143–45; professional ethical dilemmas in, 145–48; and public interest, 158–60; and publicity, 144–45; 'quality of confidence,' 149, 169, 190; remedies, 151; shield laws, xvi, 142, 154, 161, 162–63, 170; as starting point in UK, 152; unauthorised use (or planned use), 150; of vested interests, xviii. *See also* breach of confidence; freedom of information laws (FOI); whistleblowers
confidentiality clauses, 142–43
'confirmation bias,' 308
conflict, as core news value, xvii, 209
conflicts of interest, xiv, xvii–xviii, 344, 345; and ethical codes, 349–50; and friendships, 353–54

Confucianism, 11, 15
conscience, 49, 51, **55**, 58
consequentialism, xiv, 3, 9–10, *12*, *17*, 19, 20; and defamation issues, 132; and human rights, 25; and reflective tools, 56, 64; truth and deception, view of, 78, 95; utilitarianism, 9–10, 20, 25. *See also* stakeholder mapping
Constitution (Australia), 35, 37, 39, 128, 280
Constitution (US). *See* First Amendment (US Constitution)
consulting with others/referring upward, 58, 70–71, **73**, 106, **135**, 166–69, 200, 271, 301, 337, 365, 366–67
consumer law, xviii, 345; defined, 344; financial services, 344, 345, 359, 367
contempt, defined, 212
contempt of court: contempt by publication, 214, 235; contempt in the face of the court, 206, 212, 216–17, 235; lessons for communicators, 216; mobile phone ringing, 216; revealing jury deliberations, 213, 217, 227–28; scandalising the court, 206, 213, 217, 226–27, 235; *sub judice* contempt, 206, 213–16, 218, 221–25, 227, 229, **234**, 235. *See also* disobedience contempt
Contempt of Court Act 1981 (United Kingdom), 154, 214
Contempt of Court Act 2019 (New Zealand), 214
contempt of Parliament, 162
'*contemptus curiae*', 212
contextual truth defence, 127
contracts, 354–55
contractualism (social contract theory), xiv, 3, 7–9, *12*, *17*, 19, 20; and defamation issues, 132–33; and human rights, 25; and reflective tools, 8, 56, 67; truth, view of, 78
'control orders,' 296
Convention Establishing the World Intellectual Property Organization (WIPO), 249
Convention on the Elimination of All Forms of Racial Discrimination (CERD), 311, 312, 326
Convention on the Rights of Persons with Disabilities (CRPD), 311, 312
Conway, Kellyanne, 86–87
Cook, James, 176
cookies, xv, 89–90

copyright, xvii, 181; in 200BCE, 244; and artificial intelligence, 255; 'cut and paste' model, 90–91; defined, 243; duration, 251; employers' right to, 259; fair dealing, xvii, 243, 251–52, 260–61, 267, 272; fair use, xvii, 243, 251–52, 272; form of expression, 249, 258–59; key questions for, **266**; law internationally, 249–55; in a literary work, 258–59; parody, 261; registering, 250; remedies for infringement, 265; 'some rights reserved' approach, 251; symbol, 250; in translations, 251. *See also* intellectual property
Copyright Act 1968 (Australia), 91, 258, 261, 263, 272
Corby, Schapelle, 264
co-regulation and self-regulation, 5, 32–34, 45; of Australian media, 39–44, **41**, **43**; defined, 23; of discrimination, 317–20; global platform, 34; and privacy, 177–80
Cornwall, Deborah, 161
corporate codes of practice, 42
corporate communicators, 84–86, 164, 180
corporate social responsibility (CSR), xviii, 10, 34, 86, 344, 346, 347
Corporations Act 2001 (Australia), 93, 164, 359
corruption, 344, 345, 348–49, 353–56; in defamation law, 361; internationally, 352
Courier-Mail (Brisbane), 113, 231
COVID-19 pandemic, 25, 89, 228
Cox, D., 346
Crane, A., 64
Creative Commons, 251, 272
Crime and Corruption Commission (QCCC, Queensland), 256
crime and violence, xvi; 'bare facts,' 221–22; children's viewing of, 209; and confidentiality, 160; innocence until proven guilty, 29; internet viewing of, 210; law, cases and examples internationally, 211–17; media communication of, 208–9; parole, 38; 'pending' cases, 214, 215, 221–22; philosophical background and human rights context of communicating about, 207–9; 'pixelated' photos of accused, 223; sexual offences, reporting, 230; *sub judice* contempt, 221–22. *See also* justice, communicating

Crimes Act 1914 (Australia), 292–93, 296
Criminal Code (Canada), 325
Criminal Code Act 1995 (Australia), 232, 290–96, 326, 331–32
Criminal Code Amendment (Sharing of Abhorrent Violent Material) Bill (2019), 210
criminal libel, 101, 105, 136
crisis communicators, 10
Crocodile Dundee (movie), 269
Crowe, Russell, 126
Crystal, V., 214
cultural life, freedom of, 29
customary laws, 4
cyberbullying, xvii, 211, 307, 319, 331–34, 337; Adult Cyber Abuse, 332–33; image-based abuse, 323
cybersecurity, xvii, 81, 82, 90, 188, 197; defined, 277; 'denial of service' attacks, 298. *See also* national security
cyber-squatting, 257

Daily Mirror, 150, 182
Daily Telegraph, 113, 118
damages: 'account of profits,' 151, 253, 265; for breach of confidentiality, 151; for defamation, 105, 106, 107, 110, 118, 123, 127, 130; for privacy invasion, 189, 194–95; for revealing identities, 218
Darling, Ralph, 35
Dart Center for Journalism and Trauma, 61
data protection, xvi, 143; in Australia, 192–94; data breaches, 193–94; defined, 175; government breaches, 186; key concepts, 175; laws, 185–88; lessons for communicators, 187; and national security, 296–98; 'sensitive information,' 193. *See also* privacy
'death knock,' 51, 84, 177, 178–79
deception, **54–55**, 188, 350; basic Australian legal principles on, 90–93; bots and cookies, xv, 89–90; and career needs and values, 82–84; defined, 77; disguises/pretense, 56, 145, 182, 244, 256, 264; front groups, 85; and intention, 68; lying by omission, 85, 93; modern conceptions of, 81–82; philosophical and religious thinking on, 78–80, 95; religious notions of, 80–81, 95; and social media influencers, 352; and surveillance/recording, 91, 188; and terms of use, 89. *See also* truth
Declaration of Independence (US), 24, 31, 177, 309
Declaration of Rights (Bill of Rights, England), 24
Declaration of Rights of Man and of the Citizen (1768, France), 27, 177
defamation, xv–xvi, 101–41; 'actual malice,' 107; applying reflection-in-action to, 131–33; Australian law, 107–10; burden of proof, 107, 110–12, 118; case law, 108, 111, 112; and common law, 102, 107–8, 117, 120, 125–28, 136; corruption allegations, 361; court costs, 130; 'criminal,' 106; 'criminal libel,' 35, 101, 136; damages awarded, 105, 106, 107, 110, 118, 123, 127, 130; defences best handled by media lawyers, 127–30; defined, 101–2, 104–5; during discussion of political matters, 126, 127–28, **134–35**; elements of the action, 110–14; ethical and legal risks, **54–55**; as everyday occurrence, 105–6; and fictitious characters, 113; and free expression, 104; of a group, 112; imputation, 101, 109, 110, 111, 116; injunctions, 105, 130; injurious falsehood as alternative action, 91, 131; and intellectual property, 90–91; and internet, 105–6, 110, 114–15; of judges, 226; justifiable, 106, 109; key aspects of Australian law, 114–16; legal standing, 115; libel, 101, 105; limitation period, 115; in media law, 87; mistaken identity cases, 113, 119; publication to at least a third person, 106, 113, 136; publishing the comments of others, 115–16; qualified privilege, 37, 107, 109, 121, 124–28, **134**, 136–37, 361; 'reasonableness' test, 38, 109, 118, 122, 183, 355; reference to (or identification of) the plaintiff, 112, 136; remedies, 129–30, 137; and ridicule, 108, 109; right of reply, 122, 124, 125, 127, **134, 135**; and satire, 123; serious harm, xvi, 101, 106, 107, 110, 114, 136; slander, 105, 131; Specific Legal Risk Analysis, 133, **134–35**; third party comments, 77, 88–89; tools for decision-making, 108; unlawful attacks, 104, 177. *See also* defence; reputation

Defamation Act 2005 (Australia), 37, 90, 108, 114, 118, 131; qualified privilege in, 125
Defamation Act 2006 (ACT), 108
defences, legal, xvii, 90, 116–30; absolute privilege, public documents and fair report, 90, 118–20, 136; based on proper material, 121; confidentiality, 150–51; 'contextual' truth, 127; against defamation, 106; extended Lange qualified privilege defence, 125, 126, 127–28; 'fair report,' 90, 119, 136, 158–59; 'honest opinion' ('fair comment'), 90, 120–23, 136, 261; innocent dissemination, 116, 127, 129; and national security cases, 294, 296, 299, 301; offer of amends, 128; public interest, 121, 123–25, 294, 296; truth/justification, 106, 117–18, 136; UK version, 124. *See also* defamation
'delict,' 182
Denmark, 322–23
deon (duty), 6
deontology, xiv, 3, 6–7, *12, 17*, 18, 19–20; and defamation issues, 132; and human rights, 24–25; and reflective tools, 56, 67; truth, view of, 78
Department of Immigration and Border Protection (Australia), 166
Depp, Johnny, 105
Derrida, Jacques, 79
'Development' model, 28–29
Deveny, Catherine, 362
Diana, Princess, 84, 182
difference principle, 8
Digital Ethics Report (IFJ), 314
Diogenes the Cynic, 309
Directory of Intellectual Property Offices (WIPO), 249
disclosure. *See* confidentiality, secrets, sources and disclosure
discrimination, cyberbullying, and harassment, xiv, xvii, 307–43; Australian legal approaches to, 326–34; 'confirmation bias,' 308; cyberbullying, xvii, 211, 307, 319, 331–34, 337; discrimination defined, 307; fines for corporations, 325; hate speech, 314, 316–19, 337; international ethical regulation, 313–14; international legal approaches to, 322–25, 337; key concepts, 307; lessons for communicators, 318; online harassment of communicators of diverse backgrounds, 312–13; philosophical background to, 307–11; potential problem scenario, 334–37; professional ethics, discrimination and cyber-safety, 313–22; prohibited by UN declarations, 29; 'protected characteristics,' 317; racial, 36–37; self-regulation of, 317–20; slavery, 309–10; stereotyping, 307–9; types of, 311
disinformation, 77, 81, 96
disobedience contempt, 138, 142, 148, 152–53, 170; in Australia, 160–62; and justice reporting, 213, 221, 235. *See also* contempt of court
Distillers, 215
Dixon, John, 225
'D-notice' (defence notice) system, 289
Douglas, Michael, 182
Dow Jones, 114
Dowling, Shane, 160
Dowsett, John, 161
Driver, J., 6
due diligence, 85
duels, 209
Dumas, Alexandre, 181

Eatock, Pat, 327
Editorial Policies, Editorial Guidelines, Classification Standards and Code of Practice (ABC), 42
Editors' Code of Practice (IPSO, 2021), 178
egoism, 3, 9, 12–13, 20
Einstein, Justice, 220
electronic communication, 110–11
Ellenborough, Lord, 213
Ellsberg, Daniel, 281–82
EMC2, 357
employment law, 362–63, 367
Engels, Friedrich, 15
England: Bill of Rights, 24; defamation actions, 102; defamation law, 106–7; justice, history of, 207; *Magna Carta*, 24; Statute of Anne (1710), 248; Statute of Monopolies (1624), 248
Enhancing Online Safety Act 2015 (Australia), 332
'Enhancing Online Safety of Women in the Media' project, 319
Enlightenment era, 9–10, 79, 84
environmentalist approaches, xiv, 14
Environment Protection Authority (EPA, NSW), 194–95

equality, 309
Equal Opportunity Act 2010 (Victoria), 334
'equitable doctrine,' 149
equity, 67–69, 233
Erasing David (film), 186
Ericson, R.V., 208
eSafety Commissioner (Commonwealth), 332
eSafety Commissioner's eSafety Guide, 316–17
escape clauses, 148
Espionage Act (United States), 281
espionage and secrets, 88, 292–93
Essay Concerning Human Understanding (Locke), 7–8, 26, 59
Essential Media Communications, 357
Ethics Centre, 278–79
ēthikos, 5
eudaimonia (flourishing or happiness), 11
European Convention on Human Rights, 30–31, 104, 149, 177, 182, 253, 324, 325
European Court of Human Rights, 182, 325
European Union: discrimination laws, 324; *European Union Whistleblower Directive* (2021), 155; General Data Protection Regulation (GDPR), 89, 185–86
Evatt, H.V., 35
Evening Standard, 215
Evidence Act (Australia), 162
evidentiary privilege, 152–53
existential issues, 277–78
Ex parte P (Staughton), 208

Facebook, 34, 89, 121, 151, 210; Cambridge Analytica-Facebook personal data breach scandal, xvi, 186, 187; and national security, 288–89; third party comments on, 116
fact-checkers, 89
facts, 65–66, 67, 84, 94, 198, 335; and opinions, 120–21
fair and accurate report, 90, 101, 158, 214, 223, 225, 229, **234**, 236, 326, 337, 350
'fair comment' ('honest opinion'). *See* 'honest opinion' ('fair comment')
fair dealing, xvii, 243, 251–52, 260–61, 267; for news reporting purposes, 261–62, 272; for parody or satire purposes, 262–63
'Fairfax test,' 158

'fair report' defence, 90, 119, 136, 158–59
'fair summary of, or a fair extract,' 119
fair use, xvii, 243, 251–52, 272
Fair Work Act 2009 (Australia), 333
Fair Work Commission (Australia), 44, 333, 362
'fake news,' 77, 81, 89, 96; 2DAY-FM prank call, 91–92; and war, 279–80
False Advertising Law and Unfair Competition Law (California), 351
false connection, 256, 268
false innuendo, 111
false light, 181
Family Law Act 1975 (Australia), 231
fan fiction, xvii, 257–58
Farrell, Paul, 166
Federal Communications Commission (FCC, US), 210
Federal Trade Commission (FTC, United States), 186, 187; Division of Advertising Practices (DAP), 352
Felt, Mark, 281
feminist approaches, xiv, 14
Ferguson, Adele, 163
financial services, 344, 345, 359, 367
Finkelstein, Ray, 360
Finkelstein (2012) review, 178
First Amendment (US Constitution), 23, 31–32, 44, 45, 87, 107, 128; and breach of confidence, 149; 'clear and present danger,' 214; commercial speech, 351; and coverage of criminal trials, 211; hate speech protected by, 322, 323–24; and national security, 280, 281, 286; and privacy, 182
Florence, Republic of, 248
Forbes, Francis, 35
Foreign Influence Transparency Scheme Act 2018 (Australia), 38
form of expression, 249, 258–59
Forsskal, Peter, 156
Foucault, Michel, 15, 79–80
Four Corners, 37
Four Theories of the Press (Siebert, Peterson and Schramm), 23, 28
Fourth Estate, 28, 50, 83, 144
Fraill, Joanne, 213
France, and right privacy, 180–81
Francis, Bob, 227
Fraser, I., 354, 355
Freedom Act 2015 (United States), 287
Freedom and Destiny (May), 52
freedom of expression, xiv, xvi, 14, 25–28; and censorship, 25–26; and

defamation, 104; defined, 23; and intellectual property, 245; international law, 29–32; and national security, 277, 280–82, 287, 289; philosophical and historical background, 24–28; and privacy, 182; in UN documents, 29–30
Freedom of Information Act 1982 (NSW), 164
freedom of information laws (FOI), xvi, 142, 145, 149, 156–57, 170; in Australia, 164–66
freedom of the press/press freedom, 23, 25–28; and press systems theory, 28–29
free expression groups, 32
Free Press Unlimited, 315
Free TV Australia, 39–40, 179, 320
free will, 8
French, Chief Justice, 219
French Revolution, 27
front groups, 85

Gageler, Justice, 222
Gallagher, Norm, 227
Galtung, J., 285
'Gambling in Las Vegas' (Theroux), 18
Gassaway, Bob, 284
Gelber, K., 290
Gender Equity Victoria (GEN VIC), 319
General Data Protection Regulation (GDPR), 89, 185–86
general will, 8
genocide, 309
Germany, 322, 325
Getty Images, 254–55
Gibson, A., 354, 355
Giggs, Ryan, 183
Gill, Cameron, 295
Giuliani, Rudolph, 85
Glennon, Michael, 224
Global Conference for Media Freedom, the Media Freedom Coalition, 30
globalised world, xiii, xv, 34
Global Television (Canada), 350
Goldberg, D., 156
Golden Mean, 11
Golden Rule, 6–7, 80
Good, the, 9
Google, 123, 127, 129, 210, 227, 325, 358
Gorman, Ginger, 322
Gosseries, A., 144, 145
Government Information (Public Access) Act (NSW), 164
Grant, Hugh, 182
Grantham, S., 64, 69–70, 86, 88, 299, 300

Greek and Roman thought, xiv, 3, 7, 11, 24–25; on confidentiality, 143, 169; on corruption, 346; on intellectual property, 244, 272; on justice, 207, 235; military values in, 278; on privacy, 176; on slavery, 309; on truth and deception, 78, 95
Greenpeace, 261, 267; *Rainbow Warrior* bombing, 287
Gregory, P., 209
Guardian (news outlet), 165, 186
Guidelines on the Protection of Privacy and Transborder Flows of Personal Data (OECD), 185, 192
Gutenberg, Johann, 25–26
Guterres, Antonio, 14
Gutnick, Joseph, 114

Habermas, Jürgen, 15
Hall, Stuart, 208
Hampson, Bradley, 332
Haneef, Mohamed, 292
Hanson, Pauline, 123
happiness, 9–11
Hardy, K., 289, 293
Harmful Digital Communications Act 2015 (New Zealand), 325
Harry, Prince, 184
Harvard Law Review, 181
Harvey, Michael, 161
Harvie, Brittany, 224
hate speech, 314, 316, 337; protected by First Amendment, 322, 323–24; self-regulation of, 317–19
health and medicinal products and services, 360
Heard, Amber, 105
'hearsay' evidence, 117
Hegel, Georg, 244
Hello! magazine, 182
Henry IV (Shakespeare), 284
Herald Sun (Melbourne), 326–28
Here, There Are Dragons (Johns), 292
Herodotus, 24
Hewart, Lord, 208
Higgins, Justice, 247
Himma, K., 244–45
Hinch, Derryn, 221, 223, 224
Hippocrates, 143
Hippocratic Oath, 143, 148, 169
Hiroshima, 284
Hobbes, Thomas, 7, 24, 177
Hockey, Joe, 114–15
Hocking, J., 289

Hogan, Paul, 269
Holdsworth, William, 207
Holmes à Court, Peter, 126
Holocaust denial laws (Germany), 322, 329
Holsworthy Army Barracks (Sydney), 291
Homer, 284
'honest opinion' ('fair comment'), 90, 101, 120–23, 136, 261
honesty, 56–57, 84, 349
The Hotplate (television series), 263
House of Lords, 151–52, 182, 215, 216
human rights, 23–48; basic Australian legal principles in human rights and free expression, 34–36; and breach of confidence, 149; and consumer law, 348–49; defined, 23; and deontology, 24–25; dignity, 29, 78, 310, 312; and four classical philosophical approaches, 24–25; freedom of movement, 25; freedom of the press, 28; global platform self-regulation, 34; international human rights framework, xiv, 24; key concepts, 23; key laws on in Australia, 36–39; law of free expression and human rights internationally, 29–32; and national security, 280–82; and privacy, 176–77, 197; professional ethical dilemmas, co-regulation and self-regulation, 32–34; and reputation, 104; safety and security, xvii; social media policies, 34, 44
Human Rights Act 1998 (United Kingdom), 182, 214, 218
Human Rights Act 2004 (Australian Capital Territory), 36, 197
Human Rights Act 2019 (Queensland), 36, 197
Human Rights and Equal Opportunity Commission (HREOC) (Australia), 326
Human Rights and Equal Opportunity Commission Act (Australia) 1986, 326
human rights-oriented approaches, xiv, xv, 14
Hurley, Elizabeth, 182, 184
'hyper-legislation,' 290

identity theft, 188
Ignatieff, Michael, 279
ignorance as no defence, 214, 215
Iliad (Homer), 284

implied freedoms, 37–39, 45, 280, 295, 363
improper behaviour, 206, 216–17, 235
'improper motive,' 110, 127, 226–27
imputation, 101, 109, 110, 111, 116, 122, 136
Independent Commission Against Corruption (ICAC) (NSW), 161, 356
Independent Media Council (West Australian newspapers), 40
Independent National Security Legislation Monitor (INSLM), 292
Independent Press Standards Organisation (IPSO), 178
Indigenous peoples, 4, 38. *See also* Aboriginal and Torres Strait Islander peoples
Information Act (Northern Territory), 164
initial public offering (IPO), 93, 359
injunctions: breach of confidence, 149, 151, 159; defamation, 105, 130; and justice, 215–16; and national security, 281; and privacy, 183, 194
'injurious falsehood,' 91, 131
innocent dissemination defence, 116, 127, 129
Instagram, 180, 317
Institutes of Justinian, 207
integrity, conflicted interests and the business of communication, xvii–xviii, 344–71; basic Australian legal principles, 355–67; consumer law, 348–49, 367; contracts, 354–55; in different occupations, 345; and human rights, 348–49, 367; integrity defined, 344; key concepts, 344; law, cases and examples of conflicts of interest and misleading conduct internationally, 350–55; philosophical background to, 346–48; potential problem scenario, 364–67; professional ethical codes and dilemmas on conflicts of interests and misleading consumers, 349–50. *See also* consumer law; employment law; financial services
intellectual property, xiv, xvii, 243–76; attribution, 243, 244, 247, 251, 252, 254, 261; basic Australian legal principles in, 258–71; copyright law internationally, 249–55; 'cut and paste' model, 90–91; and defamation, 90–91; defined, 243, 248–49, 272;

Index 383

digital IP cases, 265; ethical guidelines and regulation of, 246–48; fan fiction, xvii, 257–58; and free expression, 245; integrity of authorship, 263–64; key concepts, 243; law, cases and examples internationally, 248–49; lessons for professional communicators, 253–54, 268; moral rights, xvii, 243, 245, 263–65, 271, 272; 'passing off,' 91, 256–57, 268, 272, 357; philosophical background and human rights context of plagiarism and intellectual property, 244–46; philosophical origins of, xvii; potential problem area, 269–71; public domain, xvii, 243, 251–55; and satire, 256, 260, 262–63, 267, 268; television format protections, 263; trade marks, xvii, 255–56, 265–68, 272. *See also* copyright
Intelligence Services Act 2001 (Australia), 295
intent (purpose), 9, 233
'intermediary immunity,' 324
International Center for Journalists, 285
International Court of Justice, 216
International Covenant on Civil and Political Rights (ICCPR), 29–30, 35, 105, 156–57, 177, 192, 208; discrimination, view of, 311, 312; and intellectual property, 245; and national security, 280
International Covenant on Economic, Social and Cultural Rights (UN), 245
International Federation of Journalists' (IFJ) Charter of Ethics, 314
international law: and copyright, 258–59; defamation law, xvi, 104–7; on discrimination, cyberbullying, and harassment, 322–25; free expression, 29–32
internet, xv, xvii, 36, 39, 81, 88–90, 96; and confidentiality, 151–52, 156, 284–85; and copyright, 252, 254–55; and defamation, 105–6, 110, 114–15; and discrimination, 316–18; identity theft, 188; and intellectual property rights, 247–48; international approaches to online safety of communicators, 314–15; and privacy, 177–78, 180; self-regulation, 34, 317–20; take down orders, 220; violent graphic material on, 210; women as targets of online violence,

313, 315, 316, 319, 321–22. *See also* cybersecurity; intellectual property; social media
Internet Corporation for Assigned Names and Numbers (ICANN), 257
intrusion, 181
Iraq war, 288
Irish Republican Army (IRA), 287
Islam, 80, 103, 310–11, 322–23
Italy, Renaissance, 248

Jefferson, Thomas, 24, 309
Jesus, 6–7, 80, 310
job references, 105, 125–26
John, Elton, 184
John, King, 24
Johns, Alan, 291–92
Johnson, Krystal, 206, 224–25
Johnson, Samuel, 282, 284
Jones, Alan, 320–21, 330, 361
Jones, Bernard Patrick, 219
journaling, xv, 49, 62, 70–71, **73**, 74, 131
journalism: and confidentiality, 147–48, 152–53; 'death knock,' 51, 84, 177, 178–79; deaths of journalists in course of work, 32, 284, 322–23; as Fourth Estate, 28, 50, 83, 144; jailing of journalists, 7, 142, 153, 160–61, 163, 213, 296; 'mindful journalism,' 285; peace journalism, xvii, 28, 277, 302; public interest journalism, 363–64; 'public's right to know', xiii, 27–28, 83, 132–33, 145, 176–77, 210, 300; truth and deception in, 82–84; women as targets of online violence, 313, 315, 316, 319, 321–22. *See also* justice, communicating; media law and ethics
The Journalist and the Murderer (Malcolm), 84
Judaism, 80, 103
judges and magistrates, 208
Judicial Proceedings Reports Act 1958 (Victoria), 230
jurisdiction, 114; defined, 77
Jury Act 1977 (NSW), 228
jus ad bellum ('justice towards war'), 279
jus in bello ('justice in war'), 279
jus post bellum ('justice after war'), 279
justice, communicating, xiv, xvi, 8, 206–39; absent juries, withdrawn questions and the *voir dire,* 231; appropriate coverage, 229; basic Australian legal principles and cases,

219–32; British-based system of law, 209; contempt of court, 206, 212–13; court reporting privileges and practice, 217–19; covering court cases and performing court communication roles, 228–29; crime reportage time zones, xvii, 223, **234**, 235, 236; defined, 207; ethical codes, regulation of crime and court coverage and a solutions approach, 210–11; identification restrictions, 218, 229–32, 236; improper pressure, 227; key concepts, 206; law, cases and examples internationally, 211–17; lessons for professional communicators, 225; 'open justice,' 145, 206, 208, 211, 217, 219–20; philosophical background and human rights context of, 207–9; potential problem areas, 232–35; and publicity, 207–8, 214; 'real and definite tendency' to prejudice, 206, 214, 222, 225; reasons for examining, 206–7; secrecy provisions, 220; *sub judice* contempt, 206, 213–16, 218, 221–25, 227, 229, **234**, 235; suppression orders, 206, 211, 220, 221, 235. *See also* crime and violence
'justice as fairness,' 8
justification, 106, 109, 117–18, 136; 'public justification,' 68, 94; for war, 277, 278–79. *See also* truth
just war theory, 277, 278–79
Jyllands-Posten, 322–23

Kant, Immanuel, xiv, 6–7, 11, 24–25, 78, 144, 167, 365
Kashtanova, Kristina, 255
Keane, Justice, 222
Kelly, Desmond, 161
Khomeini, Ayatollah Ruhollah, 323
King, Larry, 284
Kirby, Justice, 219–20

Lahey, Kate, 119
Lange, David, 37
law, 57; commercial, 91; ethics and morals related to, 5; formal legislation and court decisions, 33; jurisdiction, 77; and reflective tools, **54–55**, 70
law and ethics across communication careers, 77–98; applying reflection-in-action techniques, 93–95; basic Australian legal principles on truth and deception, 90–93; communicating via the internet, social media and artificial intelligence, 88–90; communication careers – different needs, different values, 82–87; corporate communicators and PR consultants, 84–86; journalism careers, 82–84; key concepts, 77; lessons for professional communicators, 92; modern conceptions of truth and deception, 81–82; non-government organisations (NGOs), 86–87; philosophical and religious thinking on truth and deception, 78–80, 95; potential problem scenarios, 95; publication, law of, 88; public relations careers, 84–86; religious notions of truth and deception, 80–81, 95; specialist fields, 93
Law of Nature, 8
Laws, John, 228, 330–31
lawyers, 27, **73**; defences best handled by, 117, 127–30; legal escalation policy, 70–71
leaks, 146, 149, 151, 154–55, 162, 288; Wikileaks, 88, 151, 155. *See also* whistleblowers
legal escalation policy, 70–71
legal risks, **54–55**
legal standing, 115
Lenah Game Meats case (2001), xvi, 157–58, 183, 189, 190–92, 201
Lesotho Diamond Corporation, 357–58
#LetHerSpeak campaigning, 230
Leveson Inquiry (2012), 178
libel, 105–6, 136, 189
Liberal Party (Hockey's), 114–15
libertarian approach, 13, 25, 44; and marketplace of ideas, 26; and press systems theory, 28; in United Kingdom, 87
liberties, basic, 10
liberty principle, 8
Lippman, Walter, 308
lobbyists, 146
Locke, John, 7–8, 24, 26, 59, 176, 309; intellectual property, view of, 244
loyalties, 66, 67, 94, 199, 335
Lying – Moral Choice in Public and Private Life (Bok), 82, 103

Machiavelli, Niccolò, 10, 79
Macquarie Concise Dictionary, 104–5

Magna Carta, 24
Mail on Sunday, 184, 253
majority opinion, 8, 25
Malaysian Airlines flight MH370, 85
Malcolm, Janet, 84
malice, 101, 127, 131, 361
malinfomation, 77, 81, 96
malware, 89
Mandela, Nelson, 23
Manning, Chelsea (formerly Bradley), 155, 156, 288
'man of straw,' 106
marketplace of ideas, 26, 84
Markle, Meghan, 184, 252–54
Markle, Thomas, 252–53
Martinson, D.L., 67–68, 233
Marx, Karl, 15
Marxist, structuralist, post-structuralist and postmodernist perspectives, xiv, 15
Mason, Anthony, 158
Mason, Justice, 224
May, Rollo, 52
Mayhem – Violence as Public Entertainment (Bok), 209
McGarrity, N., 290
McIntyre, Scott, 362–63
McKenzie, Nick, 162–63
McKinnon, Michael, 164
McLean, Hamish, 85
McMahon, Cait, 284
McManus, Gerard, 161
Media, Entertainment and Arts Alliance (MEAA, Australia), 39, 356; Code of Ethics, 33, 40, **41**, 91, 147, 179, 246, 319, 349–50; Ethics Complaints Panel, 40; Ethics Review Committee, 247; National Ethics Committee, 91
media law and ethics, xii–xiv, 101–41, 133–37; Australian defamation law, 107–10; basics of defamation law internationally, 104–7; broad definition of, 4; crime and justice, communication of, 208–9; independent investigations, 215; key concepts, 101; lessons for professional communicators, 105, 110; prior restraint, 26, 130, 191, 281, 287; and privacy ethics, 178–79; religious origins of reputational ethics and defamation, 102–3; reputation in moral philosophy, 103–4; reputations and human rights, 104; truth and deception in, 87, 96. *See also* defamation; journalism; reputation

Media Watch (ABC), 42, 121–22, 247, 320, 361–62
Menken, Adah Isaacs, 181
mens rea (guilty mind), 222
mental health, 15; fake news as impetus for suicide, 91; and justice reporting, 232; of media professionals, 5, 50–52, 61; Mindframe Guidelines, 211; and moral injury, 51; and national security, 283–84; post-traumatic stress disorder, 51–52, 283–84, 302; reporting on, xvii, 317–18, 337; suicide, 91, 125, 211, 232, 337; vicarious trauma, 209. *See also* mindful approaches
Merck pharmaceutical company, 347
Meta, 34, 89, 187, 325; Oversight Board, 317–18; Terms of Service (2022), 248
Meta Transparency Report (2022), 288–89
Milat, Ivan, 112, 223
Mill, John Stuart, xiv, 9, 20, 25, 27, 144, 154, 167, 176
Miller, Judith, 153
Miller, S., 245–46, 347–48
Milton, John, 25, 26
Mindframe Guidelines, 211, 232, 317–18, 337
mindful approaches, xiv, xv, 15, 28, 70, 93, 131, 299
'mindful journalism,' 285
mindful reflection, 59–62; defined, 49
mindmapping, 49, 62–63, *63*, 74, 131
misinformation, 77, 81, 89, 96, 319
misleading and deceptive conduct, 57, 91, 268, 272, 357–58, 366
Mitchell, Robert, 190
Mohammed, Prophet, 310, 322
Monis, Man Haron, 38
Moore, A., 244–45
moral acts, 8
moral compass, xiv–xv, 3, 5, *16*, 20, 50, 51, 57; applying to ethical decisions, 16–17; and defamation issues, 133
moral consciousness, 8
moral genealogy, xiv
moral injury, xv, 49–51
moral muteness, xv, 49–51
moral myopia, xv, 49–50
moral panic, 208
moral philosophy, 5–6
moral psychology, 8
moral rights, xvii, 243, 245, 263–65, 271, 272

morals, defined, 5
Morel, Daniel, 254–55
mores (morals), 5
Moriarty, J., 347
Morse, Valerie, 30
Mosley, Max, 182
Mundey, Jack, 227
Murdoch, Iris, 60, 347
Murdoch, Rupert, 188, 266
Murray, William, 106
Musk, Elon, 34, 89
My Kitchen Rules (MKR) (television programme), 263

National Broadband Network (NBN), 158
national security, xiv, xvii, 220, 277–306; 'control orders,' 296; 'D-notice' (defence notice) system, 289; espionage and secrets, 292–93; ethics and law in action, 299–301; and freedom of expression, 277, 280–82, 287, 289; human rights dimensions to, 280–82; just war theory, 277; key concepts, 277; law, cases and examples internationally, 286–89; lessons for professional communicators, 296; philosophical background to communication about war, defence and national security, 278–80; 'preventative detention orders' (PDOs), 296; professional ethical dilemmas in, 282–85; and propaganda, 279–80, 283, 284, 286; and public interest, 294, 296, 299, 301; 'recklessness' in disclosure, 290, 291–93; restrictions on media, 280, 286, 287, 302; secret trials, 291–92; security classifications, 293, 298; and social media, 288–89; surveillance, data retention and source protection, 296–98; and surveillance, 296–98; treason, 290; treason and sedition laws, 277, 286, 289; 'voluntary restraint' system, 289; and whistleblowing, 155, 156, 278. *See also* cybersecurity; terrorism; war
National Security Agency (NSA, United States), 186, 288
National Security Information (Criminal and Civil Proceedings) Act 2004 (NSI Act) (Australia), 291
National Union of Journalists Code of Conduct (NUJ), 349

National Union of Journalists (NUJ) Code of Conduct (United Kingdom), 147, 178, 179
natural rights, 8
Network Enforcement Law (Germany), 325
Network Ten, 260
Neuberger, Lord, 207
Neville Jeffress Pidler, 261
News Corp Australia Editorial Professional Conduct Policy, 42
News Corporation, 266
News Deeply, 60–61
News Media and Digital Platforms Mandatory Bargaining Code, 363–64
news media bargaining code, xviii, 344, 363–64
News of the World, 188
Newspaper Acts Opinion, 35
newspaper rule, 163
New York Times, 31–32, 153, 186, 281, 350
New Zealand, 30; *Bill of Rights Act 1990* (BORA), 30, 280, 325; *Contempt of Court Act 2019*, 214; discrimination laws, 325; massacre (2019), 210
Ng, Mary, 353
Nicomachean Ethics (Aristotle), 207
Nietzsche, Friedrich, 79
Nike, 351
Nine Network, 195–96
Nixon, Richard, 77, 281
Noll, Shannon, 358
non-government organisations (NGOs), 14, 32, 324; truth and deception in, 86–87, 96
normative ethics, xiv, 3. *See also* consequentialism; contractualism; deontology; virtue ethics
NSW Independent Commission Against Corruption (ICAC), 161
'nuisance,' 189, 195–96

Obama, Barack, 288
obligations, 3, 25; of confidentiality, 150, 151, 169
Ochlik, Remi, 284
Oderberg, David, 103
Office of Communications (Ofcom, United Kingdom), 178
off-the-record, xvi, 142, 155, 162
oikos (family or private), 176
Onions, Paul, 223
On Liberty (Mill), 10, 27

Online Safety Act 2021 (Australia), 332
Online Safety Bill (United Kingdom), 325
Online Safety of Diverse Journalists (Vallencia-Forrester et al., 2023), 313
Online Violence Response Hub, 315–16
'open justice,' 145, 206, 208, 211, 217, 219–20
opinion: 'honest opinion' ('fair comment'), 90, 120–23, 136, 261; public, 308
organisational policy stances, 66
Organisation for Economic Co-operation and Development (OECD), 185, 192
original position, 8

pacifism, 278
Palmer, Clive, 262–63
pamphleteers, 26
Panama Papers (2016), 288
Papua New Guinea, 346–47
Parfit, Derek, 6, 12
Parfit's mountain, *12*, 12–13
Parker-Bowles, Camilla (Queen Consort), 84
Parliament (England), 24, 26, 84
Parliament, contempt of (Australia), 162
parody, 261, 262–63
Parr, T., 144, 145
'passing off,' 91, 256–57, 268, 272, 357
PATRIOT Act 2001 (United States), 287
Patterson, P., 65
peace journalism, xvii, 28, 277, 285, 302
Pearson, M., 64, 69–70, 86, 88, 299, 300
Pell, George, 221
Pember, D.R., 286
Pennells, Steve, 163
Pentagon Papers case (1971), 156, 280, 281–82, 287
People magazine, 253
personality rights (rights in publicity), 182, 256–57
'perspectivism,' 79
persuasion professions, 68
Perth Now news website, 328–29
PETA, 250
philosophical approaches, 5–11; moral philosophy, 5–6. *See also* consequentialism; contractualism (social contract theory); deontology; normative ethics; solutions journalism; virtue ethics
photographs: copyright in, 254, 259, 264–65; at courthouse, 228;
'pixelated' photos of accused, 223; and privacy, 181–83
Pitch Perfect 2, 107, 109
plagiarism, xvii, 121–22, 272; defined, 243, 245–46; ethical guidelines and regulation of, 246–48; philosophical background and human rights context of, 244–46
Plan of Action on the Safety of Journalists and the Issue of Impunity (2017), 316
Plato, 11, 346
polis (public), 176
political advertising, 37
political power, 145
Politico, 87
Porter, Christian, 130
Posetti, Julie, 285, 312–13
positive rights, 37
post-structuralist approaches, xiv, 15
'post truth,' 81, 96
Potter, Ralph, 65
Potter Box, xv, 49, 53, 65–67; for discrimination, 334–37; in privacy cases, 197–99; for truth and deception, 94
power relations, 79–80
prank calls, 91–92
prejudice, 307
'prescribed information provider' exception, 357
PRESS Act bill (United States), 154
press councils, 33
press systems, xv, 23, 33; theory, 28–29
Price, Steve, 330
principles, 66, 67, 94, 199, 335–36
print licensing laws, 26
prior restraint, 26, 130, 191, 281, 287
prison and jailing of journalists, 7, 142, 153, 160–61, 163, 213, 296
prisoners, and justice reporting, 231
privacy, xiv, xvi, 37, 175–205; Australian law, 189–92; and breach of confidence, 182, 190, 191; and celebrities, xvi, 143, 181–83; in corporate and public relations, 179–80; corporate policies, 180; damages for breaches of, 189, 194–95; 'death knock,' 51, 84, 177, 178–79; in international law, 149, 197; invasion of, 143, 175, 183–85, 190–91, 194–95; key concepts, 175; law, cases and examples internationally, 180–88; lessons for professional communicators, 185, 191–92; media

and privacy ethics, 178–79; in media context, 175–76; other Australian laws, 197; personality rights, 182; philosophical background and human rights context of, 176–77; potential problem scenarios, 197–200; professional ethical dilemmas, co-regulation and self-regulation, 177–79; remedies for invasions of, 190; right to, 180–85, 189; tort of invasion, 143, 183–85, 191; trespass, xvi, 181, 188–89. *See also* data protection; surveillance
Privacy Act 1988 (Australia), 37, 189, 192–93, 201
Privacy and Safety Center (Instagram), 180
Privacy Guidelines for Broadcasters (ACMA), 179
Private Eye, 153
'privileged access,' 114, 176
propaganda, 279–80, 283, 284, 286
'proper material,' 121
property, 244; and privacy, 176; reputation as, 103. *See also* intellectual property
publication, law of, 88, 114–15
public disclosure of embarrassing facts, 181–82
public documents, 119
public domain, xvii, 149, 243, 251–55
'public figure,' 107
Public Information Officers (PIOs), 212, 228
public interest, xiii, 27–28, 101; and confidentiality, 158–60, 169; and defamation defence, 90, 121, 123–25, 136; and national security cases, 294, 296, 299, 301; and *sub judice* contempt, 214; and whistleblowing, 155. *See also* freedom of information laws (FOI)
Public Interest Disclosures Act 2022 (NSW), 164
public interest journalism, 363–64
publicity, 144–45; and justice, 207–8, 214
'public justification,' 68, 94
Public Opinion (Lippman), 308
'public reason,' 145
public relations: behavioural boundaries for practitioners, 33–34; codes of ethics, 84–85, 145–46; confidentiality in, 146–47; and job references, 125–26; lobbyists, 146; MH370 disappearance, 85; posing as volunteers, 85; potential problem scenarios, 166–69; and privacy, 179–80; TARES test for, 67–68; truth and deception in, 84–86
Public Relations Consultants Association (PRCA) Professional Charter, 146, 247
Public Relations Institute of Australia (PRIA), 39, 356; Code of Ethics, 33, 42–44, **43**, 133, 147, 247, 319, 349; College of Fellows, 44; Consultancy Code of Practice, 42
Public Relations Society of America (PRSA), 84, 146, 313–14, 349
'public rules,' 145
'public's right to know', xiii, 27–28, 83, 132–33, 145, 176–77, 210, 300; and privacy, 176–77, 210
'publish and be damned,' 25, 83
publishing/ amending/ deleting/ correcting/ apologizing/ compensating, 71, **73**, **135**, 169, 200, 271, 301, 337, 367
Pullan, R., 289

qualified privilege, 37, 107, 109, 121, 124–28, **134**, 136–37, 361; common law, 125–26, 127–28; extended (Lange defence), 125, 126, 127–28; statutory, 126–27; three forms of, 125
'quality of confidence,' 149, 169, 190
Queensland Human Rights Commission, 36, 333
Queensland Right to Information (RTI) laws, 158
Queer Eye for the Straight Guy, 331
'questioning and detention' warrants, 290
'questioning' warrants, 290

Racial and Religious Tolerance Act 2001 (Victoria), 331, 334
Racial Discrimination Act 1975 (Australia), 36–37, 326–29
racial vilification, 307
Rand, Ayn, 13
rationalisation, xv, 49–50, 80–81, 93
Rawls, John, xiv, 7, 8–9, 145
'real and definite tendency,' 206, 214, 222, 225
'real and substantial risk,' 214
'reasonable belief,' 124, 128
'reasonable person' test, 38, 109, 118, 122, 183, 355
reasoning, approaches to, 9
reciprocal duty–interest relationship, 125, 126, 136–37

Index 389

'reckless disregard,' 32, 107
recordings, 117, 178, 196–97, 201
Redbubble, 263, 266
reflection, tools for, xiv, xv, 4, 5, 8, 11, 49–76; Bok's model, xv, 53, 57–58, 65–66, 74; building resilience through ethical practice, 50–52; consulting with others, 70–71, **73**; examples, 52–53; journaling, xv, 49, 62, 70–71, **73**, 74; key concepts, 49; key professional communication situations, **54**–**55**; mindful reflection, 59–62; mindmapping, 49, 62–63, *63*, 74; potential problem scenarios, 56–58, 61, 63, *63*, 66–67, 69, **72**–**73**; Potter Box, xv, 49, 53, 65–67; reasons for, 50; reflection-in-action three-step process, 131–33, 169; routine process, 51, 52; Specific Legal Risk Analysis, 49, 53, 69–71, 74; stakeholder mapping, xiv, xv, 49, 64–65, **65**, 70; step/ status/ action approach, 71, **72**–**73**; 'STOPS and Take STOCK' tool, 60, 299; TARES test, xv, 49, 53, 67–68, 74. *See also* Bok's model; journaling; mindful approaches; mindmapping; Potter Box
religion, freedom of, 29
religious approaches, xiv; media law and ethics, 102–3
remedies: for breach of confidence, 151; for copyright infringement, 265; defamation, 129–30, 137; for privacy invasions, 190
Renaissance politics, 79
Reporters Committee for Freedom of the Press, 154
Reporters Without Borders (RSF), 284, 315; World Press Freedom Index, 31
reputation, xiv, xv–xvi, 101–41; defined, 101; and human rights, 104; in moral philosophy, 103–4; as property right, 103. *See also* defamation
resilience, 50–52, 345
respect, 67–69, 233
'ride-alongs,' 195
Right Concentration ('*samadhi*'), 60
right of reply, 122, 124, 125, 127, **134**, **135**
rights, as alien to the good, 25
Right Speech (Buddhism), 80, 102
Right to Information (RTI) Act (Queensland), 164
Rinehart, Gina, 163

Riskin, L.L., 60, 299
Roach, K., 290
Roberts, Leslie, 350
Roberts-Smith, Ben, 90, 118
Roe v Wade abortion decision (United States), 288
Rohingas (Myanmar), 310
Rolph, D., 103
Rousseau, Jean-Jacques, 8, 24
Rowling, JK, 183, 258
Ruebottom, T., 64
Ruge, M., 285
Rush, Geoffrey, 118, 130
Rushdie, Salman, 323

Sacco, Justine, 308
'safe harbour' exemptions, 357–58
Samoan protocols, 4
The Satanic Verses (Rushdie), 323
satire, 123, 256, 260, 262–63, 267, 268
Scanlon, T. M., 7, 8–9
Scholz, Tyson 'ASX Wolf,' 359
Schön, Donald, 50, 59
Schopenhauer, Arthur, 13
secrecy, xvi, 143, 144–45; in Aboriginal and Torres Strait Islander practices, 157; espionage and secrets, 88, 292–93; secret trials, 291–92; spy agencies, 290–91; and war, 279. *See also* confidentiality, secrets, sources and disclosure
Secrets: On the Ethics of Concealment and Revelation (Bok), 145
securities law, xviii, 344–45
Security Intelligence Organisation Act 1979 (Australia), 290
sedition, 106, 277, 286, 289, 302
self-interest, xiv, 3, 12–13, **54**, 57, 133
self-regulation. *See* co-regulation and self-regulation
separation of powers, 86
September 11 terrorist attacks (United States), xvii, 85, 286, 287, 302
serious harm, xvi, 101, 106, 107, 110, 114, 136
Seven Network, 165
Seven West Media, 40
Sex Discrimination Act 1984 (SDA) (Australia), 333
Shakespeare, William, 78, 101, 284
Shanks-Markovina, Jordan, 123, 227
shield laws, xvi, 142, 154, 161–63, 170; in Australia, 162–63
Sidgwick, Henry, 144

Sikkhism, 103
Sins of the Father (book), 264
Sisalem, Aladdin, 331
Sister True Dedication, 61
slander, 105, 131
Slater, David, 250
slavery, 309–10
Smethurst, Annika, 294–96
Smith, Neddy, 161
Smith, S., 333
Smith Act 1940 (United States), 286
Snowden (film), 155
Snowden, Edward, 155, 156, 186, 288, 293
social contract, 3, 7–9, 19; and human rights, 25; 'public reason' and 'public rules,' 145; and truth-telling, 78. *See also* contractualism (social contract theory)
The Social Contract (Rousseau), 8
social media, xv, 44; bloggers, 154, 223; bots and cookies, xv, 89–90; 'bubble' or 'echo chamber' effect, 82; Cambridge Analytica-Facebook personal data breach scandal, xvi, 186, 187; and commercial speech, 352; and confidentiality, 151–52; and discrimination, 316–18; financial influencers ('finfluencers'), 359; influencers, 5, 307–8, 352, 357–60, 362, 364–66; law and ethics in, 88–90; and libel, 105; and national security, 288–89; online harassment of communicators of diverse backgrounds, 312–13; and privacy, 180; self-regulation, 34, 317–20; and shield laws, 154; terms of use (terms of service), 34, 89, 316; third party comments, 77, 88–89, 136; truth and deception in, 81–82, 96
social responsibility model, 28, 66–68, 84, 233
Society of Professional Journalists' (SPJ) Code of Ethics (United States), 33, 83, 148, 178, 246; 'Minimize Harm' clauses, 178; *Resolving Ethical Conflicts in Wartime,* 282–83
Socrates, 7, 11, 25, 50
solitude, 59, 176
solutions journalism, xiv, xvi–xvii, 15–16, 28, 210–11, 285
Sossin, L., 214
sources. *See* confidentiality, secrets, sources and disclosure

South Australian Tourist Commission, 358
South Los Angeles, reporting on, 211
Special Broadcasting Service (SBS), 321
specialist fields, law and ethics of, 93
Specific Legal Risk Analysis, 49, 53, 69–71, 74; and confidentiality, 166, 168–69; and defamation issues, 133, **134–35**; and discrimination, 336–37; and intellectual property, 270–71; and national security, 299, 301; in privacy cases, 199–200; for truth and deception, 93
Spicer, Sean, 86–87
Spigelman, James, 35, 219
spy agencies, 290–91
stakeholder approaches, 169, 200, 336–37, 366
stakeholder mapping, xiv, xv, 49, 64–65, **65**, 70, **72**, 233, 271; and national security, 299, 300, 301; for truth and deception, 93
stakeholder theory, 10, 86
Stallone, Sylvester, 257–58
Star Entertainment, 361
'State of Nature,' 7
Staughton, Christopher, 208
step/ status/ action approach, 71, **72–73**
stereotyping, 307–9
Stoics, 11, 309
'STOPS and Take STOCK' tool, 60
sub judice contempt, 206, 213–16, 218, 221–25, 227, 229, **234**, 235
suicide: by defendants, 125; fake news as impetus for, 91; reporting on, 211, 232, 318–19, 337
Sullivan, L.B., 31, 107
Sullivan's case (1964), 31–32, 107, 351
Sun (United Kingdom), 105
Sunday Herald Sun, 37
Sun-Herald, 112, 264–65
Sunshine Coast Regional Council, 158
suppression orders, 206, 211, 220, 221, 235
surveillance, xvi, 91, 178, 188–89, 196–97, 201; defined, 175; and national security, 287, 296–98; recordings, 117
Surveillance Devices Act 2007 (NSW), 91
Swedish Edict of the Freedom of the Press (1766), 156
Sydney Gazette, 35
Sydney Morning Herald, 121, 161, 362
Sykes, Trevor, 268–69

Talking About a Revolution (Abdel-Magied), 322
Tame, Grace, 230
Tamils (Sri Lanka), 310
Tang Dynasty (China), 156
TARES test, xv, 49, 53, 67–69, 93; and justice reporting, 232–35
Tasmania, 38, 229, 230
Telecommunications (Interception and Access) Act 1979 (Australia), 196
teleology, 9
television, 210
telos, 9
terms of use (terms of service), 34, 89, 316
terrorism, 280; 7/7 London attacks (2005), 287; anti-terrorism laws, xvii, 284–91; Bali bombings (2002 and 2005), 287; and confidentiality of sources, 284–85, 289–90; Irish Republican Army (IRA), 287; September 11 attacks (United States), xvii, 85, 286, 287, 302. *See also* cybersecurity; national security
theoretical lenses, 3, 13–16, 57, 133
A Theory of Justice (Rawls), 8
Therapeutic Goods Act 1989 (Australia), 93, 360
Therapeutic Goods Administration (TGA), 93, 360
Theroux, Louis, 18
third parties: comments by, 77, 88–89, 115–16, 136; and confidentiality, 151–52
Thomas, Imogen, 183
The Three Musketeers (Dumas), 181
three-step proportionality test, 38–39
Timor-Leste, 163
Tjukurpa, 157
Toben, Frederick, 329
Tomlinson, Gary (Wit-boooka), 226
Toronto Star, 350
torts, 106; breach of confidence, 149; 'delict,' 182; negligence, 355; privacy invasion, 143, 183–85, 191; trespass, 194
Totem, 315
trade marks, xvii, 255–56, 265–68, 272
Trade Marks Act 1995 (Australia), 265–68
transparency, xvi, 58, 144, 145, 156
trauma, 51; and 'death knock,' 179; post-traumatic stress disorder, 51–52, 283–84, 302; vicarious, 209

treason, 277, 286, 290, 302
Treatise on the Laws and Customs of the Kingdom of England ('Glanvill'), 212
trespass, xvi, 181, 188–89, 194, 201; defined, 175; digital, 188; 'nuisance,' 189, 195–96
Trkulja, Michael, 129
Troll Hunting (Gorman), 322
'true innuendo,' 111
Trump, Donald, 81, 86–87, 89
truth, xv, 77–78; basic legal principles on, 90–93; 'contextual,' 90, 127; as defence, 106, 117–18, 136; defined, 77–78; in marketplace of ideas, 26; modern conceptions of, 81–82; philosophical and religious thinking on, 78–80, 95; 'post truth,' 81; religious notions of, 80–81, 95; as social construct, 79; during wartime, 284. *See also* deception; justification
truthfulness, 67–69, 68
Truth Social, 89
Tryckfrihetsförordningen (TF), 156
TV Parental Guidelines (US), 210
Twisted Sister (band), 262–63
Twitter (now 'X'), 34, 89, 114–15, 152, 183, 254–55
Two Treatises of Government (Locke), 8
typo-squatting, 257

Uber data breach, 186
Ulpian, 24
UN Commission on Human Rights, 156–57
'unconscionability,' 191, 194, 195
Understanding Copyright and Related Rights (WIPO), 249
United Kingdom: Brexit referendum, 187; discrimination laws, 324–25; libertarian approach in, 87; privacy rulings, 182–83
United Nations, 29–31, 310, 312; and freedom of information, 156–57; *International Covenant on Civil and Political Rights* (ICCPR), 29–30, 35, 105, 156–57, 192; privacy rights, 104
United Nations General Assembly, 316
United Nations Guidelines for Consumer Protection, 348, 349
United Nations' Office of the High Commissioner on Human Rights (OHCHR), 348
United States: burden of proof in, 107; *Declaration of Independence,* 24, 31,

177, 309; January 6, 2021 riots and attack on US Capitol, 81, 89; personal information protected online, 323–24; presidential election (2016), 187; right to privacy, 181–82; September 11 terrorist attacks, xvii, 85, 286, 287, 302
Universal Declaration of Human Rights (United Nations, 1948), 14, 29–30, 29–31, 35, 156, 310, 312; Article 19, 29–30, 45; on freedom of human beings, 29, 310, 312; 'inherent dignity' of all people, 29, 312; privacy in, 177; right against defamation, 105
universal law, 6–7, 18, 25, 167
unlawful attacks, 104, 177
UN Special Rapporteur on Freedom of Opinion and Expression, 156–57
'urging violence,' 290
US Code of Federal Regulations (1989), 245
US Constitution, Bill of Rights, 23
US Copyright Office, 249, 255
US Press Freedom Tracker, 153
utilitarianism, 9–10, 20, 25, 144, 176, 244
Utilitarianism (Mill), 10

values, 66, 67, 94, 198, 335; military, 278
veil of ignorance, 8
victims, 143; and breach of confidentiality, 158; identification restrictions on, 218, 229–32, 236; privacy of, 189; reflection tools for decision-making, 64, **65**; in sexual offence cases, 230
Victorian Equal Opportunity and Human Rights Commission, 36, 334
Vietnam War, 156, 286
Vilks, Lars, 323
A Vindication of the Rights of Woman (Wollstonecraft), 14
virtue ethics, xiv, xvii, 3, 10–11, *12*, *17*, 19, 20, 309; and authenticity, 68, 69; and defamation issues, 133; and human rights, 25; and reflective tools, 56, 67; and self-reflection, 50; truth, view of, 78
The Virtue of Selfishness – A new concept of egoism (Rand), 13
voir dire, 231
vulnerable people before the law, 197

Walkley Awards, 165, 166

wantok (reciprocal relationship, Papua New Guinea), 346–47
Wantok Niuspepa, 347
war: 'ethical restraint' in, 279; First World War (1914–1918), 286; just war theory, 277, 278–79; peace journalism, xvii, 28, 277, 285, 302; professional ethical dilemmas in, 282–85; proportionality in conduct of, 279. *See also* national security
Ware, Michael, 284
warning of publication, 159, 215
Warren, Samuel D., 181
Washington Post, 281
Watergate, 281
Weil, Simone, 25, 59, 176
West Australian, 37
Wex Legal Definitions, 286
'What is Truth?' (Cash), 77–78
WhatsApp, 151
whistleblowers, xvi, 117, 142, 154–56, 170; as bravery, 278; criminal charts, 281–82; laws, 149; lessons for professional communicators, 282; protection in Australia, 163–64
Whitman, James Q., 181
Wikileaks, 88, 151, 155
WikiLeaks, 151, 293
Wikimedia Commons, 250, 251
Wilk, Richard, 18
Wilkins, L., 65
will, 13
William, Prince, 188
Williams, G., 289, 293
Williams, Mary Elizabeth, 61
Wilson, Rebel, 107, 109–10
Wohl, R.A., 60, 299
Wolf, Josh, 153
Wollstonecraft, Mary, 14
Woman's Day, 107, 109
Worksafe Queensland, 333
World Intellectual Property Organization (WIPO), 249; Arbitration and Mediation Center, 257
Wotton, Lex, 38

'X'. *See* Twitter.

Yahoo!, 129, 190, 206, 224–25
YouTube, 123, 316

Zeno of Citium, 309
Zeta-Jones, Catherine, 182

Milton Keynes UK
Ingram Content Group UK Ltd.
UKHW022035240124
436653UK00003B/17